The Gender of Freedom

Elizabeth Maddock Dillon

The Gender of Freedom

Fictions of Liberalism and the Literary
Public Sphere

Stanford University Press, Stanford, California   2004

Stanford University Press
Stanford, California
© 2004 by the Board of Trustees of the
Leland Stanford Junior University
Printed in the United States of America

Library of Congress Cataloging-in-Publication Data
Dillon, Elizabeth Maddock
    The gender of freedom : fictions of liberalism and the literary public sphere /
Elizabeth Maddock Dillon
        p. cm.
Includes bibliographical references and index.
ISBN 0-8047-2941-7 (acid-free paper)
        1. American literature—Colonial period, ca. 1600–1775—History and
criticism. 2. Liberty in literature. 3. Dickinson, Emily, 1830–1886—Criticism
and interpretation. 4. American literature—1783–1850—History and
criticism. 5. Politics and literature—United States—History. 6. Women
and literature—United States—History. 7. Sentimentalism in literature.
8. Liberalism in literature. 9. Sex role in literature. 10. Marriage in literature.
11. Women in literature. I. Title.
PS169.L5 D55   2004

810.9'3552—dc21   2003025733

This book is printed on acid-free, archival quality paper.

Original printing 2004
Last figure below indicates year of this printing:
13   12   11   10   09   08   07   06   05   04

Typeset in 10/13 Minion

The Hilles Publication Fund has provided support for the publication of
this book. We gratefully acknowledge this assistance.

FOR JOHN

Contents

Acknowledgments

While writing is a solitary endeavor, the pleasures of thinking have always been eminently communal for me. I'm grateful to the series of communities that engaged, provoked, and guided my thinking in the many years this manuscript has been in gestation. I first began to write about liberalism and gender in the company of teachers and graduate student colleagues at U.C. Berkeley. I'm grateful to Mitchell Breitwieser and Nancy Ruttenburg for their early support and continued friendship these many years. Frederick Dolan introduced me to the intriguing complexities of liberal political theory, and Judith Butler, Carolyn Porter, and Avital Ronell provided support at crucial moments. I don't think I could have learned to think without the company of Lisa Freinkel, who will remain my earliest partner in the pleasures of philosophy. Thanks as well are due to Jennifer Culbert, who attended both early and late to the progression of this project. At Cornell University, I received generous support from the fellowship of the Center for the Humanities under the guidance of Dominick LaCapra. I'm also grateful for the support and intellectual example of Walter Cohen, Jonathan Culler, Natalie Melas, Shirley Samuels, and Mark Seltzer. Irene Tucker's friendship and intellectual company were indispensable in Ithaca and remain invaluable. At Yale University, I've benefited enormously from the friendship and shared ideas of colleagues: I thank Nigel Alderman, Richard Brodhead, John Demos, Laura Frost, Mokhtar Ghambou, Amy Hungerford, Catherine Labio, Pericles Lewis, Ken Minkema, Joseph Roach, Katherine Rowe, Michael Trask, Mary-Floyd Wilson, Ruth Bernard Yeazell, and Bryan Wolf. I am also grateful for the collegiality and friendship of Ivy Schweitzer, Jonathan Elmer, Donald Pease, Leonard Tennenhouse, and Robyn Wiegman. Megan Pugh supplied skilled research assistance in the final stages of preparing the manuscript. I am appreciative of support for the research and writing of this book generously provided by the Mellon Foundation and the Morse Fund at Yale University. My deepest thanks to Laura Wexler, who has exemplified generosity at every turn, and to Serene Jones, who has covered many a mile, many a mountain, and every idea in this manuscript with me in the past two years.

Finally, I thank my parents, Stephen and Margot Maddock, for their unfailing moral support; my daughters, Charlotte and Sophie, with whom I think anew about so many of the oldest things; and my husband, John, whose companionship has been sustaining.

The Gender of Freedom

Introduction

The Gender of Freedom and
Women in Public

Shortly after I married, I began to stumble over words, over a new vocabulary of marriage that suddenly seemed to belong to me, though it was too new to my tongue to feel at home there. Along with the difficulty of pronouncing the words "my husband" as if they were not in quotation marks, I remember experiencing as odd the thought that my relationship with my partner was now a "marriage." In uttering the exemplary performative statement "I do" we had enacted our marital tie, but this pronouncement had also brought into being a new *thing*—a marriage.[1] I was surprised by precisely the *thingness* of the marriage—its foreign and objectlike character. I mentally prodded and poked at this new thing, rehearsing the terms in which it was often invoked: "How is your marriage?" "Marriage is hard work." "Their marriage is on the rocks." What was this thing that we had created? It seemed, to my mind, to have the structure of a black hole: that is, it had a prominent public exterior that announced a mysterious, deeply private, unknowable interior. Our lives had changed little from pre- to post-marriage: we lived in the same apartment where we had lived before, we had the same jobs, the same friends. Yet marriage seemed to erect a state-sponsored wall around us, within which our sexual activities were now, strangely enough, state-sanctioned as well (all those new sheets for wedding presents!). I contracted a profound interest in stories of divorce at this point. I suppose my question was this: at what point can these walls be breached?

Pamela Haag argues that the sphere of privacy—of sexual intimacy—became a central site of modern liberalism at the turn of the twentieth century.[2] American freedom and citizenship became increasingly defined in terms of the *free* acts occurring in the protected sphere of privacy marked out by heterosexual marriage rather than in terms of the free acts of economic activity occurring in the marketplace that had characterized earlier, classic liberalism of the eighteenth and nineteenth centuries. As a nineteenth-century missionary argued, "marriages based on mutual consent and mutual love" embody "the highest ideal in modern America."[3] Mutual consent in marriage thus indexed the freedom of the American citizen, and the right to be left alone in marriage, elaborated in the twentieth century as the legal doctrine of privacy, confirmed that freedom.[4] Yet as my own sense of uneasy interpellation into the institution of marriage had made evident, the state's legal demarcation of marriage as a site of privacy and freedom brought a disconcerting structuring force with it. Indeed, as Haag and other critics have made clear, the legal boundaries of the arena of privacy in which freedom takes place are drawn in such a way as to give the state extraordinary power over "private" freedom: the state's historical interdiction of both interracial marriage and homosexuality are glaring instances of this authority.[5] The freedom granted by liberalism thus involves a structuring force, and it is the claim of this book that gender is one of the key categories through which liberalism scripts the interrelated public and private lives of citizens of the liberal state.

I use the term "liberalism" here not in the contemporary vernacular sense (liberal versus conservative), but with broad reference to the political tradition inaugurated by theorists of the social contract such as John Locke and Jean-Jacques Rousseau. The innovation of liberal political theory lies in the claim that individuals have the right to exercise political choice or consent (as well as dissent) with respect to governing authority: the freedom, or the fundamental right to liberty, ascribed to the individual in this theory defines the politics of liberalism. In ascribing the capacity to consent to the individual, liberalism also, by implication, constructs and relies upon a strong definition of the modern subject as one who is free, autonomous, and capable of self-government and rational behavior. Despite the proclaimed universality of such a subject, women have historically been understood to lack the independence necessary to function as liberal subjects. Since the founding of the U.S. state, women have been overtly excluded from the purview of liberal citizenship in a variety of ways: under the law of "coverture," for instance, married white women had no independent legal standing before the law and were unable to own property (including property in their own bodies and the wages of their own labor) prior to the mid-nineteenth century. The capacity to exercise political consent, in the form of the franchise, was not extended to white women until 1920 and only fitfully to women of color from that point forward. Critics of women's suffrage argued that women would be too subject to the suasion of others (such as their husbands) and thus unable to exercise independent choice in the ballot booth. Legal, political, and cultural definitions of femininity identified women as incapable of acting autonomously, incapable of achieving liberal subjectivity.

Feminist critics have thus argued that liberalism is flawed insofar as it excludes women.[6] While it is indeed the case that the figure of the woman within liberalism often stands opposed to the autonomous, white male liberal subject, this book explores the proposition that this opposition is itself crucial to liberal thought and culture. As such, I argue that liberalism does not exclude women so much as it creates and reserves a discrete position for women within its structure. The position marked out for women—particularly white women—within liberalism is private and familial. Yet rather than simply standing as external to liberalism, this private position—and indeed, the entire notion of privacy and private property—must be seen as crucial to the structure and meaning of liberalism. This is why, for instance, sexual intimacy (coded as privacy) comes to be linked to freedom in the twentieth century, as Haag argues. The focus of this book is on the development of liberalism in relation to gender prior to the twentieth century, and I argue that women's private position has been integral to liberalism since its inception. Indeed, liberalism relies heavily on a binary model of sex and gender: liberal doctrine both creates and sustains a rigidified opposition between male and female bodies and subjectivities. Rather than focusing on women's exclusion from liberalism, however, I argue that one can, with a dialectical turn, locate women *within* the broader structure of liberalism, and discern, as well, the way in which liberalism historically helps to create the very meaning of the word "woman" as we know it today. Race, too, assumes a prominent position within this account of liberalism and gender insofar as the figure of the private woman is insistently defined as white.

The association of women with privacy and the domestic sphere is one that has been vigorously contested of late: historians and literary critics alike have demonstrated the lack of clarity of any demarcation between public and private spheres and the extent to which women of all races routinely engaged in public speaking, paid labor, and political endeavor in a variety of historical periods. Yet liberalism, as a political system, insistently draws an ideological distinction between public and private spheres, and gender has historically been a central element of this mapping of space as well. While it may be possible to demonstrate a lack of functional boundaries between public and private roles for both men and women, the ideological organization of liberal social space relies, in both cultural and juridical terms, upon a perceived distinction between public and private spheres. The political philosopher Judith Shklar argues, for instance, that liberalism is based, in its essence, upon an insistent division between public and private realms:

> Liberalism has only one overriding aim: to secure the political conditions that are necessary for the exercise of personal freedom. . . . [Liberalism] must reject only

those political doctrines that do not recognize any difference between the spheres of the personal and the public. Because of the primacy of toleration as the irreducible limit on public agents, liberals must always draw such a line. This is not historically a permanent or unalterable boundary, but it does require that every public policy be considered with this separation in mind and be consciously defended as meeting its most severe current standard.[7]

According to Shklar, then, liberalism has the primary aim of protecting "personal freedom" that occurs on the private side of the public/private divide. As such, liberalism must always draw a line between public and private realms, although the location of this line may shift at different historical moments. Shklar's analysis thus indicates that the private sphere, whether it is defined in terms of religion or sexuality, must necessarily remain untouched and uncontaminated by the intervention of public control in order to maintain the central mandate of liberalism.

Although Shklar usefully sketches the way in which liberalism relies upon the public/private division, I would disagree with her characterization of the private sphere as independent from the public sphere. Rather than view the public/private division as one that preserves a private realm as sacrosanct from public intrusion, I would describe the two spheres as mutually articulating one another. Privacy, I argue in this book, is constructed and articulated in the public sphere. The privacy of women is the product not of women's seclusion within their homes, but of a public articulation and valuation of women's domestic position. Images of women, books written for women, and books written by women circulated in abundance between the seventeenth and nineteenth centuries; women were not without ample representation in the literary public sphere. Yet much of what was established in public sphere discourse concerning women addressed the value (if not the sacred nature) of women's association with domesticity and privacy.[8] In the first chapter of this book, I cite Nathaniel Hawthorne's awkward account of the logic that precludes women from appearing in the print public sphere. Hawthorne contends that when women write for public venues, there is "a sort of impropriety in the display of woman's *naked mind* to the gaze of the world, with indications by which its inmost secrets may be searched out." This, he concludes, is "an irregularity which men do not commit in appearing there."[9] Although I discuss this passage at greater length in the first chapter, it is worth citing here for the iconic image it strains to articulate: women who appear in public (even in writing) are naked. Hawthorne here *constructs* for us the nakedness of the female mind, of femininity itself; he creates the private status of women's words, minds, and bodies by publicly displaying the image of the naked woman. Hawthorne's image is both symptomatic and enduring: in a Supreme Court decision on issues of privacy rendered as recently as 2001, Justice Antonin Scalia, delivering the majority decision, constructs a similar image of the naked woman in order to give legal meaning and clarity to the debated term "privacy." The case, *Danny Lee Kyllo v. United States*, revolves around whether police use of infrared technology to locate heat-producing lamps employed for growing marijuana constitutes an illegal search, an illegal invasion of the privacy of the home. Although much of the debate in the case concerns whether the infrared technology is "through-the-wall" or "off-the-wall" surveillance—whether it truly invades the home—Scalia ultimately argues that infrared technology is invasive because it might be used to gather information about "intimate details" of the home: "the [infrared scanner] might disclose, for example, at what hour each night the lady of the house takes her daily sauna and bath—a detail that many would consider 'intimate.' "[10] While Scalia argues that all details of what occurs inside the home are intimate, the iconic image of privacy—a naked woman, publicly invoked—is crucial to the rhetorical construction of that argument. In the case of the images of naked women and privacy wrought by both Scalia and Hawthorne, we can see how the public sphere is used to create and circulate images that define women as private. More importantly, we can also see the way in which women are displayed (even when "naked," particularly when "naked") *in public* at the very moment when their private identity is seemingly articulated. Thus to say that women are absent from the public sphere because they are consigned to the private sphere is incorrect: rather, powerful *public* images of femininity identify women as private. In this book, I argue that both images of women (such as those cited above) and writing *by* women have been central to the workings of the literary public sphere from its inception in the seventeenth century. Part of what I seek to illuminate, then, is why that presence has so often been understood as an absence.

My argument thus relies heavily upon an understanding of the public sphere as the location of speech and writing—as the sphere of publicity most fully described by Jürgen Habermas. Habermas has linked the emergence of a public sphere of open debate to the historical development of liberalism. When individuals attained the means to debate their ideas in public (in newspapers, in coffeehouses), they created a social space separate from the state in which they were able to monitor the state critically and thus restructure the political organization of the society. The sphere of publicity described by Habermas is one that he diagrams as a third space (which we might call "the social") standing between private individuals in their familial space and the state.[11] However, Habermas's typology is confusing given that the "public sphere in the world of letters" is defined as a third space, yet it also seems, at various moments in the text, to be assimilated to both the public and the private sphere. As Nancy Fraser points out, the term "public sphere" as it is commonly used (in broad theoretical and often feminist terms) tends to conflate three separate entities: the state, the paid economy, and the realm of public discourse.[12] The nomenclature of the "public sphere" and the liberal dichotomy between public and private has tended to cause the social space of the print public sphere to be assimilated, in theoretical models, to the public side of the public/private divide. Rather than relocate print culture on one side or the other of this divide, I want to argue that more attention should be paid to the way in which print stands as an intermediary location that helps to generate the meaning of both the private and public domains. In this book, I thus seek to open up and explore the space of the literary public sphere as a social space that links the public and private and mediates between the two.

In focusing on this intermediary space, I take explicit issue with a more standard liberal (and Habermasian) narrative that describes citizens as subjects created and fully constituted in private, familial spaces who subsequently emerge into the public sphere to debate rationally their (already constituted, already known) needs and desires. This temporal narrative (first private, then public) is one that has been used to taxonomize the disability and oppression of women under liberalism: as individuals who are primarily located in the private sphere, women never emerge into public, never attain the status of full participants in the rational, critical debates of the public sphere. Against this narrative, I suggest that the public sphere has never operated as a disinterested realm of reasoned debate. Rather, private subjects do not exist in advance of their entry into public debate with fully formed agendas ready at hand. I argue that public sphere culture ("public opinion" in Tocqueville's terms, or the intermediary space of the social) is not only directed toward monitoring the state, as in Habermas's model, but toward shaping or constituting private subjects who seek to emerge into public recognition. This public sphere, which I describe as particularly linked to literary forms of culture, is not only concerned with rational political debate but with the desire for recognition. In the space of the social, I argue, versions of private subjectivity are publicly articulated and individuals seek to emerge into public recognition by deploying publicly available codes of subjectivity. On this model, privacy has no ontological priority over publicity, and privacy, moreover, is itself the back formation of social negotiation. Rather than a Habermasian public sphere of rational critical debate, then, I describe the public sphere as governed by desire—by the desire of subjects to emerge into the space of subjectivity or social recognition. This model of the public sphere blurs the distinction between public and private in part because it points toward the mutual constitution of public sphere recognition and private subjectivity. Reconfiguring the public sphere in this fashion causes some difficulty with terminology because the public sphere no longer appears quite so public, nor the private quite so private. I thus define the space of public sphere activity concerned with private subject production as the space of "sociality," a term that I use to point to the public circulation of the desire for recognition that structures the liberal public sphere.[13]

As I demonstrate throughout this book, women are not in the least absent from the public sphere of desire: rather, their presence there is significant in both cultural and political terms. While I do not argue that women have historically had access to the same forms of public power that men have wielded, I do suggest that gender is a constitutive element of liberal political structure and that women are thus very much present, at every historical moment, in the public workings of sociality. The presence and importance of women (as well as the very definition of the term "woman"), I argue in the coming pages, emerge in a number of distinctly recognizable literary forms. In the chapters that follow, I trace specific historical instances of the shifting relations between liberalism and gender in the public sphere of the United States from the seventeenth through the nineteenth centuries. In so doing I aim to supply a prehistory to the nineteenth-century sentimentalism that has long served as the primary genre identified with women's writing in American literature. Instead of locating the nineteenth century as a point of emergence for women writers, I will describe it as a point of convergence, at which many of the terms I have sketched here assume their most densely associated form— at which, for instance, privacy is most clearly related to gender and political subjectivity, and at which a binary model of gender is most strongly naturalized. In moving further back in time to show how this terminology arises, we see that it is not a question of women stepping out of privacy to become writers at this point, but of a tradition of gender formation in the public sphere that most fully naturalizes its own terms and divisions in the nineteenth century. For instance, although the nineteenth century may see an intensification of domestic affect around heterosexual marriage, in the eighteenth century, the family often seems hardly able to organize itself into a "natural form," ready instead to violate its own uncertain premises through incest, seduction, and adultery.

Unearthing this prehistory changes the story of American literature in an additional fashion: it places writing by American women less squarely within a nationalist framework than most previous accounts of such work. Beginning with a discussion of Anne Hutchinson and the antinomian controversy, I locate the gendered terms animating this debate both within English religious history and in relation to the new communicative norms governing colonial conditions. John Winthrop's *Short Story* concerning the antinomian controversy, for instance, is clearly written for an English rather than an American audience. In broader terms, a concern with gender and a new set of exchange relations can be seen to emerge out of the colonial condition in its orientation toward both English and American public sphere identity. Indeed, the notions of exchange, commerce, and sympathy that inform English fiction of the eighteenth century are arguably one effect of the economic and political revolutions set off by colonialism and early forms of global capitalism. Colonialism is the opening wedge of the world of commercial exchange and the "imagined communities" of Benedict Anderson's print capitalism. I relate these material developments to the ideological pressures brought to bear on the family and gender—the pressures that bring into being modern forms of the family and gender—and thus see literature as bound less to the nation than to developments that both cross and create national boundaries. The Anglo-American colonial world thus stands more at the origin of my account of liberal desire and subject formation than does the founding of the U.S. nation.

My account of the value and meaning of a literary public sphere in which women are full players is meant to challenge both a masculinist tradition of American literature (that has, indeed, long been under attack), and an account of the separation of public and private spheres that views women as external to a public sphere of print culture from its inception. A chorus of critical voices has recently argued not only that women have been excluded from the public sphere, but that the contemporary political public sphere is dangerously narrow or has collapsed altogether. The left has thus often had recourse to a republican rallying cry: if the public sphere were to be reanimated and made truly inclusive, it would enable a commitment to civic rather than individual interest. Iris Young voices one of the more compelling versions of this claim when she argues that we should not only imagine a more inclusive "heterogeneous public sphere," but that we must reconsider the way communication functions in the public sphere. Rather than conceiving of a public sphere in terms of rational critical debate in which we presume "the unity of the speaking subject, that knows himself or herself and seeks faithfully to represent his or her feelings," we must understand the affective force of language as well:

> Communication is not only motivated by the aim to reach consensus, a shared understanding of the world, but also and even more basically by a desire to love and be loved. Modulations of eros operate in the semiotic elements of communication, that put the subject's identity in question in relation to itself, its own part and imagination, and to others, in the heterogeneity of their identity. People do not merely

hear, take in and argue about the validity of utterances. Rather we are affected, in an immediate and felt fashion, by the other's expression and its manner of being addressed to us.[14]

Young's argument clearly resonates with the animating theoretical claims of my study: the literary public sphere and its concern with forms of private subjectivity and subjectification must be understood as central to the politics of the liberal public sphere, not as external to them. Young thus speaks, here, to the issue of desire that is critical to my analysis of liberalism, yet I think she falls short of fully realizing the force of her own diagnosis. It is not merely affect that must be understood to matter in the public sphere (as opposed to reason); rather, affect and desire must be understood less as the effusions of certain kinds of subjects than as constituting all subjects. In other words, the desire for recognition shapes individuals in their most private dimensions. Thus the argument for a more inclusive "heterogeneous" public sphere falls short of directing attention to the ways in which heterogeneity is itself the product of public sphere dynamics of subjectification that are primarily coded as private.

Public sphere discourse, through the modalities of desire, creates subjects; thus what needs to be brought into public is not just difference, or different kinds of subjects, but different forms of desire and exchange together with an analysis of the structuring effects of desire. Lauren Berlant has argued that the public sphere has been collapsed into the private sphere, creating an "intimate public sphere" in which the workings of private life are tacitly understood as the basis of political identity but do not, insofar as they are private, make themselves available to forms of political and collective contestation.[15] It is in the name of such contestation that the structural effects of desire call for analysis. The liberal desire that gives us the rich and textured terrain of private life does indeed individuate the subjects of mass culture, but it does so in relation to a structure—in relation to fictional moments of supposed identity, and thus in relation to mechanisms of mediation and exchange. It is the workings of this liberal desire that appear most prominently in the literary public sphere, and to which I turn in this book.

1

Gender, Liberal Theory, and the Literary Public Sphere

> It is wrong to say God made *Rich* and *Poor*: He made
> only *Male* and *Female*.
>
> Thomas Paine, *Agrarian Justice*

THE BODY OF LIBERALISM

The importance of gender within the founding fictions of liberalism emerges with particular clarity when we contrast the location of political authority within liberalism to its position within an earlier, feudal political order. Although a feudal political order committed to a divinely ordained social hierarchy understands women as lesser beings than men—beings situated lower than men on the Great Chain of Being—liberalism does not. Organized around voluntaristic relations of contract rather than ascriptive relations of status, liberalism (in theory) does not particularize women on the basis of status. Indeed, the shift from status to contract is fundamental to liberalism: liberalism imputes an equality of agency among all individuals who engage in contracts and thus defines the subject in terms of his or her fundamental human capacity to make choices.[1] Liberalism thus presupposes an equality among individuals at the level of liberty (all individuals are equal insofar as they have the capacity and right to exercise free choice), if not at the level of social and economic condition. Yet because women's bodies have been seen to constrain and encumber them, women have been understood to lack the constitutive agency that would enable them to participate in liberal subjectivity. Within the universalizing theory of liberalism, then, women are particularized in such a way as to stand outside of the political prestige accorded to the individual. The logic of this particularization of women involves not simply pulling rank—arguing that men are more authoritative, muscular, rational, or closer to God than women—rather, it requires defining women as individuals constitutively unable to exercise choice and agency.

The demarcation between male autonomy and female dependency within liberalism is typically grounded in a discourse of biological determinism: that is, the difference between men and women is construed as natural (rather than cultural) and as derived from physiological distinctions between male and female bodies. Women are defined as essentially (biologically, ontologically) *prepolitical* beings whose very bodies and psyches preclude them from attaining the independence necessary for entry-level competence in the liberal political arena. In the simplest of terms, for instance, women's bodies have been described as insufficiently bounded; the penetrable female body is understood to be inherently lacking in autonomy, conjoined to children and dependent upon men.[2] Yet it is important to note that the strong binary distinction between the sexes is less biologically than historically grounded: as Thomas Laqueur has argued, a fixed division between male and female anatomies only emerges in the eighteenth century. The dimorphic construction of sexed bodies thus corresponds historically to the period in which liberalism emerges.

According to historians of the body such as Laqueur and Londa Schiebinger, a one-sex model of the body was commonplace prior to the eighteenth century: anatomical pictures of this body depict male and female sexual organs as identical, save that the female genitalia are inside rather than outside the body. On this model, then, the body is not inherently sexed: rather, the similarities between the bodies of men and women indicate a continuity of substance, a single sex that assumes a variety of forms. Differences among bodies were articulated in terms of class and status rather than gender: moreover, the *ground* of difference was not the body itself but a divinely sanctioned hierarchy that placed the king's body at the top of the political and social order.[3] Anatomy textbooks from the eighteenth century forward, however, emphasize the divarication of male and female bodies rather than their similarity: more importantly, a host of psychological and social distinctions between men and women are derived from the now utterly distinct male and female bodies. "Not only are the sexes different," writes Laqueur of the eighteenth century, "but they are different in every conceivable aspect of body and soul, in every physical and moral aspect."[4] On the two-sex model, social difference is understood as *grounded* in (deriving its authority from) biological difference. The shift in the ground and meaning of sexual difference from the early modern to the modern period is succinctly illustrated in the profound transformation in the social coding of sexual difference among children in the two periods. Phyllis Rackin points out that children in sixteenth-century England were dressed in skirts until they reached the age of seven because class, rather than gender, was the central signifier of social identity: "The physical difference that separated boys from girls was insignificant: what mattered was the difference in social rank that separated one man from another. . . . But we wrap our children in pink or blue blankets even in the hospital nursery, insisting on the innate, biological difference between male and female."[5] Our contemporary sense that gender is a fundamental episteme of subjectivity—a crucial element of knowledge about any individual—should thus be understood to have significant historical and cultural parameters.

Although gender did matter prior to the eighteenth century, it mattered in a far different way than it does for the modern, liberal subject. For instance, claims about the meaning of gender with respect to political authority change dramatically when sex is understood to be grounded in biology rather than divine hierarchy. In 1559 the Scottish Reformation leader John Knox famously inveighed against the rule of women, arguing that such rule violated the hierarchical order ordained by God: "Against God can nothing be more manifest than that a woman shall be exalted to reign above man. For the contrary sentence hath He pronounced in these words: 'Thy will shall be subject to thy husband, and he shall bear dominion over thee' (Gen. 3:16)."[6] Knox makes no argument about the physical capacities of women: rather, he straightforwardly asserts that because men occupy a higher rung on the divine order than women they should not be governed by women. If we jump forward to 1795 in the early days of the American Republic, we find Federalist publisher and pamphleteer William Cobbett similarly arguing (albeit in a satirical vein) that women should not govern men. Unlike Knox, however, Cobbett bases his argument on the anatomical differences between male and female bodies: "Who knows but our present house of Representatives, for instance, may be succeeded by members of the other sex? . . . If the speaker should happen to be with child that would be nothing odd to us . . . and if she should even lie in, during the sessions, her place might be supplied by her aunt or grandmother."[7] Cobbett thus imagines a scene in which the political order is disrupted by the presence of a female body that cannot function autonomously. For Cobbett, a woman's body is likely to literally burst open when placed in the public sphere, necessitating a chain of substitutions (aunts, grandmothers) that announce dependence upon and association with other bodies. According to Cobbett, then, the female body incapacitates women for positions of political authority. By way of contrast, we might note that Knox argues that a woman's ability to have children is a *sign* (not the ground) of her subjection to man and God: "Hereby . . . [we] see that God by His sentence hath dejected all women from empire and dominion above man. For two punishments are laid upon her: to wit, a dolour, anguish and pain, as oft as ever she shall be mother; and a subjection of herself, her appetites and will, to her husband and to his will."[8] Under an early modern dispensation, then, women are excluded from governing because they must not violate the divine hierarchy that locates men above them. Under a modern, liberal dispensation, on the other hand, women *cannot* participate in politics because their bodies prevent them from doing so: the pregnant body is the ground that dictates women's exclusion from the public, political sphere.

William Cobbett's description of the female body as biologically unsuited for political subjectivity might be seen to inaugurate a long American tradition in which the woman's body is understood to incapacitate her for the duties of citizenship. Indeed, as Lauren Berlant argues with respect to recent Supreme Court decisions concerning abortion, "[For the justices] heterosexual femininity [in its reproductive capacity] in the United States is an undue burden":[9] according to Berlant, femininity is effectively construed as a bodily handicap to citizenship insofar as the woman's body (in particular, the female reproductive system) is understood to exercise upon women a kind of constraint not experienced by men. The notion that a woman's reproductive system is an undue burden for citizenship indicates, most obviously, that the male body is taken as normative for citizenship. Less obviously, it indicates the way in which the pregnant female body (an image that represents a condition that some, but not all, women experience for a relatively brief time in their lives) comes to stand as a synecdoche both for femininity itself and for constraint, dependency, and the limits of volition.

In serving as the ground of political agency, then, the sexed body bears a great deal of theoretical weight within liberalism. Yet liberalism does not simply deploy the terms of a preexisting ontological division between men and women; rather, it works to effect this division. Viewed historically, we might say that liberal thought relies upon the *transformation* of sex and gender into ontological categories; these essentialized categories, in turn, underwrite the delimitation of women's activity to a prepolitical, private sphere together with the discursive production of men as idealized occupants of the public sphere.[10] Yet if it is indeed the case that biology becomes the grounds for adjudicating political participation—for excluding women from political participation in the liberal state—we must wonder *why* this is so. What purpose is served by differentiating male and female bodies within liberalism and by relegating women to a prepolitical position? To answer this question in very schematic terms we might say that a prepolitical terrain is necessary to form the support and the origin (in both material and theoretical terms) upon which the liberal political field is constructed. In theoretical terms, the figure of the prepolitical woman serves as an ideological foil to enable the emergence into intelligibility of the autonomous liberal male. In material terms, the distinction between male and female bodies serves as the basis of a crucial division of labor in which women perform domestic work that, in turn, provides the economic support for the production of masculine autonomy. In effecting this division of labor, the ostensibly descriptive terms of biological essentialism thus attain a prescriptive force.

In equating women, and particularly the reproductive capacity of the female body, with biological constraint and an absence of self-determination, liberalism places women outside of the realm of choice that constitutes the political sphere. Women thereby become the cultural placeholders of *constraint* (as opposed to volition), or what Wendy Brown refers to as "encumbrance":

> The liberal formulation of liberty is thus not merely opposed to but *premised* upon encumbrance; it is achieved by displacing the embodied, encumbered, and limited nature of existence onto women. . . . [T]he autonomous subject of liberalism requires a large population of nonautonomus subjects, a population that generates, tends, and avows the goods, relations, dependencies and connections that sustain and nourish human life. . . . [T]he putative autonomy of the liberal subject partakes of a myth of masculinity requiring the disavowal of dependency, the disavowal of the relations that nourish and sustain this subject.[11]

Although men as well as women live in an encumbered world—a world in which social and physical constraints and dependencies shape our lives—the masculinized liberal subject is established in what I will call a "line of fiction,"[12] a fiction in which men do not occupy bodies that encumber, constrain, and limit them. Moreover, as Brown suggests in the passage cited above, liberalism enacts this fiction in both theoretical and material terms. In theoretical terms, liberalism tends to disavow forms of dependence experienced by men by locating dependence *in general* in the figure of the biologically constrained female body. In material terms, on the other hand, liberalism is historically associated with a division of labor between men and women that helps to give substance to the theory (rendering descriptive theory prescriptive, and hence self-actualizing): the prepolitical woman serves as the domestic support of the autonomous male, providing the "invisible," nonwaged labor of nourishing, housekeeping, and reproducing that serves as the prerequisite to men's ability to function "autonomously" in the public sphere.[13] In other words, men's participation in the public sphere is dependent upon an array of support services that are located outside the political sphere in the realm of necessity—a realm designated as prepolitical, and, in the fiction of liberalism, populated primarily by women, and, as I will argue, people of color.

In theory, then, liberalism posits equality in the political field, yet it simultaneously relies upon a biology of incommensurable difference that functions to circumscribe, in advance, the field of political participation. Difference—both sexual and racial—is thus located in an extrapolitical terrain where it is naturalized, rendered a mute truth of the physical world rather than a political assertion subject to negotiation among contracting individuals. The circumscription of the political field selects out a relatively homogenous group of individuals as political subjects to share in the theoretical equality of liberalism; indeed, the very homogeneity of this group might be seen to facilitate the creation of a horizontally organized field in which vertical relations of status and difference are displaced outside the field altogether. For example, while race slavery would seem to violate the basic liberal premises of freedom and equality, the liberal displacement of the meaning of racial difference from the realm of politics to that of biology might be seen, paradoxically, to have historically fostered political equality only among white men. Edmund Morgan has thus argued that race slavery in the early Republic *facilitated* rather than contradicted political claims to equality among the colonists. Because slaves performed the labor that the British lower classes might have performed in England, there was less class disparity among the white men of Virginia. Race, understood as a biological rather than social or political difference, thus offered a convenient means to circumscribe the polity such that equality and republican politics obtained among the white planters of Virginia. Morgan explains that "the most ardent American republicans were Virginians, and their ardor was not unrelated to their power over the men and women they held in bondage.... Racism thus absorbed in Virginia the fear and contempt that men in England . . . felt for the inarticulate lower classes. Racism made it possible for white Virginians to develop a devotion to the equality that English republicans had declared to be the soul of liberty."[14] Biological essentialism enables the differential relations of status—which would have been understood as class difference in a previous period—to be defined as apolitical, and thus not susceptible to political debate.

In its recourse to biological essentialism, liberalism is the more insidious for defining as *natural* what is in fact a *political* distribution of power among those who will count as subjects and those who will not. As Judith Butler points out, drawing the limits of the political field is itself a fundamentally political act, despite the fact that this circumscription (and its political valences) appears invisible once it is completed: "The act which unilaterally establishes the domain of the political functions, then, as an authoritarian ruse by which political contest over the status of the subject is summarily silenced."[15] The contest over the political authority of white women and nonwhite Americans is summarily silenced by biological discourse: sexual anatomy, craniology, phrenology, and theories of polygenesis proliferate in the nineteenth century as discourses that police the fundamentally political, fictively biological, line between male and female, between white and nonwhite identities.[16] The shift toward biological essentialism enables liberalism to posit a theoretical equality among all individuals (to seemingly eradicate status relations), while simultaneously reinstantiating status relations by grounding them in biological, rather than political or religious, terms. Insofar as liberalism disavows the status-based divisions at its origins, it is founded in a line of fiction; moreover, located as it is in a foundational position, this fiction is particularly difficult to contest.[17]

Biological essentialism would seem, then, to exclude women and African-Americans from liberalism.[18] Yet I would argue that this exclusion can be reversed in dialectical terms: that is, it is demonstrably the case that this exclusion *includes* white women and African-Americans in an externalized—but foundational—position. More specifically, this foundational position might be seen as related to *private property*. In the colonial Atlantic world and in the United States, the emerging biological discourse of race served to classify Africans and African-Americans as property rather than persons: slaves were thus relegated to the status of private property and decisively excluded from public, political participation. As Houston Baker points out, blacks historically did not have access to the public sphere precisely because they were culturally and juridically conceived of as property rather than persons.[19] The 1857 Dred Scott decision by the Supreme Court notoriously ruled that free African-Americans could not be considered U.S. citizens; Chief Justice Roger Taney's ruling insisted that because Africans were first brought to the United States as property, their descendants could not be considered persons with political standing in the nation. In his simultaneous insistence on the essential character of African-Americans as property, and the political duty of the state to protect the right of white men to own property, Taney's decision dramatizes the binary nature of the division between property and persons and the extent to which the two sides of that binary are mutually constitutive. That is, the decision indicates that white personhood and an adherent political subjectivity are predicated on the ownership of property: moreover, slaves become a particularly sacred form of property insofar as they sustain a connection between whiteness, property ownership, and political subjectivity.[20] In material terms, the labor of African-American slaves produces the capital that underwrites the independence from constraint of the white male property owner. In both these material terms and in the theoretical terms articulated in the Dred Scott decision, biological essentialism enables black bodies to be understood as a form of property that *produces* the political personhood of the white, male liberal subject.

I have thus far argued that biological essentialism operates within liberalism to establish the extrapolitical status of both African-Americans and white women. However, the analogy between the essentializing discourse of race and that of sex is far from absolute and, indeed, it breaks down in an instructive fashion when we consider the starkly different positions held by black and white women within liberalism. On the one hand, the biological discourses of race and sex bear a structural similarity to one another: the fictive whiteness that is the historical property of the American liberal subject requires blackness for its production in both theoretical and material terms, and the fictive autonomy of the idealized male participant of the public sphere depends upon the white woman's theoretical and material status as private. Yet the African-American's status as property renders him or her *apolitical* within liberalism, whereas the white woman's status as private renders her *prepolitical* within liberalism. White women, although historically conceived of as property under the law of coverture, increasingly appear, over the course of the eighteenth and nineteenth centuries, as figures not merely of property but of privacy as well. As domestic privacy becomes increasingly central to liberal narratives of freedom, the white woman's position in the domestic sphere becomes sacralized: political authority in liberalism from the eighteenth century forward is located in a tightly symbiotic relation between private and public spheres in which domesticity produces a kind of privacy that serves as an origin for the fiction of liberal masculinity. As property, African-American women were not granted a private status similar to that of white women. Indeed, as Hortense Spillers argues, African-Americans who were categorized as property were "ungendered." Enslaved black women in particular were denied the social-symbolic position of motherhood: "even though the enslaved female reproduced other enslaved persons, we do not read 'birth' in this instance as a reproduction of mothering precisely because the female, like the male, has been robbed of the parental right, the parental function."[21] Spillers points, here, to the socially (rather than biologically) reproductive function of the mother, and particularly to parenting as the reproductive origin of social subjectivity. The role of mother as socially reproductive is granted to white women, but denied to black women. Insofar as white women are located in a prepolitical space, they are also positioned within a temporal narrative concerning the production of male, liberal subjectivity: men form and sustain their identities in the private sphere, and, sequentially, emerge from this prepolitical space into the political sphere. Insofar as African-American women are located in an *apolitical* space, defined as property rather than persons, they are not visible as gendered subjects, not visible as signifiers of the privacy that produces public identity.

Much of this book will focus on the prepolitical position of white women, and more specifically on the temporal trajectory of liberalism's line of fiction as the liberal subject moves from a private sphere origin to a public sphere agency. At this juncture, however, it is important to note that whiteness is a constitutive element of the category of gender within this fiction. Moreover, the fact that black women historically do not have the social-symbolic function of "woman" indicates both the racial determination of "woman" as linked to whiteness, and the social, noncorporeal nature of this position.[22] That is, the biological determination of women's identity as private is exposed as fictive at the moment when biologically female black bodies are not similarly identified as private. For instance, the black woman's reproductive capacity is historically *not* used as an argument for disqualifying her from participation in labor outside the home. Through the lens of race, then, the ideological quality of white women's privacy becomes more evident; moreover, we will see, too, that discourses of racial identity assume importance in both defining and challenging the private identity of white women, particularly in the nineteenth century, when the binary opposition of black and white becomes increasingly sharply drawn, as does the binary opposition between private and public spheres.

THE TEMPORALITY OF LIBERALISM

The prepolitical space to which white women are consigned (putatively on the basis of biology) is, then, not simply a spatial location but a *temporal* one. The private, familial space that women occupy serves as the origin and staging ground of male liberal identity insofar as the *narrative* of liberal subjectivity begins in privacy and moves forward into public agency. Conceived in temporal, narrative terms rather than spatial ones, women's location in a prepolitical realm can be understood less as an exclusion from the public sphere than as an inclusion within a liberal narrative, albeit a narrative that tends toward the end of masculine agency. Liberalism might be described in terms of a fundamental antinomy between the embodied, constrained nature of subjectivity and the idea of the subject as free and autonomous. Both gender and the temporality of narrative are resources deployed in liberal thought to resolve this antinomy.[23] As I will argue below, the temporal trajectory of the liberal narrative is an important element of liberalism's line of fiction; moreover, I will suggest that we might productively reverse this narrative and consider women's private and familial role as the back-formation of a masculinized public agency. Rather than viewing privacy as the natural origin of public identity, we might thus view privacy as *coproduced* together with public identity in the print public sphere. In this sense, I will argue that privacy and private property constitute a fabulous origin rather than the temporal starting point of the narrative of liberal subjectivity. For the moment, however, I want to sketch out the ways in which liberalism has constructed and relied upon precisely this line of fiction (a movement from private to public) in both theoretical and historical terms.

Historically, liberal theory and liberal politics emerge in tandem with new forms of property relations and specifically with the growth of private property ownership. In the transition from feudalism to capitalism, land tenure shifted from feudal property relations in which land was held in tenancy in the ruler's name, to absolute, or individual ownership. In seventeenth-century England, where agrarian capitalism was central to the transition from feudalism to capitalism, private land ownership assumed enormous political significance.[24] Indeed, the ownership of property was understood as the source of an individual's political independence and thus of the individual's authority to participate in the political life of the nation. Because landowners could support themselves, they were understood to be independent from the will of other men—from governmental or commercial influence and manipulation. As J. G. A. Pocock argues, the ownership of land is the predicate of republican political authority: "Personal independence . . . could only belong to men whose property was their own and did not consist in expectations from the men in government; and the moral quality which only propertied independence could confer, and which became almost indistinguishable from property itself, was known as 'virtue.'"[25] In the liberal tradition, which supervenes or competes with republicanism, property ownership is similarly at the root of political agency.[26] As C. B. Macpherson, among others, argues, the so-called "Putney debates" between Oliver Cromwell and the Puritan Levellers following the English Revolution framed the character of the political authority of citizens in terms of property ownership. Cromwell and his fellow Independent, Henry Ireton, argued that the franchise of the new government should be restricted to owners of freehold land and freemen of trading corporations: Ireton thus states, "If there be anything at all that is a foundation of liberty it is this, that those who shall choose the law-makers shall be men freed from dependence upon others."[27] Macpherson argues that the Levellers, too, imagine property relations to stand at the root of franchise rights insofar as they don't propose universal manhood suffrage, but propose excluding from the franchise servants and alms takers who, as one Leveller states, "because they depend upon the will of other men . . . should be afraid to displease [them]."[28] In theoretical terms, liberalism proposes that equal political rights inhere in the condition of being human and are thus universal despite differences among individuals in their material conditions; yet historically, the notion of a political authority located in the independent agency of the citizen is closely linked to property ownership.[29]

This historical grounding of liberalism in property ownership, particularly in its English roots, casts a long shadow over liberalism in the United States. The property-rights limitations on the franchise debated at Putney in 1647 remained in place in England through 1918, and, although less restrictive in the United States, nonetheless formed the basis for suffrage in the British colonies prior to the Revolution, and persisted in some states through the middle of the nineteenth century. Significantly, as property requirements for the franchise were abolished, they were replaced by voting limitations defined in terms of race and gender.[30] As such, the whiteness and masculinity that qualify one for political participation come to serve as biological markers of self-possession and independence. Understood themselves as property rather than as independent property owners, white women and blacks could not vote. Liberalism is a political doctrine that construes the role of the state as that of protecting the freedom of citizens, yet the freedom that underwrites the authority of the liberal political subject, and the freedom that the liberal state is understood to protect, is linked to private property ownership.[31] The state thus has an interest, as we have seen, in protecting the raced and gendered divisions of labor that define the white male as the inviolable owner of private property and white women and blacks as producers and species of property. In narrative terms, private property thus stands as the origin of liberal autonomy: property ownership enables one to move forward into the public sphere.

I have just sketched a historical narrative in which the public agency of the liberal subject emerges from the creation of private property. The early theorists of liberalism expound a temporal narrative of liberalism as well, yet they rely less on the historical demise of feudalism and the advent of absolute property as the framework of this narrative than upon overt fictions of origins: the "states of nature" postulated by Hobbes, Locke, and Rousseau are the starting points of liberal theory. In each instance, a fictive "state of nature" precedes civil society and determines the need for civil society. In each of these theories, women are associated with the state of nature rather than with civil society. In Locke's theory in particular, it becomes clear that liberalism is premised both upon a separation of private and public spheres and upon the narrative movement from a more primitive state of nature (associated with the private sphere) to the fully developed public sphere of civil society. In his *Second Treatise*, Locke develops the terms of liberal theory as he argues against Sir Robert Filmer's claim that the authority of the monarch is patriarchal, like that of a father over a family. While Locke agrees that fathers have a natural right to power within the family, he argues that the political power of the state cannot be understood in analogous terms: properly *political* power is not grounded in patriarchy but in mutual contract or consent among independent, self-possessed citizens. Yet in arguing that political power should not be understood on a patriarchal model, Locke performs an incision on the social body crucial to liberalism: he dissevers a private, domestic sphere—a prepolitical sphere in which paternal power still obtains—from the properly political sphere of consent: "These two *Powers, Political* and *Paternal, are so perfectly* distinct and separate; are built upon so different Foundations and given to so different Ends, that every Subject that is a Father, has as much a *Paternal Power* over his Children, as the Prince has over his [children] . . . and can therefore contain not any part of degree of that kind of a Dominion, which a Prince, or Magistrate has over his Subject." While the ruling of the family "naturally falls to the Man's share, as the abler and the stronger," this kind of ruling is not considered political, but natural or prepolitical: "The *Society betwixt Parents and Children*, and the distinct Rights and Powers belonging respectively to them . . . is far different from a Politick Society."[32] Locke thus proposes a developmental narrative operative at two levels: in the general evolution of society from the state of nature toward a civil compact, and at the level of each individual who leaves the natural authority of the family behind to enter into civil society upon reaching the age of reason. As feminist theorists have pointed out, however, women do not emerge from Locke's prepolitical realm into political adulthood: women are located in this narrative at the origin of liberal subjectivity but remain behind while men progress toward full political participation as they enter into property-owning contractual relations.

The above account of Locke's narrative of liberal origins is informed to a large degree by the work of Carole Pateman, a feminist critic of liberal theory who has persuasively argued that the exclusion of women from the public sphere is constitutive rather than contingent with respect to liberalism. Specifically, Pateman argues that the social contract, which necessarily obtains only among men, is subtended by a sexual contract in which men establish authority or conjugal sex-right over women. By the time the social contract is made, Pateman argues, a *prior* contract—the sexual contract—is already in place. The sexual contract is one in which men are given sexual access to women and granted patriarchal authority over them: "The assumption must necessarily be made that, by the time the social contract is made, all the women in the natural condition have been conquered by men and are now their subjects (servants). . . . Only men who stand to each other as free and equal masters of 'families' will take part."[33] Invoking Freud's mythic social origin scene of parricide in *Totem and Taboo*, Pateman argues that the fraternal organization of liberalism is posited upon the demise of a patriarchalism (parricide) that establishes equality among brothers *who seek equal access to women*. Fraternity—the horizontal political field of liberalism—is thus predicated on a shared masculine authority over women. Moreover, because this authority is established before the social contract in which men enter as equals into civil society, women's subjugation (in the prepolitical private sphere) under the sexual contract remains hidden. Underlying and preceding the social contract, Pateman argues, lies the sexual contract: "During the genesis of civil society, the sphere of natural subjection is separated out as the non-political sphere. . . . Sex-right or conjugal right, the original political right, then becomes completely hidden."[34] Against the origin stories of the liberal theorists, Pateman thus posits an alternative origin, one that exposes gendered forms of oppression as the prehistory of fraternal contract.

Pateman's theory is extremely powerful insofar as it acknowledges the structural relation of the public/private division to liberalism, and thus the structural role of gender within liberalism. Yet I disagree with Pateman's approach in one key regard: Pateman, like other liberal theorists, proposes a *narrative* of liberal identity in which women are located temporally prior to men, and in which men emerge from their association with women into a public, liberal status. Pateman intentionally responds to the founding fictions of liberal theorists—the state of nature tales—by proposing an alternative narrative in their stead. Clearly, this narrative is not intended as normative but is designed to make women's position more visible, to help women emerge from a hidden, foundational status beneath the social contract.[35] Nonetheless, I think Pateman thereby mistakenly enacts a premise of liberalism—namely, that the antinomies of the liberal subject are ameliorated by recourse to narrative. If the liberal subject must insist upon autonomy, self-possession, and volition in a world where all bodies are subject to forms of biological and social constraint, discipline, and exchange, liberalism ameliorates this contradiction by recourse both to gender division (men have volition, women embody constraint) *and* by narrative (constraint that once obtained in the state of nature or the private sphere no longer obtains when the liberal subject emerges into civil society). In separating out the contradiction over time, narrative both temporalizes and temporizes the contradiction of liberalism. In recasting the narrative of liberalism to account for a prior moment of oppression, Pateman reinforces the temporal movement of liberalism's line of fiction.

Contrary to Pateman, however, I would argue that women occupy a position in the narrative of liberal subjectivity that is less hidden and repressed than she indicates. Indeed, far from being written out of social contract theory, women are written in, albeit in a problematic fashion. More importantly, I would argue against the linear emplotment of the fiction of liberal origins that Pateman presents us with. First, as I discuss below, the narrative of liberal development tends to double back on itself once the liberal subject emerges into the public sphere. This is so because the purpose of government and public sphere activity, on the liberal model, is the protection of private freedom. As such, liberalism returns toward property and privacy for a continued justification of its public sphere activity: because private property is both origin and telos, the private sphere is not simply left behind in a progressive narrative of liberal development as Pateman proposes. Second, I would argue that it is important to understand the origin tales of liberal theory as bearing little reference to history. While articulated in the form of history, the "state of nature" stories are also clearly fictions. As such, we should understand that what they narrate is the ideology of liberal subjectivity, not the developmental history of mankind's social organization. In other words, these origin stories do not describe events that have happened in the past, but rather describe the construction of subjectivities, a process that occurs in a repetitive rather than linear fashion.

Judith Butler's description of the recursive nature of subject formation points us toward a model for thinking about the *nonlinear* force of the story of the liberal subject: "If the subject is constituted by power, that power does not cease at the moment the subject is constituted, for that subject is never fully constituted, but is subjected and produced time and again. That subject is neither a ground nor a product, but the permanent possibility of a certain resignifying process, one which gets detoured and stalled through other mechanisms of power, but which is power's own possibility of being reworked."[36] Butler's reference to "resignifying" is particularly resonant in this case: because the liberal subject emerges from the private sphere, and bears constant reference to that sphere in his public activity, privacy (and femininity) is not located resolutely in the past as the narrative model would imply, but must be repeatedly invoked (resignified) in order to serve as the ground of liberal identity. I would thus argue that the temporal force of the narrative of liberal origins is subject to reversal; rather than a narrative movement from privacy to public identity, we can understand public sphere identity to call for the production and reproduction of privacy rather than for it to be left behind. Understood in these terms, we can see that the privacy of women's bodies and labor must be constantly produced in order for the autonomous liberal male to emerge, on a daily basis even, into his public sphere identity. As I will argue below, the print public sphere relies upon and reproduces fictions of liberalism. Moreover, women are highly visible both within these narratives and as producers of these narratives.

THE TEXTUALITY OF LIBERALISM

The woman writer, Nathaniel Hawthorne tells us, faces a peculiar danger in entering into the print public sphere: there is, he writes, "a sort of impropriety in the display of woman's *naked mind* to the gaze of the world, with indications by which its inmost secrets may be searched out." This, he concludes, is "an irregularity which men do not commit in appearing there."[37] In order to insist on the private nature of women's every thought and action, Hawthorne here describes the words of women as essentially fleshlike, as insistently attached to the carnal figure of the woman who can only appear in public as an indecently exposed body. Hawthorne's recourse to catachresis (the "naked mind") indicates the conceptual stretch he must make to attach the embodied figure of woman to the abstractive nature of ratiocination and print. Indeed, print—a medium in which bodies are, precisely, absent because only words remain present—theoretically produces the writer as an abstract liberal subject. Yet as we have seen, the unencumbered liberal agent emerges with the help of a powerful narrative, one that defines the liberal subject's agency as grounded in his possessive relation to privacy. This relation, I will argue, does not disappear in print: rather, print produces privacy—makes it visible, comprehensible, meaningful, and locates it within a narrative—as much as it produces the public nature of the liberal subject. Ironically, with respect to Hawthorne's lament, then, the searching out of inmost secrets—the creation and exposition of interiority—and the construction of women as the cultural bearers of secrets and privacy occur precisely within the print public sphere. For this reason, we might say that women have been indecently exposed in print at the origins of liberalism: print constructs women's privacy and relies upon this privacy to articulate the narrative emergence of the masculine liberal subject at the same time that it renders women's authorship both potent and vexed as a public act.

In arguing that privacy is constructed in the print public sphere, and thus that the antinomies of liberal subjectivity (embodiment/abstraction, private/public, female/male) are proposed in the structure of print, I turn to a body of theory that locates the origins of liberal subjectivity less in property ownership than in political relations connected to technologies of print and publicity. The most prominent of these theorists, Jürgen Habermas, argues that the print public sphere, which had its advent in the eighteenth century, was the birthplace of the liberal subject. The print medium blossomed in this period, Habermas tells us, in the form of newspapers, journals, and novels, all of which dissociated writing and print from state and church power and associated it instead with commerce, private property, and the concerns of a bourgeois citizenry. This new public sphere stood outside state control, and served as a meeting ground for bourgeois citizens to engage in rational, critical debate concerning politics and civic life. Public opinion, refined and rendered rational through exposure to the light of publicity, came to be understood as the ground of political authority, thus dismantling the claim to authority of absolutist regimes and positing instead a government subject to public scrutiny and the rule of law and reason. The institutions of the public sphere—salons, coffeehouses, journals, newspapers—were spaces in which individuals gathered to express their ideas as individuals and as equals. These institutions, Habermas writes, "disregarded status altogether. [They] replaced the celebration of rank with a tact befitting equals. The parity on whose basis alone the authority of the better argument could assert itself against that of social hierarchy . . . meant . . . the parity of 'common humanity.' "[38] We thus find the tenets of liberalism— the equal freedom of each individual to exercise agency, the liberty to assent to forms of government, the autonomy of subjects guided by reason—embedded less in an independence arising from property ownership than in specific institutions (salons, newspapers) in which individuals were able to freely express their ideas. Foremost among these institutions in the eighteenth century is the printed word and its increased public circulation in new literary forms.

How does such a model of textual liberalism configure the gender relations that we have seen are embedded within liberalism? While feminist theorists have argued that Habermas's public sphere constitutively excludes women, I will argue that Habermas actually proposes two different models of the public sphere, one of which locates women as far more central than does the other. Critics have often noted the tension in Habermas's work between his description of the public sphere as a normative model of a democratic society (an ideal according to which democracy should function) and as a historical description of the rise of print culture and liberalism in eighteenth-century Europe. In what follows, I suggest that the historical model is far more attentive to the central position of women, privacy, and desire within liberalism than is the normative model. In its normative form, Habermas's public sphere would seem to instantiate a Kantian ideal of rational communication or "procedural rationality"[39] in which the institutions of public sphere communication (through their openness to public debate) make access to reason, or "common humanity," possible. For contemporary political theorists such as Seyla Benhabib, the normative dimension of Habermas's public sphere remains the central ideal of democracy: "the normative principle of 'free and unconstrained dialogue among reasoning individuals,' . . . after all is the principle of democratic legitimacy for all modern societies."[40] Moreover, for Benhabib, it is precisely the "radically proceduralist" nature of Habermas's public sphere that promises social change, since one of the premises of the public sphere is its openness to all speakers. In part because Habermas's later work emphasizes the normative dimension of the public sphere, critics have typically identified the public sphere with an ideal of procedural rationalism and given less attention to his historical description of the eighteenth-century public sphere.[41] In the readings that follow, I argue for a reassessment of the relation of women to the print public sphere on the basis of Habermas's description of literature in the eighteenth-century public sphere: in so doing, I claim less to be faithful to the overall trajectory of Habermas's work than to elucidate, for my own purposes, a particular model of print culture buried within Habermas's work that speaks to the presence (rather than absence) of women in the print public sphere.

Habermas's model of the normative public sphere accords with what I have called the temporality of liberalism. He emphasizes that private subjectivity is the prerequisite of public activity: "it was private people," he argues repeatedly, "who related to each other . . .as a public" (28). Habermas would thus seem to follow the model of the other liberal theorists we have seen in tracing the narrative emergence of the liberal subject from out of the private into the public sphere. Indeed, for this reason, Joan Landes critiques Habermas very much along the lines of Pateman's analysis of Locke: "the exclusion of women from the bourgeois public was not incidental but central to its incarnation," she argues. According to Landes, the bourgeois public sphere claims to eradicate status relations through the abstract discourse of reasonable debate, but access to the public sphere is "predicated on one's having a certain position in the property order."[42] As such, the hidden status relations of liberalism—including those of gender, which locate women as particular (rather than universal), propertyless, and unreasoning—determine who emerges from privacy into public and who does not. The proceduralist model of the public sphere works, according to Landes, to banish women to the domestic sphere and to silence them: the bourgeois public sphere functions to "confine women to the interior," she concludes.[43]

Yet if the interior, domestic realm (the "intimate sphere" in Habermas's terms) appears as a space of confinement hidden away from the light of reason and publicity according to the proceduralist model of the public sphere, it

assumes a different status according to Habermas's *historical* model of the public sphere. Specifically, Habermas's historical model locates the intimate sphere
as the site of the production of a new form of subjectivity that is the prerequisite of public sphere activity. In emphasizing the importance of the intimate
sphere in its co-relation with the public sphere, Habermas proposes a model of
liberal identity that is not, I would argue, wholly linear. Historically, Habermas
tells us, the bourgeois public sphere is predicated upon the new organization
of the family as a conjugal unit that produces the subjectivity of the bourgeois
homme. The conjugal, patriarchal family was the "wellspring of a specific subjectivity," the breeding ground of "privateness in the modern sense of a saturated and free interiority" (43, 28). The public, in turn, is comprised of individuals with precisely this sort of individuality and interiority: "privatized
individuals . . . formed the public sphere of a rational-critical debate in the
world of letters within which the subjectivity originating in the interiority of
the conjugal family, by communicating with itself, attained clarity about itself"
(51). While this passage emphasizes the complementarity of the private individual and the public sphere, it does so in such a way that the linear movement
from private to public, so characteristic of liberal theory, becomes less than
clear. For instance, the interiority created in the conjugal family only seems to
fully come to fruition—to "attain clarity about itself"—in the public sphere.
Indeed, public communication seems to concern interiority itself, suggesting
that interiority may be less the predicate of rational communication than its
result.

Habermas also indicates that the family is less the site of constraint and
embodiment—a place to be left behind with childhood—than a site where
freedom is realized in its link to the "interiority" of the liberal subject. Freedom
consists in engaging in the voluntary relations, such as companionate marriage
and parental love, that characterize the intimate sphere. The family, writes
Habermas, "seemed to be established voluntarily and by free individuals and to
be maintained without coercion; it seemed to rest on the lasting community of
love on the part of the two spouses; it seemed to permit that non-instrumen-
tal development of all faculties that marks the cultivated personality" (46–47).
As the locus of choice and voluntary social bonds, the intimate sphere allows
the emergence of a "concept of the humanity that was supposed to inhere in
humankind as such and truly to constitute its absoluteness" (47). Two issues of
note emerge here: first, bourgeois liberalism, as Habermas describes it, circles
back upon privacy as both the wellspring of liberal subjectivity *and* the ends
that it works to articulate and sustain. In other words, the intimate sphere
becomes both the origin and the telos of liberal subjectivity. Second, the fami-

ly here serves as the site where the "concept of humanity" is expressed and realized. This formulation stands in explicit tension with the claim that "common
humanity" is discovered in the exercise of reason in the public sphere.[44]

Habermas adds a further dimension to his discussion of freedom in the intimate sphere when he subsequently posits—in seemingly contradictory fashion—that freedom in the intimate sphere is illusory, or a mere representation
that masks constraint *and* that the representation of this illusory freedom has
real effects. In other words, Habermas stages a sort of double reversal of his
position, the result of which, as we will see, is to route the "freedom" of the intimate sphere through the representational practices of a literary (and historical)
public sphere. As we might note in Habermas's language cited in the previous
paragraph, the liberty that occurs in the intimate sphere is repeatedly qualified
as "seeming" rather than real. While freedom would *seem* to be located in privacy, it is "illusory" insofar as it works as the ideological mask of economic
constraint. Specifically, Habermas argues that the family is the place where
property owners represent their freedom, or view their freedom as being enacted:

> In a certain fashion, commodity owners could view themselves as autonomous. To
> the degree that they were emancipated from governmental directives and controls,
> they made decisions freely in accord with standards of profitability. In this regard
> they owed obedience to no one and were subject only to the anonymous laws func-
> tioning in accord with an economic rationality immanent, so it appeared, in the
> market. . . . Such an autonomy of private people, founded on the right to property
> and in a sense also realized in the participation in a market economy, *had to be capa-
> ble of being portrayed as such*. To the autonomy of property owners in the market *cor-
> responded* a self-presentation of human beings in the family. The latter's intimacy,
> apparently set free from the constraint of society, was the seal on the truth of a pri-
> vate autonomy exercised in competition. . . . Thus it was a private autonomy deny-
> ing its economic origins . . . that provided the bourgeois family with its conscious-
> ness of itself. (46; emphases added)

With respect to this fairly dense passage, we might begin by noting that the
function of property ownership has shifted considerably from the model proposed by both Pocock and even Macpherson in his discussion of the Putney
debates. Property ownership is not described here as directly enabling political
participation. Recall that on Pocock's republican model, in particular, property ownership enables one to remain independent from manipulation, and thus
capable of acting in a virtuous, high-minded fashion within the public
sphere—capable of pursuing a politics directed toward the common good
rather than private interest. On Habermas's more explicitly liberal and capitalist model, property ownership makes one autonomous, but only insofar as one

submits to the laws of the market. This apparent freedom *gains ground* by being reflected in a sense of personal freedom that is exercised in the intimate sphere.[45] Habermas thus argues that a sense of economic freedom, itself perhaps misguided ("owners *could view* themselves as autonomous"), displaces itself onto the intimate sphere of the family. The nature of this displacement is somewhat obscure: Habermas says that the family functions as a means of "portraying" or representing the bourgeois subject's freedom. He also argues that the autonomy of the market "corresponds" to the representation of freedom in the family. From this language we might draw two conclusions: First, on a liberal (in contrast to republican) model, property ownership and economic autonomy eventuate in a freedom enacted in terms that are private and domestic, rather than public and political. Second, the relation between economic autonomy and freedom within the family is not causative but, roughly speaking, mimetic. In other words, economic freedom does not enable or cause freedom in the family (as it enables free political participation on the republican model); rather, the freedom that occurs in the family is ostensibly the image or representation of economic freedom. We might, then, see the "correspondence" between economic autonomy and intimate sphere freedom as one of a shared epistemology: both the market and the family are sites where the subject experiences a "sense" of freedom, however misguided such a sense might be.

Yet the "real" function of the bourgeois family, Habermas argues, is to play a "precisely defined role in the process of the reproduction of capital" by serving as a genealogical structure for inheritance and by functioning as an agent of social control in bringing about "strict conformity with societally necessary requirements" (47). While the family may be the site of constraint—a cog within both patriarchy and capitalism—Habermas here suggests that the very effectiveness of the family in serving these functions is linked to its capacity to represent a site of freedom. More importantly, if we follow Habermas through one more turn of his exposition on this subject, the freedom *represented* (albeit not really existing) in the family creates very real social effects: "the ideas of freedom, love, and cultivation of the person that grew out of the experiences of the conjugal family's private sphere were surely more than just ideology. As an objective meaning contained as an element in the structure of the actual institution, and without whose subjective validity society would not have been able to reproduce itself, these ideas were also reality" (48). In a somewhat wistful formulation ("surely" this is more than ideology), Habermas effectively reconcretizes what he had formerly derealized as fiction or illusion. Yet note that he does so at the level of the subject: the "subjective" validity of the idea of free-

dom exercised in familial relations becomes the driving force of social reproduction. In other words, because subjects believe in the fiction of freedom, they
continue to freely consent to the constraints of the intimate sphere and thus act
in "strict conformity with societally necessary requirements." Moreover, in
emphasizing the *representational* (fictional, yet objective) nature of the social
meaning of the intimate sphere, Habermas underscores the fact that the representations produced in the public sphere concern more than the exercise of
reason: these representations portray the freedom of the intimate sphere. It is
for this reason that Habermas cites the domestic novel, and particularly the
epistolary form of a novel such as *Pamela*, as illustrative of the print public
sphere in its function of introducing (or creating) the "terrain of subjectivity"
(50). The literary public sphere, which comprises part of Habermas's account
of the historical public sphere of the eighteenth century, thus does not serve the
same function as the public sphere of procedural rationalism. What is exposed
in the literary public sphere is subjectivity as interiority and affect, not rationality.

The tension evident in Habermas's vacillating account of the family as the
location of individual freedom and/or of social constraint resonates through a
great deal of contemporary debate concerning culture and politics, as well as
the history of liberal theory. Is the modern subject a free agent or a social construction? On the one hand, the social construction model (generally of a
Foucauldian inflection) suggests that individuals are determined by culture
rather than vice versa; on the other hand, Habermas's normative public sphere,
and liberalism in general, relies upon the model of a subject who can freely
choose, articulate, and pursue his or her self-determined vision of the good or
moral life. Habermas's description of the family and the literary public sphere
suggests that agency and social determination meet in the intimate sphere. To
understand how this occurs, we might begin by examining the Marxist element
of Habermas's argument, one in which the family is the agent of capital accumulation rather than the site of freedom. In the *Grundrisse* Marx argues that
capitalism enables individuals to see themselves as free insofar as they are each
equal players in the market and thus able to choose to pursue their own interests in an exchange economy.[46] This, then, is the freedom of which Habermas
speaks when he argues that the bourgeoisie saw themselves as autonomous to
the extent that they were governed only by the anonymous laws of the market.
Yet as Marx argues, the laws of the market are such that they utterly compromise freedom and equality: "It is forgotten, on one side, that the *presupposition*
of exchange value, as the objective basis of the whole of the system of production, already in itself implies compulsion over the individual, since his imme-

diate product is not a product for him, but only *becomes* such in the social process. . . . [H]e is therefore entirely determined by society."[47] In other words, because value is determined through exchange, the "free" individual must constantly produce himself in accordance with the standards of value held by others. I would highlight here what I have called an epistemological moment linking Habermas's account of the marketplace and representations of the intimate sphere: in both cases a sense of freedom is experienced, but in both cases a moment of abstraction is required in which one imagines what it is that the other wants such that one can become that. In its thematization of desire and the heterosexual marriage contract, the domestic novel of the eighteenth century directly deals with imagining the abstract other—imagining how one might attain value by existing as the object of another's desire.

The relation between a system of economics and a system of affect is suggested by Habermas when he argues that the freedom of the marketplace is represented as an affective ordering of one's relationships within the family. Adam Smith's *Theory of Moral Sentiments* (1759) is also a useful and historically influential text in which we can locate the relation of affect to economy that I mean to specify here. Smith points to the way in which the sympathetic exchange of positions between the self and other is critical to the function of liberal society. In order to understand, shape, and value ourselves, we imagine ourselves as seen through the eyes of another:

> Our first ideas of personal beauty and deformity are drawn from the shape and appearance of others, not from our own. . . . We begin . . . to examine our own passions and conduct, and to consider how these must appear to [others], by considering how they would appear to us if in their situation. We suppose ourselves the spectators of our own behaviour, and endeavour to imagine what effect it would, in this light, produce upon us. This is the only looking-glass by which we can, in some measure, with the eyes of other people, scrutinize the propriety of our own conduct.[48]

Smith's sentimental exchange of subject positions describes not just a procedure of social interaction, but an episteme of liberal-capitalist (exchange) culture: one must engage in an *imaginative* exchange with the other in order to acquire value and social identity. One must imagine the desire of the other—what the spectator feels, thinks, and wants—in order to forge an identity and value for the self. Moreover, in so doing, one also engages oneself, as Marx argues, in being determined from the outside. As John Bender states, "The sympathetic interchange of 'I' and 'other' is, for Smith, the fundamental psychic mechanism establishing social order. The freedom of the deep, first-person subject and the invisible web of power functioning as third-person presence in individual conscience are indissolubly fused."[49] Smith's model of sympathy thus conjoins the volition of the subject with the infusion of social structure; it does so, I would emphasize, through a process of *imagining the desire of the other*. In routing the freedom of the domestic sphere through publicity—through the literary public sphere—Habermas thus offers not only an account of the way in which social norms (heterosexuality, patriarchy) become inscribed as individual desire, but also an account of the way in which understanding oneself through this structure of desire establishes a sense of agency and freedom in the liberal subject. As opposed to a classical republican model, on which property sets one free from the state, on the liberal-capitalist model, property is always determined within a system of exchange, and thus freedom is displaced onto the family as the site of noninstrumentality (as an even more deeply ideological relation of freedom to constraint). The family thus becomes the grounds of privacy and subjectivity that create liberal agency, rather than the site of simple property ownership as on the republican model. A fictional moment, a moment of abstraction into understanding the desire of the other, specified by Smith as sympathy, is here the moment that enables economic and domestic links between freedom and external determination; it gives an account of how the outside becomes the inside—an account of what we might call subjectification, or the moment when the individual becomes a subject who exercises agency and choice and also becomes subject to social structure through the mechanisms of exchange.[50] While existing for and through the fictional other is a political and economic reality of the liberal/capitalist exchange society, it is relocated in Habermas's account of the bourgeois family into a story of individuality rather than one of structure, and specifically into a story of heterosexual desire and marital consent.

The subjectivity established in the intimate sphere is thus complex and far from merely private. Privacy and subjectivity are established through a relation with the abstract other (the public), that is characterized by imagination and desire. Moreover, if we take the imaginative exchange relation to be central to establishing private subjectivity, we can understand why forms of print culture, such as the epistolary novel, are important to this process. The role of literature in the historical public sphere, then, is far different from the expressions of reason that characterize the normative public sphere. And indeed, Habermas describes the historical public sphere as itself divided into two different realms (which we might characterize as modalities): a literary one where interiority and subjectivity were imagined and displayed and a political one where rational debate over private property and the civil sphere occurred. Women, Habermas tells us, were central participants in the literary public sphere but were excluded from the political public sphere.[51] Habermas's dual taxonomy of the public sphere implies a significant revision of the terms of the public/private divide, particularly as it is generally construed in feminist theory. Feminist theory has tended to describe the domestic sphere as private and the market and the state as public. On the other hand, classic liberalism (particularly the economic, laissez-faire version of it) views the market as private rather than public: in this case, the public sphere of the state is understood as directed toward protecting the freedom of individuals to operate in a private, economic realm. Habermas's model of the public/private divide contrasts with both the feminist and classic liberal accounts: Habermas's political public sphere stands between the state and the private market economy, and the public sphere thus enables critical debate concerning the state and the private sphere.[52] The literary public sphere, as an element of Habermas's public sphere, would stand, as well, between the state and private sphere, albeit with its concerns directed toward the intimate sphere rather than the state. As such, the literary public sphere introduces a model of publicity that includes, rather than excludes, women. Moreover, it imagines women engaged in the public production of privacy, rather than "confined" or silenced within the private sphere.[53]

To what extent does Habermas's model of the literary public sphere offer a genuine modification of the fiction of liberalism and its temporal and gendered terms? One might argue that it offers little in the way of modification on two accounts: first, as some critics argue, the literary public sphere may be understood as merely preparatory with respect to the political public sphere. In other words, it is possible to see the literary public sphere as helping to form both institutions (coffeehouses, libraries) and a type of subjectivity that was necessary for creating the political public sphere, but that also no longer needed to be maintained once the full force of procedural rationalism governed the political public sphere.[54] Second, one might argue that this model of the literary public sphere effectively grants woman a "public sphere of her own" but serves no purpose other than a renewed confinement, particularly given that the content of the literary public sphere for women seems to be centered on domesticity. Thus Kathryn Shevelow argues, for example, that "authorization within writing not only does not contradict women's political powerlessness but actually reinforces it" because it is "predicated upon the cultural reaffirmation of a conception of feminine values that, as the product of a patriarchal ideology, gives women a kind of literary visibility, a place in print culture, but a place defined within the terms of that ideology."[55] Yet both of these criticisms miss the mark, I would argue, insofar as they fail to understand the looping or circular nature of the relation between the literary public sphere and the political public sphere.

Building upon or borrowing from Habermas's description of the literary public sphere, I will make two claims: First, the exposition of subjectivity in the literary public sphere works to produce privacy and bourgeois subjectivity and this subjectivity is the predicate for participation in the political public sphere. As such, we see a recursive loop between privacy and publicity in which the intimate sphere "prequalifies" certain subjects for participation in the political public sphere, and in which the public sphere in turn produces the very privacy understood as the predicate of public sphere participation. The public sphere produces privacy insofar as it looks to the intimate sphere as both origin and end of freedom: exercising freedom of choice in love and marriage, for instance, serves to illustrate the freedom and basic humanity of the bourgeois subject. Second, while the political public sphere may host rational debate concerning the disposition of private property (or, on a more republican model, debate concerning the public good), the literary public sphere models and produces subjectivity through what I will call an epistemology of desire (rather than reason). The literary public sphere produces subjectivity not by way of tutelage or by way of a blunt imposition of values and norms, but by way, as I have suggested, of desire and identification.

Although I develop the latter point at greater length below, I would point here to the way in which a circular (rather than linear) relation between public and private spheres significantly modifies existing feminist responses to Habermas. Benhabib, for instance, has largely embraced Habermas's normative model of the public sphere on the grounds that rational proceduralism entails the radical openness of the public sphere—an openness that can and should be used to broaden the concerns of the public sphere to include issues formerly seen as private, and thus issues concerning women. Yet because subjects must be prequalified for access to the public sphere, Benhabib overlooks the moment of subjectification crucial for determining who will count as a procedural rationalist. The circular model of the public/private sphere accounts for this moment of subjectification that can only occur offstage, as it were, on the normative account of the public sphere. Landes's rejection of Habermas, on the other hand, indicates that this offstage subjectification summarily renders women private and thus forever excludes them from the public sphere: yet if privacy is itself determined from the outside, through publicity, then this binary opposition, and its linear movement, is more susceptible to analysis and revision than she imagines. To summarize my claim, then, I use Habermas's model of the literary public sphere as the grounds of a critique of the temporal narrative of liberalism. This critique cracks apart the rigid dualism of the public/private coupling that insists upon women's exclusion from the public sphere, and cracks it less by arguing that there is no such dualism than by arguing that the two sides of this dyad are mutually constituting at every moment, and thus that women figure on both sides of the divide.

THE DESIRE OF LIBERALISM

Literary criticism has tended to describe women writers as silenced by the mechanisms of the liberal division between public and private spheres. Historically, however, this is simply not the case. In the United States, the best-selling literary works of both the eighteenth and nineteenth centuries—Susannah Rowson's *Charlotte Temple* and Harriet Beecher Stowe's *Uncle Tom's Cabin*—were written by women. We might note, as well, that Hawthorne's invocation of a private feminine ideal, of the need for women to be sheltered from exposure in the public sphere, occurs only in the face of the fact that women authors are outselling him. Indeed, as a burgeoning field of critical work on women writers in the eighteenth and nineteenth centuries indicates, women's writing was not absent from the historical public sphere so much as absent from twentieth-century critical accounts of literary history. The model of the literary public sphere that I propose here aims to account, then, not for the silence of women writers in the United States, but for their prominence.

The literary genre of the novel, which gained ground in the eighteenth century, is heavily identified with women (as both readers and writers) and with an intimate sphere in which women are principal figures. What is often described as the first American novel, *The Power of Sympathy* by William Hill Brown, was published in 1789; the novel explores the workings of epistolarity, sentiment, and the marriage contract, all defining elements of the domestic novel in the literary public sphere. Yet despite the neat historical conjunction between the first American novel and the birth of the American nation,[56] the literature of sentiment (and its feminized, intimate content) has often been seen to mark a falling off from a more original and authentic masculine tradition of American letters. Perhaps the best-known author of this claim is Ann Douglas, who argues that the sentimental novels of the nineteenth century represent an unfortunate feminization of a previously rigorous, masculine and Calvinist American culture. Although Douglas's work has been the subject of fairly heated debate since its publication, a second version of a similar narrative that has received less criticism can be found in Michael Warner's account of the eighteenth-century republican public sphere.[57] On Warner's account, the print public sphere of the eighteenth century is comprised largely of white male writers and readers; the advent of a feminized reading public coincides, for Warner, with a turn away from a republican civic-mindedness toward privatized, liberal forms of print, including the feminized genre of the novel.[58] Contrary to this narrative of an unfortunate fall into feminization, I argue that domestic literature and its female producers and consumers are central to both the literary and the political culture of the early United States.[59] Moreover, understanding the presence of women as writers and readers in the literary public sphere dramatically changes our understanding of the shape of literary culture in the United States, and of the relation between gender and liberalism.

If we turn to Michael Warner's influential account of the print public sphere in the early eighteenth century, we find a public sphere that resembles the normative Habermasian model, yet emphasizes a model of republican rather than liberal citizenship. In the early eighteenth century, Warner argues, individuals enter into the public sphere in order to rationally debate the public good. Indeed, republican virtue consists in precisely this procedural or performative engagement in the public sphere: entering into debate in the public sphere defines one as concerned with the public good. This is the case, in part, because the structure of the public sphere corresponds to a republican ideal: both require that one divorce oneself from private interests in order to engage in civic-minded activity. According to Warner, the structure of the print public sphere requires as much because it operates according to a "principle of negativity" in which one assumes a kind of abstract or fictional status, divorced from one's material and private existence, simply by entering into print. Republican print is "normally impersonal," Warner argues, because in the print public sphere, one imagines oneself as a generic, national reader or writer: "it becomes possible to imagine oneself, in the act of reading, becoming part of an arena of the national people that cannot be realized except through such mediating imaginings."[60] On Pocock's model, we have seen the independence and virtue of the republican citizen established with respect to property ownership: only white, property-owning men were free from influence and governmental control, and thus able to divorce themselves from personal concerns and devote themselves to public concerns because of their very economic and social privilege. By mapping virtuous, independent civic-mindedness onto the print public sphere, Warner would seem to extend the republican franchise beyond the group of white male property owners. Yet despite the apparent accessibility of such a model, Warner argues that only white men were de facto granted access to the print public sphere. This is the case because a "covert identification of print consumption with the community of propertied white males" took place, such that abstraction remained, in fact, a resource limited to property-owning white men (48). How this covert identification takes place, however, is not entirely clear. Warner suggests, on the one hand, that material barriers, such as literacy and access to printed texts, may have served to limit public sphere activity to the well-educated and propertied. Yet given the high literacy rate of white women in the colonies (over fifty percent), this seems of limited explanatory value. Elsewhere, Warner suggests that femininity has been understood as synonymous with embodiment and particularity, and thus abstraction into the public sphere would be constitutively at odds with female identity.[61] While the latter claim seems more compelling, I would argue instead that the public sphere is used to *establish* the very terms of masculinity and femininity invoked here, and thus this claim attests more to the presence of women in public discourse than their absence. While attentive to the very real limitations of an idealized accessibility, Warner's model of republican print tends to describe privacy and embodiment as inert—as that which can be left behind in the act of abstraction—rather than as that which is produced in and through the public sphere, in and through the very process of abstraction.

If we turn to Warner's discussion of the feminized genre of the novel, this treatment of privacy (together with gender) becomes more evident. In contrast to a republican civic-minded form of print, Warner sees the novel as a kind of publicity that is principally not civic-minded, but is instead oriented toward privacy: "The turn toward sentiment can be seen as a key element both in the extension of the national imaginary to the female readership of novels and in the emergence of a liberal paradigm for appreciating printed texts" (174). The novel, as a feminized and privatized form of publicity, involves an imaginary extension of political identity, but not civic-minded debate; as such, it is associated not with a republican concern for the good of the polis, but with a liberal care for the self:

> This imaginary participation in the public order [found in the novel] is . . . a precondition for modern nationalism, though it is anathema to pure republicanism. The modern nation does not have citizens in the same way the republic does. You can be a member of the nation, attributing its agency to yourself in imaginary identification, without being a freeholder or exercising any agency in the public sphere. Nationalism makes no distinction between such imaginary participation and the active participation of its citizens. In republicanism that distinction counted for everything. (173)

While Warner draws a strong distinction between imaginary and real participation in the public sphere, I would argue that this distinction doesn't hold, even within Warner's own account of the republican public sphere. Recall that the moment of abstraction that defines entry into the republican public sphere is described by Warner as an imaginative exercise. Given that entry into the print public sphere (republican or liberal, public-minded or privately oriented) requires an act of imagination, what would seem to distinguish the two acts is the content of what is imagined rather than the active or passive nature of the engagement. The republican abstraction, as Warner describes it, is directed toward a generalized idea of the public or a *sensus communus*, whereas the liberal imagination is devoted toward individuation and particularization, toward representations that specify the workings of desire and sentiment in all of their subjective and characterological depth.

Rather than distinguishing temporally or historically between republican abstraction and liberal individuation as Warner does, I would argue that the literary public sphere always operates in both directions simultaneously. Typically the mechanisms of abstraction (of procedural rationalism) receive the most press within theories of the public sphere: however, the workings of individuation and desire, as I argue below, are necessary to account for the "new subjectivity" that Habermas describes as the predicate of the public sphere. If we return to Adam Smith's account of sympathy for a description of how the subject relates to the other, we can see the proximity of the two models to one another as well as their difference. On the one hand, Adam Smith can be read as proposing that a kind of abstract, liberal universalism operates through the workings of sympathy. This line of thinking emerges most clearly in his discussion of the way in which individuals internalize an "impartial spectator." Smith writes:

> We can never survey our own sentiments and motives, we can never form any judgment concerning them, unless we remove ourselves, as it were, from our own natural station, and endeavour to view them as at a certain distance from us. . . .We endeavour to examine our own conduct as we imagine any other fair and impartial spectator would examine it. If, upon placing ourselves in his situation, we thoroughly enter into all the passions and motives which influenced it, we approve of it, by sympathy with the approbation of this supposed equitable judge. If otherwise, we enter into his disapprobation, and condemn it.[62]

According to John Bender, this internalized "impartial spectator" is notably generalized and impersonal. This "juridical self" internalizes a concept of justice through measuring himself against the views of an impartial spectator. As Bender writes, the juridical self is "the focal point of inspection by a potentially infinite number of imagined spectators—all collected into Smith's personification of the impartial spectator."[63] The impartial spectator thus insures the internalization of social norms in a disciplinary fashion. As such, this view of the impartial other resonates with liberal doctrine concerning the impartiality of law and its internal availability, as in, for example, Kant's notion of a "moral law within." The impartial spectator thus has a generalizing function, operating to insure social cohesion among diverse individuals who imagine themselves in relation to a generality.

Yet while Bender emphasizes the impartial nature of the internalized spectator, another reading of sympathy in Smith's formulation might see particularization rather than generalization as a guiding principle of the interchange. In a passage shortly after the one cited above, Smith argues that other individuals perform a mirroring function that confers upon each individual their sense of self:

> Were it possible that a human creature could grow up to manhood in some solitary place, without any communication with his own species, he could no more think of his own character, of the propriety or demerit of his own sentiments and conduct, of the beauty or deformity of his own mind, than of the beauty or deformity of his own face. All these are objects which he cannot easily see, which naturally he does not look at, and with regard to which he is provided with no mirror which can present them to his view. Bring him into society, and he is immediately provided with the mirror which he wanted before. It is placed in the countenance and behaviour of those he lives with, which always mark when they enter into, and when they disapprove of his sentiments; and it is here that he first views the propriety and impropriety of his own passions, the beauty and deformity of his own mind.[64]

This passage suggests that the subject is not only regulated through his imagination of how others see him, but that his very *existence* as a self-conscious subject is founded in this interaction. In this revised version of the Cartesian *cogito* (which might be worded as follows: "I think he thinks I am, therefore I am"), being is guaranteed only by the mirroring gaze of the other. What is at stake in this case, then, is not the work of a preexistent subject attempting to conform to an idealized and impartial judge, but the act of a subject coming into being through identification with the eye of the beholder. We can thus relate this back to Marx's model of exchange: one has value within this system only insofar as one corresponds to the desire of the other; the desire of the other constitutes the self. If we imagine sympathy as partiality, then the desire of the other is individualizing, not generalizing or abstract. On this model, it is thus the desire of the other (not the other's impartiality) that makes one a self rather than faceless. While Bender's model emphasizes sympathy as a force of social control and cohesion, the model of a particularizing desire suggests that sympathy enables individuation.[65] The procedural rationalist operates according to a law of reason that we have seen to be figured by Smith as an impartial spectator: yet this model presupposes that a self already exists that can be measured in relation to the views of the impartial spectator. The model of the desiring other, on the other hand, suggests that the subject only comes into existence through the mediation of the other. This mediation, then, is original and particularizing rather than secondary and generalizing.

The imaginative moment of mediation I have described begins to bear a great deal of weight in the eighteenth century with the changing configuration of political and economic relations—with the advent of democratic liberalism. In political terms, I would advert here to the work of Claude Lefort, who argues that the demise of monarchy sees the eradication of a representational system in which the body of the king served as a visible, organizing principle of social cohesion. In contrast, democratic power does not reside in any visible body; the locus of democratic power, according to Lefort, "is an empty place, it cannot be occupied—it is such that no individual and no group can be consubstantial with it—and it cannot be represented."[66] The empty place of democratic power is the "people," a people that remains unrepresentable because it is at once collective and individual, though the collectivity is available only by the imaginative mediation staged between the individual and his others. In democracy, the "people" is always a fictive construct, circulating in the abstractive (imaginary) relation between the individual and the collective.

In economic terms, as numerous critics have argued, the shift to a capitalist, credit-based economy entailed a new horizon of suppositional relations. During the economic revolution experienced in Britain in the early eighteenth century, finance came to involve an array of speculative forms: credit promissory notes, joint-stock companies, and paper notes issued by the new Bank of England. Entering into the speculative contracts that structured this economy involved making commitments based on assumptions about the future— assumptions about the probable outcome of future events. Such an imaginative calculus involved a great deal of anxiety and generated critique: in 1720, for instance, the famous "South Sea bubble" ruined many investors who had placed money in the slave-trading South Sea Company. The Whig writer "Cato" describes credit as based in "gilded clouds [and] . . . fleeting apparitions": credit is likely to collapse at the "story of a Spanish frigate . . . or the sickness of a foreign prince, or the saying of a broker in a coffee-house."[67] Indeed, as Pocock argues, the economy of credit was initially seen as feminizing insofar as it made one dependent upon the actions and desires of others as well as upon one's own passions.[68] In later configurations (as we saw Habermas contend earlier), the autonomy of the bourgeois capitalist is asserted in his ability to pursue his own ends without external constraint. As Pocock points

out, however, this commercially autonomous man is at a far remove from the
virtuous "unity" of the republican citizen who did not suffer his identity to be
mediated through the relations of the market or of representation.[69] Let me
point, then, to the suppositional nature of these new relations of commerce
and politics: the moment of abstraction and imagination—of imagining the
desire of the other—is central to the credit economy and to democracy where
power circulates in the relation of subjects and does not stand embodied in a
single figure. Smith's model of sympathy as well as the mediated models of politics (democracy) and economics (capitalist exchange) all require the imaginative labor of the subject to specify his value and identity as mediated through
others. As a literary form, the novel corresponds to the new exigency of engaging in imaginatively mediated representations of the subject. As both Michael
McKeon and Catherine Gallagher have argued, what distinguishes the novel as
a new literary form in the eighteenth century is precisely its fictionality: only
in the eighteenth century did people begin to find value in reading about persons who had never existed. Yet if we see the widespread logic of Smithian sympathy at work in both political and economic terms, the desire to imagine one's
way into the minds of suppositional subjects suddenly becomes of central
importance in navigating the terrain of liberalism.[70]

Returning to Warner's description of the print public sphere, we might say
that the liberal, novelistic moment of identification is as much a part of the
structure of the print public sphere as is the abstractive moment that Warner
identifies as republican. Indeed, we might characterize the imaginative
moment of entry into the print public sphere as one of sympathetic mediation,
and thus as a moment that functions both to generalize the subject and to particularize him. Moreover, to the extent that this imaginative moment is one of
mediation (of imagining the self in relation to a particular or general other), it
augurs against a republican ethos, at least in the terms that Pocock has
described a republican concern for virtuous self-unity and an aversion to
mediation as a form of dependency.[71] If we imagine these two forms of identification—abstraction and individuation—both occurring through the workings of the public sphere, we see that the literary public sphere emerges as a
pivotal location of subjectification in its dual meanings—that of creating a free
subject and of constraining the subject to an existing social structure.

THE GENDER OF LIBERALISM

I now wish to argue that the primary form of constraint, or "structuration,"
effected in the literary public sphere of the eighteenth century concerns the

becoming binary of gender and the becoming heterosexual of desire: in other words, the structure to which the subject consents (in order to become a subject) is one that primarily concerns newly configured forms of gender and sexuality. The eighteenth-century domestic novel, largely centered around issues of courtship, might be seen as an elaboration of the imagined desire of the other and of the way in which the subject accrues subjectivity and interiority through the coarticulation of desire with the other—through an elaboration of subjectivity that results in the marriage contract as the seal of what Habermas identifies as a new bourgeois subjectivity. In its emphasis on heterosexual marriage as the sign of subjectivity, however, this model of bourgeois subjectivity ratifies *sexual difference* as the primary axis of difference organizing the subject and social relations. This is a point worth underscoring, given that most critics of American literature who explore the intersubjective workings of sympathy tend to ignore sexual difference or imagine that sexual difference is overcome rather than established through sympathy. For instance, discussions of the political valences of sympathy have tended to be ranged on alternative sides of a debate as to whether sympathy is democratic or imperialist. On the one hand, sympathy would seem to extend fellow feeling to others (insofar as sympathy circulates through the other) and thus would seem inclusive and democratic. On the other hand, insofar as sympathy requires a self to imagine how the other feels, one can see it as an impositional gesture in which one grants subjectivity to the other on the condition that he or she agrees to resemble or imitate the self.[72] Yet both of these models tend to see the work of sympathy as homogenizing—as directed toward creating similarity between the self and others. In the model of a sympathy as particularizing, however, the self and the other are not the same—rather, they desire one another. Insofar as sexual difference and heterosexuality are taken as the determining elements of the desire of the other, sexual difference stands as a key element of individualization and subjectification. In the domestic novel focused on courtship, one is differentiated through the *uniqueness* of one's emotions, particularly through love. As Habermas argues, the voluntary and noninstrumental nature of this desire demonstrates one's freedom and interiority. In related terms, Niklas Luhmann argues that romantic love of the eighteenth century differs significantly from earlier ideologies of love (courtly love, for instance), insofar as it is oriented toward the production of autonomy through social reflexivity.[73] In romantic love, Luhmann demonstrates, one is singled out by the desire of the other, and thus becomes an individual subject. Indeed, Luhmann argues that this model of romantic love had the effect of diminishing the difference between the sexes insofar as it enabled a kind of subjective reciprocity between the man and woman in the romantic couple. Against Luhmann, however, I would argue that the fact that the romantic couple is comprised of a man and woman (and not, say, two women) indicates that sexual difference counts *more* rather than less on this model of individuation. Indeed, on this model, sexual difference becomes the organizing difference of the bourgeois subject and liberal society.

The latter point—the extent to which sexual difference comes to stand in for a range of other social and economic differences—is a central claim of Nancy Armstrong's groundbreaking work on eighteenth-century fiction, *Desire and Domestic Fiction.* According to Armstrong, the novel creates a "modern form of desire," a desire oriented toward the individual subject rather than toward wealth and social status. More specifically, this desire is first mapped onto the figure of the middle-class woman and a new definition of feminine value. Armstrong argues that

> narratives which seemed to be concerned solely with matters of courtship and marriage in fact seized the authority to say what was female, and . . . they did so in order to contest the reigning notion of kinship relations that attached most power and privilege to certain family lines. This struggle to represent sexuality took the form of a struggle to individuate wherever there was a collective body, to attach psychological motives to what had been the openly political behavior of contending groups, and to evaluate these according to a set of moral norms that exalted the domestic woman over and above her aristocratic counterpart.[74]

In the domestic novel, status ceased to matter and "only the more subtle nuances of behavior indicated what one was really worth. . . . It is only by thus subordinating all social differences to those based on gender that these novels bring order to social relationships" (4). Armstrong thus marks two crucial changes that become visible within the domestic novel: first, the bourgeois subject is individuated or valued in terms of interiority and depth rather than in terms of external status. And second, difference is now primarily construed in terms of sex rather than class. More importantly, the two changes are intimately linked to one another: interiority is articulated and made visible by way of new models of gender that are, in turn, developed and articulated through fictions of heterosexual desire, courtship, and marriage.

Armstrong emphasizes a number of points that are important to my argument: first, as gender comes to stand as the defining difference structuring society, other differences, such as those of class and wealth, are rendered less visible. As such, the fundamentally political shift from aristocratic authority to bourgeois liberalism is effected through developing a set of terms (gender, subjectivity) that present themselves as apolitical—as domestic and private rather than public and political: "the power fiction would come to exercise depended

entirely on denying the inherently political aim of fictions of personal development; the production of the modern individual required above all else a specific form of political unconscious" (36). Middle-class fictions of personal
development thus come to function as the "unconscious" of bourgeois power.
In terms of my argument, we might say that these fictions are crucial for pre-
qualifying the subject for entry into the political public sphere. Moreover, in
emphasizing the political function of the domestic novel, Armstrong offers a
radically different model of the sexual contract than that proposed by Carole
Pateman. Rather than seeing the marriage contract as standing behind or
beneath the social contract, Armstrong sees the marriage contract as the most
enduring version of the social contract: "novels were supposed to rewrite political history as personal histories that elaborated on the courtship procedures
ensuring a happy domestic life" (38). Entering into the marriage contract
involved a consent to the social order—a consent to a version of bourgeois subjectification, albeit one construed as personal rather than political.[75]

Yet as critics have noted, there is a certain tension in Armstrong's account
between the notion that gender becomes a reigning discourse of difference and
the claim that women were empowered by their role in the contracting of heterosexual marriage and the creation of a domestic sphere linked to subject formation. We can see this, for instance, in Armstrong's discussion of the novel
Pamela, in which she describes the authority Pamela accrues to herself through
insisting that Mr. B. engage in contractual relations with her: "she penetrates
into the heart of the dominant culture to appropriate its material as the stuff
of her own subjectivity. Even before her letters are publicly aired and authorized, Richardson grants them a reformist power that is actually the power to
form desire" (119). On the one hand, the mutual desire that circulates in the
courtship narrative would seem to imply a mutual subjectivity, and hence a
form of authority that resides as much in women as in men. On the other
hand, the single guiding rule of this desire is sexual difference: as such, the one
difference authorized by the courtship marriage is the fundamental distinction
(rather than parity) between men and women. This distinction, in turn, will
serve not only to guarantee subjectivity, but also to authorize a sexual division
of labor and the association of women with a private subjectivity configured as
apolitical and domestic. If subjectivity accrues to Pamela at the moment when
she says "no" and insists on her autonomy, the force of Mr. B's desire also subjectifies her as a private, domestic woman, a role to which she, in turn, will say
"yes."

And indeed, Armstrong herself indicates that the structuring power of gender involves far more than the claim that women become contracting subjects

through marriage. "The modern female body," she writes, "comprised a grammar of subjectivity capable of regulating desire, pleasure, the ordinary care of the body, the conduct of courtship, the division of labor, and the dynamic of family relationships" (95). The definition of "woman," then, involved a range of behaviors extending well beyond eliciting male desire; these behaviors link that desire to what Habermas calls the "real" function of the family, the preservation of capital, and to this we might add the capacity to individuate the liberal subject within an economy that threatens to homogenize its subjects through the generalizing force of exchange. That is, gender difference enables the very particularization that the homogenizing force of sympathetic identification threatens to obliterate. Within mass culture, Mark Seltzer argues, gender can serve as the modality of difference that sustains the subject in his individuality: "In the translation of a traumatic failure of self-difference into an absolutized sexual difference, the vanishing of the distinction between self and other is corrected in the radicalized polarization of male and female."[76] Heterosexual desire, grounded in absolute difference, thus ratifies both subject and structure. As such, the coupling of social constraint and freedom through binary gender roles finds its happiest fiction in the heterosexual courtship narrative. To modify Armstrong, then, I would suggest that if eighteenth-century fiction sees the elevation of the domestic woman, it sees the elevation of heterosexual desire to new social heights as well. Lawrence Stone describes, for instance, the growth of companionate marriage and its emphasis on the naturalness of heterosexual desire in this period. Henry Abelove argues that during this same period, homosexuality takes shape as a category in opposition to the newfound normativity of heterosexuality. Jill Campbell's work on eighteenth-century masquerade has demonstrated as well the extent of conflict over the naturalization of gender differences that often seemed to be roles rather than internal truths of subjectivity in the eighteenth century. As Campbell's work indicates, the historical work of naturalizing gender difference itself took place in public sphere debates and in a range of literary and dramatic representations.

Women's consent to the marriage contract and to the structuring force of gender division thus both grants women the status of subjects ("I'm 'wife' . . . I'm Czar—I'm 'Woman' now—" writes Emily Dickinson) *and* locates them firmly on the private side of the public/private divide. Insofar as relations in the private sphere are understood as *free* and consensual, women thus become defined in terms of privacy's extralegal status. Thus, for instance, as Reva Siegel writes,

[Sentimental] marriage was an affective relation that subsisted and flourished in a private domain beyond the reach of law. A wife could not enforce a contract with her husband compensating her for work performed in the family sphere because such labor was to be performed altruistically, rather than self-interestedly: for love, not pay. A wife could not bring a tort claim against a husband who battered her because such conflicts were to be resolved altruistically, by marital partners who would, or should, learn to forgive and forget. Adjudication of intramarital contract or tort claims, courts reasoned, would destroy marital harmony and expose private aspects of the conjugal relation to the corrosive glare of public scrutiny. . . . By the turn of the century, courts seeking to justify wives' continuing legal disabilities described marriage as an emotional relationship subsisting in a private realm "beyond" the reach of law.[77]

Siegel here points to the paradoxical position of women as signifiers of freedom in the intimate sphere, women who are themselves constrained by a discourse of sexual difference that inhibits them from assuming a legal status before the court. If we return to Habermas's description of the intimate sphere, we might say that the freedom and constraint of the subject of an exchange economy is writ large in representations of the intimate sphere, and that women, in particular, come to bear the contradictory effects of subjectification through liberal desire. Women, then, might be said to be intimate with liberal desire, intimate with subjectification: their "consent" to a private identity prohibits recourse to the temporalizing and temporizing fictions of liberalism in which the masculine subject emerges into the public sphere after attaining identity in the private sphere.

Over the course of this chapter, I have attempted to dematerialize the boundaries of liberal identity, to describe both the guiding fictions of liberalism and the means of their production and reproduction. More importantly, in locating the generative power and necessity of these fictions in the public sphere, I have also shown that women are not summarily banished from the production of meaning and power within liberalism. If women are historically absent from rational procedural debate, particularly in its civic forms, they are nonetheless eminently present in the literary public sphere and wield signifying force with respect to property, privacy, desire, and subjectivity. It may seem, however, that I have ended exceedingly close to where I began: while women, on my account, may now emerge as central to the workings of the public sphere and the production of liberal subjectivity, I also argue that this very public production subjectifies women as private and apolitical. That is, I may seem to have elevated women to the level of a public sphere identity only to tether them the more tightly to a private sphere identity over the course of the last forty pages. But the mechanism of the tethering is far different than that of the temporalizing narrative of liberalism precisely because this mechanism operates by way of publicity, exchange, and desire rather than by way of biology, linear narrative, and liberal self-possession. The model of the feminine literary public sphere indicates that women have a voice, albeit not the voice of the liberal subject: rather, we might describe such a voice as that of liberal subjectification, a voice that bespeaks the public and literary construction of private subjectivity.

2 Puritan Bodies and Transatlantic Texts

The Puritan Anne Hutchinson stands as a solitary female figure in early American history, famously exiled from the Massachusetts Bay Colony for her claim to have direct access to God and for her ostensible leadership of a group of "antinomian" colonists who rebelled against the ministers of the church—ministers who, she and her followers claimed, preached a covenant of works rather than one of grace. Hutchinson stands, too, as an originary figure in many accounts of American history: she is described as inaugurating a tradition of American individualism or, alternatively, as originating a line of feminist rebellion against patriarchal authority in the New World. In this chapter, I describe her less as the progenitor of an Emersonian self-reliance than as a figure who helped to catalyze new models of gender formulated within an emergent, transatlantic literary public sphere. In the trial against Hutchinson and in the written accounts of it that circulated in England for financial and religious reasons, I suggest that we can trace a set of horizontally organized relations of authority that emerged out of the economic and political structures of the colonial enterprise. These horizontal relations—evident, for instance, in the predominance of contractual metaphors governing both colonial finance and religious and political discipline—stood in stark contrast to traditional, hierarchical modes of authority. In this chapter, I delineate the way in which a literary public sphere took shape out of the economic, religious, and political situation of transatlantic colonial adventure. In doing so, I aim to locate the significance of the antinomian crisis and the figure of Anne Hutchinson less within a theological debate that points to the Puritan origins of American identity than within a much broader historical shift toward modes of liberal subjectivity and gender articulated in and through colonialism and the advent of public sphere discourse.

Anne Hutchinson migrated to the Massachusetts Bay Colony from England with her husband and children in 1634. A follower of the minister John Cotton, she crossed the Atlantic and resettled in New England after he did so, demonstrating her deep attachment to his ministry and, in particular, to his doctrine concerning the nature of spiritual or free grace from God. After moving to Massachusetts, she eventually began to hold religious meetings in her home (known as "conventicles") to discuss the sermons of the colony's ministers. These discussions evidently began to assume a critical edge with respect to ministers who seemed not to sufficiently emphasize spiritual grace, and members of the group began to publicly express criticism of a number of the colony's most prominent ministers. With the colony divided between those supporting Hutchinson's views (including then-governor Henry Vane) and those opposed (John Winthrop among them), the General Court called for a day of fasting in January of 1637 to resolve tensions in the colony. However, the Reverend John Wheelwright, called upon to preach the fast-day sermon, inflamed rather than soothed tensions with a lecture that emphasized the divide between those preaching a "covenant of grace" and those preaching a "covenant of works." The General Court responded to Wheelwright's provocation by examining him at length on his theological doctrine; he was convicted of sedition and later banished from the colony. A petition was presented by members of the Boston Church in support of Wheelwright, but John Winthrop and other magistrates rejected the petition. Moreover, Winthrop was soon able to gain the upper hand, winning the governorship away from Henry Vane, and, eventually, at a General Court session in November 1637, moving with other magistrates to banish and disenfranchise many of the signatories of the petition and visible leaders of the "antinomian" faction (including Wheelwright). In addition, all those who had signed the petition were disarmed. Hutchinson herself was placed on trial in civil court in 1637 and sentenced to banishment: a church trial in 1638 resulted in excommunication. Hutchinson subsequently moved to Rhode Island with a group of supporters; following the death of her husband she moved to Long Island Sound, where she was later killed in a raid by Native Americans.[1]

The transcript of Anne Hutchinson's civil trial in 1637 opens and closes with Hutchinson's demand to know what crimes are charged against her. At the outset of the trial, Hutchinson is able to push her judges toward their most succinct answer to this question: Governor John Winthrop tells her that she stands accused of breaking the fifth commandment—of dishonoring her parents. As a central participant in the so-called antinomian faction that generated popular criticism of ministerial authority throughout the Massachusetts Bay Colony, Hutchinson most certainly had breached the constraints of an existing religious and social hierarchy, dishonoring the colony's religious "fathers." Over the course of the trial, however, Hutchinson argues with wit and wile against this charge. Nonetheless, with the same words, she performs the very violation she refutes anew insofar as she asserts the authority of her theological reasoning, her proximate experience of God, over and against those of her religious and social superiors. At the close of the trial, as Winthrop announces the court's decision to banish her from the colony, Hutchinson repeats the plea to have the charges against her enumerated: "I desire to know wherefore I am banished." This time, Hutchinson's question remains pointedly unanswered: "Say no more," states Winthrop, "the court knows wherefore and is satisfied."[2]

The legal and theological debate in which Hutchinson participates so skillfully is thus forcibly foreclosed by Winthrop's assertion of the court's knowledge and authority: we might say he ultimately performs his legal authority by commanding silence in order to put an end to Hutchinson's own self-authorizing performance. The questioning voice of Hutchinson would thus seem to be summarily silenced. And indeed, Winthrop's admonition to silence has often been taken as the primal scene of the antinomian controversy: that is, the controversy has been read as a sort of foundational silencing of women, a historical moment when patriarchal authority is established in the very act of stifling the speech of a woman.[3] In this chapter, I argue against what the evidence of the governor's final words seems to insist upon: that is, I argue that although Hutchinson may have ceased to speak in the courtroom in November 1637, in a larger cultural context, she has remained far from silent.

In the pages that follow, I examine the antinomian controversy in relation to the origins of liberalism and a nascent transatlantic print public sphere. In this context, Hutchinson in particular and women in general are neither absent nor voiceless. Rather, Hutchinson's words and the figure of Anne Hutchinson are produced in print for an audience extending far beyond those who heard Winthrop admonish her in Boston. Moreover, Winthrop himself is the author of much of what will circulate in print concerning Hutchinson. As such, it is less the subversive voice of Anne Hutchinson as it has survived in print that I aim to trace than the way in which particular figurations of gender are produced in print as a result of this early colonial crisis of authority and governance. I thus aim to delineate in the antinomian controversy the emergence of new representations of gender that correspond to an incipient politics and culture of liberalism. Given their general reputation for intolerance and social stricture, it may seem counterintuitive to identify the Puritans of Massachusetts Bay as liberal. Yet, as I argue below, the Puritans stand on the cusp of the divide between early modern and modern social orders. Understood less as grim, Hawthornian forebears than as one faction of religious radicals among the array of dissidents who would soon foment the English Civil War, the

Puritans of Massachusetts can be seen to have embraced political, economic, and religious innovations that augured for a modern liberal order. At the heart of Puritan religious reform lies the assertion that each individual stands free to enter directly into his or her own relation with God—a relation unmediated by the brokerage of bishop, priest, Latinate ritual, or baroque image. While Calvinist theology does not advocate the eradication of social or divine hierarchy, it does accord a broad authority to the individual conscience. In this emphasis on the individual conscience, New England Puritanism brings into view an active, volitional, contracting subject—a subject who, I argue below, is recognizable as proto-liberal. More broadly, I suggest that the religious and political innovations of New England Puritanism need to be read in the context of colonialism and larger English Puritan designs to establish an empire in North America in order to crush the advances of Catholic Spain in the New World and reinvigorate England in religious and financial terms. Critics have tended to view the New England Puritans as rigidly opposed to a liberal politics: they construe Anne Hutchinson as giving voice to a courageous individualism—a "primitive feminism"[4] based upon liberal values—over and against the conservative, hierarchical rule of the colony's elders. I argue the reverse: that is, I show that gender emerges as a category of knowledge through which liberalism effects social order on behalf of the Puritan fathers. As such, I see the elders themselves as proto-liberal, as attempting to articulate the shape of a new social and political order and finding in gender one of the terms through which they can do so. Moreover, the liberal order I describe here is not only or even primarily theological, but is linked to the restructuring of political authority through colonial innovations in finance and print communication.

I do not want to overstate my case here: I aim less to identify New England Puritanism as a decisively liberal break with a feudal past than to locate the emerging lineaments of the liberal subject in a period when many of the tenets of liberalism would have been anathema to the dominant culture. As I have indicated, the theological presuppositions that shade toward liberal subjectivity are one piece of a more complex picture that includes the loosening of monarchical power over both England and the colonial outposts of the first empire, as well as the ascendancy of a commercial, transactional (rather than hierarchical) authority in the developing transatlantic marketplace. The growing print public sphere—what Benedict Anderson has called the print capitalism of modern nationalism—is entwined in this complex of developments as well, and stands as both index and agent of a shift toward new modes of subjectivity and political authority.[5] The central concern of this book is the relation between liberalism and gender: I thus turn to the early seventeenth century in order to examine the way in which gender begins to be articulated as more central to subjectivity—less flexible, more determinate—at the very moment when a more volitional subject is proposed. With broad reference to the conditions of colonialism, the English Civil War, and the rise of capitalism, and more particular reference to the theological terms of the antinomian debate and the print materials emerging from that debate, I trace the uneven articulation of a gendered liberal subject in seventeenth-century Anglo-American culture. I begin the chapter with an analysis of the transcripts of Hutchinson's civil and ecclesiastical trials, where I examine the relationship between Hutchinson's heresies and liberal subjectivity and describe the creation of an oppositional public sphere within the Massachusetts Bay Colony. I subsequently turn to an examination of the transatlantic publishing history of documents related to the antinomian crisis in order to consider broader relations of authority, print, and gender with respect to the structural conditions of the English Puritan colonial enterprise.

"THE RULE OF THE NEW CREATURE": LIBERALISM AND THE TRIAL OF ANNE HUTCHINSON

The antinomian controversy presents a strange mix of arcane theological debate and overt civil unrest. On the one hand, the controversy turns on the distinction between the covenant of grace and that of works and, more particularly, upon the fine interpretive line that divides the two in practice. According to Governor John Winthrop, the distinction between the two positions was such that "no man could tell (except some few, who know the bottom of the matter) where any difference was."[6] On the other hand, the debate over this elusive distinction—a debate fueled in large part by Hutchinson—seemed at one point to have a portion of the colony on the brink of armed rebellion. In his introduction to Winthrop's *Short Story*, the minister Thomas Weld writes that "after our Sermons were ended at our publike Lectures, you might have seene halfe a dozen Pistols discharged at the face of the Preacher, (I meane) so many objections made by the opinionists [antinomians] in the open Assembly against our doctrine delivered . . . [as to cause] the marvellous weakning of holy truths delivered" (209). The force of the theological challenge posed by the "opinionists" is thus felt by the ruling faction as far more than a doctrinal debate: rather, in publicly challenging the ministers over their religious tenets, the antinomians contested the authority upon which the entwined religious and political hierarchy of the colony rested. As such, the figurative pistols described by Weld were, in the mind of the Puritan court, very close to wielding literal force. Following an incendiary fast-day sermon by the antinomian minister John Wheelwright—a sermon that, in a series of violent tropes, descried an unbridgeable gap between those who preached a covenant of works and those who didn't—the Boston court moved in 1637 to disarm all members of the faction in order to prevent a wholesale uprising. Weld's figurative pistols thus point toward two central concerns of mine: first, to the link between the theological debates involved in the controversy and the political organization of the colony. This link, as I argue below, is more than circumstantial—that is, the antinomians raised a profound challenge to the colony not simply because they disagreed with the ministers who were in power, but because their theological disagreement raised the question of who legitimately wields political power—of where religious, and by extension secular, authority lies. And second, Weld's metaphor points to a deep anxiety about the force of publicity manifest in a loss of distinction between literal and figurative acts. The sense that figurative violence is tantamount to literal violence corresponds to a sense of the increasing force wielded by public speech and publicity. I suggest, then, that as Puritans began to authorize new forms of contractual subjectivity, new forms of speech erupted with unique and sometimes frightening force.[7]

What, specifically, was the nature of Hutchinson's heresy? How did her theological claims gain such force as to threaten the very stability of the colony? Critics have long debated these questions and have found them difficult to answer definitively in part because Hutchinson's "heresies" arguably do not lie outside of Puritan doctrine at all.[8] In the analysis below, I suggest that answers to questions concerning the meaning and force of the antinomian crisis do not lie solely within theology, but rather can be found in the volatile interaction between Hutchinson's theological claims and the colonial setting of the crisis. Specifically, I suggest that Hutchinson used Puritan theology to authorize a new form of private subjectivity that in turn had the effect of unsettling existing models of public authority on colonial terrain. Ultimately, I argue, Hutchinson and her followers created an oppositional public sphere that bore a striking resemblance to a modern, non-state-identified public sphere historically associated (as we saw in the first chapter) with the culture and politics of liberalism.

The theological terms of the debate are nonetheless not irrelevant to my claims, and it is worth examining the way in which they lay the groundwork for Hutchinson's account of her own private subjectivity. First and foremost, Hutchinson's developed capacity for self-authorization (her account of the authority of her private subjectivity) is clearly rooted in her sense of the immediacy of her relation to God. Because of the intimacy of her knowledge of God and her experience of the saving grace of Christ, the chain of mediating religious and political authorities who govern the colony in the name of God hold little sway over her. "But now having seen him which is invisible," she states at her civil trial, "I fear not what man can do unto me" (338). While Puritanism authorizes this immediacy, it also has little capacity to regulate the political consequences of it. The crucial distinction between the covenant of works and grace, upon which so much of the theological debate hinged, might be understood in terms of mediation and immediacy as well. Following Calvin, the Puritans believed that each individual was predestined for salvation or damnation. As such, one could not hope to change one's foreordained status by performing good works—by entering into a covenant of works. Rather, salvation was the free gift of God, a gift of grace to the elect saints and thus solely available through a covenant of grace. Yet the New England Puritans also held that good works and living a godly life, while not capable of *effecting* salvation, might nonetheless serve as *evidence* of salvation. Righteous behavior, together with the subjective experience of one's relation with God, would serve as the testimony of one's salvation; moreover, this testimony was required in order to gain membership in the church, or status as "sanctified." Whether sanctification (saintly behavior in the visible world) could be taken as evidence of justification (true sainthood in the invisible world of God) became a central issue in the antinomian debates. For Hutchinson and her followers, the mediate signs of sanctification held little value: rather, the immediate and subjective experience of grace was the only true indication of election. According to her critics, Hutchinson's emphasis on immediacy extended to a contempt for the mediating power of the language of the Bible itself.[9] More broadly, in trumpeting her direct access to God, Hutchinson eradicated the power of the ministry and magistracy to exercise authority over her. Thus as Winthrop complains, "she walked by such a rule as cannot stand with the peace of any State; for such bottomless revelations . . . being above reason and Scripture . . . are not subject to controll" (274).

Antinomianism—a belief that, through election, one is above or beyond the law (hence *anti-nomos*)—was a clearly defined heresy in the Puritan church, yet Hutchinson did not see herself as committing this heresy. Rather, she represented herself as hewing more closely to the truths of Calvinism than did others who remained satisfied with works instead of grace. At her trial, for instance, her opening request that the court state the charges against her is in effect a carefully staged rhetorical ploy. Less a request for information than an aggressive verbal parry, Hutchinson's query *follows* Winthrop's laundry list of charges against her. Winthrop has only just listed her infractions in explicit terms:

> Mrs. Hutchinson, you are called here as one of those that have troubled the peace of the commonwealth and the churches here; you are known to be a woman that hath had a great share in the promoting and divulging of those opinions that are causes of this trouble . . . you have spoken divers things . . . very prejudicial to the honour of the churches and ministers thereof, and you have maintained a meeting and an assembly in your house that hath been condemned by the general assembly as a thing not tolerable nor comely in the sight of God nor fitting for your sex. (312)

When Hutchinson responds to these accusations by stating that "I hear no things laid to my charge" she peremptorily denies the legitimacy of Winthrop's indictment; according to Hutchinson, the laws that Winthrop claims she has broken are no law to her.[10] In a strict sense, she is on solid legal ground, given that no legal code had been established in the colonies, and that the Bible was taken as the law of the land.[11] In his rejoinder, Winthrop defers to Hutchinson's implicit argument and reframes his allegations against her in biblical terms: Hutchinson has, he states, violated the fifth commandment. This time, Hutchinson responds to the accusation rather than denies that any charge has been made. As such, Hutchinson does concede that she is governed by law, yet she also refuses to see the court as the legitimate embodiment of this law since the law is biblical. Thus when Winthrop says "the Lord doth say honour thy father and thy mother," Hutchinson responds "Ey Sir in the Lord." In this semantic quibble, she indicates that she will honor authority only so far as she believes that authority to be consonant with God's law. She thus repeatedly draws a line between "what God hath appointed" and the appointees of the court.

Hutchinson's implicit claim that honoring the law of God and honoring the law of the state are not one and the same is certainly not an argument foreign to Puritanism. We might recall, for instance, the Puritan response to the state-sanctioned directives of Archbishop William Laud in England. Or, indeed, the Cromwellian regard for the authority of the English crown. As the English Civil War testifies, Puritan doctrine contained within it terms that authorized moral opposition to state power. The immediacy of the individual congregant's relation to God together with his or her access to the vernacular text of scripture worked to legitimate an individual understanding of the will of God that effectively deauthorized mediate authorities, particularly those who claimed to derive their right to rule over others from God (such as bishops and kings). As Philip Gura, among others, argues, Hutchinson's ideas are less an abrupt departure from Puritan orthodoxy than part of a primal Puritan mix of competing doctrines that were the topic of ongoing debate among English Puritans at the time. "Those who held antinomian beliefs were no heretical invaders from outside the colony," writes Gura, "but a significant minority that . . . grounded their faith and piety in the moment of justification, not in its consequent effects."[12] As Stephen Foster argues, English Puritanism contained within it a "corrosive zeal": yet in New England, this zeal could operate against state authorities identified with Protestant reform rather than those arrayed in opposition to it.[13] Thus, as critics such as Kai Erikson and Perry Miller have pointed out, what served as effective oppositional discourse in England proved problematic when the Puritans were in power in New England.[14]

In British historiography, the oppositional discourse of English Puritanism has long been characterized as liberal (albeit not without some recent challenges to this orthodoxy). Historians such as R. H. Tawney, A. S. P. Woodhouse, Michael Walzer, and Christopher Hill, among others, have linked the theology and practice of English Puritanism with the political causes of liberty and democracy.[15] Yet the sea change occasioned by crossing the Atlantic seems to have marked New England Puritans as a distinctively different political species: in the tradition of an American historiography, New England Puritans are typically characterized as illiberal. Vernon Parrington, writing in the 1920s, describes the New England Puritans as adhering to a feudally aligned Calvinism that eradicated the liberal elements of Protestant reform: "In New England . . . by virtue of a rigid suppression of free inquiry, Calvinism long lingered out a harsh existence, grotesque and illiberal to the last. In banishing the Antinomians and Separatists and Quakers, the Massachusetts magistrates cast out the spirit of liberalism from the household of the Saints."[16] Anne Hutchinson and her followers have thus been memorialized as a liberal faction fighting against the illiberal conservatism of the Puritan fathers. This account of the illiberal character of the Massachusetts Puritans defines liberalism in terms of tolerance; insofar as they are intolerant of religious difference, the Puritans are illiberal. Yet if we understand the force of liberalism to lie less in a doctrine of tolerance than in the relocation of authority away from divinely ordained identity to an individualized and internalized relation to God (and/or natural law), the Puritans stand more clearly as progenitors of the theories of a liberal such as John Locke. A number of factors thus argue against dichotomizing Hutchinson and the elders across a liberal/feudal divide, even in theological terms: first, the New England Puritans shared in the theology of the English Puritans and, indeed, were often criticized for being more radical than their metropolitan cohort. Second, Hutchinson's theological views represented a strain of thought internal to Puritanism rather than one external to it: as such, it seems accurate to characterize Hutchinson as sharing with the elders certain volatile liberal (or proto-liberal) presumptions that emerge with new force in a colonial setting. As against the claims that identify Hutchinson as liberal and the elders as feudal, then, I would argue that Hutchinson compels the religious and civil leaders of the colony to acknowledge the force of their shared liberal presumptions and thus obliges them to begin to articulate their authority in fundamentally liberal forms—forms identified with subjectification, exchange, and publicity rather than with an older punitive era of feudalism.[17]

It is the larger claim of this book that gender is a key form of liberal knowledge and subjectivity, although it is often a hidden dimension of liberalism. As we saw in the first chapter, liberalism, in theory, does not rely upon gender as a guarantor of social order. In theory, liberalism offers a level playing field to all individuals; liberal accounts of the public sphere, in particular, emphasize the fact that the authority of public speech or writing stands or falls on the quality of the argument advanced, not the quality (or gender) of the speaker or writer advancing the argument. In contrast, an early modern concept of gender understands male/female differences as manifestations of a divinely instituted hierarchical order. How, then, does gender emerge in the trials as a term through which liberalism is articulated? In what follows, I argue that Hutchinson and Winthrop both struggle, at times, to deploy liberal definitions of gender as they seek to define the relation between a developing private subjectivity and a new political order. In other words, rather than placing Hutchinson and Winthrop on opposite sides of a liberal/feudal divide, I argue that both accept liberal premises that will ultimately reconfigure the significance of gender in relation to public authority. The new terms of private and public authority emerge fitfully and sometimes furtively within the trial and the documents related to it: neither Hutchinson nor Winthrop gives voice to liberal doctrine in an unmixed key. Nonetheless, I would suggest that one can trace, in the tenor of their arguments, a fundamentally new set of presuppositions that are decidedly those of a liberal politics and a liberal subjectivity.

For her part, Anne Hutchinson has surprisingly little to say about the authority of women in religious or political terms: rather, she repeatedly argues that her gender does not matter before God. As such, however, Hutchinson deploys Puritan doctrine with respect to gender in a proto-liberal mode: that is, she uses her direct access to God to fashion herself as an authorized public speaker, contending that it is her godliness, not her gender, that determines the authority of her actions and arguments. Indeed, Hutchinson refers to the text of Galatians to support her claim to a new subjectivity that eradicates the exterior and insignificant difference between men and women. Her reference is evidently to Paul's letter to the Galatians: "There is neither Jew nor Greek: there is neither bond nor free: there is neither male nor female: for you are all one in Christ Jesus" (Gal. 3:28). Winthrop reports that "to justify this her disordered course, she said she walked by the rule of the Apostle, Gal. which she called the rule of the new creature": in other words, in merging with Christ, Hutchinson imagines that a new creature emerges, a creature guided by a rule that no longer grounds itself in distinctions between male and female.

If Hutchinson advances a liberal account of herself as a "new creature," Winthrop, in contrast, would seem, at least initially, to resort to a feudal notion of a gendered social order. As we have already seen, Winthrop's opening accusation against Hutchinson at her civil trial refers to her violation of standards of feminine deference: in holding public meetings and, worse still, in holding forth upon her own theological views in public, she has acted in a manner not "fitting" to her sex. Winthrop thus recognizes male and female individuals more readily than the "new creature" Hutchinson declares herself to be. During the trial, Winthrop repeatedly states the need for gendered hierarchy as a form of social order necessary to the well-being of the state; in particular, he finds that public speech by a woman is contrary to gendered notions of civil order. When asked to justify her behavior in holding "weekly publick meetings" Hutchinson defends her meetings as private scenes of instruction. Moreover, she contends that she adheres to both the Bible and common custom among Puritans in holding these "conventicles": "I conceive there lyes a clear rule in Titus," states Hutchinson, "that the elder women should instruct the younger" (315). Winthrop, in turn, contends that her meetings violate the biblical rule provided in Corinthians, where Paul instructs women to be silent in church and specifically to save their questions for their husbands rather than air them in public. Winthrop thus cites the need for women to stand in a subordinate relation to men. Moreover, this subordination should itself be the proper matter of instruction among women, according to Winthrop: "you must take [Titus] in this sense that elder women must instruct the younger about their business, and to love their husbands and not to make them to clash" (316). Hutchinson's attempt to publicly teach theology, according to Winthrop, places women above men and fails to teach or embody the proper terms of a hierarchical social order. In response, Hutchinson argues that her instruction is licensed as a form of prophecy, not as public ministry: "[Meeting attendees] must not take [instruction] as it comes from me, but as it comes from the Lord Jesus Christ, and if I tooke upon me a publick Ministery, I should break a rule, but not in exercising a gift of Prophecy, and I would see a rule to turne away them that come to me" (269). In her own defense, then, Hutchinson rejects descriptions of her actions in terms of a public, social hierarchy—an order that she has clearly violated—and instead emphasizes the private relation between herself and God: it is this relation that, in turn, authorizes her speech before the audiences gathered in her home. Indeed, Hutchinson's claims in this respect are far from singular: accounts of women who used the spiritualist side of Puritanism in the seventeenth century to authorize activity unacceptable according to gendered social norms are numerous.[18] In his insistence on gender as a key term of social hierarchy, on the other hand, Winthrop would seem to align himself with feudal notions of order over and against Hutchinson's claims to a developed private (and gender-neutral) subjectivity formed through her merger with God.

Yet despite the fact that Winthrop and the other magistrates cling to the language of hierarchy in their verbal scuffles with Hutchinson throughout the trial, they do not, finally, rely upon these hierarchical norms in adjudicating her case. Indeed, I would suggest that they are far more liberal in their final judgments than they initially appear to be. It is a commonplace of critical commentary on the civil trial that Hutchinson is ultimately convicted on the basis of her claim to have had direct revelations from God: on this reading, Hutchinson suddenly loses her articulate sensibility in a moment of fatigue during the trial and, in a fatal and foreseeable misstep, announces that her authority is grounded in immediate revelations from God.[19] This account of the trial emphasizes Hutchinson's liberalism over and against the "grotesque illiberalism" of the magistrates: Hutchinson's revelations are taken as evidence of an "unrestrained subjectivity"[20] that in turn gives the magistrates license to convict and punish her. As against this long-standing interpretation of the trial, however, I would argue that Hutchinson is convicted less because of the *form* of her relation with God (direct revelation) than because of the *content* of the revelation she announces to the court. Hutchinson's revelation is troublesome not simply because it is (possibly) "above nature," but also because it foretells the destruction of those who prosecute her: she announces to the court, "if you go on in this course you begin you will bring a curse upon you and your posterity, and the mouth of the Lord hath spoken it" (338).[21] In Winthrop's account of the trial he reports a slight but significant variation of this statement: Hutchinson, he writes, proclaims that "for this you goe about to doe to me, God will ruine you and your posterity, and this whole State" (273). Once Winthrop redacts her prophecy in these terms—asserting that she predicts not just the ruin of the magistrates' posterity, but of the *state* itself—it is abundantly clear that Hutchinson is guilty of sedition: that is, she is guilty of undermining and attempting to destroy the very existence of the colony. Winthrop's account of her revelation thus emphasizes its *seditious* content rather than simply its formal status as immediate communication from God. If we read the court as, finally, banishing her because of her seditious claims rather than for having revelations of any sort, this would suggest that the court is *unable* to convict her on the grounds of her claims to self-authorization (by way of God) because these claims are doctrinally sustainable within Puritanism. Hutchinson is thus not punished as a liberal subject: indeed, it is precisely on these grounds that the court has so much trouble indicting her; rather, it is only in more explicit political terms—as a seditious element within the state—that the court finally finds the grounds to move against her. Put in stronger terms: Hutchinson compels the magistrates to acknowledge, at least implicitly, that Puritanism allows an authority to accrue to private subjectivity that they cannot regulate in the overt terms of hierarchy. Regulation will occur, rather, in terms of a concept of the public good and in terms of a new understanding of publicity.

It is not possible to put an excessively fine point upon the distinction between the magistrates' concerns with Hutchinson's revelations due to their form and their concerns due to seditious content. Clearly the magistrates endorse the notion that social hierarchy is consonant with the public good and they view immediate revelations, in general, as illegitimately enabling individuals to evade the chain of authority. Nonetheless, as one trial participant points out, Puritans have not been wholly censorious of revelation and prophecy in the past; the fact that more illustrious Puritans such as Thomas Hooker have prophesied on the basis of revelation indicates that in and of itself, revelation is not a clear infraction of Puritan doctrine.[22] Moreover, once Hutchinson claims to have had a revelation predicting her own salvation and the ruin of her prosecutors, a lengthy debate follows as to the legitimacy of her revelations— indicating, once again, that the revelations themselves were in no way the clear-cut violation that critics have presumed them to be. In terms of the sequence of the trial events, the content of the revelations seems less to immediately condemn Hutchinson than to embolden Hutchinson's prosecutors against her. Thus, for instance, following her announcement concerning the revelations, the ministers who had previously been unwilling to take an oath to testify against her are now willing to do so.[23] This additional testimony from the ministers, in turn, seems to shore up the evidence of her seditious behavior toward which the revelations also point.

More importantly, however, Hutchinson is typically able to defend herself against the (feudal, hierarchically based) charges of having violated the gendered terms of the social order: she does so, as we have seen, by invoking notions of privacy and the sanctity of conscience. The debate between the claims of privacy (advanced by Hutchinson) and the state's right to constrain public behavior (advanced by Winthrop) is thus central to the antinomian controversy.[24] The terms of this debate indicate, moreover, the extent to which shifting definitions of public and private authority are decisive elements of the new social order developing in the Bay Colony. The right to a private conscience beyond the bounds of state control is asserted repeatedly in the antinomian debates by both Hutchinson and her supporter and coagitator John Wheelwright. Because the Puritans themselves had recently defended their own religious beliefs in England in these terms, the language of conscience is a sacrosanct defense—a trump card, if you will—for the antinomians to play against the Puritan magistrates. Yet while Winthrop, for instance, must concede the inviolability of conscience, he nonetheless insists that conscience must be kept privately in order to avoid troubling the public peace. In his account of Wheelwright's trial for sedition, Winthrop thus distinguishes between private conscience and public sedition: "[Wheelwright] pretended there was nothing could be laid to his charge, but a matter of different opinion . . . it was answered, that if he had kept his judgement to himselfe, so as the publike peace had not beene troubled or endangered by it, we should have left him to himselfe, for we doe not challenge power over mens consciences, but when seditious speeches and practises discover such a corrupt conscience, it is our duty to use authority to reforme both" (259). The hands-off policy that protects matters of private conscience is thus declared null at the moment when conscience translates itself into publicity and a threat to public order. Similarly, when Hutchinson states that the reasons for her actions are "a matter of conscience," Winthrop replies, "Your conscience you must keep or it must be kept for you" (312), thereby imagining a succinct boundary between the legitimacy of private belief and the illegitimacy of disruptive public action. And as Winthrop's statement further indicates, he clearly understands it to be the state's right and duty to police this division.

Yet despite Winthrop's insistence to the contrary, the clarity of the boundary between private conscience and public order is not always so evident: indeed, debate rages, even after Wheelwright's examination, as to whether he was legitimately prosecuted in civil court given that his concerns were theological and doctrinal—matters of conscience best interrogated in ecclesiastical rather than civil procedures. One of the documents included in Winthrop's *Short Story* is an "apologie" written in defense of the court's actions in prosecuting Wheelwright following his sermon: a document produced, in other words, to counter a sense of public outrage at the proceedings themselves. Primary among the defenses of the magistrates' actions is the claim that Wheelwright's case

> was not matter of conscience, but of a civill nature and therefore most proper for this Court, to take Cognizance of, and the rather for the speciall contempt which had beene offered to the Court therein, and which the Church could not judge of. . . . The heat of contention and uncharitable censures . . . began to over-spread the Countrey, and that chiefely by occasion of [Wheelwright's] Sermon, and the like miscarriages, did require that the Civill power should speedily allay that heat. (283)

In both Hutchinson's and Wheelwright's trials, then, an idea of public good—and specifically of public order—is invoked to define and prosecute sedition. Private conscience is sanctioned, but only insofar as it remains, precisely, private and unpublished. Moreover, as the passages cited above indicate, the magistracy believed in the state's absolute authority to intervene in any action bearing upon the public order. Indeed, we might say that publicity and the state are considered coextensive; publicly espoused doctrine cannot differ from that of the state without being seditious.

Equating any form of public debate with sedition implies an understanding of publicness that is entirely antithetical to Jürgen Habermas's influential concept of the liberal public sphere. Rather, the Puritan understanding of publicness evinced in the antinomian trial reports is of a piece with a preliberal, prepublic sphere model of state and society in which publicness is equated not with public opinion but with the representation of state authority. As David Zaret, among others, argues, Habermas's notion of an oppositional public sphere, in which individuals emerged from established private identities to engage in public, rational debate, was nonexistent in early seventeenth-century England.[25] To be public before the advent of the liberal public sphere meant not to publish one's own thoughts or ideas, but to embody state authority, to be representative of the state in its corporate nature. Habermas thus speaks, for instance, of a "representative publicness"—a public individual who represents the state or the commonwealth—which precedes the later notion of a public sphere defined as "the sphere of private people come together as a public."[26] The concept of the public good invoked by Winthrop in the trials of both Wheelwright and Hutchinson clearly equates publicness with a unified state authority rather than with competing individual voices governed by reason. Indeed, in his famous sermon "A Model of Christian Charity," delivered shipboard while crossing the Atlantic, Winthrop states, "the care of the publique must oversway all private respects . . . perticuler estates cannot subsist in the ruine of the publique."[27] To be public, then, does not involve making one's private ideas known to others (publication), but it rather involves abandoning one's particular estate in favor of embodying the common cause of the commonwealth.

We might schematize the early and later versions of the concepts of public and private as follows: for Winthrop publicness involves representations consistent with the unanimity of the state and the authority granted the state by God. "Privacy," in turn, defines what lies outside the public good and, moreover, is often seen as refractory to the public good. Particular estates and private interests must, on this model, be subordinated to and excluded from any form of representative public identity. Indeed, the use of the term "private" in the Massachusetts Bay Colony in this period typically refers to that which stands outside the unified representational practices of the commonwealth; "privacy" often designates a place where differences are worked out prior to announcing a unified public position among colony leaders. Thus, for instance, in January 1636, in response to a concern with perceived factions among the rulers of the colony, the magistrates draw up a set of articles including one ordaining "that the magistrates should (as far as might be) ripen their Consultations before hande, that their vote in public might be one. (as the voyce of God.)"[28] The magistrates imagine themselves to embody a public, divine authority: their voice must therefore be unanimous "as the voyce of God." Privacy, on the other hand, represents dissent and exile from this authority and unified voice. While authority is infused from above in the model of state-identified publicness, if we turn to the model of the liberal public sphere, we see a sharp contrast: here, authority derives from below, from the privacy of individuals who join together to debate ideas in public. Consider Habermas's definition of the liberal public sphere:

> The bourgeois public sphere may be conceived above all as the sphere of *private people* come together as a public: they soon claimed the public sphere regulated from below *against the public authorities* themselves, *to engage them in a debate* over the general rules governing relations in the basically privatized but publicly relevant sphere of commodity exchange and social labor. The medium of this political confrontation was peculiar and without historical precedent: people's public use of their reason.[29]

With the advent of the liberal public sphere, Habermas indicates, authority shifted from the state to a public sphere comprised of private individuals defined by their capacity to use reason. Further, the liberal public sphere constituted an *oppositional* public space that not only did *not* coincide with the state but actively monitored and critiqued state policy as well. For Winthrop, publicness involves embodying God's authority in the univocal representations of the state: in the liberal public sphere, publicness involves the authority of the individual who emerges from privacy to engage in public debate.

Winthrop and the magistrates are thus clearly opposed to a liberal political sphere in which state policies are openly debated, yet they are nonetheless not so clearly opposed to a key presupposition of the liberal public sphere—namely, the authority of privacy. As indicated earlier in the chapter, a crucial proto-liberal assumption of Puritanism lies in the claim that each individual has the capacity to *privately* contract a relationship with God without the intervention of mediating authorities. The sanctity of conscience derives from this individual relation between the congregant and God. In this respect, then, Puritanism does grant a good deal of authority to the private individual, despite a commitment to a political order opposed to open forms of debate.[30] Indeed, according to Christopher Hill, English Puritans used theological claims related to this immediate and private contract with God to shift the meaning of publicness as well. Hill argues that when the Puritan congregant contracted with God, he achieved the public status of a representative man that had previously been reserved only for those representing God by way of embodying the state:

> The godly were public persons because Christ was a public person, and they were part of Christ. So they could not only oppose but even judge their sovereign, now a public person no longer. . . . the theory of the public, common, or representative person helped to liberate from the constraints of a traditional status society those who believed themselves to be the elect. If such men could demand their rights from God, could extort the promises from him, they would hardly be more deferential to princes.[31]

According to Hill, then, Puritans individually claimed a representative status insofar as their contract with God allowed them to embody authority. In other words, Puritanism authorized the individual over and against the state and relocated public authority in the private contract with God rather than in conformity to divinely authorized state powers.

Hill's account adverts to an English Puritanism that overtly challenged state authority during the English Civil War rather than New England Puritanism that embodied state authority. Nonetheless, I would argue that the shift toward new forms of public authority occasioned by new forms of Puritan private authority occurred in New England as well as Old. Definitions of privacy and publicness are inextricably linked: in shifting the meaning and value of privacy, or, more specifically, in locating authority in a form of privacy, the New England Puritans invited upon themselves radical shifts in the meaning and value of publicness as well. In the case of both Hutchinson and Wheelwright, we see precisely this equation drawn between an authorized privacy and a new-found form of publicity. I have argued that Hutchinson deploys the liberal force of her private relation with God to authorize her own disruptive activities in the colony. Despite the very public effects of these activities, Hutchinson repeatedly insists that her actions—including teaching and leading conventicles—are defensible because they are private. As such, she shies away from challenging the Puritans to accept new modes of publicness and defends herself, instead, by insisting that she is only following accepted models of private activity. John Wheelwright, on the other hand, argues quite explicitly that he has a right to "publish" his opinions because the authority of these opinions derives from his private relation to God. In other words, Wheelwright makes explicit the claim that a new form of authorized privacy results in new forms of publicness. Winthrop thus reports that during his trial, Wheelwright asserted his right to publicly express his private views without regard for the good of the state:

> That [Wheelwright] did know (as he himselfe confessed) that divers of the Ministers here were not of his Judgement in those [doctrinal] points, and that the *publishing* of them, would cause disturbance in the Country, and yet he would never conferre with the Ministers abut them, that thereby he might have gained them to his opinion, (if it had beene the truth) or at least have manifested some care of the publick peace, which he rather seemed to slight, when being demanded in the Court a reason of such his failing, hee answered that he ought not to consult with flesh and bloud, about the *publishing* of that truth which he had received from God. (290–91; emphases added)

Winthrop indicates that Wheelwright should follow the model of state-identified publicness: differences of doctrine should be resolved in private in order to maintain public unanimity. Wheelwright, on the other hand, is effectively announcing his belief in a kind of publicness far closer to that countenanced by the liberal public sphere: the private truth he has received from God authorizes him to announce his personal ideas publicly and, indeed, to oppose and debate the policies of the state. In fact, Wheelwright's use of the word "publish" uncannily presages the terminology and logic of the print public sphere, despite the fact that his reference in this case is clearly not to publishing in print, but to making public in oratory. As such, Wheelwright would seem to claim a Puritan (and proto-liberal) authority of privacy and, from there, to derive the right to a critical and oppositional (liberal) public sphere.

While Hutchinson herself eschews the terminology of publicity that Wheelwright argues for here, it is nonetheless the case that her use of the authority of her private relation to God enables her to organize an oppositional public sphere within the colony. If we return to Hutchinson's trial transcript, it becomes evident that Hutchinson's offense, in the eyes of the magistracy, is less the unrestrained subjectivity announced by the fact of her revelations than the seditious (non-state-identified) force of the public gatherings or conventicles she convenes in her home. In effect, Hutchinson creates an oppositional public sphere within the colony; that is, she does not simply criticize the ministers, but on the basis of Puritan doctrine, mobilizes a public that operates outside state-sanctioned publicness. Rather than using the conventicles to reinforce the ministers' sermons by repeating them, Hutchinson argues with (monitors, critiques) the doctrines of these state-identified figures on the authority of her private contract with God and her specific, *personal* knowledge of the terms of God's saving grace. Winthrop thus reports that "Shee kept open house for all commers, and set up two Lecture dayes in the week, when they usually met at her house, threescore or fourescore persons, the pretence was to repeate Sermons, but when that was done, shee would comment upon the Doctrines, and interpret all passages at her pleasure, and expound dark places of Scripture, so as whatsoever the Letter held forth . . . shee would bee sure to make it serve her turn" (264). Similarly, at the trial, he accuses her of gathering an *oppositional* public: "you do not . . . search the Scriptures for their confirming in the truths delivered, but you open your teachers points, and declare his meaning, and correct wherein you think he hath failed, &c. and by this meanes you abase the honour and authority of the publick Ministery" (268).[32] As a result of these meetings, members of Hutchinson's "party" begin to criticize the ministers by debating their points in church after the sermon or by simply walking out of church when the ministers begin preaching. By adumbrating an alternative source of authority in Puritan privacy, Hutchinson thus mobilized a non-state-identified public sphere. It is worth emphasizing the liberal lineaments of the oppositional public sphere Hutchinson helps to foster. Habermas makes it clear that a liberal public sphere arises as private individuals begin to have a sense of authority that allows them to critique the state. While Habermas locates this authority in the growth of capitalism and the contractual relations of private property ownership, we have seen that Puritanism relocates divine authority into a private realm and thus creates a similar condition of private authority from which the right to criticize the state emerges. In developing notions of the private self and the self's relation with God, the Puritans set the stage, in effect, for an oppositional public sphere.

One of the primary social sites for developing the private religious subjectivity so central to Puritanism was the conventicle, the private meeting of believers held for worship and study outside church. Conventicles, such as the meetings Hutchinson would eventually be condemned for holding, were encouraged by Puritan authorities in both Massachusetts and Old England. As Patrick Collinson has shown, conventicles were commonplace in English Puritanism from the sixteenth century forward. Indeed, according to Collinson, these voluntary "meetings of the godly" were important to developing the lay-oriented, independent nature of the Puritan movement against the existing parish structure of the Anglican church.[33] Extracurricular meetings of devout individuals were held to both repeat sermons and read scripture, but also to develop the private subjectivity central to Puritan faith. Stephen Foster, for instance, describes conventicles as virtual laboratories for refining the morphology of personal conversion: by John Cotton's time, he argues, "the godly had passed well beyond simple scriptural exegesis to probe into one another's spiritual affairs under the guise of personal application of the doctrine. . . . Part of the learning by participation came through the example and conversation of the godly, with whom one compared experiences at those much praised fruitful Sabbath conferences."[34] In effect, the conventicle allowed one to join with others in the work of personal probing and seeking necessary to discern and make meaning out of one's private relation with God. Indeed, John Cotton, in discussing Hutchinson's conventicles, argues that her meetings initially seemed to him to perform precisely the desired work necessary for bringing converts to knowledge of their salvation in Christ:

> All [Hutchinson's teaching] was well . . . and suited with the publike Ministery, which had gone along in the same way, so as these private conferences did well tend to water the seeds publikely sown. Whereupon all the faithfull embraced her conference, and blessed God for her fruitfull discourses. And many whose spirituall estates were not so safely layed, yet were hereby helped and awakened to discover their sandy foundations, and to seek for better establishment in Christ. (412)

Cotton thus describes Hutchinson's conventicles as a form of private inquiry that is the companion piece of public work performed by the ministers. Ideally, then, conventicles align public and private religious meaning: conventicles develop a private subjectivity in each individual that accords with the state-identified public theology of the colony's ministers.

Yet in the development of a private subjectivity also stands the possibility of empowering the laity or private individuals in ways unauthorized by public ministry—of developing a new public. Thus, as Foster argues, conventicles in England quickly assumed the shape of a counterpublic: "Without departing too much from their first purposes, these gatherings rather easily became forums for the criticism of official policy in church and state."[35] When Hutchinson's meetings, too, acquire this character—and in terms of their structure, it should be no surprise that they do—the ministers convene a synod to condemn the practice. Rather than condemning conventicles outright, however, the synod insists on demarcating public and private meetings, effectively attempting to eradicate the possibility of any oppositional content in the private meetings. The synod's ruling reads as follows: "That though women might meet (some few together) to pray and edify one another; yet such a set assembly, (as was then in practice in Boston,) where sixty or more did meet every week, and one woman (in a prophetical way, by resolving questions of doctrine, and expounding scripture) took upon her the whole exercise, was agreed to be disorderly, and without rule."[36] From the language used here, it is evident that the distinction between acceptable and unacceptable conventicles is somewhat difficult to draw. On the one hand, the conventicles seem necessary to enable the development of a private relation with God and to shape this relation into an acceptable and comprehensible form. On the other hand, precisely the empowerment of this privatized relation between God and congregant opens the possibility for "expounding" rather than "repeating" doctrine. The conventicles thus have an important and double-edged function: on the one hand, they are disciplinary in an almost Foucauldian sense—through them, individuals learn to interpret their lives in light of the fixed morphology of the conversion narrative. On the other hand, they are profoundly subversive of a hierarchical social order insofar as they lay the groundwork for an oppositional public sphere.[37]

The emphasis placed on conventicles within Puritanism points to the important new role of privacy in relation to public identity. Privacy is no longer entirely external or marginal with respect to the public order, but begins to serve as its grounds. With this shift in the meaning and importance of privacy, women—previously understood as excluded from representative publicness—begin to have a new public authority precisely because of their important private identities. Consider, for instance, the position of women within conventicles in England and New England. Foster cites the account of one Oliver Heywood, a Lancashire minister who in the 1640s joined a conventicle convened by a woman: "We were above 20 young men and others, who joyned together by the instigation of an ancient godly widow woman, and propounded necessary questions and held up a conference every fourtnight and prayed our course about, where I was (tho being young and raw) some time exercised, this was maintained a considerable time in winter nights."[38] Collinson points, as well, to the link between the domestic, private space of the conventicle and the greater role of women therein: "Since these meetings were an extension of normal family worship, there is every reason to suppose that laymen took a lead in prayer and even in expounding doctrine. . . . In the Dedham minutes, we even find a brother inquiring, 'whether it were convenient a woman should pray, having a better gift than her husband?' "[39] As this anecdotal evidence indicates, women were able to assume authority when it came to developing private subjectivity and to conducting private meetings in the home. As Hutchinson's own experience indicates, moreover, this developed privacy assumed important public dimensions.

It is worth noting that, as we have seen, Hutchinson herself studiously avoids claiming any public role for her private meetings, despite the noticeable changes in public behavior that seem to stem from them. As such, Hutchinson claims that she is adhering to an established form of gendered behavior: because she is not seeking to represent or embody the state, she is not seeking a public role for herself. But in deploying the older model of representative publicness, she also willfully ignores the new public role that her private self-authorization has enabled her to assume. Wheelwright, by way of contrast, does not hesitate to claim that he has a new public authority based in his private relation to God: he argues for his right to publish his ideas, whereas Hutchinson defends herself on the grounds that she has never sought to be public. Both Hutchinson and Wheelwright thus conform to an older set of gendered expectations concerning public and private norms, while at the same time, their actions demonstrate the new public power afforded to privacy, and thereby to women as well as to men.

At the close of her trial Hutchinson is banished from the colony; later, she is excommunicated from the church as well. In addition, her followers are disarmed and placed on trial for sedition. Winthrop and the ministers thus respond to Hutchinson's agitations—to her oppositional public sphere—with acts of overt repression. Yet as I have argued, the shift toward a new model of the liberal public sphere is one that is grounded in the structure and theology of Puritanism; as such, I would argue that Winthrop's most significant actions against Hutchinson are ultimately not punitive but are themselves related to publicity and the public sphere. In other words, Winthrop responds, in part, to Hutchinson's challenge by engaging in the new terms of publicity and exchange, the power of which she herself has made evident. Shortly after Hutchinson leaves the Bay Colony for Rhode Island, Winthrop relates in his journal that he immediately wrote up all the documents relevant to the controversy to send back to England "to the end that all our godly friends might not be discouraged from coming to us."[40] The next section of this chapter examines the documents that Winthrop and others circulated in the transatlantic print public sphere following the controversy. For the moment, let me note that Winthrop's representations of Hutchinson in the print public sphere will serve as his own entry into public debates over the political and religious future of England and its colonies; moreover, these documents bespeak an attempt to deploy liberal accounts of gender in circuits of exchange and desire and thus mark a politics of gender of an order quite distinct from overt norms of hierarchy and repression. It is the argument of the remainder of this chapter that the way in which both women and men are authorized by and through privacy will ultimately not be contained or controlled through top-down modes of authority—through punishment and banishment—but through publicity itself turned back upon privacy.

TRANSATLANTIC PRINT AND IMPERIAL DESIGNS

When Winthrop writes up his account of the antinomian controversy, he does so, in part, with the intentions of a publicist, that is, he is concerned with presenting the colonists' governing of the crisis in the best possible light. Moreover, he is not simply interested in producing what might be called a "winner's" version of history for posterity; rather, he has the more immediate aim of reassuring potential investors and immigrants to the colony that Massachusetts Bay remains worthy of their commitments. His intended audience, as he writes in his journal, is thus less the colonists of Massachusetts Bay than the home crowd in England—"our godly friends"—who might eventually join the colony or, alternatively, invest in the colony. Winthrop's concern with impressing this audience favorably was acute, and justifiably so. The Massachusetts Bay Colony was far from self-sustaining in the 1630s; rather, the colony depended for its economic livelihood upon the infusion of monies brought to its shores by new immigrants from England, immigrants who typically liquidated their English properties before sailing for New England. Yet this influx of people and funds began to slow at the close of the 1630s, and when the Long Parliament was convened in 1640 and Archbishop Laud's persecutions of Puritans in England ceased, the flow of immigrants abruptly halted. Indeed, by the early 1640s, there were more colonists returning to England than emigrating to New England.[41] As a result, the colony was plunged into financial crisis. Massachusetts suffered a severe economic depression and was hard-pressed by an inability to purchase manufactured goods from England due to lack of currency. In addition, former financial backers in England as well as colonists themselves began to look toward the West Indies for the possibility of greater profit and warmer climes for settlement. As Raymond Stearns reports,

English financial supporters, seeking profits as well as godliness in the enterprise, urged the colonists to move farther south, either on the American coast or to the West Indies, where they could be more comfortable, more nearly self-sufficient, just as godly, and perhaps less expensive. . . . Only widespread poverty and the faith and dissuasive force of Governor Winthrop, backed by Endecott and prominent elders, prevented a wholesale departure of colonists from Massachusetts shores.[42]

Winthrop's force was not only dissuasive—that is, he attempted not simply to keep colonists from abandoning the colony—but also persuasive insofar as he continued to court Puritan support in England. While Winthrop's *Short Story* has typically been read as the orthodox party's account of the theological arguments waged in Massachusetts over antinomianism, the *transatlantic* context of the narrative is a primary (and largely unrecognized) influence in the document's creation and publication.[43] News of the antinomian controversy reached English ears quickly. Indeed, following the crisis, Winthrop received a letter reporting that Massachusetts was "spoken of disgracefully and with bitternes in the greatest meetings in the kingdome" because of negative reports concerning the repression of the antinomian party.[44] While Winthrop's narrative tends to focus on Anne Hutchinson, it is worth noting that numerous colonists were banished from the colony during the controversy (primarily those who had signed the petition in support of Wheelwright), some of whom returned to England rather than following Hutchinson to Rhode Island. Those who returned to England included prominent and wealthy Puritans such as Henry Vane, the former governor of the colony who had close connections to Puritan aristocrats in England. Winthrop's history is thus an attempt to reassure Puritan supporters that justice and religious orthodoxy prevail in Massachusetts. Although the manuscript undoubtedly circulated privately for a number of years, the actual publication of Winthrop's *Short Story* in England occurred some seven years after its composition, in 1644, through the offices of Thomas Weld.[45] Weld, a minister from Roxbury, arrived in England in 1641 having been deputized by the Massachusetts Court of Assistants to return to England to garner additional financial support for the colony and to mollify angry creditors concerned about the lack of return on their investments in the colony. Neither Weld nor Winthrop's motives for publication can be described as wholly monetary—that is, both individuals saw the account of Hutchinson's trial as evidence of the work of God in New England. But their desire to publicize this information conjoined economic and religious motives, as was often the case for Puritans. When Winthrop wrote the document following Hutchinson's banishment, he did so in an effort to present the colony in the best light to English supporters; when Weld published the document in 1644, he did so in the context both of his mission to secure additional investment in the colony and more specifically to promote the New England Way in the context of ongoing theological debates in England over the future shape of the Protestant church in England.[46]

The transatlantic context of the *Short Story* is important for understanding Winthrop's relation to liberalism because it points to Winthrop's own necessary engagement with public sphere discourse, a public sphere organized according to the horizontal, contractual terms of liberalism and nascent capitalism rather than the vertical terms of patronage and state representativeness.[47] While Winthrop is aligned with state authority in the colony of Massachusetts, he is not aligned with the state outside the colony. His deliberate distance from state authority in England is evident in the fact that he does not turn to the crown or Parliament for support of the colony at its moment of desperate economic need, but to the religious and financial investment community of wealthy Puritans in England and to Puritan supporters interested in emigrating to the colony. Indeed, when the Massachusetts court first contemplates sending agents to England to seek financial assistance, the magistrates worry that even an appeal to Parliament (presumably more sympathetic to Puritan colonization than Charles I) will jeopardize the favorable terms of the colony's charter. Winthrop reports in his journal, "we declined the motion [to appeal to Parliament] for this consideration, that if we should put ourselves under the protection of the parliament, we must then be subject to all such laws as they should make, or at least such as they might impose upon us; in which course though they should intend our good, yet it might prove very prejudicial to us."[48] Ironically, then, while Winthrop invokes a need for the suppression of a public sphere that is not identified with the state during the antinomian crisis, his own work and writing depend upon the circulation of publicity in a transatlantic public sphere that is increasingly not aligned with state representation.

The appeal the colonists make to England, then, is ultimately one that is directed to a community of wealthy investors who are guided by a set of *private* or non-state-aligned interests (godliness and wealth) that they pursue in public forms that oppose state authority. As Robert Brenner demonstrates, the entwined financial and religious motivations of the "colonizing aristocrats" among the Puritan elite clearly broke with the policies and interests of the British state. Historically the British crown had granted charters to trading companies and maintained close alliances with an elite merchant class: the Company of Merchant Adventurers and the East India Company developed symbiotic relations with the crown that granted them monopolies while they, in turn, garnered funds for the crown in the form of import and export tariffs. The colonial merchants in the Americas were, however, of a different stripe. According to Brenner, the elite, crown-supporting merchants abandoned efforts to colonize North America in the 1620s because of the difficulty of extracting rapid profits from the region.[49] In the wake of their withdrawal, a new class of less elite merchants became involved in trade *and* settlement; this class of individuals did not rely upon the crown for protection and, indeed, often sought free trade rather than increased regulation from the state. Unallied with the interests of the monarchy, the new merchants often made common cause with Puritan dissidents who sought to settle elsewhere because of persecution in England.[50] In both religious and economic terms, then, the colonization efforts made by English Puritans in the 1630s were founded upon the attenuation of state authority—upon the development of independent sources of authority (wealth, godliness) not identified with existing state powers.

The Massachusetts Bay Colony was founded as a joint-stock trading company and chartered from the king much as earlier trading companies such as the Levant Company and the Virginia Company. However, the Puritan aristocrats involved in founding the colony were able to exert their power to effect something of a coup in the terms of this charter: rather than being required to hold company meetings in England and to govern the colony through an emissary, the Puritan settlers were able to denominate themselves as company officers and to take their charter with them.[51] As a result, Winthrop and other settlers were able to govern themselves independently with little direct accountability to the crown. Historians have justifiably made much of this independence from direct ties to English government and, indeed, the colonists themselves (as we have seen) placed enormous value on this freedom. Accounts of the charter transfer tend to emphasize the essential transformation of the trading corporation at this point into a self-governing religious enterprise.[52] Yet despite the political independence enabled by the charter transfer, links to the investment community in England remained strong: as a result, the connection between the Massachusetts Colony and England was maintained primarily through investment relations rather than through the state. Given that many of the investors in the company understood themselves to be contributing to religious rather than strictly financial ends, the accountability of the colonists to these investors was not strictly financial. Rather, it was *both* religious and financial. As such, it seems important to emphasize less the lack of connection between the colonists and England than the distinct nature of this connection: the hierarchical relay of state authority from the crown downward through the charter and an outside appointed governor may have been dismantled, but in their stead we find a set of horizontal, contractual relations associated with early capitalism.[53]

As Habermas's model of the origins of the public sphere indicates, the development of authoritative forms of privacy (new forms of bourgeois subjectivity) helped to establish a liberal public sphere in which the public good is the subject of rational debate. In my discussion of Anne Hutchinson's trial, I argued that Puritan theology—the doctrine of direct access to God—allowed Hutchinson to locate the authority of her religious ideas in her private experience; this, in turn, enabled her to speak and argue publicly against the state in a new way. Like Hutchinson, Winthrop and the investors locate their authority to attenuate their bonds with the British state in religious claims. Yet in addition to their religious authority, they claim authority to pursue their interests as property owners—as investors with private financial interests in the balance. We might recall Habermas's argument about the effects of capitalism on property owners: "In a certain fashion," Habermas contends, "commodity owners could view themselves as autonomous. To the degree that they were emancipated from governmental directives and controls, they made decisions freely in accord with standards of profitability. In this regard they owed obedience to no one and were subject only to the anonymous laws functioning in accord with . . . economic rationality" (46). For Habermas, the public sphere emerges out of commodity ownership as property owners "engage . . . in a debate over the general rules governing relations in the basically privatized but publicly relevant sphere of commodity production and social labor" (27). According to Habermas, then, the realm of private interest and the creation of an authority located in private identity (the predicate, as I have emphasized, of the new public sphere) is associated with capitalism. In contrast, David Zaret argues that the origins of the public sphere lie less in capitalism alone than in the development of Protestantism in England: "Not simply protestantism but its lay initiative created the first body of public opinion, the public sphere of religion, whose participants saw it in terms of 'critical reflections of a public competent to form its own judgments.'"[54] Habermas and Zaret thus both locate the origins of the public sphere in the new independence and competency of private individuals as defined, respectively, by property ownership and religion. In the case of the Puritans, it seems particularly evident that both financial and religious discourses contribute to a sense of private, non-state-sanctioned authority.

For Habermas and Zaret, the authority of the individual (whether grounded in religion or capital) results in a public sphere governed by rational debate.

As I argued in the first chapter, however, it may be useful to think of the public sphere created in light of both Protestant theology and capitalist investment in terms of desire rather than simply reason. For instance, arguments over the antinomian controversy were not simply penned in order to debate the rationality or even the justness of the Puritan rulers' actions in handling the crisis: rather, these documents were written in part to generate desire (or antipathy) among readers for the colonial project itself. Winthrop's *Short Story* was written not for the sake of historical accuracy and rationality alone, but in order to make English readers believe that the Massachusetts Bay Colony was a thriving, godly enterprise that they might wish to join. In emphasizing the component of desire in the public sphere, I mean to point to the somewhat invisible regulatory function of new public sphere relations: while top-down forms of governance may be attenuated or vitiated with respect to the crown's control of the Bay Colony, the regulation of the colony shifts to a set of market terms governed by desire and publicity. Rather than answering to the king, Winthrop must now answer to the desire of his readers and Puritan investors in England. While he is free from the immediate control of the state, he is tethered to the more amorphous regulation of private desire circulating in the market. Moreover, the Puritans in Massachusetts understood that it was important that their religious and economic stock continue to rise or at least maintain its value with an English audience in order for the colony to survive, and they deliberately produced and circulated many texts to appeal to this audience. Hence, as Phillip Round argues, "the act of reporting facts to a metropolitan reader . . . recapitulated in discourse the transatlantic mercantile network in which the colonists themselves, their furs and timber, and their much-needed English provisions every day participated" (20). Reports to metropolitan readers not only recapitulated a mercantile network, but also shaped the terms of this network of economic, religious, and political relations.

Traditional accounts of American history that emphasize the foundational role of the Puritans in shaping America—the "Puritan origins" model—tend to pay scant attention to the determining network of connections between Old England and New England. Rather, the journey across the Atlantic is figured as a break with the Old World and the origin of the New World: hence, for instance, the removal of the charter to Massachusetts is understood to confer complete independence from England rather than to establish alternative forms of connection and dependence. Yet the colonists themselves were not only culturally connected to England, as recent accounts have emphasized (they certainly considered themselves "English"), they were also acutely aware of their dependence upon English support and viewed themselves as wholly connected to, and even constituted by, a network of economic, religious, and literary connections with the metropole. Indeed, Winthrop's famous description of the colony as a "city on a hill" spells out the Puritan mission in terms that rely upon a notion of the transatlantic public sphere: with the image of the "city on a hill," Winthrop implies that an English audience is watching the activities of the colonists, and that the colonists' work in founding a godly community will be exemplary in reforming the Anglican church. This image reveals not only the work of founding that he imagines himself to be undertaking, but, conversely, that the settlers are reliant, in their central mission, upon the gaze of this English audience. In more concrete terms, it is clear from their actions that Massachusetts leaders were tremendously concerned with their British audience. In 1631, for instance, one Henry Linne was whipped and ordered banished from Boston "for writinge Lettres into England, full of slander against our government, & orders of our Churches."[55] In 1635, an immigrant named John Pratt was called before the court for having written back to England that the land was barren; his letter lamented "the improbability or impossibility of subsistence for ourselves or our posterity without tempting God, or without extraordinary means."[56] The court seized the letter and required him to write another letter repudiating these claims. The antinomian crisis—precisely because it was a theological and political crisis for the colony that resulted in major upheaval, including the banishment of many colonists— was clearly a subject that required careful handling of public relations with England. Indeed, the letter writer who reported to Winthrop that news of the crisis was tarnishing Massachusetts's reputation in England recommended that Winthrop pay mind to "how [colonists] doe answeare the lettres (such as they may be) of theire friends sent ower from vs to you."[57]

The colonists did indeed pay mind to the reports of the colony that reached England, yet they were not ultimately able to control the flow of information across the ocean. While ships could be, and indeed were, searched for letters containing derogatory information, individuals who left the colony and returned to England (some of whom were banished, others of whom found the colony lacking promise) were free to publish their opinions in England without fear of colonial regulation. Precisely because the colony was not allied with the British state, British censors had no interest in controlling information about the colonies. Round argues that an awareness of the need to control information shaped colonial policies and led to repressive measures. Yet as Round's discussion indicates, these measures were not successful because of the new nature of the public sphere:

> Within a year or two of their founding, both Plymouth and the Bay Colony reacted to cultural imperatives demanding that the management of information being exchanged in transatlantic letters be centralized in an authorized elite. . . . Soon after

its establishment, the Bay Colony government began meting out harsh punishments for 'disinformation.' In 1631 . . . Philip Ratcliffe was found guilty of uttering malicious speeches and had his ears cut off. . . . [B]y cropping the culprit's ears—instead of, for example, the hand that had written the offensive matter—the authorities were signaling the importance of paying attention to a reader's or listener's response. Reading and interpretation were becoming important sites of social and political control in both England and New England during the early decades of the seventeenth century, a time when governmental proclamation barred "lavish and licentious talking in matters of state."[58]

The emphasis on audience reception and the desire to control this reception points to a concern with the effects of the circulation of information in a growing public sphere that can not, in fact, be regulated from above. Cutting off the ears of the offending writer may signal a concern for reception, but it certainly doesn't achieve the effect of controlling the reception of information among listeners or readers. Indeed, as historian David Cressy argues, attempts to regulate the flow of information back to England often backfired by increasing enmity toward the colony among its detractors. Cressy categorizes the accounts of New England that appear in England as follows:

By the middle of the seventeenth century the English could draw on four main sets of opinion about New England: first, that the land was marvelous and that the saints were planting there a model of godliness and good government; second, that the land was indeed wonderful, but the Puritan experiment was gravely in error; third, that the environment was difficult and disappointing but worth enduring because of the righteousness of God's cause; and fourth, that both cause and environment were worthless and ought to be abandoned.[59]

As Cressy's categories indicate, privately and publicly circulated descriptions of the Massachusetts Bay Colony proliferated in England. This proliferation of competing accounts of the colony indicates the inability of the colonial rulers to control the dissemination of news in England; that is, it shows precisely the public nature of the literary sphere in England concerning colonial representation. Ultimately, the *inability* of the Massachusetts authorities to regulate the flow of information back to England concerning the colony required that they, too, add their voices to the chorus of competing accounts in an attempt to accrue public sentiment to their vision. Unable to fully regulate accounts of the antinomian controversy, Winthrop, in writing the *Short Story*, produced and circulated his own. In other words, despite their best efforts to the contrary, the Puritan leaders were pushed to participate in a liberal public sphere.

The *Short Story*, then, is a text that is created out of Winthrop's awareness of his need to participate in a transatlantic public sphere. Winthrop's journal indicates that his intention was to circulate this account among Puritan sup-

porters in England—a form of limited or what might be called "coterie" publishing. When the text was published in London seven years later by Thomas
Weld, it was even more clear that publication occurred because of a desire to
enter into transatlantic print public sphere debates over representations of the
colony. Indeed, as noted above, the entire mission that Thomas Weld and fellow minister Hugh Peter undertook in 1641 was an explicit attempt to improve
support for the colony among English investors. Their mission was evidently
fourfold: to reassure creditors who had not received the promised return on
their investment, to gather additional funds and goods to support the colony,
to seek relief from British tariffs on commerce, and to abet "the work of reformation of the churches" in England.[60] All told, we might see this mission as a
lobbying effort—a publicity excursion to England on behalf of the colony. And
indeed, one of the many activities Weld and Peter engaged in upon returning
to England was the publishing of numerous documents written by
Massachusetts Puritans, including the glowing report of the colony titled *New
England's First Fruits*.[61] Interestingly, colony governors debated for some time
as to whether sending such a mission would have positive or negative effects:
John Endecott worried that an official mission from the colony would serve as
a public advertisement of the colony's straits and would thus discourage additional investment. Endecott complained to Winthrop that such a mission
would put off new immigrants, "The report of our povertie having bene
alreadie a manifest cause of debarring most from us." Moreover, he argued, "it
will conferme my Lord Say and others of his judgement that New England can
no longer subsist without the helpe of old England; espetiallie they beinge
already informed of the forwardness of divers among us to remove to the West
Indies because they cannot heere maintayne their families."[62] Endecott suggested, alternatively, that the colonists should "privately" ask for funds from
English supporters. Yet the public mission, aborted once in 1640, eventually
took place in 1641 as the colonists felt a pressing economic need for additional
funds.

Endecott's concerns about Lord Say and Sele's judgments proved to be prescient, as indeed was his more specific objection to the person of Hugh Peter,
a man whom he saw as "too well affected to the West Indies" rather than devoted to the New England cause alone. Although Peter did not ever participate in
West Indian colonization, he also did not ever return to New England but
became embroiled, instead, in the English Puritan cause, a cause with far different concerns than the single goal of sustaining the New England colony. As
Endecott indicates, from the perspective of New England, English Puritan colonization of the West Indies became a threat to the very existence of

Massachusetts, particularly by the early 1640s, when the economic difficulties
of the Bay Colony caused the wealthy colonizing Puritans of England to withdraw their support from Massachusetts in favor of projects in the West Indies
such as Providence Island. From the perspective of the Puritan grandees, New
England held no particular claim to their support save insofar as it conformed
to the needs of a larger, imperialist Puritan plan. English Puritan colonizing
efforts were not simply an attempt to find a safe haven from the rising
Arminian tide in the 1630s, but also part of a grand plan to increase the power
of an English Protestant nation by crushing Spanish dominion and wealth in
the colonies, and thereby also destroying the Catholic force in Europe. The aim
of Puritan colonialism was thus to turn a profit for England and Protestantism
at the expense of Spain and Catholicism. As Karen Kupperman explains,
Massachusetts was far from central to this grand design:

> English puritans of high rank and national prominence were interested in the suc-
> cess of Massachusetts and often helped the colony materially, but they never believed
> that New England could ever be anything but the merest sideshow while the real
> action was carried on elsewhere. . . . Only ventures [in the West Indies], they
> believed, could truly serve England by helping to solve the country's crippling eco-
> nomic problems and, more important, by stemming the flow of gold to Spanish cof-
> fers that fueled the great war machine harrying European Protestants back into
> Roman Catholicism. With England economically strong and independent, and with
> Spain weakened, true religion would be made secure.[63]

Viewing the Massachusetts Bay Colony within this imperial schema, rather
than seeing it standing securely at the origin of a new American history, effects
something of a Copernican revolution in our understanding of the New
England Puritans' location in the seventeenth-century colonial universe. That
is, it enables us to see that the battle the Puritans in Massachusetts fought in
their first decades of existence was not simply one of founding a godly
Christian community in the "wilderness," but rather one of competing for the
resources of an English public, and in particular, the resources of Puritan
imperialists who had begun to believe that the main chance for wealth and
redemption lay elsewhere than in New England.[64]

Hugh Peter and Thomas Weld, chosen for their mission on behalf of
Massachusetts precisely for their connections to the Puritan grandees and their
facility in the worlds of business and publicity, were nonetheless ultimately
drawn toward the imperial center of the English Puritan cause and away from
pursuing the specific needs of the Bay Colony. Hugh Peter, in particular,
despite his intermittent efforts on behalf of the colony, is exemplary of a cosmopolitan English imperialist Puritan who engaged in a variety of transatlantic adventures on behalf of Puritanism. Peter himself had been involved in

bringing together the group of merchants, settlers, and Puritan aristocrats who first formed the Massachusetts Bay Company while he was in exile in Holland under Laud's repressive regime. Emigrating to Massachusetts and assuming a prominent position there as a minister in Salem, he nonetheless quickly became involved in other imperial adventures when he returned to England as Massachusetts's emissary in 1641. In 1642 he left England for Ireland as part of a new Puritan venture, the "Adventurers for Ireland," a company organized to "reduce the Rebels in the said Realm of Ireland" (and turn a tidy profit) following the 1641 uprising there. The Adventurers for Ireland was in effect a Puritan mercenary band, deputized by Parliament to fight the Irish at a time when Parliament distrusted Charles I and was loath to authorize funds to raise an army under his banner. The same group of Puritan grandees who funded colonization in Massachusetts, Providence Island, and Bermuda stood behind this venture as well: Lord Brooke, Lord Say and Sele, the Earl of Warwick, and John Humfry included. In return for their services in raising a private army, Parliament agreed that they might "hold and enjoy to their own Use, without any Accompt whatsoever, . . . all Ships, Goods, Monies, Plate, Pillage, and Spoil" they laid hands upon.[65] In other words, in return for fighting the Catholic Irish, the Merchant Adventurers were authorized by Parliament to seize their property. Not entirely different from Puritan colonizing ventures across the Atlantic, this investment similarly promised both religious and financial rewards and, further, was distinctly outside the control of the crown. Indeed, Peter's own propagandizing efforts regarding his success in the Irish adventure (after a mere three months there) helped to cement sentiment against Charles I at the outbreak of civil war in England as Peter reported that the English king and his soldiers were in league with the Irish papists.

Upon his return to England, Peter asserted himself at the center of public sphere debates over the course of Parliament's relation to the Crown, arguing against the moderate voices of the "peace party" at every turn and thereby furthering critique of the monarchy and fanning the flames of civil war. Through sermons, repeated petitions to Parliament, and pamphlets, Peter's voice became prominent in the emerging oppositional public sphere in London.[66] For a period of years, some of his publishing efforts were related to the New England cause, but he was unquestionably more taken by the larger Puritan design and was centrally involved in the rise to power of the group of Puritan colonizing aristocrats during the civil war, in no small part due to the persuasiveness of his public voice. Peter later served as chaplain to the New Model Army, chaplain for Cromwell in battles in Ireland in 1649, and was appointed chaplain to the Council of State by Cromwell in 1650. Following Cromwell's

death and the restoration of Charles II to the throne, however, he was exempt-
ed from the Act of Indemnity and in 1660 was executed after having been
found guilty of abetting the execution of Charles I.[67] It seems significant that
the word historians and biographers most often resort to in their descriptions
of Peter is not "minister" or "chaplain" but "propagandist." Above all, Peter
exerted authority through the new mechanisms of publication available to
him; indeed, he was ultimately convicted of the crime of regicide, not because
he sat on the court that determined Charles's fate, but because he repeatedly
urged the cause of regicide with powerful sermons before the court.[68] Not
entirely unlike Anne Hutchinson, then, Hugh Peter eventually was punished
for his success in galvanizing public sphere opposition against a ruling authority. I dwell on the career of Hugh Peter here because it so aptly illustrates the
world of a cosmopolitan Puritanism that is not often visible in accounts of the
Massachusetts Bay Colony. Peter was an important figure in Massachusetts,
and, as we have seen, was chosen to represent the colony's interests in England.
But his work for Massachusetts was only one episode in a much longer and
larger career in the greater English Puritan world. Peter's career thus makes
visible the position of the Massachusetts colony within broader, transatlantic
religious and economic structures. Aspects of his career—his transatlantic
venturing in finance and religion (to New England, Ireland, and earlier to
Holland), his wholesale engagement in an oppositional public sphere, and his
commitment to a set of horizontal, contractual relations rather than to the
vertical terms of monarchy—indicate the defining structures of this larger
world. John Winthrop and Anne Hutchinson, too, belong to this world of
transatlantic Puritanism. The proto-liberal public sphere emerging in Massachusetts and England around Puritanism is related, as I have tried to suggest,
to both economic and religious developments, developments embodied in and
shaped by the colonization efforts of the Puritan aristocrats and the transatlantic travelers (many of whom crossed the Atlantic in both directions) who
lived in the colonies and lived to see their accounts of the colony in print in
England.

Hugh Peter was executed for the crime of beheading the king, that is, for
advocating what we might call a "headless" new political order tending in the
direction of liberalism.[69] Moreover, the zealousness of his advocacy in beheading the king was associated by some members of the English public with his
attachment to colonial endeavors. Stearns reports, for instance, that one
English listener protested against the "new Gospell, which teacheth us (as
[Peter] saies) to rebell and resist the King." He complains of "the ministers who
brought [these ideas] over from New-England, the Land of *Canaan*, As Mr.

Peters, whose zealous Doctrine we have stayed so long to heare on a Fast Day" (213). On the face of it, the listeners' report is simply incorrect: it is not the case that Massachusetts divines ever openly advocated regicide.[70] Rather, Massachusetts authorities tended to be wary of attracting any attention from the crown for fear that their valuable charter might be revoked. Yet despite being literally incorrect as to the provenance of regicidal doctrine, this listener is nonetheless correct in associating Puritan colonialism with antimonarchical ideas. Puritan colonialism, as I argue below, *effected* a "headless" political order and thus pointed toward the possibility of a reformed political body that did not have a king standing at its head. Thomas Lechford, a disaffected colonist who returned to England after repeated clashes with the ruling elders in Massachusetts, excoriated the democratic tendencies in both church and civil government in the colony: "I thank God: that Christians cannot live happily without Bishops, as in England, nor Englishmen without a King. Popular elections [as in Massachusetts] indanger people with war and a multitude of other inconveniences."[71] As his account of the colony indicates, Lechford sees a headless order emerging in both the church and state of Massachusetts with the eradication and attenuation of both Presbyterian and monarchical forms of government. As I have indicated, the Puritan colonial endeavor is predicated upon the creation of new, horizontally structured forms of political, economic, and religious power. The specific events surrounding the publication of Winthrop's *Short Story* in 1644, to which I now turn, shed light on the nature of the new "headless" or liberal form of order that is beginning to fitfully materialize from this set of horizontal relations. Moreover, as I will suggest below, gender begins to manifest itself as a key term in articulating the new relations structuring this headless order.

THE 'SHORT STORY' IN CONTEXT, OR, THE HEADLESS BODY AND THE CIRCUIT OF LIBERAL SUBJECTIVITY

Thomas Weld published Winthrop's *Short Story* in 1644 in the midst of pamphlet wars concerning the debates of the Westminster Assembly, the body of prominent divines and parliamentarians convened by Parliament in 1643 to dismantle the policies of the Laudian church and determine the structure of a new, purified Anglican church. Chief among the charges laid to the Westminster Assembly was reforming church government. Those gathered were in full agreement that the hierarchical structure of the prelacy should be eradicated. Indeed, in convening the assembly, Parliament underscored the necessity of destroying the vertical power structure of the existing church: "the present Church-government by Archbishops, Bishops, their Chancellors, Commissaries, Deanes, Deanes and Chapters, Archdeacons, and other Ecclesiastical Officers depending upon the Hierarchy, is evill, and justly offensive and burthensome to the Kingdome, a great impediment to reformation and growth of Religion."[72] Yet while prelatical church hierarchy was clearly the enemy, the antidote to this evil was less clear. In the early years of the assembly, an opposition emerged between those aligned with the Scottish Presbyterians and the so-called "Independents" or Congregationalists. Schematically, one might say that the Presbyterians favored a top-down structure of church governance in contrast to the bottom-up model of the Independents: whereas the Presbyterians sought a framework of synods and officers that would unify a national organization, the Independents favored placing control in the hands of the individual congregations or "gathered" churches.

To demonstrate the viability of a purified church not ruled from above, the Independents turned to the example of New England Puritanism; the Presbyterians, in turn, painted the New England Way as an abject failure of governance. As such, New England Puritanism and particularly the structure of Massachusetts church government served as a focal point of the public sphere debate that erupted over the proceedings of the Westminster Assembly. Weld and Peter published at least three texts about church government in New England explicitly aimed at intervening in the Westminster Assembly debates; indeed, New England divines, as a whole, were active and important contributors to the wealth of publications concerning church governance that appeared in relation to the assembly. On the one hand, then, the Westminster Assembly was a forum in which New England Puritanism might function precisely as Winthrop had imagined, as an exemplary "city on a hill" pointing the way toward church reform in England. On the other hand, the New England Way was subject to the harsh light of inspection by unfriendly observers and found wanting in many respects. Central to the debate over what lesson might be derived from the colony of Massachusetts was the antinomian controversy itself. Simply put, did the events of the antinomian controversy demonstrate the success of New England church governance or its failure? Weld clearly published Winthrop's *Short Story* to demonstrate the colony's ability to overcome heresy and schism, yet Presbyterian critics saw in the same narrative evidence that New England's lack of proper church governance *produced* schism within the church rather than contained it.[73]

Among the tropes circulating in the pamphlet war over the New England Way, bodily figures predominated. Presbyterian authors described the church as a body; properly ordered, the body was governed by the head. More specifically, the organs of the head—eyes, ears, tongue—dominated the lower organs such as arms, hands, and feet. The organic metaphor of the body applied to civil government in early modern England as well: as numerous studies have shown, the English king was described as the head of the body of the state.[74] But just as Peter and other radical Puritans would stand accused of beheading the body of the king and thus of dismembering the body of the state, so too were the radical New England Puritans accused of advocating a "headless" and disfigured body of the church. Robert Baillie, the influential Scottish Presbyterian minister in the Westminster Assembly, argued that New England congregationalism invested too much authority in the laity thereby distorting the natural structure of the church body. "The Lord *is the God of Order*," wrote Baillie, "but the putting of the power of Jurisdiction in the peoples hand, brings confusion into the Church, for it makes the feete above the head, it puts the greatest power into the hand of the meanest, it gives power to the Flocke to depose and excommunicate their Pastour."[75] The New England policy of allowing members of the congregation to elect and depose pastors appeared, to Baillie, to turn the world upside down. According to Baillie, church officers needed to have absolute (rather than provisional) authority over members of the congregation because

> they are the eyes, eares, hands, and principall Members of the Body of Christ; for the eminent persons and Officers of a Church are compared to these Members, because of these actions. But the people are not the eyes, eares, hands; are not the principall Members of the Body of Christ: for if so, there should be none left in the Church to be the feete, or lesse principall Members: all should becomes eyes, and hands, and the Church should be made a Body *Homogenous*, contrary to the doctrine of the Apostle. (184)

Thus Baillie and other Presbyterians such as William Rathband saw the disfigured "body homogenous" as the result of a colonial disease, a disorder bred in Massachusetts and imported to England through the voices and pens of ministers such as Hugh Peter and Thomas Weld. Moreover, the antinomian controversy, in which Hutchinson and her followers shouted down ministers in church and disdained their authority, was the precise result of the placing of feet above the head: the crisis was the inevitable product of colonial congregationalism that located too much authority in the people and distorted the organic body of the church.

The debates over church government at Westminster mirror debates taking place during this period (and in the tumultuous decades to come) concerning civil government and liberalism. Sir Robert Filmer's *Patriarcha*, which defends the patriarchal structure of monarchy and describes the king as the indis-

putable head of the political body, is written (although not published) during
roughly this period. Filmer's text will become axiomatic to Tory politics in
years to come; John Locke's influential liberal theory in *Two Treatises on
Government* is, in turn, an explicit attack on Filmer's ideas. Locke locates the
ground of civil government not in the top-down authority of the king, but in
a bottom-up theory of natural law—specifically, in each individual's interior
access to reason and natural law. In the debate over church government, New
England Puritans thus prefigure many of the terms of Lockean liberalism.[76]
When Thomas Weld lays out his defense of church order and discipline in New
England, then, he is delineating the workings of a nascent liberal system of
authority. In defending the New England Way, Weld states that he will demonstrate that "our Discipline bred [heresies and schism] not, but destroyed them
rather."[77] Yet he is careful to indicate that a *new* species of discipline is being
deployed that is not that of the top-down Presbyterian order. Rather than
argue that ministers and elders do, indeed, exercise punitive authority over
their congregations, Weld advances a strikingly different model of how discipline operates in New England: for Weld, control of the church operates at the
level of individual agency and subjectivity, not at the level of external hierarchy. Much as the Lockean liberal subject will engage in the social contract,
Weld's Puritan subject engages in a religious contract with God and his fellow
congregants and it is ultimately this *contract* that exercises control over each
individual body within the church.

Weld thus explicitly eschews the metaphor of the hierarchically arrayed
body as a description of the church. In its stead, however, he proposes an equally powerful and evocative organizing image—namely, the figure of the hand.
Weld begins his defense of the New England churches with an explanation of
the methods of "gathering" or founding a new congregation in which new
members of the church produce a covenant and "subscribe their *hands* to it."[78]
In this account of convening a new church, he emphasizes that the authority to
do so lies explicitly within the private and *subjective* state of the individuals
gathering to create the church. The church thus originates not as a structure or
grid imposed upon the people of the nation from above (as in the Presbyterian
model), but rather as the result of the volitional and contractual acts engaged
in by each individual member of the church. Weld describes the founding
("gathering") of a new congregation in New England as follows:

> [The new members assemble.] Then one of them (chosen to order the work of the
> day) stands up and speaks to the other of the Brethren. . . . Then himself begins, and
> makes confession of his faith in all the principles of Religion, and then a declaration
> of his effectuall calling to Christ, and how God hath carried on the work of grace
> . . . in his soule to that day. Then all the rest do the like, which done to the satisfac-

tion of the Brethren present, they give testimony of the godly and approved life and conversation of each other. After this, they enter into a sacred and solemn Covenant . . . and then . . . subscribe their hands to it. . . . Then the Brethren of other Churches . . . reaching forth the right hand of fellowship to them, bear witnesse to their proceedings to be according to God, [and] testifie their acceptance of them into brotherly fellowship.[79]

The image of the hand appears repeatedly in this passage and in the surrounding pages of the text: Weld represents the hand as subscribing to the covenant, reaching forth in fellowship, laid upon others in testimony, and raised in plebiscite. As an alternative to the heterogeneous organs of Baillie's church body, the trope of the hand reconfigures the Puritan church in a number of ways. First, it points to the individual agency of each congregant: the hand expresses the private and autonomous will of the subject who engages in contracts, votes in elections, and signs his name to documents. Second, the trope points to the equal status and authority of all of the individuals in the church: the hands of various individuals are not distinguishable from one another in contrast to Baillie's carefully differentiated organs with the church body. Finally, the hands of the individual congregants are understood in terms of an important relation of connection to one another: that is, the acts of covenanting, reaching, and gathering seem to require the conjoining of hands with one another. While the hand points to individual agency, then, it also functions in importantly communal ways within Weld's text. Weld further invokes the trope of the hand in the specific context of church governance when he likens the system of congregational church officers to fingers on a hand:

And here behold . . . the faithfull and tender care of our blessed Lord, that fully provides in those officers for the necessities of all his saints: viz. By Pastors, Teachers, Elders, Deacons, Widowes [Deaconesses], and hath given them their names, works, and titles in his House, which are fully sufficient for the perfecting of the saints, for the work of the Ministry, for the edification of the body of Christ, lesse then which would be too little, more then which would be too much . . . these we have, and more than these, were like six fingers to an hand.[80]

Weld here directly counteracts Baillie's image of the church body in which church officials stand as the organs of the tongue, ear, and eye. Weld suggests, rather, that the five officers of the New England church function as five fingers in a hand, not as the differentiated organs of the head. The hierarchically organized body of the national church (and, by extension, the monarchical state) is thus replaced, in Weld's liberalizing language, with the figure of the hand, thereby proposing a structure of government formed through the covenanting, contractual relations of equal individuals rather than through vertical relations of power.

For Weld, then, church order emerges from the *contracts* engaged in by each individual and in the conjoining of hands in these contracts. This concept of order would seem to accord a high degree of autonomy and authority to each individual who may freely choose whether to enter into any given contract. Yet a reading that emphasizes only the individual choice inherent in the contract would misunderstand the two-sided nature of the covenant Weld describes. While each individual must testify to the work of grace within his soul, that testimony is carefully scrutinized by the other members of the congregation before the contract is offered. Indeed, the church members must "give testimony of the godly and approved life and conversation of each other" at the founding of the church. The private experience of each individual determines his or her authority to engage in the contract *but* this private experience must be made publicly visible. Moreover, the other members of the church have a hand (a testimonial hand) in judging the truth and value of the evidence of private experience presented to the public. The liberal structure of order and discipline proposed here is thus one that circulates through public sphere representations; liberal discipline operates by requiring the production of privacy in publicly comprehensible and acceptable forms. Liberal discipline operates, then, at the level of the very *production* of subjectivity rather than at the level of punishing, organizing, or controlling existing subjects. Each individual must produce a description of his or her interior state that the community, in turn, is asked to ratify. In order to participate in the church contract (and by extension—because only church members could vote or hold office—in the social contract of the colony), individuals were required to craft an account of their inner state—to produce themselves as subjects—conforming to public norms and the expectations of the gathered church.

Thomas Lechford thus complains of the stringency of "this new discipline" that has deprived him of standing within both the church and the state because of his refusal to conform to public norms: "I am kept from the Sacrament, and all place of preferment in the Common-wealth, and forced to get my living by writing petty things" (144). Indeed, as Lechford and other critics such as Baillie and Rathband make clear, the new discipline is at once too lax and too harsh. On the one hand, they argue that the members of New England congregations have too much power over the ministers; on the other hand, they argue that the churches are far too strict in excluding and banishing members from the congregation over minutiae of behavior or doctrine. Lechford concludes (perhaps wishfully) that the "new discipline" of the Bay colony is "impossible to be executed, or long continued" (144). Yet as his own experience demonstrates, it is precisely within the "anarchicall" structure of liberal authority (governed from the bottom up) that new and exacting forms of discipline are embedded. In short, liberal discipline is embedded at the level of the circular production of subjectivity rather than at the level of administrative control.

In publishing Winthrop's *Short Story*, Weld offers the gathered divines at the Westminster Assembly less a theory of congregational government than a case history of how discipline functioned in the colony. For my purposes, then, Weld's version of the *Short Story* is also a case history of proto-liberal forms of social order in the making or, more precisely, of what I described in the first chapter as the looping or circular constitution of the liberal subject. While Winthrop's own version of the *Short Story* consisted in the main of a collection of documents (the list of errors determined by the synod, the report on the civil trial, etc.), Weld superadds a lengthy preface in his own name to Winthrop's document that effectively summarizes the events of the antinomian crisis in Massachusetts. His preface, Weld tells us, is needed for the purpose of "laying down the order and the sense of this story"—an order and sense "omitted" in the original collection of documents that comprise the story. Weld's summary, then, might be seen as an attempt to pencil in the causal relations or connective tissue linking the diverse documents Winthrop compiled in this text. He thus intentionally imposes a stronger account of just how and why heresy bloomed and was eradicated in New England.

What, then, is the precise method of the New Englanders' triumph over the antinomians? What is the root cause of their success? We might begin to answer this question by noting first what Weld does *not* say: at no point does he describe any punitive action taken by the ministers against the antinomians. Indeed, he is careful to emphasize that no members of the antinomian faction were ever punished for their "opinions" but rather were counseled to reform their ideas and finally subject chiefly to civil law for traducing the peace of the commonwealth. In Weld's narrative, the primary cause of the eventual downfall of the antinomian party is not intervention by church officers but rather intervention by God, who makes manifest the error of Hutchinson to her followers by causing both her and another follower, Mary Dyer, to miscarry pregnancies. The account of these miscarriages, or "monstrous births," as Weld calls them, is not missing from Winthrop's narrative but receives key etiological status in Weld's narrative reworking of the crisis. Moreover, the miscarriages serve as the turning point in the downfall of Hutchinson and her followers primarily because the deformed births *make public* the deformed religious opinions of Hutchinson. Weld recounts the births as follows:

> Then God himself was pleased to step in with his casting voice, and bring in his owne vote and suffrage from heaven, by testifying his displeasure against their opin-

ions and practises, as clearly as if he had pointed with his finger, in causing the two fomenting women in the time of the height of the Opinions to produce out of their wombs, as before they had out of their braines, such monstrous births as no Chronicle . . . hardly ever recorded the like. . . .This loud-speaking providence from Heaven in the monsters, did much awaken many of their followers (especially the tenderer sort) to attend Gods meaning therein; and made them at such a stand, that they dared not sleight so manifest a signe from Heaven, that from that time we found many of their eares boared . . . to attend to counsell.[81]

The hand of God does not strike Hutchinson or her follower Mary Dyer in a punitive fashion: rather, God *casts a vote* against Hutchinson's theological doctrines. God is thus figured as a hand that points and votes much as the hands of men in the church congregation. Yet God has superior interpretive abilities; he knows that Hutchinson's private, interior authority is corrupt and is able to make this corruption visible to other congregants. In effect, the miscarriages here function as publicity or evidence of heresy rather than as punishment for heresy. God's finger functions, then, much as the drawings of disembodied hands often printed in the margin of seventeenth-century texts pointing to a particular passage to emphasize its importance to the reader: God's pointing finger underscores the importance of a sign that others then have an obligation to read and understand. In response to this private truth made public, other individuals are now able to reform themselves away from Hutchinson's heretical beliefs—"to attend to counsell" for the first time. Weld thus delineates what we might call the circular structure of liberal discipline: an empowered or authorized private subjectivity (that of Anne Hutchinson) leads to publicity (in this case, negative publicity), which in turn leads to reformed subjectivity (among Hutchinson's followers) or subjectivity produced in conformity with the norms of public sphere discourse.

This circular structure is equally manifest in a second example that bears directly upon the church's role in disciplining Hutchinson. When Weld turns to an account of Hutchinson's church trial (which follows the civil trial), he again does not emphasize, contrary to what one might expect in a text on church governance, the role of the ministers in punishing or excommunicating Hutchinson and thereby restoring order to the church. Rather, Weld reports that Hutchinson's testimony at the church trial exposes her as a liar to her followers, and this public exposure causes them to attempt to reform *themselves*: "When [her followers] heard her defending her twenty nine cursed opinions in Boston Church, and there falling into fearfull lying, with an impudent forehead in the open Assembly, then they beleeved what before they could not, and were ashamed before God and men. . . . Now no man could lay more upon them, *then they would upon themselves*, in their acknowledgment."[82] Publicity (here, Hutchinson's lying in court) has a disciplinary function on antinomians, who must reform themselves in light of what has been revealed about the nature of the private ideas they had cultivated. There are, indeed, very real punitive consequences for their failure to reform themselves; they may be banished from the colony or excommunicated from the church if they continue to support Hutchinson. Yet Weld's account emphasizes that the structure of discipline in the church is organized at the level of the contracting individual; thus it is neither the court nor the ministers who are credited with reforming the church through punishing or threatening the antinomians, but the antinomians who are credited with reforming themselves in light of publicity (including publicity from God) concerning Hutchinson.

THE GENDERED BODY IN PRINT

If we consider the power accorded to Hutchinson and Dyer's miscarriages in Weld's text, it becomes clear that bodily parts other than the hand carry rhetorical and imaginative weight within his narrative. While Weld relies upon the metaphor of the hand to characterize the workings of the church, he also invokes a powerful bodily image in his description of the deformed fetuses miscarried by Dyer and Hutchinson. Indeed, the power of these images, both in Weld's preface and in Winthrop's narrative, lies in the graphic and detailed nature of the description of the fetuses:

> Mistris Dier brought forth her birth of a woman child, a fish, a beast, and a fowle, all woven together in one, and without an head. . . . Mistris Hutchison, being big with child, and growing towards the time of her labour, as other women doe, she brought forth not one, (as Mistris Dier did) but (which was more strange to amazement) 30. monstrous births or thereabouts, at once; some of them bigger, some lesser, some of one shape, some of another. . . . And see how the wisdom of God fitted this judgement to her sinne every way, for looke as she had vented mishapen opinions, so she must bring forth deformed monsters; and as about 30. Opinions in number, so many monsters.[83]

Weld makes clear the evidentiary status of these births: they stand as external proof of the internal monstrosity of Hutchinson's beliefs. Yet another figurative topography might be associated with the deformed bodies he describes: namely, that of the headless (liberal) body. Weld (like others) emphasizes that Dyer's fetus has no head—an image that brings to mind the description by critics of the colony of the monstrous, headless New England church and body of state.[84] And while no specific mention of a head appears in the account of Hutchinson's fetus, we might infer that the monstrosity of this birth lies not in the lack of a head but in its many-headed form: thirty monsters might be presumed to have thirty monstrous heads. Indeed, Hutchinson is later described by both Edward Johnson and Cotton Mather as a "hydra," a monster with many heads.[85] As Marcus Rediker and Peter Linebaugh have shown, the image of the hydra circulated widely in the seventeenth-century transatlantic world as a figure of anxiety about popular uprising. Associated with radical political movements, piracy, and witchcraft, the many-headed hydra effectively symbolized the placing of the feet (the people of nation) above the head (the ruler): rather than being ruled by one head, the social body was distorted by the rule of the people into the monstrous shape of a hydra. As such, the images of the hydra and the headless monster point to similar anxieties about social disorder. Indeed, the interchangeability of the two images with respect to Hutchinson and Dyer is evident in the cover image of a pamphlet that circulated in England concerning Dyer's miscarriage: the pamphlet reports the monstrous birth of Dyer's headless fetus in detail, yet the cover image shows a body with two heads rather than none.[86] In sum, both the body of state with no head and the body with too many heads are images that distort the hierarchical body—in which proper order, figured as organic subordination (feet below a single head), has not been achieved.

Weld's detailed description of both fetuses thus would seem to point to an anxiety about the distortion of the hierarchical body in the colonies. Yet given Weld's rejection of the figure of the hierarchical body as a model of order, it seems odd that he would evoke it (even by way of antithesis) at this crucial point in his narrative. However, we might note that Weld uses the image in a somewhat covert and significantly displaced fashion. That is, he deposes the image of the headless hierarchical body from its central position in the Presbyterian schema by associating it with the specific and individuated bodies of two heretical women and not with the body of the church as a whole. In Weld's text, the deformed, headless (or many-headed) body is no longer a figure of the church body or the body politic as a whole, but is the figure of the specific interior state of Anne Hutchinson or Mary Dyer. The opinions of these women, in all their hideousness, are made legible in these miscarriages; the miscarriages thus serve not as evidence of the deformity of the church but as evidence of corrupt female interiority. The association between the woman's womb and the production of this evidence points to a concern with interiority. The specter of social disorder is thus attached to specific female bodies. In broad terms, then, I would suggest that in the place of the corporate body, liberalism offers individuated bodies capable of self-reform and self-governance; the monstrosity of collective deformation and misgovernance, in turn, is replaced with the specificity of individuated female bodies.

Weld's use of fetal imagery seems, then, to be a strategy of displacement: the disorder attributed to Puritan forms of government is blamed, instead, on women's bodies. And indeed, many critics have argued that Hutchinson is condemned primarily because she is a woman. As David Hall, among others, notes, many of the theological opinions held by Hutchinson were close (if not identical) to those held by John Cotton, yet Hutchinson nevertheless serves as the focal point of Winthrop's account of the crisis. Moreover, it is a commonplace of criticism of the antinomian crisis to read the particular focus of Winthrop (and Weld) on the figure of Anne Hutchinson as an attempt to associate her guilt with her gender.[87] Why is this an effective move on Winthrop's part? According to Phillip Round, Winthrop's association of social disorder with women's bodies is meant to appeal to existing preconceptions about women in Old England:

> New Englanders would argue that the outbreak of antinomianism was not the fault of their theology, their "Church discipline," or even their towns but purely and simply the fault of women, those weak links in the civic discursive structures that New England men had erected against the pressures of new contractual social hierarchies, market-based economics, and geographic and cultural distance from the mother country. It was an argument to which almost every Englishman could subscribe, for despite the many violent disagreements between reformers and traditionalists that scarred early modern English society, both groups fundamentally agreed that female disorder was something that had to be controlled if either reform or tradition were again to take hold of England. (148)

Round thus sees the scapegoating of women as part of an appeal to a transatlantic audience, an appeal made not by way of arguing for the terms of a new order, but by invoking the shared terms of the old. In other words, Round's argument concurs with mine concerning the importance of contractual relations in restructuring colonial Puritan society, yet it diverges insofar as he argues that recourse to misogyny effectively papers over the emergent contractual forms of social and political power in an effort to make common cause with English critics in the seemingly universal desire to oppress women. Somewhat similarly, Jim Egan argues that the oppression of women—the placement of men in status relations above women—is meant to demonstrate the orderly nature of New England society to an English audience. According to Egan, Winthrop constructs a new model of the body politic that nonetheless "retains the pre-Elizabethan insistence on the masculinity of the monarch's body and the monstrosity of female rule. Whether in charge of the household or church, the female body represented an inversion of the metaphysical order—an unruly household, political order, and soul."[88] Both Egan and Round, then, see the virulent attack on women as an association of New

England order with older preexisting forms of gendered hierarchy, as an attempt to placate and find common ground with those in England who view order as indissociable from the hierarchical body.

On my reading, however, Weld and Winthrop's focus on the female body is not simply a return to the hierarchy of the past, but is rather symptomatic of a new form of liberal authority in which gender matters in a very different fashion. Indeed, while arguing that a gendered hierarchy is part of an older social order, Egan also points to the way in which a new emphasis on gender in the colonies restructures existing notions of the social body. Specifically, Egan argues that gender replaces class as the paramount principle organizing the hierarchy of the colonial social body: "Winthrop's rhetoric suggests that the elevation of the common body to the status of a figure for the nation itself must be accompanied by a rather rigid internal division and hierarchy of that body along gender lines: for Winthrop, only the subordination of female to male members can ensure that this body politic does not revert to the older figure of the popular body as unruly or carnivalesque" (69). Egan thus argues that gender and particularly a biological understanding of the gendered body assumes new importance in the colonies. While I ultimately agree with Egan's conclusion concerning the new significance of the biology of gender, I would locate the cause of this change elsewhere than in the desire to reinstate hierarchy in the social body. Rather, I would argue that the colonists are engaged in displacing the corporate body and imagining contractual relations as structuring social cohesion instead. In effect, Egan's reading suggests that Hutchinson is the figure of the liberal individualist who stands opposed to a ruling party in favor of corporate hierarchy. As I have suggested throughout this chapter, I view both Hutchinson *and* the ruling elders as engaged in working through the terms of a new, proto-liberal order. Thus Weld and Winthrop, as I have sought to demonstrate, are searching for a vocabulary to explicate alternative models and metaphors of social cohesion than that of the hierarchical body.

Weld, as we have seen, develops the metaphor of the hand as a central figure for governing structures oriented around the contract. Despite some evidence to the contrary, I would argue that Winthrop, too, is engaged in shifting away from the metaphor of the hierarchical corporate body. In his famous speech delivered aboard the *Arbella*, "A Modell of Christian Charity," Winthrop dwells at length upon the metaphor of the colony knit together in the corporate body of Christ. He opens his speech by insisting upon the justness of a world in which some are rich and others are poor. Both the image of the colony knit together in Christ, and the image of economic hierarchy invoked in the speech, would seem to contravene my thesis. Yet a closer reading indicates that

Winthrop emphasizes the distinction between rich and poor so that he can urge the rich to share their wealth with a community in need. More importantly, the language used to describe the corporate body of the community is never that of vertical ordinance. The body parts to which Winthrop makes repeated reference are "joints" and "ligaments"; he never speaks of the head or the feet of the corporate body. Winthrop concludes, "All true Christians are of one body in Christ. . . . The ligamentes of this body which knitt together are love. . . . Noe body can be perfect which wants its propper ligamentes. . . . All the partes of this body being thus united are made soe contiguous in a speciall relacion as they must needes partake of each others strength and infirmity, joy, and sorrowe, weale and woe."[89] While Winthrop emphasizes the corporate nature of the community as they travel across the Atlantic to New England, he does so in order to insist upon their interdependence and relative equality rather than to invoke the metaphor of a body politic ruled by a religious or civil "head." Corporate imagery is certainly not lacking in Puritan colonial documents; indeed, given the currency of this imagery in both political and theological doctrine of the seventeenth century, it would be surprising not to find it in circulation in the colonies. Nonetheless, it does seem possible to trace a decided shift in this language away from its traditional use to justify top-down structures of government. The language of contract deploys, instead, images of hands and joints, and particularly the language of self-reform. In conjunction with a shift toward contractual language of the self and social relations, the body of the Puritan subject assumes a less corporate and a more enclosed, autonomous, and individuated status than before.

It is thus Anne Hutchinson's particular body that is infected by antinomianism, as well as the bodies of her followers, but not the corporate body as a whole. It is plausible to argue the opposite. Egan contends, for instance, that Winthrop invokes a corporate and hierarchical body in his description of the antinomian crisis:

> In England, the King's body stood at once for the secular government and for the Church of England, as if there were no difference between them. Winthrop invokes this figure of national leadership and puts the Church in the place of the King in making the claim that "the whole Church of Boston" was "infected with [Anne Hutchinson's] opinions." . . . Thus Winthrop sets the magistrates and Elders in the place of the monarch as the protectors of the body politic. (70)

If we examine the passage Egan quotes, however, we see that Winthrop says the "the whole Church of Boston (some few excepted)" becomes infected with Hutchinson's opinions. The parentheses here indicate that Winthrop does not refer to a corporate body that is infected, but to individual members of the church, of whom many are infected, but a number of whom are not. Moreover, when Winthrop concludes his brief discussion of this infection, he does not refer to either ridding the corporate body of infection or eradicating part of the infected body, but rather invokes the same figure of the hand used by Weld: "But blessed bee the Lord, the snare is broken, and wee are delivered, and this woman who was the root of all these troubles, stands now before the seat of Justice, to bee rooted out of her station, by the hand of authority, guided by the finger of divine providence, as the sequell will show."[90] God's finger, again hovering in the margin next to man's hand, points the way toward colonial discipline and reformation. In general, Egan argues that the colonial social body comes to be figured as a common body rather than the king's body: thus the thrust of his argument is that a shift in the identity of the social body occurs, substituting magistrates for kings and, in particular, locating authority in masculinity rather than in class distinction. I am sympathetic to Egan's claims, in part because the discourse of the body does not simply resolve itself wholly in one direction or another at a historical moment when it is in the process of revision, yet I would argue that an important shift toward a social iconography of the *individuated* body occurs at this moment, and this shift helps us to understand the new significance of the female body in accounts of the antinomian crisis.

In tracing the liberal lineaments of Puritan colonial society, I have been pointing to new structures of authority that are instituted in a variety of overlapping fields—religious, economic, and political. In the first section of this chapter, I argued that Anne Hutchinson relied upon her private relation with God to authorize her role in creating an oppositional public sphere. Further, I argued that a new form of authorized privacy was central to Puritan theology and that the definition of privacy as an essential ground of religious and political authority had the effect of potentially promoting women into public roles that had previously been closed to them. Indeed, women's historic association with domestic space and privacy served to strengthen their claims to self-authorization through privacy; we have seen, for instance, that women were able to become important figures in conventicles in England and New England precisely because of the domestic and private origins and settings of these new publics. Yet if the new importance of privacy within liberalism oddly catapults women into positions of public authority (as was the case with Hutchinson), then the possibility of controlling this threat to existing authority lies in the liberal vein as well, that is, it lies in controlling the production of subjectivity through public sphere representation. As I argued above, Winthrop is fundamentally not able to oppose the liberal premises of Hutchinson's authority: he cannot deprive her of the right to her "conscience" or to her relation to God because of the centrality of these doctrines to Puritanism. While he does banish her from the colony on civil grounds, perhaps more importantly, he engages in extended transatlantic publicity in relation to Hutchinson's threat to his authority. Embedded himself in the world of contractual, transatlantic relations, Winthrop cannot fully control representations of the colony in the emerging public sphere, but he can contribute to them. Hence if women's private status promotes them, within liberalism, then public representations of corrupt female bodies serve, in response, to simultaneously demote them. If power no longer radiates from above, within liberalism, but from below, then discipline will also occur from below: in other words, the unfitness of women for authority will ultimately radiate from their biologically specific bodies rather than from a divine hierarchy made manifest in the corporate social body. I am suggesting, then, that it is precisely because liberalism grants women new sources of authority, a new centrality to political and religious authority, that public sphere representations actively work to define women as incapable of sustaining that authority. Weld and Winthrop indicate that Hutchinson has that within which de-authorizes her; Hutchinson is deformed, they suggest, but not the whole of Puritan society.

If we return to the specifics of the antinomian crisis, we can see, as I have argued, that Winthrop and Weld respond to the threat of Hutchinson's newfound authority by circulating new representations of the female body in print. In particular, both Winthrop and Weld aggressively seek to expose Hutchinson and Dyer's miscarried fetuses to public view with a determination that Weld, at least, recognizes as somewhat untoward. The corpse of the Dyer fetus was literally exhumed through the offices of Winthrop after he overheard reports of the birth among Hutchinson's followers. Unearthed five months after its burial, the fetal corpse was badly decomposed when it saw it the light of day, yet Winthrop took it upon himself to display the corpse and to examine it at length in order to produce numerous detailed written accounts of its deformation. According to the *Short Story*, more than one hundred people viewed the body after Winthrop had it exhumed. Winthrop eventually produced at least four written accounts of Dyer's fetal corpse, and more than eight reports based on Winthrop's are extant in print. Thus while Winthrop was clearly intent upon displaying the prodigal nature of this "monstrous birth," we might note, as well, the prodigious number of written accounts of the birth that circulated across the Atlantic.[91] In Weld's account of the Dyer miscarriage, he inserts something of an apology for the lurid nature of his description of the fetus: "These things are so strange, that I am almost loath to be the reporter of

them, lest I should seeme to feigne a new story, and not to relate an old one.
... [But] these things are so well knowne in New England, that they have beene
made use of in publike, by the reverend Teacher of Boston, and testified by so
many letters to friends here, that the things are past question" (214). Weld thus
indicates some reluctance in relying upon such implicitly private and
grotesque material to advance his narrative: his defense, however, is that the
event has *already* been "made use of in publike." Weld thus claims not to be
revealing anything that has not already entered the public domain. Yet I would
suggest that it is precisely the private nature of the birth—its association with
the interior of women's bodies, and with the domestic space of female reproduction—that generates its efficacy for public narrative at this point. As we
have seen, the incident generates meaning because of the manner in which it
exposes the private truth of antinomian doctrine in public, the manner in
which it links private and public truths.

The representations of the fetal corpses were clearly not received in England
in wholly the spirit in which Winthrop penned them. While some circulated
accounts of the monstrous births as scientific curiosities without religious
meaning, others overtly criticized Winthrop's attempts to derive religious
meaning from the births. In a text written in direct response to the *Short Story*,
John Wheelwright (the antinomian leader who left for England after having
been banished by Winthrop) contends that the linking of the interior states of
private bodies to public debate is itself objectionable behavior. Wheelwright
argues, first, that Winthrop has little business examining a deformed fetus in
the first place: "I question not his learning &c. but I admire his certainty, or
rather impudence; did the man obstetricate?"[92] He thus suggests that any
knowledge of the meaning of the deformed fetus would require a medical
understanding of the corpse and the birth rather than a religious understanding of heretical opinions. His further critique of the passage concerning the
Hutchinson and Dyer miscarriages indicates his suspicion of the public reading Weld and Winthrop derive from the private materials they bring to light:

> As for his *Analogy* [between Hutchinson's heresies and her monstrous births] ... It
> is a monstrous conception of his brain, a spurious issue of his intellect, acted upon
> by a sweatish and Feaverish zeal, which indeed beats almost in every line; and
> resolves his in themselves imperfect sometimes, if not feigned facts into phanatique
> meditations. For first, the proportion is not exact, for he reckons not 30. opinions
> which he calls Mrs. *Hutchinsons,* and those many of them coincident too, made more
> I suppose to prepare for his conceit. Secondly, but admit it were, yet his Notion is
> impertinent, for he brings defects of Nature, amongst defects of Manners. All he can
> say (if he were so acute) is, that those are these *reductive* and as they are effects of sin.
> A poore plea, by the same reason he may under the same title discover all the weak-

nesses and naturall imperfections either of man or woman, and fix a kind of morality upon them: But he will say perhaps, that this birth was an extraordinary defect: It avails nothing, unless he will either raise it to a miracle, or at the least prove a supernaturall remission of the *formative virtue in her*. That will require a most accurate physicall inspection which I think his learning will not reach, although (for ought I can see) his modesty might: for he tels us of women *purging and vomiting*, what if the distemper we usually call *Cholera* did for the present oppresse those women? must it needs be proclaimed? must it needs be in print? (196–97)

Wheelwright presents a number of interesting claims in this passage: first, he objects to Winthrop's attempt to link the "natural" defect of a miscarriage with the defect in "manners" or theological opinions and behavior of Hutchinson. Wheelwright thus objects to the publishing analogy we observed earlier in which the deformed fetuses are taken as evidence of Hutchinson's interior state. Wheelwright argues that the epistemological value of the fetuses here ascribed to them could only be located in a miracle, that is, God might have punished Hutchinson by causing her to miscarry, but this miracle would need further proof. In other words, Wheelwright indicates that a miracle would be "above nature," precisely the claim employed against Hutchinson in her trial with regard to her direct revelations. Perhaps more importantly, he objects to the work of Weld and Winthrop in publishing their account of the miscarried births in the first place. In particular he protests the publication of Winthrop's reports that at the birth itself, the women who attended Dyer's labor were overtaken by illness and began vomiting. Wheelwright again insists that this illness may have its cause elsewhere than in heresy, thereby attempting to sever the interpretive link between public and private that is crucial to Weld's presentation of the incidents.

Wheelwright thus argues that publishing accounts of women's bodily infirmities is a violation of both modesty and sense. His final question: "must needs it be in print?" is, then, a crucial one. Given their diligence in publishing these materials, Winthrop and Weld would seem to answer this question with a clear affirmative: the account of these women's illnesses *needs* to be in print. Why is this the case? Most obviously, publicizing the bodily disabilities of antinomian women serves to counter the public authority Hutchinson has accrued through her association with privacy and the cultivation of interiority. The authority born in the private, enclosed world of women—both the birthing room and the literal, interior space of a woman's womb—is shown to be the source of deformed public opinions rather than authorized ones. Weld and Winthrop are thus pursuing a liberal line of discipline: because new forms of authority originate in private bodies, new forms of public control will rely upon publicly producing authoritative accounts of privacy and thereby disciplining private subjects in new, essentialist terms. Because the interior space of antinomian women is corrupt, so too is their public doctrine rendered dangerous rather than compelling in its intimacy with God. As Weld reports, the ministers do not punish congregants for their erroneous opinions, rather, they labor to convince them of their errors by demonstrating publicly the truth of the ruling elders' views. Discipline thus takes the shape of publicity rather than bodily punishment; in the narrative of Hutchinson's deformed fetus we see publicity used as a form of bodily disqualification—a form of discipline that structures access to power without exercising punitive force upon bodies.

In disqualifying the vomiting, purging, and parturient female body from claiming public authority, Weld and Winthrop also participate, I would argue, in defining the new boundaries and essential boundedness of the liberal body. According to Jonathan Gil Harris, the mid-seventeenth century saw a decisive shift in English medical understandings of the body that derived from and influenced political understanding of the body politic. Whereas early, Galenic models of the body focused on humoral accounts of illness, in which disease was a function of the imbalance of elements within the body, seventeenth-century models began to describe disease as the effect of an invasion of foreign elements into the body: "For the metaphor of the body politic, therefore, the decisive paradigm shift was . . . from a humoral to an ontological mode of disease" illustrated in a new, "overwhelming tendency to regard disease as having its origins in alien invaders."[93] Harris suggestively links this shift from endogenous pathology (in the humoral body) to exogenous pathology (in the bounded, ontologized body) to the change in the body politic occasioned by colonial growth and empire: "the persistence of exogenous discourses of social pathology is inextricably linked to the growth of global capitalism" (143). While Harris does not spell out the link between global capitalism and the exogenous model of disease in the social body, the work of other historians on the colonial body is suggestive in this respect. As a number of scholars have demonstrated, early colonials were tremendously concerned that their bodies would either not survive, or would change form drastically in the New World because humoral theories of illness were held in common with climatic theories of bodily identity: the permeable humoral body was subject at every moment to the influences of the environment around it. As Gail Kern Paster writes, "Besides being open and fungible in its internal workings, the humoral body was also porous and thus able to be influenced by the immediate environment."[94] In the colonial environment, then, the humoral body might be irremedially disfigured by a change in climate and environment. Yet as Joyce

Chaplin demonstrates, the colonial experience ultimately caused dramatic change not in the English body, but in theories of the body. Settlers and promoters of colonization soon began to argue that English bodies seemed not only to survive in America, but to thrive and, above all, to remain English. Chaplin demonstrates that English colonials began to "refute assertions that an alien place would change settlers, stressing that migration and change were part of the human condition . . . [and that] corporeal types were not always prey to environmental change."[95] Colonials thus began to argue that the English body was less porous and more bounded than earlier models had proposed: the bounded English body both repelled foreign influence and retained its essence within, regardless of its geographical location. Moreover, in distinguishing English from Native American bodies, settlers began to argue for a racial essentialism that defined English bodies as less porous—less subject to outside pathogens—than Native American bodies: "Explanations eventually posited that the native peoples were less resistant than the English to disease and that their susceptibility was natural to their bodies; further, by the late seventeenth century, the English emphasized that their own physical type thrived and persisted in its original form, despite exposure to an American milieu for more than a generation."[96] The colonial experience thus effected a shift in discourse such that an essential Englishness became located within a bounded body; the body, in turn, was no longer conceived as a porous container that took on the attributes of its environmental context, but as an entity that repelled foreign invasions and carried its identity within.

While the humoral body was open to influence, allied with the environment and other individuals around it, this same porosity is understood as a threat to the bounded, liberal body. As Jonathan Harris points out, porousness becomes a form of liability to the new social body: "the growing understanding of disease as an ontological seed rather than a state of imbalance was doubtless responsible for a phobic intensification of the humoral body's openness to the outside . . . the body's porousness was being increasingly reconfigured as a disconcerting vulnerability to illicit invasion by venomous pathogens" (25–26). The new body, shaped decisively by colonial experience, thus is one in which porousness represents a lack of ability to retain private identity, coherence, and authority. As Gail Kern Paster points out, theories of the humoral body had typically seen all bodies as porous, but women's bodies as particularly porous or subject to leakiness. In the new colonial setting, the liberal, contractual body could not be porous: leakiness was a particular liability. Thus I would argue that in insisting upon the particular porousness of female antinomian bodies,

Weld and Winthrop recirculate the older trope of the leaky female body, but within a new set of horizons that ascribe to the porous female body a far more invidious status.

While Chaplin's work points to the racial essentialism inherent in the shift toward the iconography of the bounded body, we might note that a gendered essentialism begins to develop at the same time. The humoral body certainly persists in political and medical language, as does the corporate body. Yet the focus on the female body as essentially different in its physical and interior state can be linked to a reformulation of the body politic in liberal terms. It is worth noting, for instance, that Wheelwright defends Hutchinson against Winthrop's aspersions by offering a humoral rather than essentialist account of her body. Though he associates some "erroneous tenents" with her pregnancy, he argues that the pregnancy simply makes her more prey to "the quality of humors" than she might be otherwise. Indeed, her male followers were also subject to melancholy because of the New England environment (due to its lack of promise), and similarly "through melancholy fumes dispose[d] to strange fancies in Divinity."[97] Pregnancy or the grimness of New England might thus equally affect male and female humoral bodies, according to Wheelwright. Winthrop, on the other hand, insists repeatedly upon the language of interiority: he attempts to "lay open" Hutchinson at the trial, and her internal errors, in the end, seem intimately related to the particularity of her female body. The development of authority emanating from below rather than above attributes specific meaning to specific bodies; it gives them meaning from within rather than from an external hierarchy as well. While the world of the liberal subject would seem to propose a greater liberality for each individual, it is also precisely at this point that subjectivity begins to be produced at the level of the body in such a way as to qualify some bodies and not others for privileged forms of public participation.

"SUBJECT TO HIM, YET IN A WAYE OF LIBERTYE": THE CONVERSION NARRATIVE AND THE MARRIAGE CONTRACT

I have argued that Winthrop's *Short Story* is a transatlantic document that attempts to publicly expose Anne Hutchinson, in particular, as harboring a corrupt interiority as well as to associate the female body, more generally, with a condition of porousness that disqualifies women from claiming public authority. Yet the disciplinary circuit operating through the public sphere works in the opposite direction as well: that is, it produces what we might call "qualifying" as well as disqualifying narratives of subjectivity. In this section, I turn to a second form of public representation that emerged from the antinomian controversy, and that demonstrates, in a different vein than the transatlantic colonial report, the circular construction of liberal subjectivity. The formal religious innovation for which the Massachusetts Puritans are perhaps the most renowned is not simply the New England Way, but more specifically, the conversion narrative required of each individual who wished to join the church. Quite literally a "qualifying" narrative, the conversion narrative became an admissions test for church membership. Individuals who produced a convincing narrative of their personal experience of God's grace were allowed to enter into the covenant; those who failed to do so were not. The procedure of this admissions test was both elaborate and public: individuals who sought church admission met first with a minister for a personal interview. The minister then inquired of the congregation as to whether any knew of offenses committed by the candidate. Barring any failure in these initial stages, the candidate was then called upon to "demonstrate the work of God in his soul"[98] by relating a narrative of his or her inner experience of God. The public performance of this narrative before the congregation was followed by an interrogation during which church members probed the details of the narrative to be assured of its evidentiary status. Subsequent to this performance, the congregation as a whole voted on whether to admit the candidate; if he or she received a majority vote, the candidate was offered the church covenant.

According to Edmund Morgan, the New England Puritans were unique in requiring a personal narrative for church admission. While other Puritan churches, including the Separatists in Holland, had demanded a profession of faith and testimony of good character for new church members, the singular aspect of the New England admissions test was its focus on the personal, interior experience of the individual seeking to join the church. Doctrinally, such a narrative requirement made a certain amount of sense given that church membership was intended for the justified alone, that is, for the so-called visible saints in the community. Because sainthood was determined on the basis of an individual's relation to God (the experience of grace) and not on the basis of works, it seems understandable that an account of inner experience would assist in identifying the elect. In this light, Morgan describes the conversion narrative requirement as an attempt to insist as much as possible upon the alignment of the visible (worldly) church and invisible (divine) one: "While affirming the old distinction between the visible and the invisible church, [New England Puritans] thus narrowed the distance between the two far more drastically than the Separatists had done" (93). Yet as much as the conversion narrative admissions test can be (and was) seen as an epistemological tool to probe the interior state of potential church members, it can also, conversely, be seen as a formula for the production of subjectivity. In other words, rather than a tool of disclosure, one could argue that the narrative requirement operated as a tool of *composure* as individuals sought to produce accounts of their interior lives that conformed to the formal expectations of the adjudicating congregation. In distinguishing between disclosure and composure, I do not mean to argue that some individuals revealed or disclosed the truth while others fabricated false versions of it: rather, I mean to suggest that the formal lineaments of the conversion narrative served as a template for the construction of publicly authorized forms of subjectivity even for those most concerned to offer the truth of their souls to public view.

Morgan's account of the conversion narrative emphasizes precisely the formulaic shape the personal narrative quickly assumed following its institutionalization: in Morgan's evocative phrase, the "morphology of conversion" is readily identifiable from extant accounts of conversion narratives. "The pattern is so plain as to give the experiences the appearance of a stereotype," writes Morgan:

> First comes a feeble and false awakening to God's commands and a pride in keeping them pretty well, but also much backsliding. Disappointments and disasters lead to other fitful hearkenings to the word. Sooner or later true legal fear or conviction enables the individual to see his hopeless and helpless condition and to know that his own righteousness cannot save him, that Christ is his only hope. Thereafter comes the infusion of saving grace, sometimes but not always so precisely felt that the believer can state exactly when and where it came to him. A struggle between faith and doubt ensues, with the candidate careful to indicate that his assurance has never been complete and that his sanctification has been much hampered by his own sinful heart. (91)

Individuals who produced narratives that did not conform to this formal pattern were not offered church membership and thus were implicitly asked to reformulate their narratives so as to conform to the accepted morphology. Susanna Bell, for instance, attempted to join the Roxbury church in 1636 but failed at the interrogation stage. After additional preparation—listening to sermons, reading accounts of conversion—she reapplied several weeks later and was able to reformulate her experiences in such a way as to pass the admissions test.[99] The founding of the second Dorchester church in 1636 was similarly deferred when objections concerning the personal narratives of the founders (including that of Richard Mather) were raised. Morgan ascribes their failure to a lack of knowledge of the narrative form: he reports that "the proposed founders of the Dorchester church were insufficiently familiar with the morphology of conversion" (101) and thus were initially prevented from founding a new church. William Hubbard's history of the colony, written in the 1680s, indicates, moreover, that once the would-be founders learned what was expected of them, they were able to produce proper narratives. The attempt to found the church failed, Hubbard relates, "through unacquaintedness with the nature of the thing desired," yet eventually, "being better informed about the nature of that which was expected from them," the church founders succeeded in producing acceptable narratives and "were gathered into a church state, with the approbation of the messengers of the churches, then assembled for that end."[100] Historian Charles Cohen emphasizes that few were denied admission on the basis of faulty narratives, yet he also indicates that full knowledge of the formal structure of the narrative facilitated admission: "A well-prepared candidate who met a congregation's standard breezed through admission as if following a script."[101] To produce a successful narrative thus seemed to require knowledge of the *form* of the narrative—of the conversion script—as much as if not more than the experience of saving grace.

As a qualifying narrative, then, the Puritan conversion narrative is exemplary of the way in which liberalism conjoins the private and the public in circular forms of authorization and discipline. On the one hand, the conversion narrative admissions test resolutely locates authority in the private, interior space of the subject. Only the profoundly personal quality of saving grace will serve as evidence to enable an individual to assume an important public identity as a church member. Because only covenanted church members could vote in civic elections or hold public office in the government, the qualifying conversion narrative underwrote both religious and political forms of citizenship and identity. As I argued in the first section of this chapter, the liberalizing aspect of Puritan doctrine lies precisely in the relocation of authority from an external hierarchy to the inner experience of a private relation with God. Yet the conversion narrative admissions test points to a second important aspect of liberalism I have tried to clarify above as well: namely, the regulatory function of the public sphere in producing privacy. While the conversion narrative would seem to base public authority on internal experience, its fixed structure demonstrates that internal experience is shaped and determined in relation to publicity and the formal exigencies of public recognition. As a qualifying narrative, the conversion narrative both reveals and produces private subjectivity, demonstrating the circular production of the liberal subject through the interdependence of private and public identities.

The regulatory or qualifying function of the conversion narrative and its association with a liberal order emerging in and through the antinomian crisis is further illuminated in the history of its institutionalization in New England.

While Morgan has argued for dating the institution of the narrative requirement to roughly 1635, Michael Ditmore has persuasively argued that the new
requirement was only imposed subsequent to the antinomian controversy and
indeed, was the direct result of that crisis. Contrary to Hutchinson's claims for
the immediacy of God's revelation to her (which, as Winthrop lamented, made
her ungovernable), the formulaic ordering of the conversion account implicitly subjected the interior relation of God and congregant to a set of normative,
publicly mediated forms. Ditmore thus describes the conversion narrative as a
"narrative paradigm that made the social communication of religious conversion a means of effectively opposing the threatening non-conformism of radically individualized and incommunicable religious experience."[102] Ditmore
thus emphasizes the disciplinary (not the epistemological or revelatory) function of the conversion narrative: rather than revealing individual experience,
the conversion narrative serves as a means of regulating the newly authorized
privacy of Puritan men and women. If the challenge of antinomianism (and,
more broadly, the liberalizing elements of Puritan doctrine and the colonial
condition) lay in a new and potentially anarchic authorization of privacy, the
conversion narrative regulated this privacy in two novel ways: first, interiority
was controlled through the public sphere rather than through a hierarchical
chain of authority, and, second, privacy was regulated through the circular production of subjectivity. In the narrative form of the conversion account we can
recognize the way in which literary texts in the public sphere aim to describe
(and thus produce) the inner truths of the liberal subject.

The effect of the antinomian controversy has long been seen as repression,
and particularly the repression of women. We have seen that Round and Egan,
for instance, see the enforcement of hierarchical relations between men and
women as one result of the controversy, and images of Winthrop and the elders frothing with punitive rage portray them as reacting repressively with
respect to Hutchinson's proposed radical selfhood. Yet as I have argued
throughout this chapter, the antinomian controversy marks the beginning of
an institutionalization of liberalism, not its repression. With this institutionalization, new forms of discipline emerge that operate through the public sphere
rather than through punitive action from above. The conversion narrative is
precisely such a form of discipline: as such, it points to a far more complicated
story than one of simple repression, particularly with respect to the issue of
gender—a complex story in which women are granted new sources of authority while simultaneously being subject to new forms of control. The more traditional account of gender-based repression is advanced by a critic such as Ann
Kibbey, who argues that following the controversy, women were silenced: "In

the wake of the antinomian crisis [John] Cotton succeeded in establishing an ecclesiastical practice he had wanted for some time: women's narratives of their conversions were given in private to the clergy rather than before the whole congregation. With this new practice, women were banished from public religious discourse, excluded from any public articulation of religious ideas."[103] Yet evidence abounds that the role of women's speech in church was a continued issue of contention following the antinomian crisis and was not in the least settled in favor of women's silence. Although women in some churches did deliver their conversion narratives to ministers in private, the ministers, in turn, typically delivered these accounts to the congregation, thus ultimately rendering them public. Thomas Lechford addresses the distinction between procedures for male and female candidates as follows: "the [candidate], if it be a man, speaketh himself; but if it be a woman, her confession made before the Elders, in private, is most usually (in Boston church) read by the Pastor, who registred the same. At Salem, the women speake themselves, for the most part, in the Church" (22–23). Thomas Weld, in turn, comments that women are not asked to publicly perform their narratives in church because they "are usually more fearefull and bashfull" than men.[104] Yet bashful men were equally able to avail themselves of a private audience with the elders, indicating that a gendered dichotomy did not uniformly structure the presentation of conversion narratives in the church.[105] Most tellingly, accounts of women's public conversion narratives following the antinomian controversy exist in the records of both Reverend Thomas Shepherd and Reverend John Fiske. Indeed, in examining men's and women's narratives, Charles Cohen concludes that little difference exists between them: "This unity of discourse should come as no surprise," argues Cohen. "In all the exposition of grace, no one distinguished between the Spirit's operations in one sex or the other. . . . The experience of grace submerges the peculiarities of gender."[106]

The critical confusion as to whether women were allowed to speak in church following the antinomian crisis mirrors the contradictory or bifurcated opinion of scholars on the question of women's status within Puritan Massachusetts. On the one hand, scholars (including Kibbey, Round, Egan, and others) have described colonial society as organized in patriarchal terms that are overtly oppressive for women. On the other hand, a second vein of scholarship has emphasized the equalizing force of Puritan contractualism on women, tracing, for instance, the importance of models of female piety and companionate marriage in empowering Puritan women.[107] I would suggest that both views are substantially correct: the Puritans stand on the cusp of the divide between early modern and modern concepts of gender and subjectivity, and thus competing versions of these concepts operate at once. While any endorsement of women's authority over men's would be anathema in social terms, the concept of privacy (and its implicit authorization of this "new creature") nonetheless extends to both men and women, and perhaps even particularly women. Without resolving this contradiction in favor of equality, I would suggest that gender is renegotiated in Puritan Massachusetts so as to authorize status relations between men and women from an entirely new position. As we have seen, the colonial body is imagined from below, and so too is the nature of status rearticulated in contractual rather than hierarchical terms. More specifically, the conversion narrative, and women's speech (rather than silence), enabled contractual conceptions of status.

The implied equality of women and men in producing authoritative accounts of private subjectivity is revealed in church records, together with anxious attempts to limit and contain this equality. In *The Notebooks of the Reverend John Fiske*, for instance, the congregants of his newly founded Wenham church debate the question of whether a woman should relate her conversion narrative in public or not. The debate overtly raises the question of whether speaking in church "argues power" for the person speaking or, alternatively, bespeaks "submission." Fiske reports the 1644 debate as follows:

> Some agitation was about women making their relations in public, occasioned from the practice of some churches to the contrary. . . . As for the considering that place in I Cor. 14, women not to speak &c., to the scripture it was resolved to speak by way of teaching a prophecy, as it seems the scope of this place, and *such a speaking argues power*. And so the parallel place seems to expound it in I Tim. 3. Whereas it was objected, but to ask a question in public they may not so much as do that, as expressed by the text ask your husband at home. Answered, asking of questions (imparts power also) in the church, *but this kind of speaking is by submission where others are to judge* &c. and to the glory of God. . . . And resolved that they should make their relations personally in public; grounds, because the whole church is to judge of their meetness which cannot so well be if she speak not herself.[108]

Fiske's congregation thus determines that the personal narratives of women may be related in public because they represent a form of submission rather than empowerment, indicating, as I have suggested, that the personal narrative might be understood less as evidence of finding one's voice than of conforming or submitting to public norms. Yet Fiske's congregation makes it clear that women need to speak and not simply submit silently: women's speech is necessary to demonstrate that submission is an act of individual choice, the act of a volitional, contracting subject. The conversion narrative thus functions, in some respects, to finesse the opposition between models of womanly submission and women's equality: women are asked to submit to men by choice and by desire. As such, a different kind of authority underwrites gender hierarchy—not simply that of divine order, but that of contractual subjectivity.

The double nature of women's conversion narrative—volitional and subjectifying—is illustrated in the lengthy disciplining of a woman in Reverend John Fiske's congregation whom we know only as the wife of Phineas Fiske. Phineas Fiske's wife comes to the attention of the congregation when she lodges complaints against her husband for his lack of tenderness toward her. While entertaining the complaints and investigating them, the congregation eventually declares them to be groundless and effectively charges Fiske's wife with cruelty to her husband for "publishing what she should have concealed . . . to the defaming of her husband" (32). Having been found in the wrong, Fiske's wife evidently did not need to be punished, but needed to produce a new story, specifically, a narrative in which she is not the victim of her husband but the beneficiary of his kindness, a narrative in which she is submissive to him. The church thus works to reform her from the inside out rather than vice versa: Fiske reports that the congregation "concluded touching her that she should appear convinced of the evil of her accusations against her husband before we proceeded further with her and that the whole church severally should endeavor as opportunity serve to convince her in the particulars" (32). Despite the efforts of an entire congregation to bend her inner sentiments toward their version of events, it takes some time to accomplish the sought-after transformation. Three months later, she evidently reports to the church on her behavior in terms that do not seem to fully express an inner change: Fiske reports that the congregation concludes that "her acknowledgement did not satisfy, but when once a manifestation of repentance was made they should joyfully proceed with her" (34). An additional four months of attention and persuasion seem to finally yield results: in an interrogation before the congregation, Fiske's wife begins to produce the narrative that will eventually enable her to join the church covenant.

> Asked whether she had not herself seen the guilt of want of love and cruelty on her part, she acknowledged it. . . . It was asked of our brother [Phineas Fiske] whether he was satisfied in her acknowledgement and could pass by any offenses given on her part toward him. He answered affirmatively. . . . Then the same things were likewise put unto her. She answered . . . affirmatively. So it was agreed that we should proceed to propound her publicly for a church member. (41–42)

The successful account of her experience obviously requires her submission to the desires of her husband, yet it is also evidently important that Fiske's wife announce her desire to submit in tones that are sufficiently persuasive to convince the congregation that she offers more than just lip service to this idea.

Clearly, her speech is necessary to authorize her submission: submission is not by way of silence, then, but by way of speech and choice.

The necessity of women's speech in church, rather than their silence, appears as well in a provocative exchange in the Boston church in 1640 (four years after the antinomian crisis) between John Cotton and Mistress Anne Hibbens. Though Cotton is sometimes credited with insisting upon the doctrine that women were not allowed to speak in church, in this instance, he and the pastor of the church, John Wilson, demand that Hibbens speak despite her initial reluctance to do so. Hibbens is asked to speak before the church to resolve a dispute between herself and a number of laborers who have performed work on her house. Evidently a voluble and tenacious woman in these debates over labor and pricing, she nonetheless refuses to speak in church.[109] A proxy who speaks for her in church reports that she is "not resolved yet that it is Lawfull for her to speke in the church."[110] In response, Cotton urges her to speak and Wilson chides her: "It hath bine Answered allready by owr Teacher that it is Lawfull for a woman to speke, whan she is asked a qwestion . . . if a woman may not speake, how shall see declare her offence to the church and be a witnes agaynst her, or how may she that hath given the offence clear her selfe or Answr to the thinges Layde to her charge." The pastor's directive indicates the necessity of women's speech in church for the work of self-reformation and contractual subjection required of women.

Despite the invitation to speak in order to submit to the rule of church and husband, Hibbens herself uses the logic of liberalism implicit in Puritanism to legitimate not her submission to her husband but her empowerment over him. When she is accused of refusing to listen to her husband, she tells John Cotton that she had understood Cotton to have "delivered it as an Ordinance of god that a man should harken to the Cownsell of his wife from that speech of god to Abraham: harken to thy wife in all that she shall say to thee." Cotton replies as follows:

> That is to be understood, whan a wife speakes as the Oricles of god according to the mind and will of god, as indeed than the speech of godly weomen wear as Oracles and did declar the minde and cownsell of god to ther Husbands, and than thay wear to harken to them as to god. But that wives now should be allwayes gods Oracles to thear Husband and that the Husband should obay his wife and not the wife the Husband, that is a falce principle, for god hath put another Law upon weomen: wives be subject to yor Husbands in all thinges, except thay should reqwier some thinge of yow that is a playne sine or a direct breach of Rule. Yow owght to obay them, and be subject to them in all thinges.

While it does seem particularly humorous that Hibbens places words granting women authority in the mouth of John Cotton, given his general insistence on the necessity of a gendered hierarchical relation between men and women, it is nonetheless also the case that Cotton insists more than most ministers on the immediacy of grace within the private soul. Cotton thus concedes that on occasion she may be correct: if a woman "speakes as the Oricles of god," then her husband should obey her. One must confess that Hibbens's confusion seems entirely strategic, yet her capacity to make this strategic move suggests the dual and competing currency of the two modes of thought concerning women: that they are like men, authorized individually by saving grace, and that they are, alternatively, far from equal to men, but rather "subject to them in all thinges."

Hibbens's experience further embodies these contradictions insofar as she is both enjoined to speak and enjoined to subservience at once. Ideally, a proper conversion narrative, in the mode of that produced by Phineas Fiske's wife, would erase all evidence of this contradiction. Yet unlike Fiske's wife, Hibbens accepted the invitation to speak, but not the invitation to self-subjection and self-reform. Indeed, she was eventually excommunicated from the church precisely for her "want of subjection." Wilson points specifically to her refusal to reformulate her narrative in terms acceptable to the community: she is excommunicated because she has "scorned cownsell and refused Instruction" and has "Like a filthie swine trampled those perles" offered to her. Women are allowed to speak, even required to speak, to produce evidence of volition and subjectivity, but this subjectivity had to be produced in normative forms. Ideally the woman's conversion narrative seamlessly conjoins the volitional equality of the liberal subject with the subservient position of the woman ranked below man in the divine order of being. Ideally, then, a lack of subjection is not displayed in the woman's conversion narrative but a desire for subjection is seen.

Far from being silenced by the antinomian controversy, then, women were introduced into public speech and public narrative in new and important ways. Indeed, we can see that women are enjoined to speak, as are Mistress Hibbens, the wife of Phineas Fiske, and even Anne Hutchinson, who reports that she begins holding conventicle meetings as a result of being criticized for not having joined existing conventicles. In the transatlantic print public sphere, documents concerning the antinomian crisis accord women's bodies a central role in establishing the disciplinary capacities of a new form of contractually oriented church government. In the colony itself, the personal conversion narratives of men *and* women assume an important function in producing contractual subjects and constraining them to existing social norms. Women were decidedly not absent from the public sphere of the church or the conversion narrative, in part because of their privileged access to privacy. Yet they were subject to the exigencies of liberal discipline through the public sphere, a liberal discipline that emerges in the antinomian controversy and underwrites this controversy.

The conversion narrative—and its religious and political importance in the Bay Colony—points to a model of the literary public sphere that I developed in the first chapter. While the Habermasian public sphere has often been defined in terms of rational debate ("procedural rationalism"), I suggested that we might see the public sphere operating in terms of subject production and desire. Because individuals seek public recognition—seek recognition in the public sphere—they produce accounts of themselves (produce themselves as subjects) that mirror the desire of the public, or public norms. Susanna Bell, Richard Mather, and Phineas Fiske's wife sought forms of recognition and produced and reshaped themselves according to what they believed a judging public desired. And indeed, each was successful in this endeavor. In relation to Habermas, then, we can see the way in which the public sphere is not simply the space of rational debate, but the space in which privacy comes to be composed and rendered recognizable or, alternatively, rendered monstrous. As such, we see a literary public sphere that is particularly concerned with the production of privacy that will stand as the ground of public identity. Women, long associated with domestic and private relations, have access and, indeed, sometimes privileged access to scenes of privacy that carry a great deal of importance in making the public sphere possible in structural terms. In fact, it is for precisely this reason, I would argue, that Hutchinson is such a central figure in the antinomian controversy: not because she is a convenient scapegoat, but because women assume a new and unaccustomed prominence in the emerging terms of liberal political association and the liberal public sphere. Winthrop and Weld argue for the justness of a liberal order by demonstrating the corrupt interiority of Anne Hutchinson: the corruption of antinomianism, they argue, is contained in private bodies, and they effect this containment in their own public sphere representations of Hutchinson's body. The conversion narrative similarly probes and reforms this interior, embodied space. The literary public sphere is concerned with producing, revealing, constructing, authorizing, and constraining this interiority, and women are everywhere included within, not absent from, this labor of representation.

For the purposes of looking forward to the eighteenth and nineteenth centuries, I would like to adduce one final example of the circuit of liberal subjectivity production that I have described as operating in the literary public sphere, namely, the marriage contract. Often invoked as the explicit analogue of the Puritan's covenant with God, marriage, whether spiritual or earthly, emphasized the conjoining of contractual and status relations. Peter Bulkeley thus describes the congregant's marriage with God as encompassing forms of self-rule and subjection: "It is a marriage-covenant that we make with God . . . therefore we must doe as the Spouse doth, resigne up our selves to be ruled and governed according to his will."[111] Puritan scholars have emphasized the equalizing force of the Puritan marriage for women, pointing to its contractual and overtly affectionate nature.[112] Yet the companionate marriage, while it bespeaks a sense of contractual agency on the part of the wife, works much like the conversion narrative to weld the woman to a particular nonvolitional status relation. John Winthrop thus argued in 1645, "The womans own choise makes such a man her husband, yet beinge so chosen, he is her lord, & she is to be subjecte to him, yet in a waye of Libertye, not of bondage: & a true wife accounts her subjection her honor & freedome, and would not thinke her condition safe & free, but in her subjection to her husbandes Authoritye."[113] Winthrop's language here emphasizes at once the woman's choice and agency as well as her submission and lack of autonomy in relation to her husband. Winthrop's marvelous phrase, "subject . . . in a way of Libertye," perfectly captures the way in which marriage both embodies and solves the contradiction between anarchic individualism and social normativity.[114] Marriage bespeaks liberty and subjection at once: marriage bespeaks a desire for subjection. The marriage metaphor thus makes volition the grounds of status and translates equality into inequality through the language of desire. According to Edmund Morgan, the language of subjection contained in the trope of the marriage contract was one that reassured the Puritan convert or "Bride of Christ": "The idea that God was actually married to his saints was very comforting, for a marriage was not easily dissolved."[115] Marriage allowed one to assume a fixed identity, and this was, evidently, a subjection much to be desired. One is reassured, made safe, by occupying a socially recognized status position. Desire for this kind of social recognition thus accounts for being subject "in a waye of Libertye," as a choice.[116] It is worth noting, as well, that the choice of subjectification is one that applies to men as well as women, that men, as brides of Christ, desire to enter into the bonds of marriage with God much as they expect women to. The volitional marriage contract as a structure of welding private to public through the mechanisms (and even erotics) of desire and the desire for social recognition point to an evolving reorganization of authority, gender, and representation.

* * *

Many long months after she had been sentenced to banishment from the colony and waited under arrest to appear before her congregation, Anne Hutchinson stood trial again, this time before her church rather than the magistrates of the colony. As she was pregnant and evidently ill, her verbal acuity does not seem to have been what it was in the earlier trial. And indeed, at the close of the church trial she seems more clearly defeated than ever before. One crushing claim that she has denied but not forcibly parried lies upon her: she stands accused of violating her marriage contract with her husband. Here, the charge is not simply that of holding false religious ideas, but the more embodied sin of adultery and the literal violation of her contract with her husband. The terms of this charge are intriguing because they rest on no evidence that she has been adulterous—indeed, Cotton says she probably has not been—but rather upon the claim that she certainly will be eventually because of the corrupt nature of her theological views. The theological debate in the trial revolves, at this point, around the so-called "mortalist" heresy, or the claim that man's body did not rise at the resurrection.[117] Hutchinson was perplexed about the claim that man's body arose at the resurrection because she saw the spirit of Christ as it had joined with the justified individual rising to heaven rather than either the soul or the degraded flesh of man doing so. Because she thereby posited a prior union of Christ with the saint, she thus also seemed (to her critics) to posit that a resurrection occurred prior to death: such a resurrection would, then, preclude the final resurrection at death. This claim, as John Dampford argues at her church trial, suggests that human law, such as marriage, no longer applies to the saint: "Thear is no first and second Resurrection of one and the same Body . . . for if the Resurrection be past than Marriage is past: for it is a waytie Reason; *after the Reseruction is past, marriage is past. Than if thear be any Union betwene man and woman it is not by Marriage but in a Way of Communitie.*"[118] John Cotton later lends his voice to this claim, arguing that Hutchinson has propounded "that filthie Sinne of the Communitie of Women and all promiscuus and filthie cominge togeather of men and Woemen without Distinction or Relation of Marriage. . . . And though I have not herd, nayther do I thinke, you have bine unfaythfull to your Husband in his Marriage Covenant, *yet that will follow upon it.*"[119] Although Winthrop locates her violation in sedition, the church trial locates her error in the violation of the marriage contract—in her refusal to wed her personal experience to forms of socially recognized subjectivity and order. Moreover, this is a personal and sexual violation that tends to impugn her interiority, to adduce unfaithfulness and contractual failure from her theological views. In the *Short Story* Winthrop and Weld had turned Hutchinson's social miscarriage into the literal miscarriage of a pregnancy, the truth of which was lodged within her body. In this case, the church effects a similar claim, lodging the truth of her promiscuity in her body as well, suggesting that anarchic ideas are of a piece with embodied violations.

While Hutchinson struggled to articulate the bodiless and genderless identity of the "new creature" formed through Christ's union with the human soul, her critics returned to her a vision of a decisively gendered and embodied individual. In the antinomian crisis, then, we see that the new creature of liberalism inhabits an individuated body that is far from immaterial, but matters a great deal, particularly in terms of its inner state and its contractual status. The new creature of liberalism was not beyond the duty to contract herself to recognizable, embodied forms, to scripted accounts of inner experience; she was, indeed, called upon to wed herself to the morphologies and narratives that structured new, publicly mediated forms of private identity, desire, and subjectivity.

3 Contracting Marriage in the New Republic

> In the modern world everyone can, should, will
> "have" a nationality, as he or she "has" a gender.
> Benedict Anderson, *Imagined Communities*

Ichabod Crane fortifies himself with the texts of his Puritan forefathers. "No tale," writes Washington Irving, "was too gross or monstrous for his capacious swallow," and it is particularly Cotton Mather's tales of witchcraft upon which Crane seeks to nourish himself. A "huge feeder," with the "dilating powers of an anaconda," Crane consumes ghostly tales as well as enormous quantities of food throughout his brief tale, as if eager to bulk up his lanky and insubstantial body.[1] Yet neither Puritan history nor quantities of food ward off Crane's eventual disembodiment, his apparent disappearance into thin air at the close of the narrative. The body of Crane, pursued unto his demise by the headless ghost of a Hessian soldier from the Revolutionary War, is never recovered. In narrative terms, Crane's disappearance is overtly linked to his failure as the suitor of the eminently embodied and well-endowed Katrina Van Tassel, the Dutch heiress who is "plump as a partridge, ripe and melting and rosy-cheeked as one of her father's peaches" (337). Crane's fantasies of devouring "so tempting a morsel"—of increasing the size of his estate and his body with the edible property (pigs, ducks, turkeys) of père Van Tassel by way of marriage to Katrina—are brought to an abrupt halt when Katrina rejects his suit following a party thrown at her father's estate. On his crestfallen journey homeward, Crane becomes prey to the specter of the headless horseman. The cause of Crane's disappearance is thus propounded in two registers: on the one hand, a ghostly historical past is realized in the figure of the headless Hessian soldier who terrifies Crane out of existence; on the other hand, Irving clearly indicates that the horseman may be less the figure of the past than the person of Crane's rival for Katrina's affections, the masculine Brom Bones, whose presence and power index the failed marital prospects of Crane. While these two explanatory models appear to be logically distinct, I would suggest that the text indicates a suppressed connection between the two. We might understand this connection as follows: marriage embodies the subject in a male or female body in such a way that the threatening aspects of the headless (liberal) social and political order are obviated. Crane's disembodiment represents the dissolution of this personal and political structuration: his marital failure brings the terror of suppressed political ghosts and anxieties to life.

In the previous chapter, I argued that images of headless bodies in the seventeenth century registered anxiety over the loss of a hierarchical religious and political order. Critics of the liberalizing governmental forms of New England Puritanism viewed the religious or political body as horrifically deformed insofar as it lacked a central figure (such as a king or bishop) to represent the power of the church and state. Yet by the eighteenth century, the American Revolution had dissevered the head of England's King George from the American political body and images of the body politic were radically reconfigured: Jay Fliegelman argues, for instance, that fraternal tropes replaced paternalistic metaphors of governmental authority; Eric Slauter notes the decline of metaphors of the body politic in favor of architectural iconography of the nation during debates over framing the constitution.[2] Indeed, the association of an acephalic order with contractual politics was often the occasion of celebratory rhetoric rather than horror. Thomas Paine, for instance, imagines a coronation day in the United States reserved for crowning the abstract figure of the law rather than the head of a monarch:

> Let a crown be placed [on the divine law], by which the world may know, that so far as we approve of monarchy, that in America THE LAW IS KING. For as in absolute governments the King is law, so in free countries the law *ought* to be King; and there ought to be no other. But lest any ill use should afterwards arise, let the crown at the conclusion of the ceremony be demolished, and scattered among the people whose right it is.[3]

Paine here celebrates the headless nature of the new government both by replacing the embodied figure of the king with the impersonal figure of the law and, further, by imagining a figurative dismemberment of the body of the king in the sacramental fragmentation and distribution of the crown among the citizens of the nation.[4] Yet if the body is thus dismembered in the new Republic, how, then, can the nation be re-membered or offered an image of social coherence in the face of bodily dissolution? Despite celebrating the relocation of political authority from the king to the people, a wealth of literary, legal, and political texts from the early national period indicates that the dangers of failed national coherence (imagined variously in terms of factions, conspiracy, alien infiltration, sedition, mobocracy, and seduction) loomed large during the period. Written in 1820, but set in the 1790s, Irving's short story suggests that the fears of a headless social body that haunted the nation at the close of the eighteenth century were more reliably managed in the early nineteenth century through affective investments in the contractual bonds of marriage. Marriage, Irving's tale indicates, serves as a vehicle of embodiment and, by extension, of gendering the body as well. As I argue below, the gendered *individual* body, produced and administered in the mutually recognizing pledges of man and woman in the heterosexual marriage contract, thus offers a stay against the loss of shared social form and epistemological certainty that liberalism potentially effects.

The link I am drawing between marriage and the acephalic political body of liberalism may appear strained in part because marriage and the political body of the state are not entities of the same order and thus are not readily classed together: we think of marriage as a personal, affective choice and the body of the state as a collective, political form. Indeed, it is precisely in the dissonance of these categories that the humor of Irving's short story lies: the two competing narratives of Crane's disappearance (collective historical ghosts or individual marital competition) are presented as incompatible. Moreover, the marriage narrative is deflationary with respect to the ghost tale: that is, it represents a "realist" account of Crane's disappearance in contrast to a legendary one. Indeed, Crane himself is satirized for his failure to understand the "real": he is foolish in his obsession with witchcraft and Cotton Mather and foolish in his lack of interest in Katrina's femininity in favor of her father's foodstuffs. Crane is the object of satire, then, insofar as he fails to understand that his main chance for becoming a man of substance lies in heterosexual desire. Yet if by the 1820s the reader was invited to separate out the legends of a collective political past from the realities of individual marital negotiation, I would argue that this separation was in no wise so readily available in the 1790s, the period that is the focus of this chapter and the period in which Irving's tale is set: that is, in the 1790s, contested models of marriage and contested models of the political body were much more visibly entwined with one another.

Indeed, I would suggest that Irving's tale points us in the direction of something of a historical narrative of the development of this marital/political relation—ranging from Puritan witchcraft to the Revolutionary War to what we might call the "marital realism" of the 1820s (represented in the masculine figure of Brom Bones)—and I propose to follow this trajectory briefly here. I begin with Crane's interest in the Puritan figure of Cotton Mather. In the last chapter, I argued that marriage functioned, for the Puritans, in terms analogous to the conversion narrative: both marriage and conversion are codified forms for the social ratification of the subject. Whereas a feudal order imagines each subject as occupying a fixed location within the corporate political body and deriving authority from that connection, liberalism locates authority in the individual subject and his or her contractual engagements. Yet the seemingly autonomous liberal subject is also tethered to the larger community, I argued, through the circular constitution of the subject: that is, the subject must be publicly produced (even in his or her interiority) and ratified to attain the status of a contracting individual. While an emerging public sphere enabled private individuals to assume public voices and to wield new forms of authority, the public sphere, on the other hand, shaped the production of "private" subjects by offering recognition and ratification to some individuals and not to others. The conversion narrative functioned as a primary form of religious and political ratification of the Puritan subject—the qualifying narrative of the congregant secured his or her contractual relation to the church and status within the colonial polis. In similar terms, the Puritan marriage contract secured forms of social recognition or ratification, albeit in return for voluntary subjugation on the part of the wife. As we saw Edmund Morgan point out, the metaphorical position of "bride of Christ" that male congregants assumed offered a reassuring form of subjugated connection to God. Yet Ichabod Crane is interested in a particular moment of Puritan history at which the reassuring (as well as disciplinary) effect of communal ratification offered by the codified norms of the Puritan community began to dissolve. Given the increased importance of commercial relations and geographic and social mobility, the New England congregation ceased to exercise significant control over social and political ratification of subjects in Massachusetts at the close of the seventeenth century; moreover, the witchcraft trials of the 1690s may be seen to exemplify precisely the upheaval occasioned by a shift in the locus of subjectification away from congregational and Puritan forms of identity. Long described by historians as marking the death throes of the Puritan theocracy, the witchcraft trials serve as a point of historical demarcation between Puritanism and the more secular and commercial political structures that organized society in the northern colonies prior to the Revolution.

Ichabod Crane thus devotes his reading hours to a book concerning the historical moment at which Puritanism lost the "subjectifying" authority that it wielded during the early part of the seventeenth century. Rather, the locus of subjectification shifted from the congregation to a larger and less cohesive civic sphere shaped by a growing capitalist economy. During the 1690s, for instance, the basis of the political franchise in the Massachusetts Bay Colony shifted from congregational membership (visible sainthood) to property ownership. Puritan religious control of political citizenship (the capacity to vote in civic elections) was thus ceded to a new standard of economic status that henceforth determined who would count as a contracting citizen of the polity. Social and political authority—and particularly the ability to "ratify" individuals as subjects of the political community—shifted toward the powerful new merchants of the growing transatlantic economy and away from pedigreed Puritans such as Cotton Mather himself.[5] Ichabod Crane is thus particularly fascinated by a moment at which an expanding public sphere causes severe social disruption.

The second moment of history that exercises an absorptive power over Crane in "The Legend of Sleepy Hollow" is that of the American Revolution. Even more self-evidently than the witchcraft trials, the Revolution marked the expansion of liberal modes of authority and social organization at the expense of older hierarchical models of order: political authority was invested directly in the people and ties were cut with the monarchical and parental body of England. The Hessian soldier who terrorizes Crane, as well as the legendary British spy, Major John André (whose death scene figures in the haunting of Crane as well), both reference the imperial and monarchical order that held sway prior to the Revolution. Cotton Mather, the Hessian soldier, and Major André thus all embody older social orders—perhaps more coherent ones— that have been disrupted and disfigured by the shift toward liberal democratic authority. The national history to which Crane turns thus does not supply him with a coherent subject identity: rather, this history itself seems to narrate the disappearance of a collective national body. While this history fails to produce a coherent national and thus individual body, marriage—in a turn to the personal, affective realm—is clearly imagined as an alternative form of individual embodiment, albeit one that Crane fails to seize upon effectively. Yet in what sense can we imagine that individual coupling might stand in for a loss of national coherence? How might the individual, private contract of marriage shore up a dissolving religious or political order? How, moreover, might marriage in 1820 or 1790 differ from marriage in 1636? In short, why would we imagine marriage to assume a political valence in the early Republic that it had presumably not held in the past?

To begin to address these questions, we might turn to the work of Claude Lefort, a political philosopher who offers an illuminating account (by way of an analysis of the work of Alexis de Tocqueville) of the indeterminacy that characterizes personal identity under democracy. Specifically, Lefort contrasts the social indeterminacy of democracy with the guarantees of monarchy:

> Under the monarchy, power was embodied in the person of the prince . . . and it therefore gave society a body. And because of this, a latent but effective knowledge of what *one* meant to the *other* existed throughout the social. This model reveals the revolutionary and unprecedented feature of democracy. The locus of power

becomes *an empty place.* . . . [D]emocracy is instituted and sustained by the *dissolution of the markers of certainty.* It inaugurates a history in which people experience a fundamental indeterminacy as to the basis of power, law and knowledge, and as to the basis of relations between *self* and *other*, at every level of social life.[6]

Lefort thus argues that the loss of the organic metaphor of the political body attached to the figure of the king gave way to a profound uncertainty in the status of the individual in democracy. Moreover, his analysis of this shift points to an interesting displacement of individual identity away from political locations toward private and social forms of identity: the loss of assurance Lefort describes extends under democracy to "every level of *social* life." Without a corporate political body, the individual—promoted to a new status within democracy—nonetheless faces a crisis at the social and personal level: whereas once the stratification of the corporate body gave him or her a clear sense of position and identity, as an individual in the atomized social space of democracy, the subject is "dispossessed of his assurance as to his identity."

What I would like to underscore in Lefort's account of democracy is the implicit transition from an overtly political account of the subject, as seen in the model of the hierarchical political body, toward the social or "private" construction of the liberal citizen-subject. This shift is seen particularly clearly when Lefort (via Tocqueville) accounts for the way in which the democratic subject seeks to secure identity in the wake of the dissolution of the corporate body. According to Tocqueville, democracy in America has the strange effect of both freeing the individual citizen *and* making him the voluntary subject of the tyranny of the majority. The tyranny of the majority imagined by Tocqueville is *not* that of a political or electoral majority (such as that feared by Alexander Hamilton and James Madison in their Federalist writings), but rather that of a majoritarian public opinion operating in the realm of the social rather than the political. Tocqueville describes public opinion as something akin to a super-egoic voice that each democratic individual internalizes in order to achieve social recognition from his or her peers. Tocqueville here ventriloquizes the commands of the voice of public opinion to the citizen-subject:

You are free to think differently from me and to retain your life, your property, and all that you possess; but you are henceforth a stranger among your people. You may retain your civil rights, but they will be useless to you, for you will never be chosen by your fellow citizens if you solicit their votes; and they will affect to scorn you if you ask for their esteem. You will remain among men, but you will be deprived of the rights of mankind. Your fellow creatures will shun you like an impure being; and even those who believe in your innocence will abandon you, lest they should be shunned in their turn. Go in peace! I have given you your life, but it is an existence worse than death.[7]

Tocqueville thus indicates that the citizen-subject may formally retain his political identity and civil rights, yet in practice he will be excluded from the horizon of the social world altogether if he fails to conform to public opinion. In other words, he will have no recognizable status as a subject unless he constructs his private identity in socially acceptable terms. Again, what seems significant here is the shift from a set of political terms (civil rights guaranteed by law) to a set of social terms (forms of recognition and social identity) that underpin the possibility of attaining political identity and agency.

What I have described in the previous chapter as the social "ratification" of the subject occurs here by way of public opinion at the level of the social rather than in the religio-political terms of the Puritans. The ratification of majoritarian public opinion is, I would suggest, similar to that performed by the Puritan conversion narrative, yet its location and operation are far more diffuse and inchoate. Rather than a literal vote within the congregation on each personal narrative, the ratification process is here dispersed across a variety of moments of social recognition. For instance, according to Tocqueville, citizens will withhold their "esteem" from those who do not court public opinion, and without this esteem and recognition, an individual will be unable to function as a politically active member of democratic society. According to Lefort, then, Tocqueville demonstrates the contradiction of liberalism "by examining the individual, who has been released from the old networks of personal dependency and granted the freedom to think and act in accordance with his own norms, but who is, on the other hand, isolated, impoverished and at the same time trapped by the image of his fellows, now that agglutination with them provides a means of escaping the threat of the dissolution of his identity" (15). This, then, is the predicament of liberal autonomy: identity is no longer provided by the corporate political body and the social totality implied therein. However, the social realm confers a new body on the liberal subject by way of mechanisms of "agglutination." The loss of a corporate body at the political level is thus replaced by the private choices of the individual who seeks to *glue* him- or herself to the community by fashioning a recognizable body according to the dictates of public opinion.

With a shift to a liberal-democratic government following the Revolution, the operations of the public sphere and of public opinion gain increased social and political significance. This claim is entirely consonant with a Habermasian account of the public sphere: according to Habermas, the development of an active public sphere culture corresponds to the emergence of liberal forms of government. Yet the account of "public opinion" I have traced in Tocqueville differs significantly from the rational-critical "public sphere" described by

Habermas. Whereas Habermas focuses on the ability of public sphere debate to monitor the activities of the state, Tocqueville points to the way in which public opinion or publicity shapes and monitors private subjects who seek public recognition. The public sphere described by Tocqueville is not characterized by rational-critical debate but by the desire for recognition: in order to become a subject within the public sphere, the individual must receive recognition from an amorphous, majoritarian "public opinion."

Tocqueville's claims about the role of public opinion are useful in reformulating a model of the public sphere in the early Republic. Rather than a disinterested, impersonal sphere of civic debate, the print public sphere was the location of the articulation of public opinion and subject ratification. I thus mean to advance a model of the public sphere that includes both the fantasy of rational-critical debate among disinterested subjects, and the relentless desire for subject recognition that is the premise of critical debate among ratified subjects. As I argued in the first chapter of this book, the model of the public sphere I propose here is one that ultimately blurs the distinction between public and private upon which much liberal theory rests, and, indeed, upon which the concept of the "public sphere" rests as well. Because the public sphere helps to create private individuals, the private sphere is, I would suggest, colonized in advance by majoritarian public opinion—by what we might call social normativity. As such, the public sphere operates less to protect the realm of privacy from all public encroachment than to determine in advance which versions of "private" subjectivity register as worthy of recognition and protection. On this account the public sphere is thus not entirely public (rational, critical, disinterested), nor is the private sphere entirely private (inviolate, untouched by market or state). I thus want to designate the space of public sphere activity concerned with private subject production as the space of "sociality," a term that I hope will give some specificity to the public circulation of social desire that marks the emergence of a liberal public sphere. In what follows I will sketch out the double valence of this term: on the one hand, sociality is the location where privacy is publicly ratified, and this ratification covertly works to maintain the coherence of the public/private distinction. On the other hand, when sociality more overtly displays the contradictions between public and private identities and desires, or exposes the public machinations of private subject production, it becomes the site of an interesting incoherence in the liberal division between public and private. In this second sense, "sociality" may be seen to designate an indeterminate middle ground, a third term that mediates and opens up possibilities foreclosed by the liberal public/private dyad. In this chapter I suggest more specifically that sociality in the eighteenth century begins to be articulated through the marriage contract, a contract that increasingly serves to link private desires (in the form of volitional marriage) to public identity (in the form of social ratification). I argue that the marriage contract does not seamlessly conjoin public and private identities in this period as it will later in the nineteenth century, but rather is itself the subject of debate and disquiet. Literary texts of the period take marriage as their primary subject yet nonetheless represent marriage as a vexed solution to the dilemma of liberal political embodiment. As such, marriage serves as an intriguing instance of exposed sociality—as evidence of sociality in both its overt and covert forms.

MARRIAGE AND SOCIAL DESIRE

Ichabod Crane's tale designates the Revolution (in the form of the headless horseman) as a site of rupture, a rupture in which the corporate political body is dissolved and in which identity is displaced onto marital forms of sociality. As the embodying force of the marriage contract in the story indicates, marriage functions as both an intensely private relation and as a form of public ratification: as such we might think of it as an important site of social life that has not been recognized by theorists as intimately related to liberal identity. For instance, while neither Lefort nor Tocqueville mentions marriage in relation to public opinion or democratic subjectivity, Lefort's account of "agglutination" (or "a means of escaping the threat of the dissolution of . . . identity") seems an entirely apt description of the way in which marriage conjoins husband and wife, thereby enabling the public recognition of "privately" constructed identities. Historians of private life have, indeed, identified the close of the eighteenth century as a decisive turning point in the form and meaning of marriage in both Europe and the United States. Niklas Luhmann, for instance, analyzes the development of the code of romantic love in its new association with marriage in the late eighteenth century. Although he is interested in broad sociological rather than political claims, his analysis is nonetheless suggestive with respect to the history of liberalism and gender I am pursuing here. Specifically, Luhmann argues that the discourse of romantic love is a means of creating and securing "intensive" individual identity at a moment when relations between individuals are rendered increasingly impersonal and anonymous (extensive) by democracy and capitalism. "It is most assuredly incorrect to characterize modern society as an impersonal mass society and leave it at that," writes Luhmann. While "impersonal relationships are the rule" in a modern society (one not characterized by ascriptive stratification), "it is *also* possible for individuals in some cases to intensify personal relationships and to communicate to others much of what they believe to be most intimately theirs and find this affirmed by others."[8] According to Luhmann, marriage based on romantic love becomes the primary form of intensive interpersonal relation from the late eighteenth century forward. Romantic love thus enables individuality to be established in the face of a loss of social stratification: one falls in love with the person who recognizes and consents to share one's unique worldview—who recognizes the individual self in his or her particularity. As many historians argue, the codes of love and marriage shifted during the eighteenth century such that class and fortune no longer dictated the choice of partner: Luhmann contends that recognition, in the form of sympathy and understanding, became primary in the choice of a romantic partner. In this sympathy, one finds an affirmation or ratification of the self: "formulations became more explicit in indicating that by orienting himself to the other person, the lover was also invariably referring to himself: he wished to find his own happiness in the other's happiness" (137). Marriage—the consent to the individuality of the other—thus becomes an important site of what I have called subjective ratification. In the new shape and form it assumes in the eighteenth century, marriage can be seen as linked to a need for forms of social recognition generated by the beheading of the corporate political body.

Evidence of the concern with marriage in the early Republic is visible in the voluminous discussion of the topic in print. In many ways this extended discussion exemplifies sociality, that is, the need to construct (and ratify) new versions of private identity in public. And indeed, the emphasis in this discussion is insistently upon the newly private dimension of marriage—that is, upon what Lawrence Stone has called "affective individualism" or a private subjectivity defined through the exercise of new modes of affect such as sympathy and romantic love. Many early novels and short stories, a number of which I discuss at length below, can be read as extended meditations on the question of how to exercise affect autonomously or, more specifically, how to *correctly* choose a marriage partner not selected in advance by one's parents or the larger social community. The paradox that this eminently public discussion of newly privatized marital desire reveals, of course, is that making the *correct* choice means exercising individual consent in relation to socially constructed norms. Advice literature on marriage published in the early national period in the United States clearly bears out the claim that marriage is related to new forms of recognition: what writers repeatedly define as the ideal basis for marriage is the sympathy and understanding that obtains between prospective partners. An oft-reprinted article, "On the Choice of a Wife," presents the advice of a father to a son to ignore both beauty and fortune in choosing a woman to wed: "Are you not struck with a sense of the infinite consequence it must be of to you, what are the qualities of the heart and understanding of one who stands in this relation, and the comparative insignificance of external charms and ornamental accomplishments?"[9] While material conditions are not wholly irrelevant, what matters in this instance is the quality of "understanding" between husband and wife, a quality that seems essential to the kind of recognition and subjective ratification that I am suggesting that marriage begins to perform under liberalism. In the early Republic, marriage patterns shifted toward decreased parental control of the choice of a marriage partner, a decrease that is celebrated in the literature of the period (invariably in moral terms) as increasing the affective connection of partners at the expense of more venal concerns such as familial and financial status.[10] As one writer opines in 1789, "The union of a worthy man with a trifling, frivolous woman, can never, with all the advantages even of fortune, be made agreeable. How different the union of a virtuous pair, who have no aim but to make each other happy!"[11] What seems particularly striking about this quotation is not simply the emphasis on mutual agreement within the marriage, but the equation of personal happiness with virtue: making one's spouse happy and conducting a marriage full of mutual understanding and sympathy is here raised to a moral good.

The elevation of personal happiness to a moral good is further extended, in many cases, to a national good as well: that is, the ideal marriage is linked to an idealized American nation founded in consent and affection. For instance, in the article cited above, the writer argues that "Cultivation of the female mind [to make women suitable, understanding partners for their husbands] is of great importance, not with respect to private happiness only, but with respect to society at large. The ladies have it in their power to form the manners of the gentlemen, and they can render them virtuous and happy, or vicious and miserable. What a glorious prize is here exhibited, to be contended for by the sex!" Or perhaps more stridently, another writer argues that

> Nothing is so honorable as Marriage nothing so comfortable both to the body and the mind. . . . It is the most wholesome, the most beneficial, and rational law for the universal welfare of man. Marriage is the union of that glorious nature that flies above the bands of love and friendship and fixes us in reputation and felicity. It is marriage alone that knits and binds the sinews of society together and makes the life of man honorable to himself, useful to others, and grateful to the God of nature.[12]

Such early national paeans to virtue and consensual choice in marriage raise the question of why marriage—which would seem to concern primarily private happiness—is so readily connected with the moral worth and health of the nation. Why, in other words, does marriage suddenly seem to achieve a political and moral importance at this point? I would suggest that the concept of liberal "sociality"—the public construction of private subjectivity—offers one explanation. Although literature of the period indicates that marriage is increasingly a matter of personal or private choice rather than parental matchmaking, public sphere attention to marriage indicates that marriage is an increasingly important structure through which private subjects achieve social recognition. Marriage constructs privacy—the private world of the bourgeois household and romantic desire—yet does so in a wholly scripted fashion that belies the very individuality it purports to create. Moreover, marriage constructs the private (and thus publicly recognizable) subject as masculine or feminine—as husband or wife. Marriage plays a pivotal political role in defining the private subjects of the liberal state who will thenceforth have the capacity to emerge from privacy into public recognition, and to defend the sanctity of "privacy" against a seemingly exterior public sphere. In short, marriage is precisely the site where private and public lines are seemingly drawn, yet where the creation of these lines reveals the fundamental interdependence (the sociality) of public and private spheres. Marriage thus derives its political force in part from appearing to be wholly private and apolitical, from appearing to be entirely voluntaristic and affective, while nonetheless shaping subjects and their "private" desires.

My description of marriage as the locus of the intertwining of public and private spheres differs markedly from the claims of other critics concerning the shifting meaning of marriage in the early Republic. In her analysis of nationalized marital rhetoric in this period, Jan Lewis, for instance, argues that the marital couple is organized in terms analogous to the new political terms of the Republic: "Marriage was the republic in miniature; it was chaste, disinterested, and free from the exercise of arbitrary power."[13] The free consent of both husband and wife to the marriage and the cultivation of virtue within marriage, on Lewis's account, mirror the central thematics of republican politics in which commitment to the public good is figured as virtue and political authority is grounded in the consent of the citizenry. As do numerous historians of family life (including Luhmann), Lewis concludes that the marriage based on consent has the effect of promoting women to a new status of equality within the marriage: Lewis extends this claim perhaps further than others in arguing that the parallel between affectionate spouse and republican citizen is so strong as implicitly to confer a distinct political role upon women: "If the affectionate union between a man and his wife, freely entered into, without tyrannical interference, is the model for all the relationships in the society and the polity, then the wife, as an indispensable half of the marital union, is a political creature."[14] While I would agree with Lewis that marriage is reshaped in the early Republic in relation to political imperatives, I would argue that marriage does not replicate the contractual politics of the Republic. Paradoxically, the republican wife is a political being only insofar as she is represented as increasingly private—only insofar, in other words, as she conforms to new models of gendered behavior that have been coded as private rather than political.[15]

Given the model of subject ratification that I have described as operating with respect to marriage, I would thus suggest two alternative claims to the general scholarly consensus concerning the equalizing force of the new affectionate and voluntaristic marriage. First, it seems to me incorrect to argue that the consensual marriage is an analogue for republican politics. While the two are clearly related, the relation is less one of similarity than complementarity: to use Luhmann's terms, marriage offers an *intensive* relation precisely because the larger political world does not. Marriage thus provides the arena for personal recognition that republican politics do not. Classical republicanism is based on the premise that the highest virtue involves attending to the good of the polis; to attain to this virtue, personal interests must be left behind. While republican virtue is disinterested, marital virtue, in contrast, is wholly interested. Marital virtue, as defined in the discourse of the early Republic, involves promoting the happiness of the spouse in order to guarantee a return on one's affection—in order to receive reciprocal understanding, sympathy, and personal recognition. The author of a 1792 article on domestic happiness thus advises the wife to attend to her husband's idiosyncratic (that is, highly individuated and personal) needs so that he will attend to hers: "By a proper attention to your husband, you will easily discover the bent of his genius and inclinations. To that turn all your thoughts, and let your words and actions solely tend to that great point. The kindness of your attention will awaken his, and gratitude will strengthen his affection, imperceptibly even to himself."[16] The passage thus describes the aim of mutual recognition at a deeply personal (rather than generic) level: moreover, attention to the spouse is meant to cultivate the return of attention to the self, or an affirmation of the self. In this passage, it is clear that cultivating the personal "bent," or the unique "genius," of one's husband is regarded as the highest good rather than a disinterested virtue. Yet the cultivation of individuality and recognition in marriage is not unrelated to political citizenship in the Republic. The suggestion is that only by attaining a sense of self in the private sphere is a man able to function in the political realm: in the quotation above from the *Christian's Magazine*, for instance, marriage is described as making "the life of man honorable to himself, useful to others, and grateful to the God of nature," thereby describing a trajectory from the moment of private recognition in marriage (man is honorable to himself in and through the eyes of a wife) to the ability to have meaningful (or useful) interactions with a wider world. In short, the emphasis on happiness and understanding in marriage is aimed at subject ratification, a function now ascribed to private life as the prerequisite for public authority, not as its analogue.[17]

The second claim I would assert with respect to the model of affectional and equalizing marriage in the early Republic is that the primary structural axis upon which such a marriage is constructed is heterosexual desire: the axis of this imperative is thus one that tends to emphasize rather than erase sexual difference. There is a certain sense in which the heterosexuality of the marriage union has simply gone without saying in most critical work on the subject: after all, if marriage is, at base, organized around a reproductive imperative, it must necessarily be heterosexual. Yet if marriage is serving an important political function—as a model of political consent, as Lewis and others argue, or, alternatively, as a model of privatized subject ratification, as I am arguing— then the meaning and value of marriage is not simply reproductive in a materialist sense. For instance, it seems possible to imagine models of consent and subject ratification involving same-sex partners: indeed, historically, models of friendship and fraternity have embodied much of the political weight here being ascribed to the heterosexual couple. Edmund Leites demonstrates, for example, the extent to which the Puritan language of companionship represented a shift from classical language extolling the virtues of same-sex friendship.[18] Moreover, as Luhmann and other scholars note, romantic love and sexual passion began to be attached primarily to marriage for the first time in the eighteenth century: sexual passion and romantic desire were, in previous eras, not solely associated with marriage or reproduction.[19] Thus while Luhmann and Lewis (again, among others) emphasize the creation of relations of equality within the consensual marriage, the primary condition of this consent seems to be the cultivation of desire for a partner defined in sex-specific terms: one need not only find a partner of the opposite sex, but it is precisely their sex—their manliness or womanliness—that one must find desirable. Luhmann argues that conjoining sexual passion with marriage in the romantic code is simply a way of intensifying intimacy within the marriage, yet this account tends to underplay the force of the shift he describes by presenting it as an intensification rather than a significant change. I would suggest that it is not simply an intensification of intimacy that is at stake, but a retraining and resignifying of sexual desire that is required to conjoin marriage and passion. The heterosexual nature of marital desire is decisive insofar as it enables marriage to serve as what I would describe as a gendering *machine*: the discourse of marriage and marital passion produces differently sexed bodies—it masculinizes men and feminizes women in an increasingly significant fashion.

A comparison of the Puritan companionate marriage and the affectional marriage of the early Republic is instructive here. While both are heterosexual couplings, the logic underwriting this coupling—the discourse of love and marriage—is quite different in each case. As Edmund Leites has shown, the Puritan marriage is far from passionless or asexual: rather, sexual desire for one's spouse was considered an important and beneficial component of marriage. Yet sexual desire was something of an added benefit to the primary aim of companionship within marriage; a Puritan would never, for instance, be urged to choose a partner on the basis of sexual desire or romantic love. Moreover, companionship was defined not simply in terms of temperament but in terms of a sexual division of labor within the household: a Puritan man chose a wife who would be an ideal "helpmeet" in the partnership of marriage. The Puritan Thomas Gataker thus describes the ideal wife in terms of her ability to perform women's work within the household:

> It is no shame or staine . . . for a woman to be housewifely, be she never so well borne, be she never so wealthy. For it is the *womans trade* so to be: it is the end of her *creation*; it is that that she was made for. She was made for man, and given to man, not to be a *play-fellow*, or *a bed-fellow*, or *a table-mate*, onely with him, (and yet to be all these too,) but to be *a yoake-fellow, a worke-fellow, a fellow-labourer* with him, to be *an assistant* and *an helper* unto him, in the managing of such *domesticall and household affaires*.[20]

This description of the companionate marriage clearly argues against a historically prior model of marriage as property brokering. Gataker emphasizes that even the wealthiest woman should not be ashamed to work, thus indicating that what matters in choosing a wife is less the wealth a woman brings to the marriage than her capacity to labor within the marriage. While men and women were considered partners and companions within the Puritan marriage, each had a clear set of sex-specific tasks to perform, and this division of labor organized gender identity in many respects. Sexual desire and mutual affective recognition (being a bed-fellow, a play-fellow, or a table-mate) are all secondary to the division of labor. In contrast, in the affective republican marriage, the division of labor is secondary to heterosexual desire. Individual recognition is what counts in the affectional marriage, as I have argued, but recognition is based in large part on the sex-specific differentiation between husbands and wives: gender is thus imagined as an essential quality of the partner and a primary component of the partner's desirability. Rather than construing compatibility in terms of labor (as is the case with the Puritans), early nationals are directed to construe companionship in terms of the complementarity of masculinity and femininity.

In the many early national texts devoted to the topic of choosing a marriage partner, we thus see masculinity and femininity emerge as qualities that elicit desire. Royall Tyler's 1787 play, "The Contrast," focuses on the question of how to choose an appropriate spouse and the coding of this choice could not be clearer: the main character, Maria, must choose between the British-educated fop, Billy Dimple, and the American-educated Colonel Manly. While the play draws a stark contrast between the British-identified (and vilified) model of marriage for money and social position and the American match based on mutual love and affection, it is worth noting that a primary quality of the winning suitor is not simply his American independence, but the masculinity so clearly announced in his title "Colonel Manly." Moreover, masculinity is defined in the play in terms of a "manly" heterosexual desire for women. One of Billy Dimple's failings is thus his lack of sexualized interest in Maria; indeed, we learn that his name has been Americanized from his father's Dutch surname, "Van Dumpling," suggesting that, like Ichabod Crane, his taste runs more to food than to women, a signal failure for the construction of an essential masculinity. More pointedly, the foppish, Anglophilic beaux of two other women in the play, Charlotte and Letitia, are marked by their effeminacy and absence of heterosexual libido. Charlotte thus opines, "I will say this to the credit of our city beaux, that such is the delicacy of their complexion, dress, and address, that, even had I no reliance upon the honour of the dear Adonises, I would trust myself in any possible situation with them, without the least apprehensions of rudeness."[21] In other words, she has no fear that sexual advances will be made upon her because the city beaux have no inclination in that direction. In contrasting British and American modes of marriage, the play thus signals that heterosexual desire—and the essentialized gender identities of two partners who provoke this desire in one another—is central to the new American marriage.

The shift from the Puritan sexual division of labor within marriage to the early national emphasis on sexual difference as the organizer of marital desire is somewhat subtle, in part because the language of companionship is important to both models of marriage and in part because the sexual division of labor within marriage continues and is even reinforced by the new emphasis on the essentially sexed nature of each partner. Yet despite their similarity, the new discourse of the early national marriage is one that emphasizes recognition by way of sexual difference rather than according to the functional benefits of companionship. As one writer advises wives in 1792, "Every man ought to be the principal object of attention in his family; of course he should feel himself happier at home than in any other place. It is doubtless, the great business of a woman's life to render his home pleasing to her husband; he will then delight in her society, and not seek abroad for alien amusements."[22] While a clear division of labor separates husband from wife in this passage, labor itself is rearranged in terms of the attentive and mutual recognition of manly and womanly behaviors: for instance, cultivating the masculine prerogatives of one's husband (home ownership, patriarchal authority in the home) is seen as desirable insofar as it allows the wife to be appreciated as a producer of an implicitly feminized domestic "delight" (rather than the producer of more prosaic household objects such as food or clothing). Indeed, in the early national period women become increasingly engaged in what Carole Shammas calls "final stage production": the bourgeois woman would, for example, be involved solely in cooking and serving a turkey rather than in raising and slaughtering it as well. The emphasis is thus on woman's role in making the home a "center of sociability"; an important function of sociability, particularly within the home, is the cultivation of individuality, private property, and mutual recognition—forms, that is, of privately organized subject ratification.[23] While this recognition is "individual" in some sense—in its private and intensive nature—it is nonetheless far from wholly individuating insofar as gender and heterosexual desire have become the uniform terms around which mutual recognition is structured.

The gendering of bodies through the institution of marriage and heterosexual desire that I have been tracing corresponds, more generally, to an increasingly essentialized understanding of sexual difference in the early national period. As Carla Mulford, among others, has argued, early nationals seemed intent upon defining gender difference at every point.[24] More broadly, as we saw in the first chapter, Thomas Laqueur points to the eighteenth century as a period when a biological concept of the essentially sexed body gained ground over a more fluid concept of gender as the social manifestation of a divine truth. Laqueur contends that gender shifted from being a "sign" of divine truth to being ontologically grounded in the body. As such, the gendered body itself came to be seen as foundational for social and political orders. In the early American context, Bruce Burgett explains, "No longer one of many phenomena ordered through pre-existing political, ethical, and theological systems, the body becomes the noumenal grounding of existence itself—a point of origin upon which political, ethical, and theological systems are then erected."[25] In related terms, Dana Nelson argues that the propagation of a unifying concept of white masculinity played a role in garnering popular support for the U.S. constitution: the constitution "convincingly and insistently circuited the ideal of political consensus through the similarly common ideal of a vigorous, strong, undivided manhood."[26] As the wealth and depth of research on the institution of a biologically configured, and thus socially sanctioned, gender divide in this period indicates, gender difference coincided with the introduction of liberal political systems—systems that were able to authorize political inequality by locating it in the seemingly nonpolitical territory of gender and race. As this work collectively indicates, liberalism produces individual bodies in newly codified terms (those of gender as well as race) at the moment when the coherence of the social body as a whole (the organicist metaphor) no longer obtains.

Critics and historians who describe consensual marriage of the eighteenth century as equalizing thus miss the force of the bodily *differentiation* written into heterosexual, marital desire. The consensual basis of marriage occurred at a moment when gender became more essentialized, more central to marriage, rather than less so. For instance, while Puritan men might have imagined themselves as "brides of Christ," in a metaphoric subjugation to God, early national men eschewed the feminizing and gender-shifting language of Puritan devotion: in a telling revision of religious rhetoric, the "bride of Christ" gave way to the "soldier of Christ" following the Revolution.[27] "Bride" thus became a term that no longer simply connoted willful subjection, or subjection by way of love: it was a term that connoted an essential and embodied femininity. The "private" marriage narrative—a narrative increasingly about personalized and sexualized desire, and thus seemingly more voluntaristic, affectional, and individualized than ever before—nonetheless was also more thoroughly colonized by a political agenda than previously insofar as it worked to sustain the liberal subject and to produce a binarized sexual division of bodies. The political unit of the family was not an analogy for the Republic, but the resource of liberalism in cementing the reciprocal relation of public and private.

THE MARITAL GOTHIC

With the demise of monarchical authority—an authority long attenuated by colonialism but wholly overthrown during the Revolution—the political identity of the subject became more diffuse and more impersonal. The polity as a whole was no longer conceived of as a hierarchically organized body, and individuals no longer occupied a fixed position within that corporate body. Rather, the polity was understood as a collection of individuals ("the people") who engaged in contracts. The authority to contract—to be constituted as a subject capable of consent—remained important to political identity, yet this authority became increasingly located off the political stage, in the arena of privacy. In other words, the grounds of political identity were increasingly displaced onto social and private functions, such as the forms of social recognition described by Tocqueville in terms of public opinion. I have suggested that one primary form of social recognition is marriage. The marriage relation offers what Luhmann calls an "intensive" relation, one that appears to be personal, though its structuring dimension is above all that of binarized gender and heterosexuality. Thus the marriage of equals, while affectionate, is also a marriage rooted in a developing language of romance linked to sexual difference. If we return, then, to Ichabod Crane, it becomes clear that one of his failings lies in his lack of heterosexual desire: he is disembodied in the new Republic because he fails to occupy a masculine body (like that of Brom Bones) defined in terms of a sexualized desire in relation to Katrina's femininity. As indicated above, one of Crane's failings seems to be his understanding of Katrina primarily in terms of a desire for food rather than sex. Moreover, another ghost mentioned obliquely in the text is that of the British spy, Major John André—a figure, as Caleb Crain has argued, associated with models of masculine sympathy and friendship that clearly compete with the marital, heterosexual organization of desire.[28] From the perspective of the 1820s, then, heterosexual marriage seems to organize the individual body more correctly than does the (now-beheaded) corporate political body or the model of male fraternity and friendship hinted at in the reference to André. As "The Legend of Sleepy Hollow" suggests, the disembodied politics of democracy was compensated for with embodied forms of masculinity and femininity most fully organized in the "private" (though highly structured) form of marriage. When Ichabod disappears at the close of "The Legend of Sleepy Hollow," his absence remains largely unremarked: the narrator concludes that "As [Ichabod Crane] was a bachelor and in nobody's debt, nobody troubled his head anymore about him." Unmarried, and unengaged in the credit economy—that is, lacking credit in both financial and affective terms—Crane vanishes from the horizon because he is neither recognized nor ratified (accredited) by the community.

If Irving's tale suggests that "marital realism" allows us to equate reality with the embodied, heterosexualized, and gendered self, the "Legend of Sleepy Hollow" nonetheless rather tellingly points to a moment when a marital organization of identity had less stability, namely to the 1790s as a period when "marital realism" had not succeeded in organizing the desires of an Ichabod Crane. Despite the fact that, as Jay Fliegelman tells us, marriage was widely promoted as "the highest state of human felicity" in the early Republic, many of the most popular novels written in the 1790s explore the failings of the hetero-sexual marriage plot rather than its successes.[29] Indeed, any number of these novels seem to deal explicitly with the question of how to define marital desire: whom, these texts seem to ask, should one marry, and what is the nature of the desire that links one to a marriage partner? On the one hand, advice literature of the period often describes marriage as a rational coupling with a romantic edge: purveyors of marital wisdom warn against marrying on the basis of beauty or wealth alone, and thus seem to warn against sexualizing desire in favor of establishing friendship as the key component of an enduring marriage. Marriage, according to one account, is "friendship made perfect."[30] Yet even this succinct formula raises some questions: what is imperfect about friendship that requires improvement? What is the nature of this improvement and why is it linked to marriage and heterosexuality? More specifically, to what extent do friendship and sympathy (understood as relations of similarity) structure marriage and to what extent does heterosexual desire (understood in terms of sexual difference) structure marriage? An absence of heterosexual desire or its inappropriate presence is a constant theme of fictional texts of the period, sug-gesting that desire in its marital form has a far more vexed and important sta-tus than much of the advice literature concerning virtue concedes. The 1789 novel *The Power of Sympathy*, often considered the first American novel, con-cerns a woman (Harriot) and her half brother (Harrington) who, unaware of their familial connection, fall in love with one another. As the similarity writ large in their names indicates, likeness seems to be the basis of their compati-bility, but this likeness or sympathy is here diagnosed as fatal once it is revealed to be incestuous: the novel thus traces the conflicted and uncertain boundary between fraternal or sororal sympathy and heterosexual desire as organizing concepts of private identity, recognition, and union.

Few critics of the early American novel have not been struck by the pre-dominance of the themes of seduction and incest—that is, by the interest in derailed marriage plots and misdirected desire—in fiction of this period.[31] Typically the novels of the 1790s concerning seduction and incest have been read by critics as allegories of nation formation: the danger the young heroine faces in the seductive figure of the rake stands as an allegory of the challenge faced by the new nation in maintaining the virtue of its citizenry in their newly liberated state.[32] The allegorical reading proposes a homology between the domestic and the political: what occurs in the drama of courtship and mar-riage is an image of what occurs at the level of the nation and its politics. As such, these critics pursue a line of reasoning similar to that of the historian Jan Lewis concerning the new prominence of affectional marriage in the early

Republic: the family or married couple is taken as an analogue for the nation. Just as I have argued against viewing marriage as the analogue for national politics with respect to Lewis's thesis, so too would I argue that fictional narratives of seduction and incest are not primarily allegorical of nation building. Rather, these novels seem to me to delineate the difficult construction of separate-yet-entwined public and private realms that are dependent for their meaning on their *difference* from one another rather than upon their resemblance. The derailed marriage narratives of the 1790s display an uncertain shift in public understandings of privacy and domesticity, articulated in terms of desire—in terms, that is, that are presupposed to be deeply individual but thus also (at the level of structure) *individuating* and hence important to the construction of the (individuated, contract-making) liberal subject. In the confused and seemingly misdirected vectors of desire that animate these novels, these texts evince the difficulty of coming to terms with the new paradigm of affectional marriage trumpeted as desirable in advice literature. I would suggest, then, that some of the unease displayed in these texts involves the cultural disruption inherent in retraining desire toward politically efficacious liberal models of private life, namely toward the heterosexualized, affectional marriage. Ultimately these novels display, as I suggest in the readings below, the powerful structuring force of a paradigm paradoxically couched primarily in terms of voluntarism.

The popular subgenre of what I will call the "marital gothic" demonstrates these claims by thematizing a dissonance between marital structure and affect.[33] In effect, the fiction of the marital gothic presupposes the structuring efficacy and even necessity of heterosexual marital desire while nonetheless indicating its lack of affective purchase upon the characters of the fiction. Two short stories published in magazines during the 1790s introduce key aspects of the genre. The 1798 story "A Lesson on Sensibility," published in the *Weekly Magazine of Original Essays, Fugitive Pieces, and Interesting Intelligence*, invokes in its title the very heart of the matter, namely the *training* of sensibility or desire. The term "sensibility," as Julie Ellison has argued, has its roots in *masculinized* fellow feeling, that is, in the sympathy shared among men that grew out of new forms of parliamentary politics in late-seventeenth-century England: "Sensibility originates in the political and social importance of affinities other than blood, though it continually feeds back into family stories. Instead of the family, then, gender—masculinity—is the crucial term."[34] According to Ellison, the possibility of parliamentary, or quasi-liberal rather than monarchical, politics requires new kinds of social relations; specifically, a strengthening of horizontal relations between men over and against the vertical relations of hierarchical monarchy. Ellison thus argues that the new language of sensibility—of shared emotion between men—is linked to a political transformation. The language of republican fraternity is exemplary of this sensibility and is readily discernible in a range of early American sentimental texts, as Caleb Crain has demonstrated. Yet in its concern with marital desires, the "lesson on sensibility" of the 1790s is no longer an account of masculine political bonds, but one concerning heterosexual desire. As such, the short story points to something of an affective rupture that might be read in terms of a need to reconfigure "sensibility" away from masculine fellow feeling, toward heterosexual desire—namely, the same rupture narrated in Ichabod Crane's efforts to negotiate between a history of masculine sentimental relations (referenced in the figure of Major André) and a future of heterosexualized marital realism.

"A Lesson on Sensibility" thus begins by focusing on heterosexual romance, though it opens with a fairly standard warning: the central character of the short story, "Archibald," is a man, we are told, who has read too many romances. As a result, he is curiously wedded to love as a subjective state, though not particularly attached to the specific object of his love—an object that is, in any event, fairly transitory: "Though he loved for a time with every appearance of ardour, it was perceived that his affections were easily transferred to a new object and easily dissolved by absence. . . . Provided there was some object to receive his amorous devoirs, it seemed nearly indifferent what the real qualifications of the object were."[35] This account emphasizes the importance of love as a *state* that defines Archibald's subjectivity, though it also criticizes his attachment to love as a code or a structure rather than as an affective and particularized form of attachment to another individual. The events of the story unfold as Archibald trains his amorous attentions upon a young Irish noblewoman, Miss Butler, who (in just the "intensive" fashion described by Luhmann) cares more for the depth of his attention to her than for his wealth or rank and thus returns his affections. However, her family immediately insists upon separating the lovers because of Archibald's lack of pedigree. Archibald is convinced by friends to travel to the West Indies while his beloved is imprisoned by her family. In an effort to dissolve her attachment to Archibald, Miss Butler's family tells her that Archibald has abandoned her for a new mistress in the West Indies. Miss Butler then agrees to marry another man whom her parents have chosen for her, but she is found dead in her room on the morning of the wedding, leaving her family to conclude that she has committed suicide: "Whether some sudden or unforeseen stroke had overtaken her; or, whether she was the author of her own death could never be certainly determined. On the whole the latter opinion was most probable" (75). Archibald, who has indeed proven unfaithful, abandons his new mistress to return to Ireland upon hearing of Miss Butler's death. He insists upon seeing her corpse, whereupon the tomb is opened to reveal the corpse of a woman who has died, not of unrequited love, but of hunger and fear upon being locked inside a tomb: "They beheld the lady, not decently reposing in her coffin, and shrouded with a snow-white mantle, but,—naked, ghastly, stretched on the floor at the foot of the stair-case, with indubitable tokens of having died, a second time, a victim to terror and famine" (75–76). The tale thus offers two accounts of the Irish heiress's death: she (seemingly) dies at her own hand as she refuses to abandon the lover who has abandoned her, and later she dies "a second time" in an access of gothic terror, entombed within a narrative that expects her to expire of unrequited love.

I use this tale to introduce the concept of the "marital gothic" not simply because it invokes gothic conventions such as castles, imprisonment, paternal cruelty, and live burial. While deploying standard gothic tropes, the story also seems in many ways to be *about* the structuring power of convention and thus speaks to my sense that the use of gothic tropes at this moment concerns a point of disconnection between structure and affect.[36] As I have suggested, Archibald is identified from the outset of the narrative as an individual who is attached to the structure of romantic love but not to the individual object of his love: in other words, the structure of romance functions for him without any need of affective connection. The narrative of heterosexual love enables Archibald to produce himself as a certain kind of masculine individual, but his affect is connected to himself rather than to the heterosexual desire that is presumably central to marital romance. It seems worth noting that Archibald is thus not simply a "rake" who pursues women for love of money or sex without a sufficient commitment to romantic or companionate marriage; rather, Archibald is cathected to love itself: "Love . . . was his element: He could not exist without it. To sigh, to muse, to frame elegies, was the business of his life" (72). Nonetheless, in some respects the tale would seem to be a fairly standard account of seduction: the "principled" Irish noblewoman is seduced by Archibald's mastery of the romantic code into believing that his attentions to her matter more than money or rank. Yet the particularly gothic twist of the tale lies in its repetition of the structure-over-subject turn at a second moment in the tale: that is, it turns out that the Irish woman was not, like most seduced and abandoned heroines of the seduction genre, prepared to die for love. The structure of early national marital romance demands that she be so; without the recognition of the beloved, which grants her social recognition as wife or wife-to-be, she might as well be dead. And indeed, her parents are so fully persuaded of the truth of this narrative that they impute to her inert body a tale of seduction and suicide. The revelation that she was not dead when they buried her indicates her parents' fundamental misrecognition of her affective state—a misrecognition that the story imputes to the reader as well—revealing the power of structure over affect again.

The deep irony revealed by the marital gothic is thus that while the code of love is supposed to individuate the subject, it paradoxically proves here to kill the subject because it is precisely not individual but conventional. I mean to indicate a more complex relation than simply one in which convention oppresses or constrains the individual, but rather, to suggest that the very category of the individuated self is produced through overpowering narratives that at certain moments appear more deadly than enabling—which produce corpses rather than properly gendered and affectively connected husbands and wives. Indeed, the paradox of the marital gothic is evident in the double-edged "lesson" of the "The Lesson in Sensibility": on the one hand, the tale would seem to suggest that heterosexual romance is itself deadly (too much novel reading can be fatal), yet on the other hand, it suggests that an ineffectually trained sensibility that failed to attach to the love object caused the problems. In other words, it is not clear from this "lesson" whether Archibald (and the reader as well) has taken the structure of marital romance too seriously or not seriously enough. What is perhaps more clear is that there is a misalignment between structure and affect that raises questions about the individuating power of marital recognition.

A second narrative or anecdote in the gothic vein from the 1790s points, in related terms, to the killing effect of marital desire by describing, quite literally, the production of wives as corpses. The 1799 anecdote, "A New Way of Preserving a Wife," tells of a husband who boasts of developing an excellent new embalming technique that has allowed him to "preserve" an entire closet full of wives. The anecdote opens as the narrator is invited by a friend to visit a man whose wife has just died. While the narrator expresses reservations about visiting a bereaved man "at such a time," he is reassured that the widower "sees every body."[37] And indeed, "seeing" and being seen turns out to be the crux of the anecdote, as well as the crux of the marital relation at stake in the anecdote. The "preserver of wives" is able to make his recently dead wife "look as fresh and as lovely as she did while she was alive"(375), though he confesses that it is important to begin the embalming process "before she is quite cold." To the narrator's complaint that one's wife might not appreciate such treatment, the enbalmer insists that turning life into death has the beneficial and desired effect for both husband and wife of preserving the looks of beautiful women, a cause for which his wives seem quite willing to sacrifice their old age: "*they* cannot but approve of my proceedings; for as their whole time, while living, is spent in endeavouring to make themselves look as well as they possibly can, they must of course be pleased at being in *high preservation* after they are dead. And, indeed, I believe that my two last help-mates were chiefly induced to be united to me, in order to secure a beautiful *posthumous appearance*" (376). The implication is thus that a specular economy conjoins husband and wife: her looks sustain his desire, and his desire sustains her looks. The wife remains the subject of recognition so long as her looks are preserved, and here that desire for recognition is eerily literalized as embalming fluid.

> The younger, therefore, they cease to exist, the handsomer they will consequently look; and no man can frame any objection to the departure of his wife, who will also be ready to die, when she is sure of making a good appearance afterwards.—No man will remain without one; and by gradually improving his collection, he may in time have the satisfaction to see a very agreeable seraglio of mutes. . . . the looks of a wife are sufficient for the generality of husbands, who would be extremely glad to see them, without hearing them. (377)

Marriage, here lampooned as perhaps *not* the state of highest felicity on earth, at least with a spouse who talks back, is described in its more ideal form as a circuit of appearances that enable self-possession. Yet this circuit is literally deadly; while producing the wife as a marital subject, it also kills her, albeit with her consent. In this anecdote, then, marital desire is not so much misdirected, but revealed as itself a murderous structuration of the subject.

In both of these examples of the marital gothic, heterosexual love and marriage seem to be necessary for the production of subjectivity and subject ratification or recognition. At the same time, however, the very affect that is presupposed to animate romantic love is absent in the characters of these fictions, thus revealing the code itself as structure and, more ominously, as a structure that produces recognition at the cost of life itself. Neither tale gestures toward an alternative resolution to the distance between structure and affect, but in pointing to heterosexual desire as itself a deadly social code, the genre of marital gothic may make us ask why heterosexual desire and marriage are understood as such powerful structuring norms. In other words, we might ask, why is heterosexuality a privileged structure of recognition, particularly when it seems so difficult at times to generate the affective charge that would make the circuitry work rather than produce the gothic tale of misaligned structure and affect?

To respond to this question, we might return to the account of a historical shift in modes of desire developed by Nancy Armstrong in a British rather than U.S. context. According to Armstrong, eighteenth-century novels and advice books effect a shift in England in the object of marital desire away from the aristocratic woman toward a new feminine bourgeois ideal: "The new curriculum . . . aimed at producing a woman whose value resided chiefly in her femaleness rather than in traditional signs of status, a woman who possessed psychological depth rather than a physically attractive surface, one who, in other words, excelled in the qualities that differentiated her from the male. As femaleness was redefined in these terms, the woman exalted by an aristocratic tradition of letters ceased to appear so desirable."[38] Armstrong describes a shift in the object of marital desire rather than a shift in the quality or kind of desire associated with marriage (as I have been describing), but she nonetheless associates this change in the object of desire with the more intensive gendering of the female body that I have associated with new marital patterns in the United States as well. For Armstrong, the desirability of the nonaristocratic woman was equated with the quality of femaleness itself. Moreover, Armstrong indicates that the force of this new form of gendering was above all political: by making certain versions of femininity that were not correlated to class status desirable, the new form of desire was subversive of existing class models, and thus effected the political work of bourgeois capitalism: "In distinguishing male from female authority, this representation of social relationships sought to break down the prerogatives that traditionally belonged to a male aristocracy" (41). According to Armstrong, then, "the novel used a thematics of gender to appropriate political resistance" (25). This shift is one oriented toward bourgeois individualism and away from a class system or an ascriptive social order. In effect, Armstrong contends that sex replaces class as the primary social division of bourgeois liberalism; in so doing sex becomes a liberatory tool working against the power of entrenched status relations.

In the context of the early national period in the United States, however, it is difficult to see bourgeois marriage patterns and new forms of marital desire as subversive of an existing class hierarchy, in large part because this old-world class system (rooted in feudal land-holding patterns and the ascriptive social order of political absolutism) did not exist in the United States. This distinction between England and the United States might begin to explain why the narrative of heterosexual desire in the early Republic often looked more ominous and fractured than in English fiction: while Richardson's Pamela uses heterosexual desire to liberate herself from an ascriptive social order and enable her own class mobility, Archibald and the Irish noblewoman find no emotional payoff in liberation from class constraints, but instead discover heterosexual marital romance to be a deadly and coercive code. Without a pronounced, aristocratic class barrier to subvert, then, marital romance appears less libera- tory than coercive. But this perhaps only adds urgency to the question posed above: why does heterosexual marriage gain ground in the United States as a normative form of social ratification at this point? I would suggest that the answer lies in a newly emerged conjunction of three terms: privacy, property, and women. As I argue below, the family, and specifically the heterosexual cou- ple, becomes the primary site of property ownership and the production of privacy: because privacy is central, rather than incidental, to liberalism, white women and "femininity" emerge as key terms in the new social arena config- ured by liberal politics in the early Republic.

LIBERAL OR REPUBLICAN: GENDER, PROPERTY, AND PRIVACY

I have used the term "liberal" to describe the politics and culture of the early national period despite an oft-asserted claim that the era might better be described as republican. Proponents of the "Republican synthesis" have per- suasively argued that the animating political ideals of the American Revolution owed more to a classical republican tradition reinvigorated by English land- holding interests than to the liberalism of John Locke or Jean-Jacques Rousseau.[39] In schematic terms, we might sketch the difference between liber- alism and republicanism as follows: republican politics place the good of the *polis* above all other concerns. Civic virtue, the ultimate aim of the republican citizen, is achieved only by leaving personal (private) interests behind and pur- suing the public good in a disinterested fashion. The liberal, on the other hand, locates the highest "good" in personal freedom rather than in freedom *from* personal concerns and thus sees the protection of private interests (such as pri- vate property) as a primary aim of the public sphere and the state. Historians such as J. G. A. Pocock, Gordon Wood, and Bernard Bailyn have argued that the civic-minded republicanism of the Revolution was replaced by self-interested liberalism by the close of the eighteenth century as a capitalist economy was established in the United States.[40] Feminist historians of the early Republic have also looked to republican politics in order to assess the shifting role of women in the new nation. More specifically, they have sought to demonstrate that republican politics offered women a unique opportunity to participate in a civic agenda.

Although it is certainly true that the language of civic virtue reached a fever pitch during the early national period, I would nonetheless argue that the distinction between liberalism and republicanism is far less sharp than many critics have supposed. Moreover, I would suggest that a focus on the position of women in particular reveals the extent to which liberalism and republicanism are not diametrically opposed but related ideologies during this period.[41] While republican ideas of civic virtue were widely proclaimed, these ideas were mapped onto a liberal social and economic framework characterized by capitalist forms of financial exchange and public sphere representation. Moreover, the appropriation of republican language by women seeking a role in the public sphere often emphasized the private, domestic position of women as mothers and wives rather than their disinterested pursuit of civic virtue. As I suggest in the argument below, then, the elevation of privacy to a matter of civic concern was less consonant with republicanism than with emerging forms of liberal sociality. Further, the representational importance of privacy in an economy based on exchange value worked to generate a status for women as important *signifiers* of privacy and property. With an increased emphasis on heterosexual romance and marriage, women functioned in an exchange economy to represent the private and propertied status of their husbands, a status crucial for establishing masculine autonomy and agency in the newly configured liberal public sphere. Critics and historians have generally argued that as gender divisions became more distinct within American society in the eighteenth century, women were increasingly absented from the public sphere and consigned to private identities. At some level, this is indeed the case, yet if women function as important signifiers of privacy, then they must remain publicly visible, even in their "privacy." As I argue below, then, heterosexual marriage accredits men as citizens, but it relies upon the representational authority of women to do so.

The American Revolution quite obviously effected a dramatic shift in the terms of citizenship and political participation in the United States: no longer subjects of the British monarchy, Americans became voluntary citizens of a nation where political authority derived from "the consent of the governed." At the moment of this reconfiguration in the terms of political identity, the political position of women stood in the balance as well; Abigail Adams famously suggested to her husband that he "remember the ladies" in framing the governing structures of the new nation. Feminist historians of the early Republic seeking to identify the changing political status of women have focused on developing ideas of women as "republican mothers" and "republican wives," arguing that although women were not able to accede to full citizenship or participation in the public sphere, they were able to construe their private, domestic roles as imbued with civic meaning. Republican mothers "did not vote, but they took pride in their ability to mold voting citizens." As Linda Kerber explains, "In the years of the early Republic a consensus developed around the idea that a mother, committed to the service of her family and to the state, might serve a political purpose. Those who opposed women in politics had to meet the proposal that women could—and should—play a political role through the raising of a patriotic child."[42] In similar terms, Jan Lewis argues that women in the home were expected to cultivate virtue as wives and thus assumed a republican mantle despite their lack of participation in civic affairs. Kerber and Lewis thus use the term "republican" to describe a form of private engagement with a national, civic agenda, yet we should note that classical republicanism accords no similar position to women.[43] Indeed, classical republicanism, as Hannah Pitkin points out, has little place for women because they are seen as belonging to the realm of necessity (working in the household to meet primary needs for food and shelter, for instance), and not to the republican realm of freedom and disinterested civic virtue: "From the political ideals of ancient Athens to their recent revival by Hannah Arendt, republican activism seems to be linked to 'manly' heroism and military glory, and to disdain for the household, the private, the personal, and the sensual."[44] Within classical republicanism, women and the household are associated with dependence and necessity rather than with virtue, autonomy, and freedom. This point is well illustrated by an anecdotal description written by Rousseau of a true "republican" mother more interested in civic virtue than the immediate ties of family. Genevieve Lloyd recounts Rousseau's anecdote from *Emile* in the following terms: "A Spartan mother—so goes Rousseau's story—had five sons with the army. A helot arrives with news of the progress of battle. Trembling the mother asks his news. 'Your five sons are slain.' 'Vile slave,' she responds, 'was that what I asked thee?' 'We have won the victory,' comes the amended bulletin. 'She hastened to the temple to give thanks to the god.' 'That,' comments Rousseau, 'was a citizen.' "[45] As Lloyd explains, the story is meant to demonstrate the demands of a disinterested commitment to the public good exacted of the republican citizen—demands that seem directly opposed to the "natural" bond of intimacy between mother and child. For my purposes, the anecdote also illustrates, by way of contrast, the extent to which the early national "republican mother" fails to adhere to the classical republican distinction between private and civic good. The early national republican mother does not abandon private concerns (such as family) in favor of a disinterested commitment to civic virtue; rather, she construes private interests (the raising of virtuous sons) as coterminous with civic virtue.

In spite of the use of the language of civic virtue to describe it, the early national emphasis on the public value of privacy is ultimately more akin to developing liberal theory than to classical republicanism, particularly if we see liberalism less as a form of economic selfishness than as a theory that connects private and public identities in new and complex ways. As I have suggested throughout this chapter, the liberal divide between public and private is less a divide than a tightly connected interdependence in which subjects become visible and recognizable in public because their private identities are highly structured by the desire for public recognition. By way of contrast, republicanism may be seen to insist more stringently upon the divide between public and private insofar as the private, domestic life is precisely what is transcended or left behind in order to participate in the public good. Evidence of the decidedly *liberal* nature of an emphasis on training the future citizens of the nation—and of reaching directly into the privacy of the home and the psyche of the child to do so—is manifest in John Locke's writings on childhood and education. As Gillian Brown has demonstrated, the shaping of private subjects is central to Lockean liberalism: "With the rise of individualism at the end of the seventeenth century comes a newly focussed interest in childhood—in the understanding, teaching, and rearing of the children who are to be liberal subjects."[46] Brown argues that Locke's treatise on education, *Some Thoughts Concerning Education*, was widely influential in colonial and early national America.[47] In this treatise, Locke advocates the training of liberal subjects in the service of forming a nation of citizens able to exercise consent in responsible ways. In Brown's compelling formulation, then, Lockean liberalism should not be seen as antithetical to the language of civic virtue, nor as a theory promoting self-interest over public interest: rather, the training of the self and the care of the self are seen as contributing to the civic good. "Liberalism, as formulated by Locke, registers the connection between personal and political spheres," writes Brown. As such, she concludes, "the civic sense registered by republicanism stems from rather than repudiates Locke's liberal vision" (9). In short, whereas republicanism sees virtue as necessarily public, liberalism posits a private virtue that contributes to the republican aim of civic good.

Rather than understanding the language of civic virtue to mark a sharp dividing line between republicanism and self-interested liberalism, we might thus imagine liberalism to redefine civic virtue as a matter touching upon private as well as public domains. As such, we might view the language of virtue as a bridge rather than a rigid divide between liberal and republican ideologies. The developing importance of privacy (its link with public authority and civic virtue) within liberalism is one I have traced with respect to Puritanism in the previous chapter. As I argued there, privacy, for the Puritans, is defined in terms of an individual relation with God: the authority of this private relation accrued to individuals who had little prestige within the preexisting social hierarchy and contributed to reconfiguring vertical social relations in a more egalitarian fashion. Anne Hutchinson, for instance, was able to use the new authority of her private religious subjectivity to give herself an important public identity, thereby generating attempts to control the production of women's private subjectivity in the congregation and the print public sphere. Whereas an earlier tradition had denigrated and demonized women, viewing them as lesser subjects than men, liberalism proposes that women have an important subjectivity that is potentially equal to that of men. The threat this potential equality poses to a male-dominated social order is met, even in the seventeenth century, less by denying women's subjectivity than by managing its production—by defining women as not wholly lacking in authority, but as resolutely private. By the eighteenth century, the interconnection of public and private spheres shifts such that women's private subjectivity is imbued with a moral good (that of the "virtuous" woman) that has public resonances. In other words, the private status of women is increasingly established, yet so too is the interconnected nature of the private and public spheres. For the Puritans, women's presence in public was itself a violation of order (though one beginning to be authorized by shifting notions of privacy); in the early national period, women's private role was constructed as a public good and we thus begin to see increased emphasis on the moral value of domestic space—on the figure of the virtuous and moral mother. The negative injunction of early modern gender relations— women who appear in public have "stepped out of place"—has become a positive injunction in the early national period: women who remain in the home are virtuous and contribute to the civic good.[48] Yet this "promotion" of women requires an increased emphasis on the difference between masculinity and femininity: women are no longer lesser men, but are wholly distinct and thus "feminized" as never before.

Although privacy may be both more important and more thoroughly associated with a positive version of femininity in the eighteenth century than the seventeenth, an additional seismic shift in definitions of privacy occurs over this period: whereas in the Puritan colonies of New England privacy concerned a relation to God, by the eighteenth century privacy was increasingly defined in terms of property ownership and what C. B. Macpherson has called "possessive individualism." In the late seventeenth century, the basis of the franchise shifted, as I have noted, in Massachusetts Bay Colony such that church members no longer elected government officials, but rather propertied white men did so.[49] Both Helena Wall and Cornelia Hughes Dayton offer vivid accounts of the shift from Puritan communal organization in the northern colonies toward an eighteenth century "embourgeoisement" in which private property came to define the legitimacy and authority of a growing class of individuals. Dayton's extensive research on court cases in the New England colonies demonstrates that the Puritans saw it as their right and duty to monitor the private lives of men and women; by the eighteenth century, however, court-room activity shifted away from the moralistic monitoring of individual behavior toward the administration of property relations in expanding commercial networks.

> After the turn of the century, . . . the constituency served by the courts narrowed to propertied men active in the expanding economy; at the same time the volume of court business was growing exponentially. . . . Along with those trends [expanded trade, larger credit networks, increased desire for luxury goods and "refinement"] came a new ethic of privacy among the emergent bourgeoisie. The social, religious, and political values of the men who breathed life into the legal system no longer called upon them to insist that their dependents or peers submit moral transgressions—slander, premarital sex, drunkenness—to the regulation of the community embodied in the county court. In the area of regulating premarital sexual relations, for example, Connecticut officials moved toward . . . sheltering the middling classes from public scrutiny, humiliation, and penalty.[50]

As Dayton indicates, the development of bourgeois privacy occurred in tandem with the expansion of the exchange economy and the elaboration of legal property rights. If certain forms of religious privacy authorized individuals within Puritan society, it later became property rights—legally associated with men—that defined privacy in the eighteenth century.

The emphasis on property as constitutive of forms of privacy might seem to mirror both certain republican principles (property as the basis of liberty) and the long-standing notion that women are a form of private property belonging to men. But as I suggest below, the liberal conjunction of women, property, and privacy is one that differs significantly from classical republicanism and early modern claims about the necessarily private nature of women and their status as property. Because, as I have argued, privacy matters a great deal within liberalism, it attains public status, and women's privacy thus bears public, political meaning: women begin to appear less as property than as *signifiers* of property and privacy. The shift in women's status from a form of property to a signifier of property and privacy is related in large measure to a fundamental shift in the meaning of property itself that occurs in the eighteenth century: whereas "property" had once primarily consisted of income-producing land, it came to refer to mobile and alienable goods with value in an exchange economy. "The entire revolution," argues Gordon Wood, "could be summed up by the

radical transformation Americans made in their understanding of property."
Whereas property "had been considered in proprietary terms as part of a person's identity and the source of his authority, such proprietary property was
regarded not as the product of one's labor or as a material asset to be bought
and sold in the market but as a means of maintaining one's gentility and independence from the caprices of the market." In contrast, modern property "was
exclusively the product of a person's labor and entrepreneurial skills; it was
commercial, dynamic, and unpredictable and could have little to do with . . .
independence."[51] Modern property is necessarily alienable and its value is
established in the marketplace of consumer desire: within this system of property, as I argue below, women achieved a new form of signifying authority
unrelated to republicanism or the feudal status of women as property belonging to men.

In the passage cited above, Gordon Wood emphasizes the extent to which
the ownership of landed property creates independence whereas commercial
property is linked to dependence. In related terms, J. G. A. Pocock argues that
the great divide within seventeenth-century politics between the backward-
looking thought of classical republicanism and the commercial impulses of liberalism is located in the distinction between landed and mobile property. As we
saw in the first chapter, Pocock contends that landed property gave one liberty
(and thus the capacity for independence and civic-minded virtue), while
mobile property placed one in a dependent relation within a system of
exchange where value hinged upon the fluctuating desires of buyers and sellers. More specifically, Pocock suggests that the developing English system of
credit and banking in the eighteenth century tended to place owners of mobile
property in a dependent relation to government and thus to rob them of the
independence landed property conferred:

> If [seventeenth-century man] found [an] anchor in the shape of land, it guaranteed
> him leisure, rationality and virtue. If he acquired land by appropriation or by inher-
> itance, these things were guaranteed him as part of a natural order. . . . Government
> stock is a promise to repay at a future date; from the inception and development of
> the National Debt, it is known that this date will in reality never be reached, but the
> tokens of repayment are exchangeable at a market price in the present. . . .
> Property—the material foundation of both personality and government—has
> ceased to be real and has become not merely mobile but imaginary. . . . Government
> and politics seemed to have been placed at the mercy of passion, fantasy and
> appetite, and these forces were known to feed on themselves and to be without
> moral limit.[52]

Pocock thus suggests that mobile property makes one dependent both upon
the government and upon a system of exchange, and that this system of

exchange is related to "fantasy" or a representational circuitry that has little anchor in the "real" of real estate and landed property, and far more anchor in the shifting desires of other individual buyers and sellers. While Pocock here describes the economics of seventeenth-century England, he has influentially argued that a strain of this same land-based republican concept of virtue was instrumental in shaping the politics of the U.S. Republic.[53] Indeed, it is precisely the logic outlined here that Wood follows in concluding that commercial property in the colonies "could have little to do with . . . independence."

Despite the theoretical soundness of the claim that mobile property places one in a relation of dependence with respect to the marketplace, I would nonetheless argue (against both Pocock and Wood) that mobile property is often explicitly described as a source of independence and autonomy in early America. First, it seems important to note that landed estates in the colonies and the early Republic never reached the size or profitability of estates in England. As such, the truly leisured, independent property owner who relied upon others to work his land, pay rents, and sustain a lifestyle free of labor never existed in the United States as he did in England.[54] Furthermore, by the time of the Revolution, many large landowners were heavily in debt, and thus far from "independent" from the market. As Isaac Kramnick argues, agrarian interests were themselves less removed from the market than part of it: "it is by no means clear," writes Kramnick, "that the city was perceived in the late eighteenth century as standing for modernity and capitalism and the countryside for reaction and agrarianism. Yeoman farmers operated very much in the capitalist marketplace and had highly developed commercial networks."[55] Secondly, although land was an important form of property in the early Republic, it was nonetheless increasingly subsumed into the category of mobile property—that is, land was viewed as capable of being alienated and sold on the market and thus was no longer seen as distinct from the realm of commerce. Evidence of this transition can be seen in laws framed at the close of the eighteenth century to abolish primogeniture and fee tail tenure (a system of heritable ownership that forbade selling the land on the market), as well as in the widespread practice of real estate speculation. As legal historian John F. Hart points out, many of the members of the Virginia legislature who voted to abolish fee tail tenure themselves "actively bought and sold land for investment purposes," indicating an understanding of land less as a source of independence than as a species of alienable property.[56] Thus while Pocock argues that "the polemic against Alexander Hamilton which Jefferson and Madison conducted in the 1790s was to a remarkable degree a replay of an English polemic which had begun in the 1670s" (67) between (republican) virtue and (liberal) commerce, it seems to me that he has mistaken both the extent to which land was itself a form of commercial property and the extent to which virtue was not a matter of landed property in the United States as it had been in England.[57]

A striking aspect of Jefferson's and particularly Madison's support for the end of primogeniture and fee entail is the use of language describing land as a commodity. The Virginia statute abolishing fee tail states, "The perpetuation of property in certain families, by means of gifts made to them in fee taille, is contrary to good policy, tends to deceive fair traders, who give a credit on the visible possession of estates [and] discourages the holder thereof from taking care and improving the same."[58] In related terms, Madison writes in a letter to Jefferson that abolishing fee tail will foster a "less proportion of Idle Proprietors" in the population. The Virginia statute thus indicates that fee tail tends to disrupt market and credit relations because it is not alienable; more importantly, heritable property encourages "idleness" and lack of labor on the land. Jefferson and Madison's connection of land with both labor and commerce suggest an understanding of property that is far different from that of leisured republican virtue. As Isaac Kramnick has pointed out, classical republicanism is "historically an ideology of leisure" that privileges people who need not work and are thus "independent" of both the marketplace and labor. Liberalism, in contrast, is "at its origin . . . an ideology of work" (1). In Lockean terms, the right to property is one established through labor: by mixing one's labor with the land, one comes to own it. In sharp contrast to the republican view, which sees labor (and commerce) as a form of enslavement that causes a loss of independence, Lockean liberalism describes labor as the basis of mobile property and individual *autonomy*. Set free from the "entails" of inherited landownership, the laboring individual is not limited by an ascriptive social order or the accident of birth, but is able to make his way in the world on the basis of his own capacity to work. "In the world of work," writes Kramnick, "one was the author of self. Individuality became an internal subjective quality; work became a concrete test and property a material extension of self. . . . [In a market society] what one has or gets, and therefore who one is, is no longer the reward appropriate to one's prescribed place; it is what one can get, the product of what one does in the competitive market" (8).

This concept of mobile property, including property in the self and in the labor of the self, seems to predominate even in early discussions of property in the United States. For instance, in the Federalist papers, Madison famously defines the protection of property as the "first object of government." However, the exact wording of his claim concerning property indicates that he associates property with labor rather than with leisured independence. Madison more precisely states that protecting the "faculty for acquiring property" is the first object of government—a phrase that we might gloss as the "capacity to labor." Madison writes, "The diversity in the faculties of men, from which the rights of property originate, is not less an insuperable obstacle to a uniformity of interests. The protection of these faculties is the first object of government. From the protection of different and unequal faculties of acquiring property, the possession of different degrees and kinds of property immediately results; and from the influence of these on the sentiments and views of the respective proprietors, ensues a division of the society into different interests and parties."[59] While Madison is clearly arguing that property need not be equally distributed among all citizens, he nonetheless imagines the origin of disparity in property ownership to be located less in heritable wealth than in individuals' differing abilities to acquire property. His formulation in this document is thus more Lockean than republican: what needs protection from the government is the *capacity* of people to acquire property though their diverse abilities rather than structures of inheritance (such as primogeniture and fee tail) through which property had traditionally been held in England.[60]

How, then, do we reconcile liberal concepts and structures of property ownership with the apparently republican language of civic virtue that dominated public discourse in the early national period? One means of doing so is to pursue the suggestion I have made above, namely, to consider the language of civic virtue as one that is effectively appropriated and transfigured by liberalism, despite its classical republican origins. The essence of this transfiguration lies in the civic value ascribed to private and personal activity within liberalism. Isaac Kramnick traces one shift in the meaning of civic virtue to Protestant sources: the Protestant work ethic equated labor with virtue and morality, and thus allowed Lockean liberals to imagine labor not simply as a self-interested economic pursuit, but as a civic contribution.[61] Yet I would suggest that we can locate a more decisive transvaluation of the language of virtue in the pervasive influence of Scottish Enlightenment philosophy on early national thought. As a number of historians, and particularly historians of gender, have argued, the philosophy of the Scottish Enlightenment found fertile ground in the United States because of its focus on integrating the social realities of the commercial marketplace with moral philosophy.[62] Nicholas Phillipson argues that Scottish philosophers ventured in this direction following the 1707 Act of Union with England that curtailed Scottish political independence while granting Scotland unfettered access to English markets around the globe. While overt *political* forms of freedom (such as constitutionalism) were thus foreclosed to the Scots,

Scottish thinkers turned to the sphere of the market and social relations to elaborate alternative understandings of liberty and virtue. These thinkers believed that "Scotland's independence could best be preserved by strengthening the economic and moral bonds of Scottish society. And the act of participating in such a process would be sufficient to release the virtue of the patriot."[63] The resultant language of civic morality, according to Phillipson, "was of peculiar interest to those provincial communities which had sprung up in the commercial age" (202), such as, we might conclude, the British colonies of North America.[64] The central claim of Scottish theorists thus concerned the moral value of market relations: in a reversal of civic humanism, Scottish philosophers argued that the market was a site of freedom rather than dependence and the location of civilizing moral influences rather than corruption. The market, they proposed, allowed one to expand one's horizon of social and economic interaction, freeing one from the limitations of local dependency. Moreover, and perhaps more importantly, commerce exerted a civilizing influence upon those who participated in it, as their manners and ideas were refined through contact with and influence of others. William Robertson thus argued that, "Commerce tends to wear off those prejudices which maintain distinction and animosity between nations. It softens and polishes the manners of men. It unites them, by one of the strongest of all ties, the desire of supplying their mutual wants. It disposes them to peace."[65] In similar terms, the Scottish philosopher John Millar describes commerce as promoting social intercourse and moral development: "In a commercial country . . . individuals form their notions of propriety according to a general standard and fashion their morals in conformity to the prevailing taste of the times. By living much in society, and maintaining an intimate correspondence, they are led also to a frequent and ready communication of their thoughts and sentiments . . . [and to] accommodate their behaviour to the disposition and temper of their company." Increase in commerce thus "diffuse[s] a spirit of liberty and independence" as well as teaches virtue according to Millar.[66] According to the Scottish thinkers, then, participation in market relations enabled a liberation from relations of dependence, promoted a capacity for choice and discrimination, and enabled a moral self-fashioning in relation to public norms of propriety.

Pocock succinctly describes the Scottish commercial account of virtue as a move to locate virtue in the *social* rather than political realm—in civility rather than civic-mindedness:

> Edinburgh saw a proliferation of Spectatorial clubs and societies, practicing the virtues of polite conversation and enlightened taste while discussing the economic, cultural and even—given an age in which manners seemed no unimportant part of

morality—the moral improvement of Scottish life. The locus of virtue shifted decisively from the civic to the civil, from the political and military to that blend of the
economic, cultural and moral which we call the social for short.[67]

Pocock's account here resembles—at the sociological level—a Habermasian
description of a public sphere that arose in coffeehouses, clubs, and journals
such as the *Spectator*. And while David Shields has brilliantly documented the
extensive and vibrant civil space of clubs and societies in the eighteenth century United States, Pocock nonetheless argues that the Scottish account of commercial virtue had no bearing on the United States in the eighteenth century.[68]
Yet other scholars have demonstrated the strength of the Scottish influence on
the United States, an influence conveyed in no small measure through the
important role of Scottish immigrants in shaping the curriculum of American
academic institutions. The work of Scottish philosophers was widely taught in
American universities, and many of those teaching this material were themselves trained in Scottish universities: thus Thomas Jefferson, for instance,
studied mathematics and natural philosophy with a progressive Scottish pro-
fessor at the College of William and Mary from 1740 to 1742.[69] As the historian
Forest McDonald contends, it may thus be useful to think about the Scottish
Enlightenment as a mediating term in the polarized debate between civic
humanist and Lockean accounts of the politics of the early Republic.[70] Lori
Merish's discussion of the influence of the Scottish thinking on the early
Republic similarly emphasizes the mediating role that Scottish civility plays in
linking public and private notions of virtue: "While civic humanists insisted on
a strict distinction between public and private spheres, the Scots qualified that
distinction by delineating a group of mediating institutions—most prominently, commerce, property, and the family—through which individuals are
'civilized,' 'socialized,' and otherwise prepared for civil society."[71] For my purposes, the Scottish emphasis on the "social" as opposed to the political or private provides a way to theorize the link between politics and the formation of
private subjectivity; as such, it helps to make visible the organizing force of
"sociality" in liberal capitalist society.

In many respects, the Scottish emphasis on the importance of developed
"social" spaces to morality and liberty coincides with a Habermasian account
of the public sphere: that is, in the emphasis on the importance of clubs,
Spectatorial societies, and social and intellectual intercourse, Scottish moral
theory seems similar to Habermas's account of the importance of the civil
sphere in the exercise of liberty. Millar, for instance, describes the formation of
economic interest groups in towns that are able to exercise a monitory control
over the government: "The voice of the mercantile interest never fails to com-

mand the attention of government, and when firm and unanimous, is even able to control and direct the deliberations of the national councils" (339). But the Scottish account has a far different accent than Habermas's account of the liberal public sphere: for the Scots, social interaction concerns the formation of the moral or "polished" subject rather than the development of rational-critical debate. In their emphasis upon subject formation ("civility," "polishing," "refinement"), the Scots articulate the basis of what I have called a *public sphere of desire* rather than a public sphere of reason. In using the term "desire" rather than reason, I mean less to argue for libido over logic than to suggest that something like an *ontological desire* subtends any debate within the public sphere itself, including the most reasonable of debates that transpire there. This ontological desire is, simply put, the desire to *be* a subject. And this desire is gratified only when an individual is recognized as a subject, or "socially ratified" in such a way that he or she can appear as a subject to others. Among the Scottish thinkers, Adam Smith's dual line of inquiry into the topics of sentiment and economics most clearly articulates the market-based nature of social ratification and thus of subject production that occurs in and through the liberal public sphere. According to Smith, the basis of morality lies in the individual's capacity to engage in social commerce with the sentiments and judgments of others. As we saw in the first chapter, according to Smith, a moral individual is shaped by his internalized understanding of a judging spectator located in the public or social sphere of commercial society:

> We either approve or disapprove of the conduct of another man according as we feel that, when we bring his case home to ourselves, we either can or cannot entirely sympathize with the sentiments and motives which directed it. And, in the same manner, we either approve or disapprove of our own conduct, according as we feel that, when we place ourselves in the situation of another man, and view it, as it were, with his eyes and from his station, we either can or cannot entirely enter into and sympathize with the sentiments and motives which influenced it. We can never survey our own sentiments and motives, we can never form any judgment concerning them, unless we remove ourselves, as it were, from our own natural station, and endeavor to view them as at a certain distance from us. But we can do this in no other way than by endeavouring to view them with the eyes of other people, or as other people are likely to view them.[72]

One achieves propriety and, indeed, virtue, through shaping the self in response to the dictates of the "impartial spectator"—a fictional version of the person who stands watching us.[73] What is striking about this formulation of the virtuous self is its relation to the marketplace where the value of any object is determined by the opinion of the consumer, as Smith insists in his explanation of the equalizing laws of economics in *The Wealth of Nations*. "Propriety" or moral sentiment is thus something of a market commodity as Jean-Christophe Agnew has argued: "What was sympathy in this context but an ultimate commodity: a universal equivalent into which all other goods could be converted? And what was the self in this context but a speculative fiction of joint manufacture: a venture, a text, a performance in which all spectators, investors, and consumers were invited, albeit obliquely to subscribe?"[74] Agnew's language, like Pocock's cited earlier, points to the fictive nature of commercial society, but I would also emphasize the intersubjective nature of that fiction: the fiction of the speculative self is not merely a fantasy but a collective one that, as a result, has very real effects. Smith's theory of sentiment thus delineates the reconstructive possibilities of market culture: one shapes oneself in relation to a judging public in order to receive recognition or sympathy even if from an internalized version of this public. The emphasis on civilization, that is, on the reciprocal effects of the market upon the self, shows that the market shapes the individual rather than simply allows the unconstrained pursuit of commercial gain. The subject is transformed by a shared social fantasy of morality and value: the market thus "refines" and "civilizes" in a manner not dissimilar to the refining character of Habermas's rational-critical debate in the public sphere. Yet the public sphere of Adam Smith and John Millar is one constituted around human desire or interest rather than reason. If we return, then, to the notion of the public sphere advanced at the beginning of this chapter, we can see how the process of social ratification I have been attempting to describe is embedded in the marketplace and a public sphere defined as social as much as civic.

Within the public sphere of desire—the marketplace of commodities and propriety described by Adam Smith—women hold a particularly elevated position according to the Scottish thinkers. In the four-stage, conjectural history proposed by Scottish thinkers—a model that traced the progress of society in four steps from hunting to pasturage to agriculture to commerce—women's position in society served as an index of social progress. John Millar's conjectural history, *Origin of the Distinction of Ranks*, opens with the chapter "Rank and Condition of Women in Different Ages," indicating the centrality of women to concepts of civility. According to Millar and, more generally, concepts of conjectural history, the position of women evolved toward equality as society itself progressed toward a more civilized state: more specifically, in the most "polished" or progressive societies, women occupy a central position as individuals who encourage the refinement of manners and civility. Millar thus writes that in the most advanced stage of society, women are

encouraged to quit that retirement which was formerly esteemed so suitable to their
character, to enlarge the sphere of their acquaintance, and to appear in mixed company, and in public meetings of pleasure.... As they are introduced more into public life, they are led to cultivate those talents which are adapted to the intercourse of
the world, and to distinguish themselves by polite accomplishments that tend to
heighten their personal attractions, and to excite those peculiar sentiments and passions of which they are the natural objects. (224)

Interestingly, Millar contends that women assume a more public position
(quitting the "retirement" or privacy of the home associated with manual
labor) in the most civilized commercial societies in contrast to their private
position in more primitive ones. Indeed it is precisely women's public status—
their "commerce" with society—that enables them to spread a civilizing influence on those around them. The public role that Millar prescribes for civilized
women is not political but civil. Woman's public role is associated with the
social status of wife and mother, not with the status of citizen or political agent.
Nonetheless, this civil position is eminently *public* and may help to illuminate
women's public position in the literary public sphere as distinct from a
Habermasian public sphere of rational-critical debate.

The currency of these ideas concerning women in the United States is evident in the American popularity of books such as James Fordyce's *The
Character and Conduct of the Female Sex*, which is subtitled, *The Advantages to
Be Derived by Young Men from the Society of Virtuous Women*. As research by
Rosemarie Zagarri demonstrates, the Scottish understanding of the four-stage
theory of history and woman's role as civilizer "permeated American writings"
in the second half of the eighteenth century. Zagarri thus astutely points out
that the figure of the "republican mother" may be better said to have Scottish
rather than civic humanist parentage.[75] The republican mother has precisely
the "civilizing" influence on the men of her household described in the conjectural theory of history. Her role lies at the intersection of public and private
identities—in the important social (and moral) realm delineated by Scottish
enlightenment thought. Similarly, I would suggest that the emphasis on volitional, affectional marriage (and thus the "republican wife" paradigm) owes
much to Scottish philosophy of the social as well. Significantly, the model of
affectional marriage is an account of family formation that breaks with the patterns of primogeniture in which inheritance laws and marriage patterns were
aimed at maintaining large acreages of landed property, and corresponds,
rather, to a commercial society in which property is no longer primarily a matter of heritable real estate but is transactional and capitalist. In terms of family formation, the shift to a model of mobile property and labor meant that

freedom consisted in freedom *from* heritable property—not the freedom (leisure) accorded by inheritance—and this points as well to new models of family formation in the realm of market society.

The importance of this new model of capitalist family formation (and the new role of women within it) suggests that we may want to interpret the domestic dramas of early American fiction in a new light. Specifically, it seems worth questioning the predominance of the "people are Clarissa" paradigm in which eighteenth-century narratives of seduction are viewed as allegorical warnings to the new American nation of the need to maintain civic "virtue." In a striking alternative to this model, Leonard Tennenhouse suggests that the figure of the libertine—a figure who stands at the heart of the seduction narrative—may serve less as a threat than an *exemplar* for American readers once we understand that what is at stake in these early novels is the development of new models of family formation. In his comparative analysis of the figure of the libertine in U.S. and English fiction of the eighteenth century, Tennenhouse highlights the different models of family formation implied by differing models of property ownership on either side of the Atlantic. In British fiction, the libertine is irredeemable, whereas in the United States, the libertine can and often is recuperated into marriage and thus founds a new family:

> In contrast with British domestic fiction, American seduction stories condemn neither the seducer nor the woman seduced so much as the underlying cause of seduction, which it attributes to the disparity between desire and economic necessity. The American libertine finds himself trapped by the prevailing system of exchange, which neither provides a solid economic foundation for a family nor gratifies his sexual desire. . . . Indeed, the object of libertine desire is generally virtuous . . . and she arouses something like natural desire in him. . . . The omnipresence of the libertine as the embodiment of masculinity creates a situation hostile to an earlier system of arranged marriages implicitly if not explicitly attributed to the British.[76]

On Tennenhouse's reading, then, the American libertine enacts a form of liberation from traditional rules of property inheritance: that is, he eschews the landed property model in favor of "natural desire"—a natural heterosexual desire for a virtuous women who will enable him to found an American family based on labor and mobile property. While Tennenhouse does not comment on the heterosexual bent of this desire, I would supplement his claims regarding family formation with the observation that the libertine's role is in part to establish the very naturalness of heterosexual desire (particularly as provoked by the virtuous woman). The libertine's masculinity and heterosexuality thus begin to qualify him as a suitable husband under the rules governing early U.S. marriage, and, more importantly, his desire to break free of a structure of heritable property and status (in the name of natural desire) shows him to be a candidate for new forms of family formation. The new, more "worthy" U.S. family, as Tennenhouse argues, locates value in (masculine) labor and (feminine) taste rather than inheritance. As such, the key to reforming the American libertine is less to break him of his wicked sexual ways than to reform him from a leisured aristocrat into a working man. In a text such as Judith Sargent Murray's serialized *Story of Margaretta*, we see precisely this transition held up as exemplary: under the benevolent tutelage of Margaretta's parents, the libertine is transformed once he is made to understand that his natural desire for a virtuous woman must be coupled with a willingness to labor to support her. Tennenhouse's analysis thus usefully points to the way in which the figure of the libertine serves an important function in early American fiction in *establishing* the new family formation, not in threatening American virtue. The seducer is thus not an allegory of the threat to American virtue, but a model for the way in which unconstrained, "natural" heterosexual desire can be promoted as a means of restructuring the family. The choice of a spouse (on the basis of sexual desire rather than property management) thus becomes an index of freedom. More importantly, the unpropertied libertine becomes propertied by way of his desire for a woman with taste and virtue: that is, he discovers that her civility and taste call for his labor, and thus her femininity endows him with a new masculine capacity for property ownership (in the form of labor) that he had previously failed to recognize when he (mistakenly) understood property primarily as heritable real estate. A virtuous wife thus becomes the signifier of natural masculinity and of the civic identity of an autonomous male.

Further testimony to the status of women as "signifiers" of a new (commercial) version of masculine autonomy and propriety is found in the shifting terms of political enfranchisement in the early Republic. Following the Revolution, citizenship was reconfigured in terms of voluntary, contractual relationships (as opposed to hierarchical relations of dependence) that presupposed independence as a key qualification for citizenship. Joan Gunderson argues that the quality of "independence" necessary for citizenship was initially defined in a number of ways, but by the close of the century, gender became a central element in defining the term. She cites Thomas Jefferson, who writes in 1776, "I was for extending the right of suffrage (or in other words the rights of a citizen) to all who had a permanent intention of living in the country. Take what circumstances you please as evidence of this, either the having resided a certain time, or having a family, or having property, any or all of them"[77] Jefferson's argument about citizenship reproduces the civic humanist notion that property enables one to vote independently, yet in her analysis of this passage, Gunderson underscores the extent to which a propertied status is linked to the condition of being a married man. For instance, Jefferson's definition of independence describes owning real estate and having dependents (a wife and children) as equal signs of independence: "For men," writes Gunderson, "independence was essential, and they could enhance their independence by stressing the dependence of others (including women) on them" (75). Following the Revolution, Gunderson contends, there is a "growing emphasis on women as dependents" (66). Particularly telling evidence in this regard is the example of New Jersey voting laws that allowed propertied (single or widowed) women to vote from 1776 to 1807, but subsequently eradicated the right of women to vote while expanding the franchise for unpropertied white males: "The new election law increased the white male voting population and eliminated female voting. To do so, the legislature had to redefine dependency status to exclude all white men and include all white women. . . . Redefining dependency as a sex-specific trait transformed dependent males into independent voters, while subsuming single women, who were in every practical sense independent, into a category of dependence. . . . The legislature simply redefined dependency as gender specific" (66). Gunderson's historical evidence thus points to the way in which women served as signifiers of the propertied, and thus independent, status of their husbands while they themselves were increasingly defined as private and lacking in the independence necessary for public participation regardless of the amount of property they owned. Property thus no longer freed one from the necessities of life to become a civic humanist; rather, the private identity associated with bourgeois masculinity signified one's freedom and civility.

Gunderson's argument demonstrates the way in which the privatization of femininity apparently entailed the exclusion of women from political participation. As we have seen, the eighteenth century granted women subjectivity, but only at the price of defining women as essentially female and essentially private. A great deal of scholarship, such as that by Gunderson, has demonstrated the extent to which women became placeholders for dependence as a means of establishing, by way of distinction, masculine independence following the Revolution. Toby Ditz argues, for instance, that "In the eighteenth century, a man who was not a master—that is, not the head of a household or 'family' of dependents—was not a full member of the civil community of adult men. Civil manhood meant mastery."[78] Ditz indicates that marital status was crucial for establishing independent masculinity in the early Republic. Yet her language implies that mastery of women at home is what established masculine identity outside the home: Ditz thus follows Carole Pateman's influential claim that the oppression of women in the family seems to enable the equality of men outside the family.[79] Without wholly disputing these claims, I would nonetheless like to point to a shift in emphasis that offers a new glimpse of the workings of the public/private divide. Specifically, I would argue that once we understand the signifying power of women with respect to constructions of masculinity, we can also see that women's "private" status is a matter of eminently public domain. In other words, while women may be prevented from voting and thus from participating in the public sphere defined in terms of political enfranchisement, in other terms they remain distinctly public insofar as the capitalist family requires their "sociality" to establish property rights and masculine identity. The example of the civil sphere described by Scottish Enlightenment thinkers, and the important role of women therein, makes visible a public sphere defined not simply in terms of voting rights or even rational-critical debate, but defined in terms of signifying authority and subject ratification.

The enormous amount of literature produced in the late eighteenth century—articles, pamphlets, conduct books, stories, and novels—devoted to the issue of woman's civilizing effect upon man and to consensual marriage indicates the extent to which new models of gendered identity were an important aspect of the literary public sphere in the new Republic. Women's participation in this literary public sphere as both writers and textual figures is testified to at the turn of every page. Scholars have generally emphasized the severely limiting dimensions of the increasingly privatized identity of women in the early Republic. Betsy Erkkila, for instance, laments the extent to which the language of equality for women was coupled with agonizing limitations: Erkkila reports that while the first issue of *The Lady's Magazine* in 1792 excerpts passages from Wollstonecraft's *A Vindication of the Rights of Women*, it nonetheless includes in the preface the claim that women's education is primarily in the service of forming "the greatest of all treasures—a GOOD WIFE."[80] Yet the "privacy" established here is far different from the private identity of individuals before the creation of the liberal public sphere: privacy and domesticity confer social identity within liberalism and as such are not linked solely with erasure and voicelessness. Rather, as I've suggested, privacy is intimately linked to publicity—to a signifying force that admits one to the realm of subject ratification. The privacy afforded the bourgeois white woman gave her a status and a public identity rarely accorded to a slave or Native American woman who lacked this privacy. When we view white femininity in terms of sociality, we can see that liberalism in this period does not entail locking women away in the private sphere, but weaving a dense set of interconnections between the public and the private. As such, the "privacy" of women is never precisely private (for better or worse), but rather in constant exchange with public representations and forms of social ratification occurring in the medium of print culture.

'EDGAR HUNTLY' AND FEMINIZED PROPERTY

Although most scholarship emphasizes women's lack of property rights in the eighteenth century (particularly under the legal system of coverture), literature from this period concerning what I have described as the new (capitalist) family formation on occasion portrays a diametrically opposed view: that is, a number of novels describe the *centrality* of women and their signifying power to property ownership. In Charles Brockden Brown's 1799 novel *Edgar Huntly Or, Memoirs of a Sleep-Walker*, the eponymous main character's marked incapacity to retain property is clearly linked to his inability to follow the heterosexual narrative path (what I will call the *heteropathic* narrative) of "natural" masculine desire for virtuous women that is repeatedly laid out before him in the text. In the opening pages of the epistolary novel, we learn that Edgar Huntly is writing a letter to his fiancée, Mary, the sister of his recently murdered friend, Waldegrave. While the letter itself testifies to Huntly's attempt to engage himself in a marital (and, as we later learn, propertied) design for his future, the contents of the letter rather immediately announce the allure, for Huntly, of an alternative path. Huntly—a well-educated young man living in Pennsylvania with no visible means of financial support—devotes this lengthy letter (which constitutes the bulk of the novel) to describing the bizarre and tortuous course of events that have befallen him since his recent return home from a visit to Mary, since, that is, his decision to strike out headlong on an "obscure path" not directed homeward and to "procee[d] in this new direction with speed."[81] The net result of following this alternative route will ultimately prove to be the demise of Huntly's engagement to Mary. Like Ichabod Crane, however, Huntly seems to effect his own erasure at the moment when he definitively rejects marital alliance with either Mary or another potential wife (Clarice), whose hand is proffered to him at the close of the novel. In each case, marriage would entitle him to a form of social visibility *and* entitle him to money and property: in each case, he rejects the signifying authority that the married state would confer upon him, with the result that he effectively disappears from the horizon of social visibility at the close of the novel.

I use the term "heteropathic" to reference the progressive, narrative force that heterosexual courtship and marriage assume as well as the undesirable and violent face marriage presents in the text. While "heteronormative" is the

critical term coined by theorists to describe the normative force of heterosexuality in contemporary culture, I use the term "heteropathic" because the novel
Edgar Huntly (like the marital gothic genre) seems to antedate the historical
moment at which heterosexuality came to fully saturate cultural norms of subjective (and political) identity. In the 1790s, as novels such as *Edgar Huntly* and
The Coquette (which I discuss at the end of this chapter) indicate, heterosexual marriage was only in the process of becoming sentimentally yoked to politically and socially dominant ideas of subjectivity as fully as it would subsequently be in the nineteenth century. Indeed, the interesting aspect of these
novels is precisely their lack of affective investment in marriage, exemplified in
the seemingly perverse inability or refusal of characters to invest the marriage
narrative with sentimental plenitude. Rather, we see marriage represented in
these texts as a particularly powerful, but far from natural, route to social
recognition and the production of subjectivity. As such, the term "heteropathic" is meant to denote the unnatural and perhaps disfiguring force that the
marriage narrative seems to exert in the presentimental eighteenth-century
texts of liberal family formation. I thus read both *Edgar Huntly* and *The
Coquette* as exploring the ways in which public and private identities are
linked, for better and for worse, through the civil institution of marriage.

Edgar Huntly, like many of Charles Brockden Brown's novels, is often
described as a literary failure. Huntly's initial address to his fiancée suggests to
the reader that a courtship plot will determine the course of the narrative:
alternatively, the mystery surrounding Waldegrave's death indicates that detection and revelation may structure the narrative as well. Yet both of these narrative paths are quickly abandoned, and the reader must instead follow Huntly
on a bizarre journey into the wilderness that seems to have little rhyme or reason. In its abandonment of a recognizable novelistic plot such as the marriage
narrative, the novel presents itself as problematic, as difficult to follow or invest
in for the reader. Yet as I argue in my reading below, Huntly quite deliberately
abandons the path to marriage in favor of trying to secure forms of political
subjectivity and embodiment unrelated to capitalist family formation. The
scriptlike quality of the marriage narrative is one that Edgar Huntly clearly fails
to subscribe to: rather, marriage is a path that Huntly repeatedly chooses to for-
sake. As I've indicated, the opening pages of the novel find Huntly striking out
for the hills, choosing a route that is clearly seen as divergent with respect to
the courtship scenario he has begun to enter into with Mary. The "new direction" Huntly initially chooses (when he forsakes the direct route from Mary's
house to his own domicile) is one that leads him to the scene of his dead
friend's murder. It is, in this respect, an old direction, representing a return to
the keening emotions of grief and desire for vengeance that he felt upon

Waldegrave's death, a time when he was "deaf to the dictates of duty and discretion"—a time he now associates with "shame and regret" (8). Huntly draws a clear opposition between his association with Mary, during which time these shameful feelings are "suspended" (a time in which duty and discretion thus presumably do reign), and the raging emotions associated with Waldegrave and his death. Yet on his midnight journey homeward he suffers a "relapse into folly" and finds it "requisite to leave" (8) the direct route home. "I was familiar with the way [to the scene of the murder]," writes Huntly, "though trackless and intricate" (9). Yet when he arrives at the elm tree where Waldegrave was killed, Huntly discovers neither the body of his friend nor clues to his murder, but the body of a different man—one wholly unknown to him. The partially clothed man he spies digging beneath the tree nonetheless exercises a compelling force upon him: "A figure, robust and strange, and half naked, to be thus employed at this hour and place, was calculated to rouse up my whole soul," he writes (10). More tellingly still, Huntly feels compelled to pursue this (still unknown) man whose path into the wilderness will prove decidedly more "trackless and intricate" than Huntly's initial course. When the man begins a journey into the wilderness at night, Huntly follows in hot pursuit:

> [The unknown man] . . . proceeded along an obscure path, which led across stubble fields, to a wood. The path continued through the wood, but he quickly struck out of it, and made his way, seemingly at random, through a most perplexing undergrowth of bushes and briars. . . . The way that he had selected, was always difficult; sometimes considerable force was requisite to beat down obstacles; sometimes, it led into a deep glen, the sides of which were so steep as scarcely to afford a footing; sometimes, into fens, from which some exertions were necessary to extricate the feet, and sometimes, through rivulets, of which the water rose to the middle. . . . Where, said I, is this singular career to terminate? Though occupied with these reflections, I did not slacken my pursuit. (18–19)

I quote the description of this "path" at length to give a flavor of the text's interest in the physical, topographical details of the arduous, uncharted terrain that Huntly covers once he chooses this new route, as well as what seems to be his excessive, undermotivated dedication to this pursuit. In subsequent pages, we learn that the man he pursues is the sleepwalking Clithero, an Irish immigrant who has a traumatic past, which he later reveals to Huntly. Yet upon learning his identity and story, Huntly only becomes more persistent in his pursuit of Clithero, now with the apparent aim of affording Clithero sympathy rather than discovering his identity. The detailed descriptions of the fantastic geographical territory—darkened caves, precipitate cliffs, unplumbed gorges, raging cataracts, hidden glens, inaccessible summits, and twisting tunnels—that Huntly traverses at great bodily peril in his dedication to Clithero fill page upon page of the novel.

In contrast to his monumental physical commitment to placing his body near Clithero's, Huntly's investment in moving toward marriage with Mary seems slight. Indeed, he not only figuratively chooses a path diverging from marriage at the outset of the novel, but he later more literally consents to abandoning the marriage when a further pretext (in the form of yet another unknown, sympathetic male body) presents itself. After having described the many miles covered in his repeated pursuits of Clithero, Huntly recounts that a strange man arrives at his door, claiming to be an old friend of the murdered Waldegrave. More importantly, this man (Weymouth) claims to be a creditor of Waldegrave's. According to Weymouth, Waldegrave had consented to hold $7,500 for him while he was engaged in commercial activities abroad. After shipwreck and prolonged illness in Europe, Weymouth returned to collect the funds, only to find that Waldegrave was dead and that no written record of his loan to Waldegrave existed. Despite a complete lack of concrete evidence supporting Weymouth's claim, Huntly rather astoundingly believes his tale immediately and thus tells Mary that she must give Weymouth the money she has inherited from her brother. His rapid decision that the money must be given to Weymouth is even more surprising (or suspect), given that he makes it clear that the $7,500 Mary had inherited from her brother is requisite to funding her impending marriage to Huntly and their planned life together. "Our flattering prospects are now shut in," Huntly writes to Mary.

> You must return to your original poverty, and once more depend for precarious subsistence on your needle. . . . [W]edlock is now more distant than ever. My heart bleeds to think of the sufferings which my beloved Mary is again fated to endure, but regrets are only aggravations of calamity. They are pernicious, and it is our duty to shake them off. I can entertain no doubts as to the equity of Weymouth's claim. (149)

A number of points seem worth noting here: first, while Huntly presents the impossibility of their marriage in imperative terms, these imperatives are dictated solely by his choice to credit the unsupported claims Weymouth makes to the money Waldegrave held in his bank account upon his death. As such, the "equity" that Huntly grants seems dictated by the sympathy he feels for Weymouth rather than sympathy that he might reasonably be expected to feel for his fiancée. Second, the potential inequity of the "credit" he immediately extends to Weymouth—and his decision to thus perpetually postpone if not cancel marriage plans with Mary—is further evident in the suggestion in Weymouth's tale that Mary may be living in the country at the moment because she is pregnant with Huntly's child. Why, then, does he choose to immediately credit Weymouth's needs rather than Mary's, and, indeed, to thereby sabotage his own claims to a married and propertied state?

Although the answer to this question is in no way immediately evident, we can determine that Huntly's sympathy for Weymouth is produced, as with Clithero, in terms quite dependent upon physical proximity: "But what wilt thou think of this new born claim?" writes Huntly to Mary. "The story, hadst thou observed the features and guize of the relater, would have won thy implicit credit. His countenance exhibited deep traces of the afflictions he had endured and the fortitude which he had exercised. He was sallow and emaciated, but his countenance was full of seriousness and dignity. A sort of ruggedness of brow, the token of great mental exertion and varied experience, argued a premature old age" (147). The "equity" he dispense thus hinges, I would suggest, upon the sympathetic and quite physical identification or *equality* he feels with another male body—in this case, that of Weymouth. The power of this physical identification with another male body is one that we can only assume exerts a surpassingly strong influence upon Huntly. In choosing to identify with Weymouth, Huntly not only abandons Mary but ultimately deprives himself of any hope of becoming propertied: currently living with his uncle, he explains that upon his uncle's death, his cousin will inherit the home, "the first act of whose authority will unquestionably be to turn [me and my sisters] from these doors" (149). In abandoning his marital alliance with Mary, Huntly thus also abandons any possibility that he will attain a propertied state. Nonetheless the decision on Huntly's part to pursue a path recommended by the physical proximity of male bodies is one that he makes repeatedly throughout the novel. The pattern of abandoning the heterosexual marriage narrative in favor of masculine sympathy is only confirmed at the close of the novel, when Huntly rejects the offer of an Irish heiress's hand in marriage in favor of offering his sympathies, once more, to Clithero, despite increasing evidence of Clithero's criminality.

From the outset of the novel, then, it seems necessary to ask why Huntly is so drawn to men like Clithero and Weymouth, with whom he has little apparent connection. Why is the power of his interest in these men so strong that it outweighs the benefits (in real property as well as social recognition) of marriage with women? One rather obvious response would be that his interest in male bodies is sexual: that is, Huntly abandons a heterosexual path toward marriage in order to pursue homosexual desires. While such a reading has been plausibly, and indeed persuasively, offered by the critic Stephen Shapiro, I'm inclined to look elsewhere for the meaning and value of male sympathy in the novel.[82] Without discounting the fact that Huntly's interest in male bodies may be sexual, I would nonetheless suggest that to read Huntly's "obscure path" or "singular career" as homosexual is in some way to consent to the power of heterosexual marriage to fully organize the social and political field of identity: in other words, such a reading would indicate that the only available means of making sense of the nonheterosexual lies in the complementary term "homo-sexual."[83] Yet I would suggest that it is precisely the organizing power of het-erosexual marriage that the novel and the character of Edgar Huntly seek to resist. Thus while it would be possible to read Huntly's affect as homosexual, I want to suggest that the alternative to heterosexuality in this novel is not homosexuality so much as what I will call a liberal cosmopolitanism—a pleas-urable identification of male bodies with one another that is less sexual than political and that makes visible a form of liberal sociality dissociated from more stable and rigidly biologized accounts of bodies produced in and through narratives of sentimental marriage. I'm interested, then, in exploring precisely the *political* desires that animate Huntly's refusal of affective engagement in heterosexual marriage.

As we have seen, Huntly is immediately "rouse[d] up" upon viewing Clithero's half-dressed body for the first time. But his connection to Clithero is more fully established and explicitly defined as a relation of *sympathy* when he realizes that Clithero is weeping:

> He seemed wrapt in meditation; but the pause was short, and succeeded by sobs, at first low, and at wide intervals, but presently louder and more vehement. . . . Never did I witness a scene of such mighty anguish, such heart-bursting grief. What should I think? I was suspended in astonishment. Every sentiment, at length, yielded to my sympathy. Every new accent of the mourner struck upon my heart with additional force, and tears found their way spontaneously to my eyes. (10–11)

What is striking about this account of sympathy is that it is wholly physical. Clithero becomes "an object of compassion" for Huntly without having exchanged a single word with him. Huntly has absolutely no idea why Clithero is weeping, yet his tears are physically contagious and generate a bond that Huntly feels himself at a bodily (rather than intellectual) level as he, too, begins to weep. Indeed, when Huntly does attempt to speak with Clithero, during this first encounter under the elm tree, Clithero looks at him briefly but offers no verbal response whatsoever: "I had no power but to stand and silently gaze upon his motions," concludes Huntly. Not only does Clithero refuse to speak to Huntly when speech seems called for by their encounter, but even his face remains unknown to Huntly.

> Again I made preparation as for an interview which could not but take place. He passed me, however, without appearing to notice my existence. He came *so near* as almost to brush my arm, yet turned not his head to either side. My *nearer* view of him, made his brawny arms and lofty stature more conspicuous; but his imperfect dress, the dimness of the light, and the confusion of my thoughts, hindered me from discerning his features. (11; emphases added)

Although no conversation takes place between the two men, the proximity of Clithero's body (rather than any knowledge Huntly can gain as to his identity) is the salient feature of their encounter as Huntly relates it. Huntly will realize shortly that the man before him is sleepwalking, a fact that only reinforces our sense that the connection Huntly feels with Clithero has little to do with consciousness, character, or reason but is rather lodged wholly at the level of the body.

Yet why this bodily interest? Why does Huntly respond so powerfully to the presence of Clithero's body? I would suggest that it is not simply a desire *for* Clithero that is registered in these encounters, but the desire on Huntly's part to produce a body of his own—that is, to produce himself as embodied. The tears that Huntly sheds immediately upon viewing Clithero weep are only the first evidence of a kind of physical mimicry that characterizes Huntly's response to Clithero. Huntly's subsequent decision to follow Clithero on his daunting physical treks rather than to speak with him indicates a willingness to reproduce Clithero's sleepwalking, wholly somaticized being with his own body. "Instead of rushing on [Clithero]," writes Huntly, "and breaking at once the spell by which his senses were bound, I concluded, contrary to my first design, to wait his departure, and allow myself to be conducted withersoever he pleased" (23). Here Huntly abandons his plan to speak with Clithero—and thus abandons his rational design of discovering Clithero's identity—in favor of establishing a mimetic or identic contact in which he matches his conduct to Clithero's, in which he too, becomes a somatic being, unspeaking but powerfully physical. Huntly writes that as he follows Clithero, "It seemed to be the sole end of his labours to bewilder or fatigue his pursuer, to pierce into the deepest thickets, to plunge into the darkest cavities, to ascend the most difficult heights, and approach the slippery and tremulous verge of the dizziest precipices. I disdained to be outstripped in this career" (23). Rather than being outstripped by Clithero's physical prowess, Huntly establishes the identity of his body with Clithero's; his physical equality is demonstrated in his capacity to equal Clithero in penetrating the wilderness. Even when he eventually learns Clithero's story, little in the way of conversation transpires between the two; rather, Clithero's pattern of flight and Huntly's pattern of pursuit continue.

> Could I arrest his foot-steps and win his attention, I might be able to insinuate the lessons of fortitude; but if words were impotent, and arguments were nugatory, yet to set by him in silence, to moisten his hand with tears, to sigh in unison, to offer him the spectacle of sympathy, the solace of believing that his demerits were not estimated by so rigid a standard by others as by himself, that one at least among his fellow men regarded him with love and pity, could not fail to be of benign influence. (102)

Here, as repeatedly in his interaction with Clithero, words fail altogether—they are "nugatory" and "impotent"—yet in their stead, indeed, precisely because of their absence, the presence of two male bodies becomes powerfully visible and significant. In the absence of words, Huntly produces himself on the model of Clithero as an unidentified, nonsymbolizing body.

Huntly's somatic self-production and his mimicry of Clithero therein are nowhere more evident than in the central chapter of the novel in which Huntly awakens to find himself inexplicably immured in an entirely darkened cavern deep in the wilderness. Huntly and the reader will later realize that he has arrived at this location through somnambulation: that is, he has now wholly adopted Clithero's mode of unconscious, bodily transport as his own. Recalling the events of this eerie awakening in his letter, Huntly writes of the entirely sensational nature of his experience, a bodily experience that remains, even in retrospect, difficult to transpose into words: "One image runs into another, sensations succeed in so rapid a train, that I fear, I shall be unable to distribute and express them with sufficient perspicuity" (152). Yet if language and ratiocination seem distant from him at this moment, he nonetheless seems gratified in his ontological desire—in his desire to simply *be* a body: "I emerged from oblivion by degrees so slow and so faint, that their succession cannot be marked. When enabled at length to attend to the information which my senses afforded, I was conscious, for a time, of nothing but existence. It was unaccompanied with lassitude or pain, but I felt disinclined to stretch my limbs, or raise my eye-lids" (152). Although the strength of his bodily sensations—pain, hunger, and thirst—will shortly prove agonizing, at this moment, the sheer sensation of being—the feeling "of nothing but existence"—is described in almost Edenic terms. An unmarked body, held in a dark and comfortable womb of the earth, Huntly marks nothing around him save his own existence, his own somatic being. The light of consciousness and reason so graphically extinguished in the figure of the sleepwalker remain figuratively absent in the unilluminated space (he is "wrapt in the murkiest and most impenetrable gloom" [153]) into which Huntly now gropes his way, guided only by touch and the physical needs of his body for food and water.

As a number of critics have noted, Huntly thus seems to gradually *become* Clithero over the course of the novel, and at this decisive moment at the heart of the novel, Huntly clearly begins sleepwalking in imitation of Clithero. Moreover, critics have also remarked upon Huntly's apparent regression to a primitivist, bodily existence at this point: Dana Luciano, for instance, comments that Huntly seems to be "almost terminally embodied" in the scene in the cavern.[84] Yet Luciano sees the embodied states the novel works to produce as undesirable for Huntly: "Though Edgar tries to run away from his body," she writes, "carnality repeatedly catches up with him throughout the tale" (4). Luciano thus indicates that Huntly flees from the state of embodiment he arrives at in the cave.[85] On my reading, however, the terms of embodiment produced in the cave are precisely what Huntly has sought, and his awakening at this moment might be seen as a rebirth into his body rather than a regression or "fall" from the state of reason. Indeed, it seems particularly telling that the moment at which Huntly arrives at the sheer feeling of his own existence— when he comes to find himself embodied in much the same way Clithero is embodied—occurs immediately on the heels of his rejection of the hetero- pathic marriage narrative. His inexplicable awakening in the cave takes place directly following his decision that Mary must cede her inheritance to Weymouth and that he and Mary must forgo their marriage plans indefinitely. Successfully evading, then, the heteropathic marriage narrative, Huntly achieves just what he has sought in striking out in another direction: he has produced himself as a mere body.

Yet why does Huntly *seek* embodiment—particularly a form of embodi- ment that seems divorced from language and reason? I want to suggest that the body Huntly pursues and produces—the unmarked, mimetic body—is a republican one, or at least the fantasy of a republican body produced on American soil. In order to explain what I mean by this, I want to turn first to the more common case made by critics for the opposite claim: that is, to argu- ments suggesting that Huntly's embodiment is radically antirepublican insofar as republican politics are predicated upon *disembodied* forms of virtue and rea- son. Luciano, for instance, opposes the embodying force of the sensationalist stories repeated in the novel to the rationalist aims of republican virtue repre- sented in the paternal figure of Sarsefield, the enlightened tutor of Huntly whom we meet later in the novel: "The stories that get told in the novel . . . pro- duce bodies; fully embodied bodies, or what I would call carnal bodies, bodies whose desires exceed the possibility of control. And despite Edgar's most mur- derous efforts, these bodies cannot be contained; they return to haunt Sarsefield's rational republican world" (9). Luciano thus contrasts rationality and sensation, suggesting that sensational texts and the carnal bodies associat- ed with them are dangerous to republican politics. In broader terms, Michael Warner has influentially argued that the early American republican public sphere is predicated on a logic of disembodiment. According to Warner, the conditions of print culture in particular and the political logic of republican- ism are mutually reinforcing insofar as both are "normally impersonal." Warner argues that particular interests and particular bodies are (ideally) transcended in republican politics and republican print culture: "Validity in the public sphere of print holds a negative relation to persons," he concludes.[86] The mechanical duplication of print guaranteed an impersonality that came to be aligned with the republican ideal of a disembodied, depersonalized concern for civic virtue: "the impersonality of public discourse is seen both as a trait of its medium and as a norm for its subjects" (38). On these accounts, then, the sensational, embodying force of *Edgar Huntly* would seem utterly divorced from a republican literary politics.

Interestingly, one of Warner's proof texts in his discussion of the republican meaning of print is another novel by Charles Brockden Brown, the 1800 *Arthur Mervyn*.[87] According to Warner, *Arthur Mervyn* indicates that literature and print, in general, have civic value because they disclose information to the public and assist in creating a knowledgeable public that can, in turn, regulate the state and pursue civic good. The value of print in republican culture thus lies not in its expressive abilities for the individual but in its capacity to disseminate information and knowledge to a broad public. Representations of print within *Arthur Mervyn* show that writing performs the civic function of diffusing information and promoting virtue and knowledge. "Brown is able to regard that direct translation of knowledge into virtue as evidence that learning . . . is inherently virtuous," writes Warner. "Disclosing information, making things public, is understood as ensuring a civic source of validity" (161, 166). Yet if Mervyn "defines himself by the inquisitive activity and rational transcendence associated with letters" (155), we learn in the first few pages of *Edgar Huntly* that the central character in this novel by Brown views the transcendence associated with letter writing as a goal of dubious worth. As Huntly begins to write to Mary, he laments that the act of writing forces him to confront a paradox: while he would like to relate the details of his traumatic narrative to his fiancée, to do so seems impossible. "In proportion as I gain power over words," writes Huntly, "shall I lose dominion over sentiments; in proportion as my tale is deliberate and slow, the incidents and motives which it is designed to exhibit will be imperfectly revived and obscurely pourtrayed" (5–6). While the republican public sphere model links disclosure and knowledge, here the act of disclosure seems vexed, entwined as it is with the need to revive not a disembodied form of knowledge but a more sensate form of identity. The attempt to disclose his trauma in written form requires the imposition of an order that distorts rather than reveals the true nature of his experience. The abstraction or disembodiment associated with writing thus reads here not as transcendent but as disfiguring.

Indeed, in *Edgar Huntly* Brown seems bent upon demonstrating the ways in which disclosure in writing cannot be associated with virtue or knowledge. When we consider the specific instances in the novel where written texts appear, for instance, we see that the circulation of written ideas functions less to spread reason and enlightenment than disease. In two separate, albeit parallel, instances, Clithero and Huntly each dedicate sleepwalking hours to hiding rather than disclosing treasured manuscripts. In Huntly's case, the writings in question are a collection of letters penned by his murdered friend Waldegrave. Prior to hiding these letters (in his sleep) Huntly expresses anxiety about the dangerous effects of circulating the writings in question; although he had earlier promised to transcribe the letters for Mary as a means of memorializing her brother, he is anxious that in doing so he will communicate the heretical philosophy Waldegrave espoused in these letters. In the early days of their friendship, Waldegrave shared with Huntly radical political and philosophical theories that he would later repudiate under the enlightened tutelage of Sarsefield. Charged by Waldegrave to destroy the letters because of their content, Huntly has nonetheless retained them for their sentimental value. For Huntly it seems impossible to separate out the virtuous "character and history" of his friend from the subversive creeds he held at the time of writing the letters: in the letters Huntly attempts to edit he finds "mixed up with abstract reasonings, were numberless passages which elucidated the character and history of my friend. These were too precious to be consigned to oblivion, and to take them out of their present connection and arrangement, would be to mutilate and deform them" (126–127). Clearly the value of these letters does not lie in the knowledge they will disseminate: indeed, they will disseminate delusion rather than knowledge, according to Waldegrave. But the letters nonetheless have significant personal value for Huntly because they embody the memory of his deceased friend. Publication thus figures as neither virtuous nor impersonal: rather, the written word has value for only the most personal of reasons, and circulating it spreads dangerous ideas to other bodies. When Huntly explains why he will not allow Mary to read Waldegrave's letters he writes, "Thy religion is the growth of sensibility and not of argument. Thou are not fortified and prepossessed against the subtleties, with which the being and attributes of the deity have been assailed. Would it be just to expose thee to pollution and depravity from this source?" (127). To Mary, who is defined as endowed with sensibility rather than reason, Waldegrave's ideas will be physically communicated, like microbes. These letters thus have the value of material, personal objects: Huntly refers to the letters as "monuments" and later as an "invaluable relique" (128), thus indicating that meaning conveys itself metonymically through these texts, much as meaning adheres to saints' bones.

Meaning thus passes physically from one embodied hand to the next; the written text is a touchstone conveying memory, presence, or pollution; it is anything but transcendent.

While Huntly seeks to secret the letters of his friend in the attic of his uncle's home, removing them from circulation, Clithero quite literally buries a manuscript written by the woman who was once his benefactress. Indeed, we learn that Clithero was digging beneath the elm tree (where Huntly first viewed him) in order to bury this volume—actions that directly contrast with republican fantasies of virtuous disclosure in print. When he relates his strange history to Huntly, we learn that Clithero, as a poor child in Ireland, was taken into the household of the wealthy Euphemia Lorimer and rose to the position of trusted steward of her estate. Mrs. Lorimer treated Clithero as a son and eventually offered him the hand of her niece, the daughter of her evil (albeit beloved) twin brother, Wiatte. Shortly before the marriage is consummated, Wiatte returns to Dublin and attacks Clithero, who in turn kills Wiatte in order to defend himself. But beset by the fear that killing Wiatte will be the death of Mrs. Lorimer—who claims an almost mystical connection to her brother—Clithero attempts to murder his benefactress, ostensibly in order to put her out of the misery she will undoubtedly feel upon learning of her brother's death. Although he does not murder Mrs. Lorimer (who faints), Clithero evidently believes he has done so and flees to America to live out his life in guilty obscurity and misery. His most treasured possession is a book written by Mrs. Lorimer explaining the details of her relation to her brother. Like Huntly's letters from Waldegrave, the volume written by Mrs. Lorimer is a "precious monument of her genius and her virtue" that exerts more in the way of emotional than rational effect upon Clithero. As such, he seeks to privatize this relation rather than let it circulate; he wants to hide Mrs. Lorimer's text from "the profane curiousity of survivors." There is a suggestion, then, that private forms of recognition can both be polluted through public disclosure and that their improper circulation can pollute others. Disclosure as an ideal of print is thus placed in question in *Edgar Huntly* because knowledge itself is never abstract but rather is tied to particular bodies as well as particular bodily effects. The violent bodily effects of disclosure are nowhere more forcefully portrayed than in the final pages of the novel, where we learn that a letter of Huntly's concerning Clithero's desire to attack Mrs. Lorimer again (once he has learned from Huntly that she is alive and well and now married to Sarsefield) has arrived in Mrs. Lorimer's hands and frightened her to the extent of causing her to miscarry a pregnancy. Throughout *Edgar Huntly*, then, the circulation of texts is a dangerous and even deadly business: written texts communicate perilous private desires with contagious effects and thus fail to produce the public knowledge and rationality necessary for republican civic virtue.

If "letters promote [a] kind of vigilant thinking" (Warner, 156) in *Arthur Mervyn*, they would thus seem to promote, by way of contrast, private embodiment and diseased forms of sensibility in *Edgar Huntly*. How should we regard this apparent contradiction within Brown's fiction? One possible way to understand the difference between the two novels would be to suggest that *Edgar Huntly* corresponds more to the norms of a liberal than republican culture of print as it is encoded in the form of the novel. While Warner reads *Arthur Mervyn* as a novel that strives to represent the republican value of print, he also contends that the novel, as a form, tends to embody liberal values. Warner contrasts the civic virtue of republicanism with the "managed esteem" associated with the credit economy of liberalism or what he describes as "the emergent liberal-capitalist model of personality and social relations" (172). Insofar as the novel operates by structuring personal forms of imaginative identification between the reader and the characters in the novel, its formal dimensions lend themselves to the liberal aims of producing private subjectivity and social recognition. Following Warner's cue, then, we might want to read *Edgar Huntly* as expressing the liberal, rather than republican, sensibilities that were in ascendance at the time—as staging the moment when republican values relinquished their hold upon the print public sphere. As I argued in the first chapter, Warner seems to describe the shift from republican to liberal modes of valuing and engaging with print as something of a political "fall" or declension insofar as the shift marks a movement away from an ideal of an active civic engagement toward a passive and "imaginary" participation in the politics of national identity. This description of the loss of civic activism in favor of privatized concerns at the close of the eighteenth century mirrors the historical narrative set forth by historians of the republican synthesis that dramatizes the dichotomy between civic humanism and liberalism. Yet as I argue in the previous section of this chapter, the dichotomy between liberalism and republicanism seems persistently overdrawn in historiography of this period, to the detriment of making the gendered terms of republican and liberal forms of American political subjectivity visible. With respect to *Edgar Huntly*, then, I would maintain that the novel is less evidence of a liberal falling off from the ideals of virtuous models of republican print culture than an attempt to work through republican political premises in early national American terrain. Specifically, I suggest that the property relations at stake in *Edgar Huntly* alert us to the impossibility of viewing civic humanism as an operative republican model in early America. Rather, Huntly's search for modes of political embodiment, in the absence of property ownership, leads him on a tortuous journey that ends in abject failure—in a disembodied state that points to the success of liberal models of racialized and gendered subject ratification while nonetheless implicitly questioning these models.

The prologue to *Edgar Huntly* announces its concern with producing a particularly American text, one rooted in a relationship with the American land and aboriginal, Native American bodies. Rather than the "puerile superstition and exploded manners; Gothic castles and chimeras" of European novels, the passion and the sympathy of the American reader should be generated by "incidents of Indian hostility, and the perils of the western wilderness" (3) indigenous to the United States, according to Brown. The announcement of a wish to produce sensations "peculiar to ourselves" in relation to the material conditions of America points, then, to the desire to materialize a specifically American body that seems central to the text. And indeed, Edgar Huntly will emerge from a cave as if from the womb of the western wilderness midway through the novel, staging a scene of autochthony followed shortly by multiple battles with Indians, just as prescribed by the preface. Yet if Brown imagines that a material relation with the land is productive of American identity in the new Republic, the relation of citizen to land in *Edgar Huntly* bears no resemblance to that prescribed by classical republicanism. As Pocock makes clear, the opposition between the world of credit relations and social recognition of liberalism and the civic-minded independence of republicanism rests upon the ability of leisured property owners to avoid forms of interdependence consequent upon engagement in an exchange economy. Property ownership makes the republican citizen independent, and this is the root of his capacity to divorce himself from personal interests and attend to the civic good: the freeholder is free precisely because he holds land that is not subject to exchange. Yet Edgar Huntly is anything but a freeholder. Not only do we learn that he lives under his uncle's roof only until such time as his cousin inherits the property and evicts him, but we also later learn that Huntly's parents were killed by Indians when he was a child in a dispute over the land they occupied. Huntly thus has no property, no patrimony, and little prospect of acquiring any. Even the land he might have inherited from his family is property that was at the center of violently contested social relations. The Huntly family land was thus never freely held in the first place, a detail that may underscore the fact that American land never had the same role in producing republican identity as did British land.

Unpropertied as he clearly is, it is more than evident that Huntly's most rapid route to achieving propertied status is by way of capitalist family formation: like the reformable rake, he needs to pursue a virtuous woman, marry her, and work for his living. We see this model of success in a number of guises in the text. First, Clithero's story begins as just such a hetero-propriative account of attaining property, recognition, and citizenship. From an impoverished childhood, he rises to the position of the intended groom of a wealthy young woman: his credentials as sincere, desirous of a virtuous woman (Clarice), and hard-working make him ideally suited for capitalist family formation. Yet Clithero fatally lashes out against this narrative, enacting a kind of unaccountable violence against the very woman (Mrs. Lorimer) who has enabled his apparent rise to success, and suggesting, perhaps, that a certain violence lies embedded in the narrative in the first place. The more successful version of capitalist family formation in the novel is visible in the history of Mrs. Lorimer and Sarsefield. Although the two were enamored of one another in their youth, Lorimer's parents (at the urging of her brother) had forbidden a marriage because of Sarsefield's lack of wealth and social status. Mrs. Lorimer subsequently married another man and was eventually widowed, while Sarsefield credentialed himself elsewhere as a soldier of British imperialism in India and the Near East. (During a portion of his wandering years, he also served as a tutor to Huntly in America.) Returning to Dublin shortly before Clithero's fall from grace, Sarsefield succeeds this time in wedding Mrs. Lorimer. Full of "natural" and clearly unshakable desire for the virtuous Euphemia Lorimer, Sarsefield has also established himself as capable of performing the labor demanded by empire. At the close of the novel, Sarsefield returns to America to offer Huntly access to the very path and goods that Clithero has forsaken, without realizing that Huntly is aware of Clithero's (and thus Sarsefield's own) story. "I am wedded to the most excellent of women," states Sarsefield. "To her am I indebted for happiness and wealth and dignity and honour. . . . She longs to embrace you as a son. To become truly her son, will depend upon your own choice and that of one, who was the companion of our voyage" (252). Huntly, who has heard this story before, is quick to fill in the blanks: "Heavens! cried I, in a transport of exultation and astonishment. Of whom do you speak? Of the mother of Clarice?" (253). Yet Sarsefield reacts with outrage to the idea that this personal information has been publicly circulated: "His countenance was equally significant of terror and rage. As soon as he regained the power of utterance, he spoke—Clithero! . . . Has he dared to utter names so sacred as those of Euphemia Lorimer and Clarice?" (253). Sarsefield thus suggests that Clithero has somehow polluted the sacred (and private) bond that unites him to Mrs. Lorimer and her niece by speaking of it to Huntly. Yet the substitutability of the individuals within the narrative—insert Huntly where

Clithero once stood—indicates precisely its lack of particularity or privacy. Sarsefield tells Huntly that it will be up to Huntly to choose Clarice on the basis of his own personal desires (the inclusion of Huntly in the family "will depend upon your own choice," Sarsefield says), indicating that the relation of Huntly to the virtuous woman he marries will be entirely based upon private and personal desire. Yet the structural—and thus impersonal—nature of the narrative offered to Huntly is more than evident when Huntly recognizes the individuals in the narrative from having heard the story before, and thus supplies the name "Clarice" before Sarsefield does. Sarsefield is horrified that the familial desires that he wishes to retail to Huntly as wholly private have circulated publicly, yet their circulation and repetition reveals the structural dimension (and the gothic contagion) of the personal, affective identities involved.[88] To transfer these personal identities is, on the one hand, to pollute them by destroying the individual and affective aspect that is central to their structural purpose (social recognition, subjective ratification), yet the affective familial relations have a structural force precisely because they are iterable and can be transferred from one set of individuals to another. To recognize the structural force of heterosexual romantic and familial bonds is to empty them of "choice" or affect and to reveal the inherent violence (lack of choice) imposed by such a template. Revealed, then, as heteropathic—as confining rather than individuating—the marriage narrative and the model of capitalist family formation are studiously avoided by Huntly.

Huntly thus clearly does not choose to materialize himself through what will become the dominant liberal model of subject formation, the gendering machine of heterosexual marriage. Moreover, he does not have access to the traditional republican form of embodiment, which is that of freehold, or property ownership (which facilitates subsequent claims to impersonal civic action). Accordingly, Huntly chooses another path—an obscure and ultimately unsuccessful one—by which he seeks to fashion a republican body of his own through a mimetic identification with other male bodies. The republican politics Huntly pursues are thus more Jacobin than Harringtonian, that is, they resemble the politics of the French Revolution rather than those of Britain's Country party in the seventeenth century. It is precisely through an imagined *fraternity* and *equality*—the identity of fraternally aligned bodies—that Huntly seeks to materialize his own existence. As we have seen, Huntly persistently seeks to identify himself physically with other unknown men such as Clithero and Weymouth. It seems significant that these marginal, undistinguished male bodies have more allure for him than patriarchal figures such as his uncle or even Sarsefield. What Huntly hunts for, then, is less patrimony or patriarchal structures of identity than fraternity and a literal identity or sameness with other male bodies. The radical republican nature of this search is evident, from the outset, in his identification with Clithero, an individual who, as an Irish laborer, has only marginal social status. Huntly thus indicates a willingness to cross boundaries of class and nationality in pursuit of common fraternal status, in his desire to place his body next to Clithero's as a "fellow man." Moreover, as both Jared Gardner and Caroll Smith-Rosenberg point out, Clithero's Irish identity would, in the 1790s, call to mind an association with French revolutionaries. Both critics note that the rabidly antirepublican writer William Cobbett sought to paint Irish immigrants in the United States as secretly fomenting French revolution in America. Moreover, Clithero's aggression against members of the ruling class aligns him with the class-oriented violence of the French Jacobins. "Murdering and attempting to murder three members of the aristocracy [Wiatte, Mrs. Lorimer, Clarice]," writes Smith-Rosenberg, "Clithero enacts the threat the middle class posed to that aristocracy, a threat made frighteningly explicit during the 1790s by the French Revolution and concurrent Irish nationalist uprisings."[89] Huntly's predilection for the radical edge of republicanism is also evident in the attraction Waldegrave's heretical theories admittedly continue to hold for him. This doctrine, which Huntly "did not entirely abjure" even after Waldegrave's repudiation of it, is one that advocates the eradication of boundaries and traditions: "[Waldegrave's] earliest creeds, tended to efface the impressions of his education; to deify necessity and universalize matter; to destroy the popular distinctions between soul and body, and to dissolve the supposed connection between the moral condition of man, anterior and subsequent to death" (125). Like the theories of the Jacobins, Waldegrave's creed is essentially a solvent, eradicating boundaries and distinctions that have supported existing forms of social order and knowledge.

Huntly, I contend, thus seeks a *republican embodiment* or a bodily equality with other men around him, in which what matters is less any visible marker of his identity than establishing the sheer physical being that he holds in common with fellow men. And indeed, it would seem that Huntly has succeeded in producing and inhabiting this body at the moment when he awakens—sensible only of his own existence—in the cave in the wilderness. What follows upon this awakening, however, is an unremitting trail of violence that constitutes the second half of the novel. Huntly not only kills a panther to feed himself and escape from the cave, but when he attempts to emerge from the cave, he finds a group of Indians camped in its entrance. In a series of engagements, routs, and escapes marked by escalating violence, Huntly will eventually murder all of these Indians as he attempts to find his way out of the wilderness, back to his uncle's home. On the one hand, it would be possible to argue that in order to return to civilization in his republican form, Huntly must distinguish between savage and civilized bodies; he must kill the "savage" bodies of the Indians in order to produce his own identity as "civilized." Both Gardner and Smith-Rosenberg argue along these lines, indicating that "It is the project of the second half of the novel to bring Edgar back to his rightful place in society. . . . Edgar claims his ownership of the forest . . . by killing Indians."[90] Yet on the other hand, as both of these critics also note, Huntly's attempts to violently distinguish himself from the Indians he kills paradoxically establish his similarity to, rather than difference from, those he targets. His experience in the wilderness has transformed him, physically, into a half-naked and bloodied figure who wields a tomahawk and shoots to kill—who thus resembles the "savage" Indian figures he seeks to murder. As such, it would seem that his republican identification with fellow male bodies extends to Indians as well as Irishmen. In an eerie reenactment of his desire to place his body next to Clithero's form and to exchange tears, we find Huntly, in the second half of the book, placed next to Indian bodies, exchanging blood. After killing several Indians, Huntly faints only to awaken in a pile of Indian bodies, having been himself left for dead by the other white settlers.

> I found myself stretched upon the ground. . . . My head rested upon something, which, on turning to examine, I found to be one of the slain Indians. . . . My head had reposed upon the breast of him whom I had shot in this part of his body. The blood had ceased to ooze from the wound, but my dishevelled locks were matted and steeped in that gore which had overflowed and choked up the orifice. (188–89)

While Huntly may kill Indians, he also comes to physically resemble an Indian; ironically, his murderous energies only further secure his identification with and proximity to these bodies.

Killing Indians thus does not seem to prove Huntly's credentials as a white, civilized American; rather, it seems to steep him in the gore of his own body and that of those around him, dissolving boundaries between white and Irish, and white and Indian bodies in the flow of bodily fluids across and between them. We might say, then, that the republican body seems to slide or flow into other bodies: in the scene where he lies among dead Indians, Huntly's body becomes one indistinguishable form in a pile of bleeding corpses. Moreover, without distinct boundaries between his body and that of a Native American, for instance, Huntly becomes a target of white settler violence. Huntly will ultimately discover that Sarsefield, who has joined the party of settlers who are attacking the Indians and searching for Huntly, shot at him as he fled through the woods because he believed (based on the physical appearance of Huntly's body) that Huntly was an Indian. Indistinguishably foreign or domestic—neither inside the community nor outside—Huntly's unmarked body thus becomes the target of Sarsefield's border-patrolling violence. The physical distinction that would mark Huntly as white and domestic has thus disappeared or dissolved as the republican body assumes equality with those around it. It would seem, then, that a kind of violence arises from the republican slide into other bodies, a violence generated in response to the unclear boundaries between live and dead bodies, between domestic and foreign bodies, and between savage and civilized bodies. Tellingly, at another moment in Huntly's flight during the second half of the novel, we see the eradication of domestic interiority associated with the unbounded republican body. During Huntly's journey toward civilization he comes upon a cabin, hoping to find refuge and "consanguinity" with those within. "[The house] was the model of cleanliness and comfort," he writes. "It was built of wood. . . . It was painted white, and the windows not only had sashes, but these sashes were supplied, contrary to custom, with glass. . . . The door had not only all its part entire, but was embellished with mouldings and a pediment" (217). As it turns, out, however, the very impressive boundaries (windows, doors) that give the house its standing in Huntly's eyes have been violated. "I went to the door of what appeared to be a kitchen," writes Huntly. "The door was wide open. This circumstance portended evil" (217). The loss of closure of the domestic space is the sign that it has no interior, no differentiated, circumscribed space within, and thus that the house offers no privacy. Moreover, upon closer examination Huntly finds that the house is the scene of two forms of destruction: the home has been attacked from without, by Indians, and from within, through the violence of an abusive husband. Like a house without doors or a home with no inside, the republican body that would seem to fulfill a fantasy of liberty and equality here produces, instead, a nightmare of boundary failure. Furthermore, Huntly's killings seem less an attempt to reestablish those boundaries than a participation in the contagious failure of boundaries to provide any identity whatsoever.

Why, then, does Huntly's fantasy of republican embodiment fail him and fail to produce substantive equality and liberty? The political theorist Rogers Smith offers one possible explanation for this failure: according to Smith, both liberalism and republicanism require what we might call bodily boundaries at a pragmatic level yet argue against these boundaries at a theoretical level. Both liberalism and republicanism theoretically presuppose the equality of all individuals, yet as a result they offer individuals little sense of self, little sense of communal or even national identity: "In their pure, unalloyed forms, liberal and democratic republican political ideals have offered few reasons why Americans should see themselves as a distinct people, apart from others."[91] Smith's account points to a theoretical incompatibility between nationalism and republicanism, one that we might expect someone like Brown—a republican writer concerned with thinking through the new terms of American national identity—to feel quite acutely. In *Edgar Huntly*, I would suggest, Brown has attempted to produce an American, republican body only to find that the republican body is un-American. As Smith argues, the true liberal or democratic-republican body would be *cosmopolitan* (without boundaries) rather than national:

> Both liberalism and republicanism, in theory and in practice, place great strains on citizens. Liberal notions of natural rights . . . make a prima facie case that all those capable of developing powers of rational self-guidance should be treated as bearers of fairly robust individual rights. Legal systems that automatically subordinate women, blacks, Native Americans, homosexuals, and non-Christians are then presumptively invalid. *Even preference for one's countrymen over aliens is suspect* if it involves infringement of basic human rights. That is a major reason why the logic of Enlightenment liberalism points away from particular national memberships and toward more inclusive, if not cosmopolitan political arrangements. (36–37; emphasis added)

Following Smith's account of the cosmopolitan nature of "rigorous" republicanism, we might see Edgar Huntly as endued with precisely such rigor: Huntly attempts to embody a republican ideal of equality, but his success in doing so meets with disaster insofar as the republican body is antinational. Huntly is rendered suspect (by Sarsefield, for instance) because he seems to prefer aliens to his countrymen, to prefer to place his body next to Irishmen and Indians rather than virtuous white women.

According to Smith, Americans have historically found it difficult to embrace the "dauntingly high" requirements of liberal or republican theory and have instead chosen to define themselves in relation to ascriptive categories of identity or "civic myths" that make them feel "proud and confident about who they are and about their futures, both as individuals and a national community" (38). In other words, because republicanism gives individuals and communities little means of constructing a stable and particularized identity, communities and nations turn to fixed identity categories (such as race and gender) and graft these categories into their self-understanding as "civic myths" in order to fashion a defined and adhesive community. Smith's account of the pragmatic pressure to employ ascriptive categories of identity in support of nationalist aims provides a useful model for understanding the vitriolic debates that split the nation during the 1790s between the Federalist and the Republican parties. Federalist anxieties, in particular, centered upon the "cosmopolitan" designs of French-allied republicans that they saw as directly undermining particularized forms of identity such as U.S. nationalism and Christianity. Indeed, as the historian Michael Chandos Brown reports, the word "cosmopolitan" may first have been used in English in its modern sense in antirepublican propaganda that circulated theories of a worldwide conspiracy linked to the French Revolution and the so-called "Bavarian Illuminati"— a conspiracy aimed at undermining national order, morality, and Christianity. In his influential book *Proofs of a Conspiracy Against All the Religions and Governments of Europe* (1798), John Robison warned readers of the coming of a "great epoch of Cosmo-politanism."[92] Yale president Timothy Dwight and the Reverend Jedediah Morse, who would spread Robison's fears of an Illuminati conspiracy in the United States, "shared [Robison's] fear of what they saw to be a state of mind suspended above the ordinary loyalties to family, church, and state."[93] William Cobbett, writing of republican cosmopolitan conspiracy infiltrating the United States, suggests that lack of property and country are the defining characters of the spreading anarchy. In *Detection of a Conspiracy, Formed by the United Irishmen* (1798), Cobbett writes: "Real, sincere villainy . . . without property, without principles, without country and without character; dark and desperate, unnatural and blood-thirsty ruffians; these were what [the French] wanted; and where could they have sought them with such certainty of success, as amongst that restless, rebellious tribe, the emigrated UNITED IRISHMEN?"[94] Cosmopolitanism—being "without country"—is here associated with a lack of moral and ethical value, with being "without principles" and "without character." Ironically, however, much of Cobbett's description seems applicable to Edgar Huntly: initially he is without property, and later he is seemingly without country, as he identifies with foreigners and eventually assumes the form of a blood-thirsty ruffian. Huntly is a cosmopolitan republican who "without property, without principles, without country and without character" threatens the boundaries of the new nation.

As Jared Gardner points out, Cobbett and other Federalists sought to strengthen national unity by expelling alien bodies, both through the Alien and Sedition Acts in 1798 and, more importantly, through the cultural work of defining domestic and foreign bodies in newly racialized terms. As such, we could say that the Federalists resort to precisely the kind of ascriptive categories of identity that Rogers Smith describes as the commonly used resource for consolidating civic identity in the face of the centripetal forces of liberalism and republicanism.[95] The Illuminati conspiracy, for instance, is imagined in the United States not primarily in terms of a league of French Jacobins but instead becomes coded in racial terms, as we see in Cobbett's association of republican conspiracy with an image of the "blood-thirsty" Irish immigrant. In similar terms, another writer warns of the republican conspiracy as a league of blacks and Irishmen that will pollute American racial purity: "Remove your wives far from the Infernal Fraternal embrace, or you may prove witness of their violation and expiring agonies, or if reserved for future infamy, may increase your families not only with a spurious, but a colored breed. Remove your daughters . . . unless you would be silent spectators of their being deflowered by the lusty Othellos."[96] While racial categories are here central to the construction of a consolidated (white) American national identity, as Gardner argues, we might note the gender politics of this image of interracial sex as well. Racial impurity and loss of national identity are here associated with the destruction of heterosexual, monogamous marriage. The "Infernal Fraternal embrace" refers to the secret brotherhood of Illuminati within the United States, but the imagery of the "fraternal embrace" suggests a clandestine, homosexual physical contact that is also equated with an adulterous heterosexual embrace. Promiscuous sexuality is associated with promiscuous bodies and cosmopolitan (unbounded, interracial) bodily identifications: in contrast, heterosexual marriage bespeaks proper boundaries and properly structured familial and national identifications.

Thus, as Michael Chandos Brown points out, images of women were central to the Illuminati terror in the United States. According to Robison's conspiracy theory, for instance, the Illuminati targeted women in their plot to subvert governments and morality because women would more eagerly pursue promises of emancipation. "Women were, in fact, the pivot upon which the whole Illuminist plan must turn," argues Brown (399). As Brown demonstrates, Mary Wollstonecraft's writings on women's rights were painted by Benjamin Silliman as part of the Illuminist conspiracy and thereby discredited. Timothy Dwight, speaking before the Yale commencement in 1797 warned against the havoc republican conspirators would wreak upon gender roles, and thus upon the very fabric of American society, if they prevailed: "the private dwelling would be converted into a brothel and the venerable matron and the snowy virgin would change characters with the bawd and the strumpet; the purity, the happiness, and the hopes of mankind, would be buried under a promiscuous and universal concubinage."[97] Here Dwight equates heterosexual marriage and marital forms of female sexuality with the purity and freedom of the nation. As these comments indicate, then, gender was an apparently ascriptive category that gained authority as a "civic myth" in the face of anxiety about national coherence, power, and identity.

Discourses of race and gender are thus inextricably bound in defining ascriptive categories of national identity as figured by antirepublicans. With respect to *Edgar Huntly*, for instance, we have seen that Huntly's most obvious path to achieving recognition and civic identity is through marriage to a white woman. Although killing Indians fails to make him civilized and white, marriage to a white woman promises to do so. Femininity and masculinity, as produced through the gendering machine of marriage, are thus both clearly related to a racialized (white) citizenship: it is a gendered behavior (marriage) that will guarantee Huntly's white citizenship and sustain his ability to justifiably lay claim to a propertied status over and against the savages whom he eerily resembles. Yet at the close of the novel, Huntly continues to reject the possibility of marriage in favor of directing his sympathy toward Clithero. When the novel does, indeed, seem to finally recognize Clithero as criminal rather than beset by "misguided benevolence," Huntly is left abandoned, on a path leading nowhere, without social recognition or voice, misguided by his own republican desires. The final letter in the novel is written by Sarsefield, who relates the deadly effects upon his unborn child of Huntly's "misguided" letter, the letter that causes Euphemia Lorimer to miscarry her pregnancy. At the close of his own letter, Sarsefield writes "Farewell" to Huntly with an ominous finality, clearly dismissing Huntly for good and placing him decisively outside the capitalist family he had previously been invited to join. At the close of the novel, then, we know that Huntly has been written out of the narrative that would give him social visibility and property; we have no clue as to any possible future that may await him, and it is thus as if he has no future existence whatsoever. Huntly's strategy of republican embodiment has thus served him poorly: he is, ultimately, much like Ichabod Crane, disembodied or erased at the close of the narrative. Heterosexual marriage clearly stands as the one visible means of arresting the "infernal fraternal" embrace of radical republicanism or cosmopolitanism. Heterosexual marriage helps to secure national identity in the terms of private white property ownership that are embedded in the conjoint relation of man and woman. *Edgar Huntly* ultimately presents a marital nationalism as the only viable path to subject recognition and property ownership, while nonetheless presenting this path in melancholic terms. Marital nationalism, I would suggest, is ultimately a decidedly liberal formation—one which relies upon gender to make a community present to itself in a seemingly private rather than political fashion.

SOCIALITY AND 'THE COQUETTE'

One of the questions Brown's novel raises is whether it is possible to have a republican politics in an exchange economy without producing a pragmatic demand for stabilizing identity categories that take an ascriptive form. Rogers Smith offers an interesting answer to this question: he suggests that it is always necessary to have identity categories in order to fashion political agency and communal recognition, but that identity categories need not be antithetical to republican or liberal theory if they are recognized as social and provisional rather than biological and immutable—if, that is, identity categories are not seen as ascriptive but as socially scripted. Smith writes:

> Liberal democrats need to find ways to affirm the genuine value that particular political communities have for efforts to realize desirable goals in the world as it is constituted now, but they must do so without denying the dangers of these memberships. The greatest threats come from profound political and psychological tendencies to treat such communities as natural, in ways that seem to legitimate both oppressive internal hierarchies and harsh injustices toward outsiders. Hence all efforts to mythologize nations or peoples as somehow 'prepolitical,' as families or primordial kinship groups, must be rejected. . . . The answer, I suggest, is to recognize political communities as entities that are, from a moral point of view, weightier members of the same species as political parties . . .such communities are ineradicably political human creations, crafted to govern and assist some people more than others. (10–11)

In effect, Smith is suggesting a reversal in our understanding of what I have described in the first chapter as the temporal narrative of liberalism. Rather than seeing political identity as rooted in primordial and "prepolitical" categories—basing citizenship, for instance, on seemingly immutable categories such as race, gender, or ethnicity—we should understand that the need for these categories or "civic myths" is politically produced. Political identity should thus be viewed as the result of "human creation," and we might thereby understand the identity categories that underwrite civic belonging to be highly mutable and historically determined; that is, identity categories should be understood as political "parties" rather than Linnaean classes. In temporal terms, political identity is not the *result* of private, prepolitical identity, but rather itself shapes and produces forms of apparently private and prepolitical identity.

The social nexus of public and private identities is one that I have called "sociality" within liberalism: sociality is the (sometimes covert, sometimes overt) means through which apparently disconnected private and public identities are interconnected. Here I want to use Smith's theory to delineate two possible versions of sociality: an *open sociality*, in which sociality is a space for the creative configuration of subjectivity, and a *closed sociality*, which involves the covert production of seemingly immutable identity categories. Closed sociality would correspond to liberalism's standard temporal narrative: first the subject's identity is presumed to be fixed and whole in advance as formed in a private, apolitical realm; then the fitness of the subject for inclusion in public and political life is judged. "Closed sociality" is a view of politics that denies the productive force of social and political publics. "Open sociality," in turn, is a view of politics that identifies public discourse as productive of private identity—which sees the moment of social or political recognition as *creative* of private identity rather than responsive to preexisting forms of subjectivity. Sociality occurs where private identity is produced through public representation and power; if it is recognized as such (if it is open), it becomes a productive space, whereas if it is not recognized as such (if it is closed), it operates merely as a kind of relay or enforcer of ascriptive identity.

In the eighteenth century, sociality, I would argue, was recognized as a more open, productive, and fluid space than it has been since then. Versions of radical republicanism (untethered to landed property) in the eighteenth century offered the opportunity of an open sociality, but anxieties around nationalism subsequently created the closed sociality that I have associated with liberalism, or the narrative and temporalizing force of liberal fiction. Huntly's rejection of the heteropathic narrative, for instance, suggests that he is able to pursue alternate forms of sociality—to pursue male identification for pleasure and self-construction, that will be foreclosed to him by a new nationalist agenda. The early construction of civil publics in informal and varied terms testifies to the way in which sociality can and did operate in an open fashion in the eighteenth century. The work of David Shields on the importance of informal social and political clubs to eighteenth-century society in the United States is particularly instructive in this regard. Shields documents not only the large number and varied kinds of private societies that existed during this period—"tavern companies, coffeehouse fellowships, tea-table gatherings, salons, dancing assemblies, routs, card parties, gentleman's clubs, and college fraternities"[98]—but also their social significance. "[Private societies], as much as any government, seemed requisites of civil order, for in them persons entered into a sense of communal identity and found a happiness in society" (xiii–xiv) writes Shields. According to Shields, then, private societies enabled the creation of stabilizing forms of identity but remained outside state control. Shields's analysis of these groups is interesting, in part, because he does not discuss these societies in political terms: rather, he insistently describes private societies as the loci of *pleasure* rather than politics. As such, Shields differs distinctly from Habermas, who has argued that society in the coffeehouse, for instance, primarily enabled the rational operation of public opinion in the service of liberal political purposes. Writing against Habermas, Shields contends that the purpose of eighteenth-century clubs had more to do with pleasure than with rationality: " 'reason' presents insuperable difficulties as an explanation for what was and is at work in communications that founded communities. . . . The disingenuous identification of reason with one's political affections suggests that 'feeling' rather than 'reason' more accurately names what was at work in communication. . . . Many of these groups confessed wit, affection, or appetite as the grounds of community, not conscience" (xv–xvi). Yet the "moral sense grounded in shared feeling" or the "sensus communis" Shields locates in this civil society is one that nonetheless might be seen to have political import. As described by Shields, private societies gave individuals a strong local sense of identity and community. Clubs were concerned with "a form of communal identity brought into being by speech acts or writing" (xviii) writes Shields in a formulation that emphasizes that identity is "brought into being" by these clubs and does not, then, serve as the preexisting basis for their formation. I would suggest, then, that the private societies Shields describes function, in part, as forms of open sociality: defining a mutable, historically determined point of shared interest, desire, and pleasure, these clubs functioned as public spheres of desire, in which a desire for being—for recognition—was satisfied in pleasurable exchanges and the creation of a "sensus communis." In many respects, these clubs enact a form of sociality sought by Edgar Huntly as he pursued the pleasure of placing his body next to that of his "fellow man."[99]

Interestingly, Shields describes many of these clubs as guided by an antirepublican impulse: "A whole range of antirepublican values was preserved in private society and would flourish quite handsomely into and through the nineteenth century. To the extent that civility condoned pleasure, and the pursuit of pleasure evaded virtue and utility, it enabled a sense of communal enrichment freed from republican discipline" (xxi). According to Shields, then, many of these private societies are antirepublican insofar as they embrace neither the language of civic virtue (insofar as they are concerned with pleasure), nor the language of equality of a more radical republicanism, insofar as they are concerned with establishing local and exclusive forms of identity rather than cosmopolitan fraternity. But the open sociality of civil society as described by Shields suggests a potentially more creative response to the conflict between republicanism and nationalism than later liberal forms of closed sociality permit. As Shields describes them, private societies do offer a local habitation and name—forms of recognition and embodiment—that are nonetheless not ascriptive insofar as they are the product rather than premise of civil association. Shields argues that such associations indicate that "there existed other accesses to happiness in the communication and play of bodies that lay intermediate between the private person and the state" (xxvii). This "play of bodies" was both heterosocial and homosocial in its varied forms in the eighteenth century, suggesting that alternatives to what I have called "marital nationalism" were indeed plausible in this period.

Hannah Webster Foster's 1797 novel, *The Coquette*, displays forms of both open and closed sociality. As in *Edgar Huntly*, the text ultimately both produces and laments the foreclosure of a supple sociality in favor of a liberal, closed sociality that operates powerfully to produce "prepolitical" categories of gender and to sustain the narrative force of heterosexual marriage. Eliza Wharton, the tragic heroine of *The Coquette*, emerges brilliantly into the social space of bourgeois civility, but she fatally misunderstands this social space as open rather than closed, as productive and creative rather than dedicated to procuring a temporal narrative (a path) linking private to public and gendering her body through heterosexual marriage. In the opening pages of the novel she announces her allegiance to the principle that Shields describes as a guiding motive of civil association: pleasure. "An unusual sensation possesses my breast," writes Eliza to her friend Lucy Freeman, "a sensation, which I once thought could never pervade it on any occasion whatever. It is *pleasure*; pleasure, my dear Lucy, on leaving my paternal roof!"[100] Pleasure is repeatedly associated, by Eliza, not just with freedom from control by her parents, but with sociability and particularly with her ability to participate in a pluralized "sensus communis." "Sociable" is the term of highest approbation for Eliza: "social converse . . . is the true zest of life," she opines (30) and it is, moreover, directly associated with virtue: "none but virtuous minds can participate" in such converse she concludes. As such, Eliza adopts a view of society and virtue that is closely allied with the Scottish theories of John Millar and Adam Smith. By "living much in society," as Millar describes it, Eliza establishes her virtue and receives social recognition from those around her: she operates in a public sphere that grants her independence and identity precisely insofar as she produces and responds to collectively articulated forms of taste and sympathy. As the friend of one of her suitors reports, Eliza is entirely fitted to this social role: "Miss Wharton sustained her part [in conversation] with great propriety. Indeed, she discovers a fund of useful knowledge, and extensive reading, which render her peculiarly entertaining; while the brilliancy of her wit, the fluency of her language, the vivacity and ease of her manners are inexpressibly engaging" (46).

An open model of sociality would construe such sociability as constructed on the model of a "party" (a humanly crafted association) rather than a Linnaean class (a biologically defined set of individuals). And indeed, Eliza is always more than ready to form a party, ready to embrace sociability as creative of possibility, communal pleasure, and virtue. In contrast, however, the majority of her friends and suitors view sociality in closed terms: here sociability is the occasion to display (rather than create) a private, feminine subjectivity and from thence to follow a path toward marriage. Sociability thus functions less as a pleasurable social *end* that is itself virtuous than it functions as a *means* of aligning private subjects in proper (heterosexually organized) relations. Eliza's friends, for instance, clearly view social occasions as primarily forums for marketing feminine subjectivity for masculine appropriation in marriage. Yet as she is pursued by two suitors—the tedious Reverend Boyer and the rakish Major Sanford—Eliza repeatedly broadcasts her lack of interest in forming a "particular" (and particularizing) connection in favor of sustaining a wider circle of sociability. Stung by her lack of interest in his privatizing and hetero-propriative desire, Boyer laments to a friend that Eliza has eschewed his private attentions in favor of joining a larger party of sociability: "The delightful hours of mutual confidence, of sentimental converse, and of the interchange of refined affection, were no more! Instead of these, *parties were formed*, unpleasing to my taste: and every opportunity was embraced to join in diversions, in which she knew I could not consistently take a share" (75; emphasis added). While Eliza seeks "no other connection than that of friendship" (6), those around her can only envision her conduct in relation to the more particularized and gendered connection of heterosexual marriage. According to her friends, Eliza is a member of a class whose femininity determines that her future lies in heterosexual marriage: sociability is a means of progressing toward a marital future. Eliza, on the other hand, construes her sociability in terms of the pleasures of party life, in which her identity is not determined in advance, but shaped by the party itself.

Her friends thus repeatedly tell her that life is a "path" and that the moment of sociability in which she is now engaged is but a step en route to a socially and biologically determined female role as wife and mother. Her friend, Mrs. Richman, explains the clearly defined steps of this path to her as follows:

> How natural, and how easy the transition from one stage of life to another! Not long since I was a gay, volatile girl; seeking satisfaction in fashionable circles and amusements; but now I am thoroughly domesticated. All my happiness is centered within the limits of my own walls; and I grudge every moment that calls me from the pleasing scenes of domestic life. . . . I must own . . . that conjugal and parental love are the main springs of my life. (97)

Naturally, the girl becomes a woman, progressing in a directed fashion toward her anatomically determined destiny, albeit passing briefly through the less clearly directional "circles" of amusements and uncoupled sociability in order to find a mate. Another friend, Lucy Freeman, points out to Eliza that she must continue to keep in mind the direction of the path she believes her to be pursuing: "You mean only to exhibit a few more girlish airs, before you turn matron. But I am persuaded, if you wish to lead down the dance of life with regularity, you will not find a more excellent partner than Mr. Boyer" (26–27). In similarly spatial terms, Mrs. Richman sketches the dangers of prolonged sociability to Eliza as a failure of directionality: "Of such pleasures [of sociability] no one, my dear, would wish to deprive you. But beware, Eliza!— Though strowed with flowers, when contemplated by your lively imagination, it is, after all, a slippery, thorny path. The round of fashionable dissipation is dangerous. A phantom is often pursued, which leaves its deluded votary the real form of wretchedness" (13). In the language of closed sociability, Mrs. Richman can only imagine Eliza's behavior as indicative of her incorrect choice of suitors; according to Mrs. Richman, then, Eliza is in danger of pursuing a phantom down the wrong path.

Yet I would suggest that Mrs. Richman has drastically misunderstood Eliza's desires. Eliza has not made the wrong choice of suitors (in favor of Sanford rather than Boyer), so much as she has refused to follow any path whatsoever toward heterosexual coupling. Eliza is not looking for a partner to lead her on a path toward marriage; rather, she is interested in forming a party—in pursuing the pleasures of civil association. What she seeks, then, is the circular, nondirective space of sociability, what I have called open sociality. When Eliza reports, rather glumly, on Boyer's pursuit of her hand in marriage, she rejects the language of progress and heteropathic narrative: "Thus far we have proceeded in this sober business [of courtship]. A good beginning you will say. Perhaps it is. I do not, however, feel myself greatly interested in the progress of the negociation. Time may consolidate my affections, and enable me to fix them on some particular object. At present the most lively emotions of my heart are those of friendship" (32–33). Here Eliza objects specifically both to the notion of a directed path (progress) and to choosing a particular object of her desire and thus a particularizing narrative of her identity. Rather, Eliza would like to maintain an intimate connection with a *circle* of friends among whom she can exercise a virtuous civility and take pleasure in forms of communal identity and recognition. Thus while her friends construe her dalliance on the marriage market as coquetry, she understands it as virtuous. Significantly, the formation of sociable "parties" is specifically related in Foster's language (as in

Roger Smith's language) to republican politics as well as to more generalized (less heteropathic) forms of sociability. Boyer's friend Selby thus reports an incident in which the forming of parties is overtly related to politics. While Major Sanford discusses theater with Miss Laurence (a shallow-minded, husband-hunting neighbor) at a social gathering, Eliza discusses politics with her friend Mrs. Richman and her husband. Selby reports,

> General Richman at length observed, that we had formed into parties. . . . Miss Laurence simpered; and looked as if she was well pleased with being in a party with so fine a man [as Sanford]; while her mother replied, that she never meddled with politics; she thought they did not belong to ladies. Miss Wharton and I, said Mrs. Richman, must beg leave to differ from you, madam. We think ourselves interested in the welfare and prosperity of our country; and consequently, claim the right of inquiring into those affairs, which may conduce to, or interfere with the common weal. We shall not be called to the senate or the field to assert its privileges, and defend its rights, but we shall feel for the honor and safety of our friends and connections, who are thus employed. (44)

In this instance, forming a social party is directly equated with engaging in political interests—in forming a political community. Moreover, the political party formed here, on the model of civil association, is a community in which men as well as women are engaged insofar as they "feel" for the common weal. At moments such as this, Eliza's seemingly "dissipated" interest in "assemblies" (attending the theater) and forming "parties" is portrayed as intrinsically virtuous, as unsexed (not pathologized by sex) and humanly crafted—dedicated to a virtuous national community on the basis of shared interest and connection rather than scripted by a private, prepolitical identity. Indeed, Miss Laurence is here portrayed as misunderstanding the nature of civil association, believing that the social party in which she is participating exists primarily for the selfish purpose of husband hunting. At this moment in the novel, then, Foster endorses a version of open sociality, suggesting that the language of coquetry so often employed to criticize Eliza—a language that construes sociality only in terms of heterosexual desire and heterosexual coupling—has fundamentally misunderstood the value of sociability.

But the language of coquetry nonetheless triumphs in the novel. Eliza's suitors as well as her friends resolutely construe sociality as a site in which a preexisting, private (sexed) individual displays or markets herself for marriage. Boyer thus considers Eliza's capacity for engaging his attention, so eloquently described by his friend Selby in terms of the virtues of civil association, as primarily revealing the fixed truth of a potential mate. Eliza's "gaiety," he worries, may make her less than suitable as wife, though he rationalizes in her favor: "[Her friends tell me] that she is naturally of a gay disposition. No matter for

that; it is an agreeable quality where there is discretion sufficient for its regulation. A cheerful friend, much more a cheerful wife is peculiarly necessary to a
person of a studious and sedentary life" (11). As fixed in his identity—"studious
and sedentary"—as Eliza is in hers—"naturally of a gay disposition"—Boyer
seeks to match man to woman on the basis of their dimorphic complementarity. Eliza, in distinct contrast to Boyer, understands sociality as that which constructs rather than reveals and confirms her "natural" identity. Persuaded by
her friends that she should accept Boyer's suit, she nonetheless feels that to do
so will require the creation of new identity for herself: "I have just received a
letter from Mr. Boyer, in the usual style," she writes dryly to Lucy. "He expects
the superlative happiness of kissing my hand next week. O dear! I believe I
must begin to fix my phiz. Let me run to the glass and try if I can make up one
that will look *madamish*" (61). For Eliza, sociality will not confirm her naturally gay disposition in cheerful wedlock but will instead fashion an utterly new
face for her, a "madamish" persona to which she will need to conform.

The language of coquetry assumes that desire exercised in the social world
is sexual or "naturally" directed toward heterosexual ends. In contrast, a model
of open sociality would view the public sphere as a location for exercising a
desire for recognition. While heterosexual desire functions as a powerful form
of recognition, it also forecloses the possibility of other forms of intercourse
and recognition beyond the privatizing aims of heterosexual sex and marriage.
Eliza presents herself on the model of Scottish sociability, according to which
sexed behavior is as much directed toward the pleasures of social intercourse as
those of sexual intercourse: "I received [your letter] with pleasure," she writes
to Boyer,

> and embrace this early opportunity of contributing my part to a correspondence,
> tending to promote a friendly and social intercourse. An epistolary communication
> between the sexes has been with some, a subject of satire and censure; but unjustly,
> in my opinion. With persons of refinement and information, it may be a source of
> entertainment and utility. The knowledge and masculine virtues of your sex may be
> softened, and rendered more diffusive by the inquisitiveness, vivacity, and docility of
> ours; drawn forth and exercised by each other. . . . In regard to the *particular* subject
> of your's [sic] I shall be silent. (47)

Eliza thus describes writing as a means of promoting the civil position and role
of women, a civil role that stands to *transform* (rather than confirm) the gendered norms of masculine and feminine behavior. She refuses, in turn, the
"particular" connection of marital engagement that Boyer offers because this
would involve transforming public, social intercourse into private, sexual intercourse, a path that would gender Eliza in far more fixed and particular terms.

She suggests, as well, that the particularity of that sexual connection is one associated with silence: not only will she be silent on that particular subject, but particularizing herself in those terms would render her silent or exile her from the space of civil association and social intercourse that gives her a platform from which to write, to party, and to assemble in public.

Yet according to the language of coquetry, Eliza is doomed because she fails to understand that sociability is ultimately structured by heterosexual desire. Perhaps the most troubling moment of the novel lies in the transition that occurs midway through the novel when Eliza effectively withdraws from the realm of sociability. This moment corresponds with the loss of her two suitors: Boyer decides that Eliza is toying with his affections, given her apparent interest in Major Sanford, and thus withdraws from the field. Sanford, no longer finding it necessary to ward off Boyer as a rival, retreats from Eliza's company in order to repair his dwindling finances, ultimately marrying an heiress to achieve this end. Eliza reacts somewhat inexplicably to the disappearances of Sanford and Boyer, at least given my reading thus far: "I am undone! I am slighted, rejected by the man [Boyer] who once sought my hand, by the man who still retains my heart! and what adds an insupportable poignancy to the reflection, is self-condemnation!" Judging from this passage, it would seem that she did have her sights set upon a path leading toward matrimony, and for this reason, when the possibility of treading that path with either Boyer or Sanford disappears, she is "undone" or pathless. If she is, indeed, committed to enjoying the circle of sociability without more particular connection, why, then, does she not return to the sociable world of parties in order to pursue her pleasure there? I would suggest that Eliza's collapse and retreat from sociability occurs at the moment when she realizes that sociality is closed rather than open: it is this realization that spells her demise. When Boyer deserts her, she faints and loses "vivacity." Although sociability enables her to exist as a socially recognized subject, she is suddenly convinced that she has failed to understand that the only direction in which sociability operates is a heteropathic one; as such, she understands that she has misrecognized her subject ratification and misrecognized her own identity as it has been constituted through sociality. At this moment, then, Eliza reconfigures her understanding of sociability, as if to bring it in line with what her friends and family have insistently urged upon her: she writes a letter to Boyer offering her hand as a way of reconstituting her desirability, but he has continued on his own path and rather immediately found a substitute marriage partner. She then withdraws, increasingly, from the world of civil society into the private space of her home, a private space in which she is particularized and sexualized by the clandestine attentions of the now-married Major Sanford. At the close of the novel, she explains her illicit association with Sanford in terms of a desire for recognition: "I had no one to participate my cares, to witness my distress, and to alleviate my sorrows, but [Sanford]. I could not therefore prevail on myself, wholly to renounce his society" (145). In a sense, her friends have insisted on precisely this particularized and heterosexualized alignment or form of recognition since they have schooled her in the need to understand her identity as primarily heterosexual. Eliza is ultimately "sexed" by Sanford, and fatally so.

Despite her desire to avoid a *particular* connection to a man—her desire for public and social intercourse rather than private, sexual intercourse—Eliza's fall from social grace is ultimately sexual. After having finally seduced Eliza without offering to marry her, Sanford writes of his conquest to a friend, indicating that Eliza's downfall was the result of her belief that she could separate social and sexual intercourse from one another: "Indeed, I should have given over the pursuit [of Eliza] long ago, but for the hopes of success I entertained from her parleying with me, and in reliance upon her own strength, endeavoring to combat, and counteract my designs. Whenever this has been the case, Charles, I have never yet been defeated in my plan" (139–40). "Parleying" with Sanford—speaking with him in parlors, for instance—is ultimately tantamount to sexual intercourse for Sanford. He insists upon his capacity to transform social into sexual intercourse, and indeed he has been able to perform precisely what he claims with respect to Eliza. Yet the reason he has done so, I would suggest, lies less in any seductive powers of his own than in the cultural logic of coquetry that supports his view: according to this logic, social intercourse is always tantamount to sexual intercourse. It is only when Eliza realizes that she has effectively misrecognized the difference between the two that she consents to assuming the particular status of a heterosexualized female body. Ultimately she is less seduced by Sanford because of any desire he elicits in her than she is convinced that sociality will only function in closed terms—convinced that she will only receive recognition as a sexed female body. And in terms that echo those of the marital gothic, it seems that achieving recognition in this fashion spells her death as she subsequently consents to sexual intercourse with Sanford, becomes pregnant out of wedlock, and dies. At the close of the novel Lucy voices precisely this logic: "To associate, is to approve; to approve, is to be betrayed!" (168). Yet Lucy's logic—one that seemingly spells out a warning against parleying with a rake—is one that effectively pronounces Eliza's death sentence: it is this logic of closed sociality, rather than the seductive powers of Sanford, that ultimately destroys Eliza.

While the events of the novel endorse this account of closed sociality, Foster offers a second perspective that dramatizes the loss of open sociality as the central tragedy explored by the novel. The deep irony of the second half of the novel, for instance, is evident in the efforts Eliza's friends exert to return her to the space of sociability that they once warned her against tarrying within. According to the logic of closed sociality, Eliza need only pick herself up and return to the marriage market after her rejections by Boyer and Sanford in order to find another partner to join her in treading the path of life. Whereas she has been repeatedly warned against "dissipation" heretofore, she is now encouraged to engage in it—to dissipate the melancholy that marks her as a private individual with a particular history in order to market herself as an attractive marriage partner engaged in the social rounds. Lucy thus rails her: "Where, O Eliza Wharton! Where is that fund of sense, and sentiment which once animated your engaging form? Where that strength of mind, that independence of soul, that alacrity and sprightliness of deportment, which formerly raised you superior to every adverse occurrence? Why have you resigned these valuable endowments, and suffered yourself to become the sport of contending passions?" (107). Lucy urges Eliza to assume the "vivacity" she once enjoyed in civil society, yet Eliza, I would suggest, is no longer able to see sociability as the site of virtue or independence: she has little interest in joining the party once she realizes that the logic of the political party is no longer that which animates it. Eliza refuses, for example, an invitation to a ball: "I cannot yet mix with gay and cheerful circles," she writes. I would suggest that she can no longer mix in this fashion because she can no longer believe in the circularity, or open nature, of sociality. Tellingly, Eliza loses interest in both reading and writing at this point. As a number of critics have pointed out, she increasingly disappears from the circle of epistolary communication among friends that constitutes the novel itself. Moreover, she loses her interest in reading as well: "And, when I have recourse to books, if I read those of serious description, they remind me of an awful futurity, for which I am unprepared; if history, it discloses facts in which I have no interest; if novels, they exhibit scenes of pleasure which I have no prospect of realizing!" (135). Her access to public forms of private embodiment is completely blocked here because the once productive forms of identification she took pleasure in have now been foreclosed to her.

At the close of the novel, Eliza adopts the language of heteropathology, describing herself as lost upon leaving her father's home: "This night I become a wretched wanderer from thy paternal roof! Oh, that the grave were this night to be my lodging!" (154). Now pregnant and unmarried, she employs the language her friends have insistently urged upon her and describes herself as having wandered from the path of virtue. To see how much her view of sociability has changed, we might compare the figure of this "wretched wanderer" with her opening words in the novel, which announced the movement beyond the paternal home in terms of pleasure rather than loss: "[I feel] *pleasure*; pleasure, my dear Lucy, on leaving my paternal roof!" (5). Yet rather than understanding the transition that occurs over the course of the novel as one that endorses closed sociality, the sympathy that Eliza's story is clearly intended to generate among its readers indicates that a sense of loss accompanies the foreclosure of sociality. Reflecting on her social and sexual downfall, Eliza cites a poem that indicates that her pathology may be located outside of her, rather than within:

> To you, great gods, I make my last appeal;
> O, clear my conscience, or my crimes reveal!
> If wand'ring through the paths of life I've run;
> And backward trod the steps, I sought to shun,
> Impute my errors to your own decree;
> My feet were guilty, but my heart was free. (109)

Eliza indicates here that lack of virtue was not her error, but rather the error lay in the "decree" of the gods—in the rigidity of the path laid before her that she was innocently unable or unwilling to follow.

In both *Edgar Huntly* and *The Coquette*, then, the narrative force of marriage is felt quite powerfully, although both books subject this force to critical scrutiny. As a literary form being developed in the eighteenth century, the novel seems to experiment in producing the forms of subjective, personal identity that circulate in the public form of print. In analogous terms, marriage itself is increasingly used to produce private identity through public forms of sociability. As such, the aims of the novel seem entwined with the embodying needs of liberalism. The open sociality of civil society is shown in both novels to be foreclosed by heterosexual marriage and its sexualized and racialized forms of embodiment. In eschewing heterosexual marriage Edgar Huntly performs what I have described as a radical republican embodiment, but the republican body offers little in the way of national identity, little in the way of domestic boundaries that would enable liberal self-possession. At the close of the novel, as we have seen, Huntly resembles Ichabod Crane, whose lack of heterosexual desire has seemingly left him entirely without a body and without property. In *The Coquette* the pleasures of society are amply displayed, but these pleasures are shown to be colonized by liberal forms of heterosexual embodiment and an ideology of privatization. *The Coquette* demonstrates the disappearance of an open sociality—in which private identity is avowedly produced in public—in favor of a closed sociality, in which private identity is produced through a shared public presumption of sexual dimorphism. At the moment when sociality's productive nature is hidden, we see erected the apparent divide between public and private that characterizes liberalism. As I've attempted to indicate throughout this chapter, that divide is the marker of submerged forms of interconnection. The "privacy" of women is only produced through public displays of male and female subjects. Women are thus central to the narrative of liberal, propertied embodiment and must be displayed in public in moments of sociality that *produce* gender although seemingly only relay its meaning. Far from merely private, women occupy a highly visible position in the literary public sphere, but the logic that determines women's identity in public can be either creative or coercive, rendering either visible or invisible the gendering force of sociality.

4   Sociality and Sentiment

Popular eighteenth-century dramas of seduction, incest, and marital uncertainty give way, in the nineteenth century, to the domestic, sentimental novel. Creating the family through heterosexual marriage—the fraught work of the eighteenth-century novel—is an accomplished task in these texts and domestic privacy a foregone conclusion. In the sentimental novel of the nineteenth century, the family is already in place and enclosed upon itself; this enclosure obtains both within specific texts and, more broadly, in the ideological codes of the genre itself. What is at stake in the literature of sentimentalism is thus not creating the family but preserving its fixed form. As Joanne Dobson writes,

> The principal theme of the sentimental text is the desire for bonding, and it is affiliation on the plane of emotion, sympathy, nurturance, or similar moral or spiritual inclination for which sentimental writers and readers yearn. Violation, actual or threatened, of the affectional bond generates the primary tension in the sentimental text and leads to bleak, dispirited, anguished, sometimes outraged, representations of human loss, as well as to idealized portrayals of human connection or divine consolation.[1]

While Dobson generalizes here as to the nature of "affectional bonds" in sentimental literature of the nineteenth century, we might more specifically characterize these bonds as primarily familial. Moreover, the bond that bears the most weight in the sentimental text is not that between husband and wife but that between mother and child. The shift from an eighteenth-century concern with contracting marriage between man and woman to a nineteenth-century concern with sustaining the emotional tie between mother and child indicates the extent to which sociality has been increasingly circumscribed over this period. The *social* work of contracting a bond between husband and wife is here eclipsed in favor of celebrating a mother-child relation rooted in a biological connection. As such, the social determinations of affective familial bonds (a central topic of the eighteenth-century novel) are rendered invisible: familial bonds are represented as entirely natural and thus not in need of negotiation at all. The cultural significance of the mother-child bond lies precisely in the assertion of the profoundly natural and unbreakable character of this connection. The possibilities of open sociality found in eighteenth-century clubs and civil relations are absent from sentimental discourse that relies, instead, upon a closed model of sociality to define the hallowed nature of the family and domestic privacy.

The celebration of the mother-child bond and the threatened violation of this bond are thus central topics of sentimental literature. Poems with titles such as "A Mother's Love" are legion in the pages of women's journals and magazines of the mid-nineteenth century: indeed, four separate poems by different authors appeared with precisely this title in the popular women's journal *Godey's Lady's Book* between 1855 and 1858. A rather unremarkable poem, "The Mother's Prayer" by Ernest Schrick, published in 1855 in *Godey's*, usefully exemplifies the conventions of the "mother love" genre:

> On one of Liberty's most lovely spots,
> In Nature's arms lived a love-singled pair;
> Man casts his dice, the Deity allots:
> She gave to them Contentment's happy share!
> 'Twas eve; through half-drawn blinds streamed in her gold,
> Where sat the mother, wife, as richly souled,
> And on her lap her first-born child as fair!
>   . . .
> Now [the child] looks up; his eyes are fixed in hers:
> She gently draws his to her searching face
> Then to her soul, then to the child's recurs
> Through the soul's mirrors to peruse her race;
> That as two mirrors, stationed front to front,
> Would in reflecting but their likeness haunt:
> Tracing the other, they themselves did trace!

The poem opens with something of a feint as it describes a "love-singled pair" destined for happiness together—a pair we might presume to be husband and wife—only to reveal that the twosome in question is not the heterosexual couple, but the mother and child. As such, the poem both plays upon and announces the shift from a conventional (eighteenth-century) literary concern with heterosexual adult coupling to a nineteenth-century concern with the affective connection of mother and child. The poet subsequently describes the scene of a mother looking down upon her child, gazing searchingly into his face—an image that appears repeatedly in nineteenth-century poems and stories devoted to motherly love. In this particular poem, the stakes of the mother-child gaze are articulated more pointedly than in many other texts: for the mother, looking upon her child is a means of looking at herself. Schrick describes the faces of the mother and child mirroring one another, mutually producing the identity of each other in a doubly inflected "mirror stage."[2] The sentimental bond of mother and child is secured as they gaze upon each other and discover themselves in one another. We see the insistence upon a naturalized and biological bond between the two: the mother looks into her son's eyes to see her own likeness and to "peruse her race" therein. Identity is thus not presented as a social construct in this poem. It is not the result, for instance, of contractual negotiations between would-be marriage partners, or among parishioners or citizens: rather, identity is discerned as written within the body and is revealed in the mirroring likeness of mother and child.

Yet despite the biological constraints that seem to govern the emotion binding mother and child, the poem nonetheless clearly associates "mother love" with freedom. The poem begins by locating the "love-singled pair" of mother and child in "Liberty's" dominion, thereby linking maternal love to freedom in much the way we have seen freedom associated, at the close of the eighteenth century, with the affective voluntarism of freely choosing a marital partner. Yet in what sense can freedom be associated with the biological connection of mother and child? The freedom of choosing a spouse in early national literature seemingly signaled an emancipation from parental control and feudal family formation, a freedom to exercise one's emotions without regard for property but with regard for character and individual desire. Yet the freedom evinced in maternal love is of a different sort. Clearly one cannot choose one's child, or even, in the terms of sentimental discourse, choose to love a child: in the sentimental text, love of one's child is hardwired into the maternal constitution and thus not in the least a matter of choice. Although the freedom associated with mother love is thus not one linked to volition, I would nonetheless argue that maternal love does signify freedom in sentimental discourse, and it does so because it is *nonutilitarian*. Dissociated from wage-earning labor and the cash nexus of the marketplace, maternal love is divorced from a world of necessity and constraint and hence signifies a fundamental form of bourgeois liberty and emotional subjectivity.

In sentimental discourse, then, the home is "one of Liberty's most lovely spots" insofar as family members exercise freedom in loving and caring for one another there for nonutilitarian reasons. As we saw in the first chapter, Jürgen Habermas describes the bourgeois family in similar terms as necessary to the *representation* of the freedom of the liberal individual. Habermas's account emphasizes the extent to which the family seems to embody freedom insofar as the domestic realm is viewed as divorced from society: "To the autonomy of property owners in the market corresponded a self-presentation of human

beings in the family. The latter's intimacy, apparently set free from the constraint of society, was the seal on the truth of a private autonomy exercized in
competition."³ Habermas speaks broadly here of the interlinking developments
of capitalism, the print public sphere, and the bourgeois family in eighteenth-
century Europe: according to this account, the freedoms of the marketplace
and of the family develop in tandem and complement one another. Yet with
more specific reference to U.S. culture, Pamela Haag argues that freedom in the
marketplace and in the family are not necessarily coarticulated: Haag contends
that an important transition occurred in the nineteenth century in which freedom *shifted* from being ideologically located in the marketplace to being located in the home. According to Haag, classic liberalism described freedom in
terms of laissez-faire economic policies, yet this freedom began to disappear
with increased state regulation of the marketplace and labor relations at the
close of the nineteenth century. As a result, the freedom of the liberal subject
came to be increasingly defined as occurring in the private space of the home.
In 1890, for instance, Justice Louis Brandeis and Samuel D. Warren articulated
for the first time the legal "right to privacy," the individual's right to be left
alone while occupying "the sacred precincts of private and domestic life."⁴
Brandeis's formulation of a right to privacy "signaled a monumental . . . shift
in the coordinates of liberal identity and culture," writes Haag. "Whether considered as 'sentiments,' or, as in twentieth-century renditions, reproductive or
sexual rights, the gist of the right to privacy was to replicate the characteristics
of laissez-faire and individual freedom evident in economic relations to other
sorts of social relations."⁵ The social relations to which Haag adverts are almost
exclusively domestic and familial—those relations associated with "the sacred
precincts" of the home. Haag's argument indicates, then, that the home bears
increased cultural weight and meaning within liberalism as the marketplace
comes to seem more the location of constraint than autonomy.

Although Haag locates this shift from classic (economic) liberalism to modern (domestic/sexual) liberalism in the early twentieth century, the logic that
associates the nuclear family with freedom and citizenship (including that in
Shrick's poem cited above) is abundantly evident in nineteenth-century sentimental culture and indeed, I would argue, has its roots there.⁶ The first premise of sentimental liberalism—of marking the home as liberty's precinct—is
that "labor" does not occur in the household. Critics such as Ann Douglas,
among others, have argued that the concept of domesticity was transformed
dramatically in the early nineteenth century when the individual household
ceased to be the site of production as it had been in a largely agrarian economy: women who were once producers of homespun or foodstuffs in a house-

hold-based economy became primarily consumers in a market-based economy. The transition away from production altered domesticity "beyond recognition" according to Douglas: "women no longer marr[ied] to help their husbands get a living, but to help them spend their income."[7] Feminist historians
have complicated this model of economic determinism significantly, arguing
that women's labor within the household continued both to exist and to contribute to family economic standing following the market revolution: what did
change, however, was the ideology of domesticity and labor. As Jeanne
Boydston persuasively argues, a "pastoralization" of women's household labor
occurred that erased its status as labor and redefined it as a mode of feminine
being or affect.[8]

While women certainly performed domestic work in the nineteenth-century household, including the work of child rearing, this labor was represented
as sentiment or love rather than work. Reva Siegel, for instance, points out that
it was precisely a sentimental logic of de-instrumentalization (pastoralization)
that came to structure women's legal status in the nineteenth century, including their lack of access to legal standing, particularly in relation to marital
issues. Siegel, as we saw in the first chapter, argues that

> [Sentimental] marriage was an affective relation that subsisted and flourished in a
> private domain beyond the reach of law. A wife could not enforce a contract with her
> husband compensating her for work performed in the family sphere because such
> labor was to be performed altruistically, rather than self-interestedly: for love, not
> pay. . . . By the turn of the century, courts seeking to justify wives' continuing legal
> disabilities described marriage as an emotional relationship subsisting in a private
> realm 'beyond' the reach of law.[9]

Labor "for love, not pay" was not instrumental, and thus, in an important
sense, was seen as volitional rather than utilitarian—it was seen as anything but
labor. In literary terms, we see the replacement of labor with love in the sentimentalized kitchen of the Quaker matriarch Rachel Halliday in Harriet
Beecher Stowe's sentimental novel, *Uncle Tom's Cabin*. In the utopian space of
Rachel's kitchen, labor is performed out of desire and love, not necessity or
compulsion. Rachel Halliday radiates "motherliness" in a fashion that makes
everything move "harmoniously" of its own volition—which is to say, without
constraint and without labor. As the family prepares breakfast under Rachel's
direction, Stowe writes,

> Everything went on so sociably, so quietly, so harmoniously, in the great kitchen—it
> seemed so pleasant to every one to do just what they were doing, there was such an
> atmosphere of mutual confidence and good fellowship everywhere—even the knives
> and the forks had a social clatter as they went on to the table, and the chicken and

ham had a cheerful and joyous fizzle in the pan, as if they rather enjoyed being cooked than otherwise.[10]

Rachel's motherly love thus has the capacity to humanize inanimate objects—to make the chicken fairly jump into the pan, without the least work on anyone's part. In a world where the marketplace turns men into things, particularly through slavery, Stowe suggests that the home turns things (forks, knives, chickens) into people and thus humanizes the world through the erasure of profit-generating labor. No labor—only love—is required to get breakfast on the table in Rachel Halliday's utopian kitchen.[11]

Critics and historians have tended to focus on the terms in which the domestic ideal and separate spheres ideology represented the home as "haven in a heartless world," or what Nancy Cott describes as "a restorative haven from the anxieties and adversities of public life and commerce."[12] Perhaps because the domestic world appears so circumscribed—so associated with the delimitation of women's lives—historians and critics have not associated it with freedom. However, the pastoralization of labor in the sentimental household has the important effect of defining the home as the location where necessity and labor end and where voluntary individual activity, animated by love, begins. Within sentimental liberalism, the home is not simply an escape from the pressures and exigencies of market competition; rather, it is the highest political good for both men and women: home is the location where freedom is ultimately instantiated. Amy Dru Stanley's work on postbellum wage labor is instructive in this regard: as she demonstrates, the implicit promise of wage labor for the freedman lay in the assertion that this form of labor would allow a man to maintain a wife and family in his own home. "In postbellum America the promise of a home unscathed by the market distinguished the rewards of free contract and chattel slavery," writes Stanley. In other words, what distinguished labor for wages from slavery was the fact that the hireling was expected to be able to create and maintain his own domestic space. Without the home, the hireling became merely a slave to wage labor. As such, Stanley suggests that domestic privacy rather than contractual labor became the primary index of freedom in the postbellum period: "The home was viewed as a crucial measure of freedom for men who owned nothing but their own labor."[13] While Stanley indicates that a primary benefit of the home for the male wage earner lay in his patriarchal control of this space—a space in which he was king rather than slave—I would suggest a somewhat more complex account of the meaning of the domestic space. Women and children who occupy the domestic space correctly (who create and maintain a home without making their work visible as labor) wield considerable symbolic power insofar as they represent not subservience to a patriarchal male head of the family, but an abundance of voluntary affect that bespeaks the essential freedom of all who occupy the home. Needless to say, there is marked contradiction entailed in this "freedom" given the highly scripted and disciplinary nature of domesticity (indeed, the erasure of labor is itself a new form of labor), but the ideological payoff of domesticity, I would contend, is intimately related to the symbolics of freedom.

In her critique of sentimentalism, Ann Douglas has suggested that domesticity and the "cult of motherhood" ensnared women in a position that was no longer useful or productive; as a result, women sought to parasitically wield influence over men and to thereby lay (dubious) claim to an exalted moral worth. According to Douglas, then, the celebration of motherhood is essentially compensatory for the authority women have lost as producers: "Praise of motherhood could bolster and promote the middle-class woman's biological function as tantamount, if not superior, to her lost economic productivity. . . . The cult of motherhood . . . was an essential precondition to the flattery American women were trained to demand in place of justice and equality."[14] Rendered passive and superfluous, women turned to motherhood to assert their continued social value. Douglas's claims have received ample critique since they were published: critics from Jane Tompkins to Lori Merish have argued that sentimentalism was neither politically irrelevant nor did it place women in a passive position.[15] Yet I want to assert a slightly different claim with respect to Douglas's argument: if women were seen as "superfluous," this superfluity was not the result of being left out of a larger economic or political picture as Douglas argues, but the result of assuming a symbolically significant position within this picture. If women worked hard to appear "superfluous"— to seem leisured rather than belabored, animated by love rather than need— they did so because this leisure was not itself extraneous but rather related to political claims of liberalism and citizenship. The cultural function of the family was not simply to maintain capital or perpetuate patrilineal authority, but to produce the freedom of the liberal subject through affective abundance and nonutilitarianism. As such, the symbolics of sentimental liberalism exerted pressure upon women from a range of racial and economic strata, not simply upon white middle-class women. Because ideals of domesticity had immense political and symbolic meaning, they cannot be understood as a *result* of the market revolution or the prosperity of a newly "leisured" middle class, as some critics have argued. In other words, leisure and domestic liberty were matters of ideology rather than free time. While sentimental liberalism and domestic ideology may have disproportionately benefited the white middle class by consolidating the moral and economic authority of members of this group, the association of liberty with housekeeping formed an influential ideology that spurred a range of engagements—from aspiring imitation to critical revision—among African-Americans, immigrants, and poor laborers who had little in the way of resources to own or maintain a home or to represent it as a space of "leisure" for women and children.[16]

Moreover, the symbolics of sentimental liberalism incorporated not just the mother of the household, but children as well. Indeed, the debut of the child as a central figure of popular and literary culture is one of the most striking aspects of sentimental discourse. Whereas children are virtually absent from eighteenth-century popular fiction, they populate every manner of sentimental text in the nineteenth century. The child in the sentimental text is, above all, "innocent," and as such, his or her love and affection is wholly unrestrained by commerce, labor, or utilitarian motives. "The child is your one true democrat," states Augustine St. Clare in *Uncle Tom's Cabin*, thus locating the truth of American political freedom in the supposed liberality of infantile sentiment. As historians of childhood have demonstrated, the figure of the "innocent" child is new to the cultural stage in the nineteenth century, though it was thenceforth embraced with great fervor. According to the seventeenth-century Puritan minister Thomas Hooker, a young child lived the life of a "beast." By the nineteenth century, however, the child's innocence was "a model for emotion-cramped parents themselves."[17] No longer the repository of original sin in its unreformed state, the child of the nineteenth century was considered untainted by the world and thus more rather than less pure than adults. Child-rearing models shifted from eighteenth-century exercises in breaking the will of the child to nineteenth-century exercises in treasuring and preserving the playful innocence of childhood. More specifically, by the late nineteenth century, children were increasingly being shielded from the world of work rather than trained for it. Daniel T. Rodgers describes an influential child-rearing manual of 1894, providing an "account of the manner in which a child could be raised virtually on the strength of love alone—never made a 'victim to regularity,' virtually never punished, never set to tasks except those stripped of their forbidding character by transformation into play." As a result, writes Rodgers, "work as traditionally conceived retreated . . . to the vanishing point" in the life of the child.[18] In sentimental discourse, the child is thus even less instrumentalized than the de-instrumentalized wife and mother. The child's "innocence" and the mother's love for (rather than her training of) the child are spectacularly useless, and thus speak to the affective, nonutilitarian structuring of home life.

Although children suddenly become central figures in the pages of nineteenth-century novels, it is equally remarkable that the most prominent action they perform in these texts is dying. As Karen Sánchez-Eppler succinctly observes, "Dying is what children do most and do best in the literary and cultural imagination of nineteenth-century America."[19] Why is the death of a child so important in the sentimental text? If the mother-child bond is of such eminent symbolic value as the location of freedom, why is so much attention devoted to its rupture? One possible answer to this question lies in the observation that staging the child's death seems to be the best means of preserving the very innocence that distinguishes the child from the adult. The child who becomes an adult loses his or her nonutilitarian status: growing up becomes something of a tragedy when childhood is the source of freedom and moral truth. In Frances Sargent Locke Osgood's poem "A Mother's Prayer in Illness," for instance, a mother enjoins God to "take [her children] first" such that they will be free from "the shadowy train of future ills" and "the hateful, withering lesson of distrust" that they will be forced to confront without their mother's protective love. Indeed, once the "world's wild discord" that the children will surely confront as they grow older (with or without the mother) is introduced in the poem, the central desire of the speaker seems to be less sheltering the children from a world without their mother (should the mother die first) than sheltering them from the world altogether: "Ah! take them first, my Father! and then me."[20] In other words, although the speaker initially seems to plead that the children die before her, given that she is ill herself, she ultimately seems to issue a plea for the death of all of them to avoid the cruelties of the world. Osgood's poem, like many others, indicates that the innocence of the child is best preserved through death rather than defiled in the inevitable process of loss that maturation would bring.

However, if the child retains his or her innocence through death, it nonetheless seems incorrect to say that the child needs to die solely to preserve its innocence. Rather, a central function of the child's death in the sentimental text is to call for and enable the articulation of maternal grief. Specifically, the death of the child enables the *public* articulation and display of the mother's love for the child and the circulation of familial affect as a means of addressing loss. The outpouring of grief that the death of the child in the nineteenth century occasions is both prodigious and public: volumes of poetry and stories devoted to maternal grief appeared in print, such as a volume titled *Echoes of Infant Voices*, published in 1849.[21] As such volumes testify, death was a decidedly public occasion, an occasion for the extended public display of familial feeling. In a study of sentimental poetry and the keepsake album in particular, Mary Louise Kete describes mourning as central to sentimentality for a number of reasons: "Loss through death, especially the death of a child, seemed to be a sanctioned moment for articulating one's skepticism about religious teachings or even the possibility of meaning itself. In the course of a symbolic process designed to allay these feelings and to rebind the mourner to the community, sentimental collaboration entailed the creation of images of both the mourner and the mourned through a joint effort."[22] Mourning, on this account, has the function of temporarily unbinding the individual from social bonds (through skepticism, through emotional rupture) and subsequently *rebinding* the individual to a social community through the public circulation and citation of codes of familial affect. In this sense, mourning for the dead child becomes the moment for the social (re)construction of privacy and the private subject—a site of what I have described as open sociality. In the literary public sphere, maternal mourning becomes the specific location where the enduring bonds of nonutilitarian familial affect are publicly constituted in the wake of loss. Kete's analysis focuses on a particular keepsake album kept over a period of some thirty years by a Vermont woman and her circle of friends. The album contains poems written originally for or copied into the album, and mourning and loss are the unifying topic of the poems. In her discussion of the poems shared and circulated in the album, Kete points to the *social* nature of grief and mourning: "It is the threat of loss that makes the declaration of presences—of the presence of and in affection—necessary. For, these poems suggest, it is freely given affection, not blood, that holds families together . . . the characteristically sentimental utopian reconstitution of the family is driven by an initial representation of that family as threatened by loss" (33). While the death of a child rips the family apart it also opens the way for the voluntaristic, social reconstruction (or retro-construction) of enduring familial bonds. When the link between mother and child is ruptured through death, Kete would seem to suggest, the familial bond is subsequently reestablished in a new and more voluntaristic fashion. The wound within the nuclear family makes possible the articulation of family bonds that now seem *more* rather than less enduring, *more* rather than less voluntary than before.

In related terms, Sánchez-Eppler argues that the death of a child in the nineteenth century was an important occasion for the commercialization and circulation of familial sentiment. Specifically, Sánchez-Eppler considers the creation of daguerreotypes of dead children that rapidly became a popular mode of memorialization following the invention of daguerreotypy in the mid-nineteenth century. In the staged, sentimental scenes of the daguerreotype of the dead child, Sánchez-Eppler argues, the privacy of familial feeling is publicly produced: "The aim of these manipulations [in the daguerreotype] is to produce out of these dead bodies a meaning that exceeds the fact of death. This tableau measures the worth of the family, whose love and intimacy are here poignantly confirmed, even in a sense produced, in the image of the children it has lost."[23] Sánchez-Eppler thus emphasizes the fact that the memorial photograph does not simply preserve family feeling, but in some sense creates it. Moreover, rather than describing the commercialization of grief as a betrayal of the personal or private nature of the loss of a child, Sánchez-Eppler indicates that commercialization is itself a tool for the production of "private" emotion: "If commodification exploits feelings to yield profit, it is equally possible for emotions to use the commercial as a means of expression and a form of circulation" (74). Commodification and circulation of the image of the dead child thus make grief productive—productive of the sentimental family as the site of what I have described as affective abundance and freedom.

I have argued that the mother-child bond is central to sentimental fiction insofar as it signifies the natural and non-negotiable connection of members of the nuclear family. In the sentimental novel, the enclosed nature of the bourgeois family would seem to correspond to what I called in the previous chapter "closed sociality." Public representations of familial identity—and indeed the seemingly transparent prose of sentimentalism itself—indicate that the truth of private identity (nurtured in the family) is displayed in public rather than created there. Private, familial identity is likewise seen as the grounds of moral action in public, thus supporting a liberal narrative in which individuals are fully created and saturated with identity in private, and subsequently appear in public in order to protect the sanctity of privacy and the bourgeois family. Yet sociality is by definition public: sociality occurs where public and private identities are mutually constituted through the operations of a public sphere of desire. I have posited that a moment of public circulation is thus necessary for the creation of liberal privacy. In the sentimental text—and in the rigid closure of sociality in the nineteenth century around private, gendered forms of domesticity—the danger of public circulation is pronounced (since it threatens enclosure) but nonetheless requisite to the creation of social meaning. Negotiating or creating a mother-child bond is not the subject of the sentimental novel, since this bond is typically posited as given in advance of culture and in advance of social interaction; rather, doing violence to the mother-child bond is the catalyst for the plot of the sentimental novel.[24] The closed domestic space of privacy is thus violently shattered in the sentimental novel, yet only this violence enables the public "display" that will generate the very meaning and value of privacy. Ironically, then, familial bonds within sentimentalism are made to be broken in order to recharge them with affective value and recirculate them as social currency.

This, then, is one way to account for the corpses of children that litter sentimental texts, from Harriet Beecher Stowe's sainted Little Eva to Lydia Sigourney's expiring infants. The intensely naturalized (and thus rigid and enclosed) terms of familial association thus seem to *necessitate* an equally intense violence to break these bonds and open the way for the narrative movement of sentimental discourse and for the social articulation of private identities. Pain, suffering, and violence are thus intrinsic to sentimental discourse, despite—or, as I am suggesting, because of—the sentimental emphasis on the closure, privacy, and freedom of the domestic space. In his well-known criticism of Harriet Beecher Stowe, James Baldwin thus defines sentimentalism as fundamentally dishonest: "the ostentatious parading of excessive and spurious emotion is the mark of dishonesty . . . the wet eyes of the sentimentalist . . . [are] the signal of secret and violent inhumanity, the mask of cruelty."[25] Baldwin puts his finger on the contradiction that inheres in sentimental fiction: violence is at once its modus operandi and that which it seemingly deplores. Like Baldwin, other critics have denounced the suffering portrayed in the sentimental text as fundamentally dishonest. For both Ann Douglas and Lauren Berlant, for instance, sentimental suffering effectively masks rather than engages in political activity. Berlant's critique is particularly compelling in this regard: sentimentalism, she suggests, tends to privatize human interaction, including efforts to effect political change in order to stem the causes of human suffering: "When sentimentality meets politics, it uses personal stories to tell of structural effects, but in so doing it risks thwarting its very attempt to perform rhetorically a scene of pain that must be soothed politically. . . . The political as a place of acts oriented toward publicness becomes replaced by a world of private thoughts, leanings, and gestures. Suffering, in this personal-public context, becomes answered by survival, which is then recoded as freedom."[26] According to Berlant, then, the public sphere has been eradicated in favor of what she describes as an "intimate public," a public in which rational political debate is insistently erased because it is translated into personal and familial narrative. The narrative of personal suffering, Berlant suggests, cannot effect structural change and thus does not constitute an engagement in a political public sphere. In many respects, Berlant's analysis seems accurate, yet I would ultimately suggest that the model of the Habermasian public sphere she implicitly evokes (and regrets the loss of) needs to be reconsidered. If, as I have argued throughout this book, the public sphere is the location where privacy is constructed, where subjects strive to emerge into visibility, then narratives of familial construction may, on occasion, prove less closed—and less depoliticized—than she suggests. I thus want to consider the publicness of sentimental suffering as a moment of sociality—a potentially open moment of sociality—rather than simply evidence of privatization. In the next section of this chapter, I analyze a series of infanticide narratives that focus on the stories that emerge out of the wound created by the dead child—a wound that is difficult to close because it is created in (ideologically) vexed circumstances, that is, when the mother is herself guilty of killing the child. In relation to this open wound, then, I want to examine the possibility of an open sociality as it appears within the sentimental text.

INFANTICIDE AND STRUCTURAL VIOLENCE

In *The Theory of Moral Sentiments*, Adam Smith points to infanticide as a cultural dividing line between savage and civilized societies. "Can there be greater barbarity than to hurt an infant?" asks Smith. "When custom can give sanction to so dreadful a violation of humanity, we may well imagine that there is scarce any particular practice so gross which it cannot authorize." In sentimental terms, no act is more unnatural—more *inhuman*, as Smith points out—than that of a mother killing her child. "What then should we imagine must be the heart of a parent who could injure that weakness which even a furious enemy is afraid to violate?" asks Smith.[27] Characteristically, Smith asks us to imagine what is in the "heart" of another human being (the infanticidal mother) in order to pass moral judgment; in so doing, he asks us to perform the central ethical act of his theory of sentiment, namely, extending sympathetic understanding to another individual. In terms of this moral theory, however, infanticide is the grossest of violations: it entails a refusal to identify (to sympathize) with the humanity of the weakest of individuals and a decision to destroy rather than protect the neediest of beings. If civility involves the extension of sympathy and sentiment to those around one (and certainly to those closest to one, such as one's child), infanticide marks the exterior limit of civil society and the onset of barbarism.

Rupturing the sacrosanct bond of mother and child, infanticide is thus the most unnatural crime when viewed in sentimental terms. Yet infanticide is nonetheless also entirely "natural" when considered from the perspective of history or social science. Historians have demonstrated, for instance, that infanticide is ubiquitous: it occurs in virtually all societies, past and present, and across social ranks.[28] Indeed, philosophers have argued that infanticide is an evolutionarily sensible practice, "natural" rather than "barbaric." Stephen Pinker, for example, suggests that mothers may be evolutionarily fitted with an "emotional circuitry" (evidently not of the sentimental variety) to commit infanticide should they need to preserve resources for other children or for their own survival.[29] In broader terms, then, we might say that infanticide marks a structural limit of social reproduction. When infanticide occurs, it renders visible the economic and cultural norms according to which individuals will and will not devote resources to reproduction and it thus indicates the social limits of reproduction. The crime of infanticide among women is primarily one of neonaticide—the killing of an infant within minutes or hours of birth—and thus is typically linked to a mother's sense that she is unwilling or unable to nurture a child in the world. As such, infanticide marks not the limits of civility or humanity, but the culturally and economically determined reproductive boundaries of any society: the conditions (social and/or economic) under which women are willing and able to bear and sustain children through infancy.

The implicit claims of these two perspectives—one that prioritizes a moral and sentimental investment in the infant and the mother-child bond, and one that attends to the larger structural processes of social reproduction—come directly into conflict in the instance of infanticide. Since roughly the mid-eighteenth century (around when Smith wrote *The Theory of Moral Sentiments*), infanticide has been regarded both as the most horrific of crimes, and, paradoxically, as a crime that tends to inspire sympathy not only for its victim but for its perpetrator. By the late eighteenth century, juries in both New England and England increasingly refused to convict women of the crime of infanticide, despite evidence of their guilt. The lack of punitive force exercised upon the mother would seem to indicate that juries remained willing, at least to some degree, to locate guilt for the crime less in the infanticidal mother herself than in the society that seemed to dictate to her the impossibility of sustaining her infant's life. The de jure criminalization of infanticide and the de facto decriminalization of the same offense indicate the extent to which infanticide is at the crux of an ideological contradiction.[30] This contradiction, I would suggest, is especially acute for sentimental liberalism, and is visible in nineteenth-century narratives concerning infanticide. If the freedom of the liberal subject is increasingly constructed around the figure of the mother and the privacy of the mother-child dyad, infanticide indicates the extent to which this dyad bears the structural burdens of the society as a whole. As such, the mother-child bond that is seemingly the most private and internal to the family—seemingly the most nonutilitarian and untouched by the public sphere or the state—turns out to be most structurally determining for the shape and identity of the nation-state. In sentimental discourse, then, and particularly in the instance of infanticide, we can see something of a hyperbolically closed sociality: the intense (hyperbolic) closure of the family into a naturalized, private unit is accompanied by the intensely public, ideological weight that this closed unit increasingly must bear.

In the following pages, I analyze four infanticide narratives written between 1701 and 1852. The first is the account of Esther Rogers as redacted by the Puritan minister John Rogers and appended to a sermon preached on the occasion of Esther Rogers's execution for the crime of infanticide in 1701. The additional three narratives, published respectively in 1786, 1822, and 1852, are all based upon the life of Elizabeth Wilson, a woman who was convicted of murdering her twin infants in Pennsylvania in 1784. A clear historical trajectory emerges across the narratives in which the nuclear family, wholly absent in the early eighteenth-century narrative, becomes central to the account of infanticide in the final sentimental narrative of the mid-nineteenth century. The closed sociality of sentimentality, I argue, locates violence within the domestic scene: that is, in comparison with earlier accounts of infanticide, the sentimental narrative indicates the way in which the closure of sociality upon itself is inevitably linked to scenes of violence. In the final narrative I examine, Lydia Maria Child's 1852 fictionalized account of Elizabeth Wilson's life and crime, the enclosed nature of the sentimental family ultimately appears to be the cause of infanticidal violence. As such, I suggest, Child both describes and critiques the sentimental logic of domestic enclosure and points to the necessity of a more open and negotiable social identity for women.

If the contradiction between private subject and social structure is particularly sharp in the sentimental narrative, it is nonetheless not wholly absent even in the early eighteenth-century Puritan account of infanticide. Infanticide represents a rip in the social fabric, a moment when a contradiction is made visible. The infanticidal mother has, in some fashion or another, been both enjoined to reproduce and not to reproduce. It is the purpose of the infanticide narrative to negotiate this double injunction and thus to resolve or make sense of the contradiction infanticide bespeaks. As in the wake of any crime, it is possible to cast out the criminal in order to restore social order: yet the contradictory injunctions to reproduce and not to reproduce are eminently social imperatives (interior to the social order), and, because of this, the guilt for the crime of infanticide cannot be easily located outside the community. As Laura Henigman argues, "While the infanticide case is a sign of the self-destructive sinfulness of an individual who willfully estranges herself from community, it is a sign as well of community failure to enforce its norms and make its institutions of care accessible to those in its orbit."[31] The infanticide narrative must thus address or offer redress for the possible indictment of social structure that the crime itself makes evident: the infanticide narrative must, then, establish the innocence of the society. Interestingly, in each of the four narratives I consider below the innocence of the society as a whole is established by affirming the innocence of the mother. Rather than casting out the murdering mother, each of the four narratives I consider offers an account of the mother's consent to the social norms that induced the infanticide. The infanticidal mother is ultimately rendered innocent insofar as she recognizes her guilt; as such, the infanticide narrative smoothes and erases the contradiction between individual and social guilt and naturalizes the contradictory limits of social reproduction. As the exception to this pattern, Child's narrative, as I argue below, suggests instead that a structural violence may inhere in the sentimental family itself.

The innocence of Esther Rogers, condemned of and executed for the crime of infanticide in Ipswich, Massachusetts, in 1701, is assured only at the moment when she confesses fully to her guilt and, more importantly, demonstrates a sense of her own "conviction" of her sin. Rogers's narrative of infanticide is appended to a tract containing three sermons preached by the Ipswich minister John Rogers (unrelated to Esther) in 1701: the title of the tract is "Death the Certain Wages of Sin . . . Occasioned by the imprisonment, condemnation and Execution of a Young Woman who was guilty of murdering her Infant Begotten in Whoredom, to which is added, an account of her manner of life and death, in which the glory of free grace is displayed." The didactic and religious nature of the tract is quite evident here: Esther Rogers's story is meant to stand as an example of the glory of God's free grace; as John Rogers writes, her story is made public "that all others who may providentially come to the view of [her], may be stirred up to praise the Lord for his wonderful goodness, in making such an heinous Sinner such an Instance of Converting Grace and Mercy."[32] Rogers's infanticide narrative is thus clearly presented as an exemplary version of Puritan conversion. Moreover, her narrative performs much of what we have seen of the Puritan conversion narrative in the second chapter: that is, it publicly and visibly produces, through overt social machination, an account of the interior religious state of an individual who seeks communal recognition. Rogers is legally convicted of infanticide by the court after her dead child is discovered half-buried, near the meetinghouse in Newbury. Yet this legal conviction—imposed from the outside—ultimately transforms itself into a spiritual conviction generated from the inside; it is this production of subjectivity, as external force becomes internal identity, that is ultimately narrated in Rogers's conversion narrative and that finally works to produce both Rogers and the Puritan society as innocent. At the moment when Esther Rogers demonstrates her own sense of conviction—an understanding of her deeply sinful nature—she produces herself as a subject available for public recognition, a subject available for redemption by God's saving grace and available for inclusion within the Puritan community.

Esther Rogers in many ways typifies the infanticidal mother. A white woman who was bound as a servant at the age of thirteen, she had little in the way of resources or status (including marital status) to support a child when she later became pregnant. Indeed, in her narrative, she reports that she has committed infanticide more than once: "About the age of seventeen," she reports, "I was left to fall into that foul Sin of Uncleanness, suffering myself to be defiled by a *Negro* Lad living in the same House" (122). Having hidden her pregnancy and delivered the baby in secrecy, she "stop[ped] the breath" of the child and subsequently buried it outside. Some period of years later, she reports, "I fell into the like horrible Pit (as before) *viz.* of Carnal Pollution with the *Negro* man belonging to that House. And being with Child again, I was in . . . great concern to know how to hide this" (124). The delivery of the second child occurs covertly and quickly as well: "I went forth to be delivered in the Field, and dropping my Child by the side of a little Pond (whether alive, or still Born I cannot tell) I covered it over with Dirt and Snow, and speedily returned home again" (124). What is remarkable in this account of extramarital sex, childbirth, and murder is the lack of sentiment attached to any of the individuals—either to her sexual partner or her child—central to the narrative. Rogers reports that she did not even tell the father of the child that she was pregnant. The father's racial identity seems relevant insofar as it mirrors Rogers's own status as indentured and thus marginal; the racial distinction between Rogers and the father also further underscores the impossibility of a marital connection between the two and hence indicates the extent to which reproduction cannot (according to existing social norms) be associated with family formation in this instance. When a sense of personal emotion and affect enters the account, it occurs only with reference to religion rather than with reference to the familial relations that structure sentimental narrative. "The [second] Child being found by some Neighbors was brought in & laid before my Face, to my horrible Shame & Terror" (124), Rogers reports. "Thinking only of the punishment I was like to suffer, without any true concernedness as to my Sins against God, or the State of my Immortal Soul; til some time after I came into *Ipswich* Prison; when and where it pleased the Great and Gracious God to work upon my heart, as in the following Relation I have given account of." Her sins, as described here, are against God, not against her dead children. Moreover, while the account of her life of sin and crime is roughly four pages in length, the relation of her conversion once she is legally convicted of infanticide and in prison awaiting execution runs an additional twenty pages. No familial relations structure her account, her affect, or her sense of identity in this narrative. The only individuals who appear significant in the narrative are the ministers who visit her in prison exhorting her to consider her spiritual state—exhorting her, as Laura Henigman argues, to "come into communion" with them by internalizing the conviction of her sin and seeking God's grace.

During the time she was imprisoned, an additional eight months following her court trial, Rogers was thus thoroughly coached in the forms of Puritan conversion. She was, the narrative tells us, "frequently visited by Ministers, and other Christians of the Town and Neighborhood" (127). Although initially she "could not open her mind or condition at all; nor make any other answer to Questions propounded, than yea or no," she later learns to speak as the result of the ministerial attentions devoted to her: "after a while she obtained more freedom of spirit, and liberty of speech. Then would she speak of her sins with aggravation, and express sorrow for them with great affection" (127–28). As both Daniel Williams and Henigman point out, Esther Rogers gains public recognition and identity only by adhering rather meticulously to the script that is given her by the ministers.[33] Her "liberty of speech" arrives at the moment when she freely follows the models of self-articulation proposed for her by the ministers. Insofar as the narrative of her conversion is crucial to the spectacle of her execution, we might thus locate Rogers's death on the cusp of the divide Michel Foucault has drawn between disciplinary and punitive cultures. Although her execution is witnessed by "Four or Five Thousand People at least" (153), the account of her interior state seems necessary to supplement a spectacle that, understood as punishment, shows the exercise of state force upon her body. The narrative, however, internalizes that force as a disciplinary power: Rogers's "liberty" arrives at the moment when she is ready to produce the form of interiority publicly prescribed for her.

If the ministers who assist Rogers in writing her conversion narrative quite obviously seek to make public use of Rogers's crime and conversion, they nonetheless do so in a fashion that is for the most part divorced from the particular nature, and particularly the gendered nature, of her crime. Rather than focusing on the breach of the mother-child bond, John Rogers's sermons themselves focus on the ubiquity of sin among all members of the community: "The natural ways of everyone are unclean," writes Rogers. "Every child of *Adam* is born a Leper, all over defiled" (95). Rogers thus emphasizes a Calvinist notion of man's innately sinful nature and seeks to convict all members of the community of their sinfulness. Esther Rogers, then, is understood as exemplary rather than extraordinary: her sin is a figure for the innate sinfulness of every member of the community. In the introduction to the sermons, for instance, Esther Rogers is compared to the biblical thief who converts while on the cross. The analogy suggests that what is most significant about her story is neither her crime nor her gender, but the distance between the life of sin and the conversion to grace, as well as the possibility of traversing this distance. Indeed, John Rogers speaks in the introduction to the sermons of Esther Rogers's confinement and her conception, yet he uses these terms to refer to her confinement in prison (not her pregnancy) and to the conception of grace in her soul, not of a child within her womb. Accordingly, images of childbirth are deployed away from their material referents toward an ungendered image of spiritual rebirth. The transition that occurs over the course of the narrative, then, traverses a line drawn between those inside and those outside the community of Christian congregants. A formerly marginal, bound servant now receives the undivided attention of numerous ministers and visitors who spend days and weeks focusing on the state of her soul. As a result, she ultimately becomes a member of this Christian community, and her conversion is taken as exemplary of precisely the movement from outside (declension) to inside (conversion). Her marginal status seems useful in this respect; it marks the distance she has covered. Ultimately, her narrative recounts a movement from outside to inside the community that is defined in terms of sin and submission to God (and the ministerially directed community) rather than in terms of a set of affective, familial relations structuring social identity.

Rogers's narrative is useful, then, in demonstrating what an unsentimental account of infanticide might look like—an account in which a different emotional purchase and an alternative version of subjectivity unrelated to sentimental motherhood appears in relation to the crime of infanticide. By way of contrast, the next three narratives I turn to—all of which are versions of the same historically documented case of infanticide in Pennsylvania—each focus in different ways on the affective bonds structuring relations between and among family members. Elizabeth Wilson was convicted of murdering her twin infants in Chester, Pennsylvania, in 1784 and executed for that crime in January of 1786. A twenty-seven-year-old woman who had borne three children out of wedlock prior to the birth of her twins, she claimed throughout that the twins were in fact killed by their father—her seducer—and not by her hand. Two days after her execution, a sixteen-page account of her execution and her confession was published, including the text of the confession she is said to have written while in prison. Although she does not confess, in this account, to the murder of her infants, she does profess herself guilty of a number of other sins: she is guilty of "the soul-destroying sin of fornication" and, more particularly, guilty of the sin of having been seduced. Her self-conviction of these sins enables her to produce a conversion narrative that bears some similarity to that of Esther Rogers: she confesses her sin, begs for the mercy of God, and finally asserts her own pleasure and reassurance in her conversion to Christ as a result of this experience. Yet despite familiar references to the saving grace of God, the lineaments of the conversion narrative in the 1786 Wilson narrative are primarily vestigial. The narrative has shifted away from the issues of sin, grace, and communion and now focuses more resolutely on the truth and meaning of affective human relations. Like Esther Rogers's narrative, *A Faithful Narrative of Elizabeth Wilson* seeks to produce the interiority of a socially recognizable subject—one whose private emotion testifies to the truth and righteousness of public, disciplinary norms. Yet the interior truth of Elizabeth Wilson bears little relation to that of Esther Rogers because the disciplinary norms of gender and maternity have shifted dramatically as well.

As Daniel Williams points out, Wilson's *Faithful Narrative* participates more fully in the genre of criminal narrative literature than that of religious conversion. Published with an eye to commercial rather than religious results, the text engages the reader with the promise of revealing the lurid details of a shocking crime. Moreover, it poses an epistemological question at the outset of the narrative that structures the reader's engagement in the text: is Elizabeth Wilson guilty or innocent of the crime of infanticide? The author reports, "Before, at, and after the trial, [Wilson] persisted in denying the fact [that she had killed the twins]; her behaviour was such, in general, as gave reasons to conclude she was innocent of the murder of which she was charged, or was an insensible, hardened creature, and did not expect to die for this crime."[34] Wilson is placed before the bar and before the reader as either "innocent" or "insensible": as we read the text, we too will search for the evidence that will demonstrate which of these labels applies. Yet the very opposition of these terms—innocent and insensible—suggests that guilt will be legible as a lack of feeling or sensibility and that innocence will be equated with sensibility.

In its emphasis on casting the story of infanticide in terms of a tale of seduction, *A Faithful Narrative* clearly participates in the early national concern over what we have seen, in the third chapter, as the issue of capitalist family formation and marital virtue. As I argued there, new models of family formation insisted on the priority of affective recognition within the heterosexual marriage. The virtuous and desirable woman was a marital companion not in her capacity to work but in her capacity to set the stage of affective individualism, recognizing her husband's identity and masculinity by way of her own femininity. Elizabeth Wilson's narrative, I would argue, seeks to establish Wilson's innocence through demonstrating her "sensibility" and family-forming desire. At the outset of her own confession, which is set within the larger text, we hear the most damning evidence against her: before she meets the seducer in this tale, she has already "had three children in an unlawful way." As such, she has clearly conducted herself in a fashion that marks her as outside the norms of female virtue and capitalist family formation. Yet the narrative subsequently works to erase this evidence against her, to restore the virtue that is seemingly absent from her character. Her "seduction" by Joseph Deshong, the father of the murdered children, thus occurs, she explains, only because of her virtuous, maritally directed desires: "In the beginning of the year 1784, [Deshong] insinuated himself into my company, under pretence of courtship, declaring himself a single man, and by repeated promises of marriage deceived and persuaded me to consent to his unlawful embraces" (4). Being seduced by promises of marriage here works to *establish* her virtue—to demonstrate her affective susceptibility to the claims of what seems to be marital, heterosexual recognition. Conversely, Deshong's true viciousness is ultimately revealed not in his sexual advances, but in his refusal to labor on behalf of Elizabeth Wilson and their children, a refusal indicating his lack of fitness for capitalist family formation. According to her account, Deshong tricks Wilson by arranging to meet her in a secluded spot to determine the details of his financial support for her and the infants: once they meet, however, he declares, "I have no money for you, nor your bastards either" (5). Holding a gun to Wilson's head, he then takes the infants and stomps them to death. At this point in the narrative, Wilson most vividly demonstrates her emotional connection to her children, and thus her "sensibility" to the crime of infanticide: "He then requested me to strip my dear dead infants naked. Thro' fear I took off each of their little gowns, but could proceed no further; my bowels yearning over my dear children" (5). Wilson's anguished account of the death of the children stands in dramatic opposition to the unemotional description of infanticide in Rogers's narrative. Her suffering testifies both to her innocence (insofar as she is sensible to the claims of familial affect), and to the shift in codes of innocence between the two historical moments in which Rogers's and Wilson's narratives appeared.

Yet if Wilson seeks to establish her innocence by way of demonstrating her commitment to affective, familial connections, her attempt to reestablish her virtue does not seem to be fully accomplished through her description of her seduction or the death of her children. The anonymous narrator of *The Faithful Narrative* continues to amass evidence for and against Wilson following the presentation of her intercalated confession in the text. After receiving a brief respite in the date of her execution, the narrator states that questions remain about her behavior: "Her behaviour was in general consistent with her situation; but not appearing at all times so deeply affected, as when the ministers visited her, some reports of the prisoners, intimating the insincerity of her profession, gave uneasiness to her friends: but when she was informed of these reports she was greatly distressed, and accounted for them in such a manner, as to remove all scruple of her sincerity" (5–6). The narrative thus indicates that doubts remain as to Wilson's account, as does anxiety on Wilson's part as to whether she has established herself as credible. The ultimate decision of the narrator to resolve the question of Wilson's innocence in her favor hinges, finally, upon a different set of circumstances that testify to Wilson's capacity to sustain familial affective bonds. The narrator reports that Wilson's brother works to obtain a stay for his sister from execution. Although he obtains one respite, he is unable to stop the execution, and, moreover, tragically arrives with a second respite from Philadelphia twenty-three minutes after Wilson's execution. While epistemological uncertainty colors the narrator's account of Wilson up to the moment of execution, the brother's arrival after her death has the rhetorical effect of cementing her innocence. At the moment when Wilson's brother appears, the narrator shifts to a distinctly sentimental mode: "But here we must drop a tear! What heart so hard, as not to melt at human woe!" (6). The bond of brother and sister, though severed by her death, gains social currency at the moment of rupture: the emotional bond of brother and sister establishes Wilson as "sensible" and establishes her innocence as well. The reader, in turn, is asked to shed a tear in testimony of familial love, and hence Wilson's innocence (sensibility) is made visible and circulated. Moreover, we receive a clear indication that her brother's attentions have abolished any questions as to her reputation and integrated her into the community: "[Her brother] took her body home, and some efforts were made to restore her to life, but in vain. The day following she was decently interred, and a large number of respectable people attended the funeral" (7). The narrator then concludes, for the first time decisively, that Wilson is "innocent, we believe, of the crime for which she suffered" (7). The narrative as a whole stages the uncertainty of Wilson's interior subjectivity, yet ultimately produces the truth of private subjectivity by way of reference to familial affect; this truth is certified by the "respectable people" who gather around the grave, and the tear the reader sheds over the familial bonds broken and displayed within the story.

In 1822, a fictionalized version of Wilson's tale appeared in an anonymously written chapbook published in Boston under the title *The Victim of Seduction!*[35] While the name of the protagonist is slightly altered—Elizabeth

Wilson becomes Harriot Wilson—the details of the account, and most particularly the brother's role therein, indicate a connection between the texts. In the thirty-six years between the two narratives, the figure of the sentimental child had begun to emerge in popular culture. Early national concern with marital negotiation had given way to the sentimental idealization of the nuclear family and of the "innocent" child in particular. The 1822 version of Wilson's narrative retains a titular concern with seduction, and thus with the politics of marriage, yet this concern is largely absent from the text itself. Rather, the story focuses on the figure of the child, although surprisingly, the child in question is not the one that Harriot gives birth to and kills, but Harriot herself. In the 1786 tale, Elizabeth Wilson was twenty-seven years old. In the 1822 tale, Harriot Wilson is just eighteen. Moreover, Harriot is positioned from the beginning of the tale as a virtuous daughter, and she is described initially as a child: "She was early educated with the utmost tenderness, and every possible care was taken to impress on her mind sentiments of virtue and religion" (3–4). Her sentimental education resembles the nineteenth-century parenting models cited in the previous section of this chapter. Moreover, her education is described primarily in terms of directing and cultivating affect rather than in terms of discipline or training. For the sake of contrast, we might recall John Rogers's comments, cited above, concerning the natural state of children: "Every child of *Adam* is born a Leper, all over defiled." Whereas Esther Rogers's version of the infanticide narrative established her innocence by exhibiting conversion *away* from the state of childhood, Harriot Wilson's tale will ultimately establish Harriot's innocence in terms of a return to childhood and the affective bonds of the nuclear family.

Unlike her progenitor, Elizabeth, Harriot Wilson is unquestionably guilty of infanticide. Although she, too, has been seduced by a man with promises of marriage, the account of her seduction and the veracity of this account is of little importance in the story. Rather, the author's central concern is Harriot's conduct from the point of her trial forward, and in particular her relation with her family. Unlike Esther Rogers or Elizabeth Wilson, Harriot Wilson is far from socially marginal: indeed, she is exemplary of the interior of the community rather than its exterior. "Such was the respectability of the unfortunate prisoner's parents and connections, and such the sensibility cherished by all with whom she had been acquainted, that on the day of her trial, the court room was early filled with more than it could conveniently contain."[36] At the trial, she is thus located in the center of the community of sensibility and, more importantly, at the center of her own nuclear family: "During her whole trial the unhappy prisoner exhibited an uncommon degree of fortitude, and seemed more to lament the misfortunes of her wretched parents and brother, on whom she had brought disgrace than her own fate" (5–6). Her innocence will ultimately be established, I will argue, by placing her at the heart of the family as the dead child who enables the circulation of sentimental meaning.

During her imprisonment, she is visited by the clergy and "exhibited many proofs of penitence" just as Esther Rogers and Elizabeth Wilson, but the emotional weight of her prison stay, again, is placed on familial relations, and particularly the scene of her final parting with her parents: this last meeting prior to her execution is described as "affecting beyond description" (7). Yet the most highly wrought scene in the story is that of Harriot's execution. In this scene, Harriot's death becomes a spectacle presented as the sublime occasion for the outpouring of readerly sensibility. Harriot herself offers an unresisting body to the public: her body seems to consent through death to its affective structuring as a sentimental child.

> When ascending the platform, and after the fated cord had been affixed, her countenance displayed a serenity that appeared more than human, and when she gave the signal, there was a recollected gracefulness and sublimity in her manner that struck every heart, and is above words or ideas. After she had been suspended nearly a minute, her hands were twice evenly and gently raised, and gradually let to fall without the least appearance of convulsive or involuntary motion, in a manner which could hardly be mistaken, when interpreted, as designed to signify consent and resignation. At all events independently of this circumstance, which was noticed by many, her whole conduct evidently showed, from this temper of mind, a composed, and even cheerful submission to the views and will of heaven; a modest unaffected submission entirely becoming her age, her sex, and situation. (7)

What seems most eerie about this passage is the pleasure the author asks the reader to take in witnessing Harriot's submission to her execution. Because her narrative is not a conversion narrative, we do not have the sense that she is looking forward to divine redemption upon death, but rather, her submission to death seems to signal her reunion with her family and a return to the position of a child, tenderly ensconced within that family. The paradox of consent figured here—the consent registered by a dead body—mirrors the paradox of locating freedom in the figure of a child who can in no way exercise that freedom in a political fashion. This idealization of Wilson as the perfect, or perhaps perfectly dead, daughter, begins to indicate the costs of reproducing the closed sociality of the sentimental family structure. Wilson fails to reproduce this structure by not having a family of her own, yet she succeeds in reaffirming the inviolability of the nuclear family by becoming symbolic of its affective and structuring power in her death. Her death is "entirely becoming" to her situation according to the narrator, but we might also say that her submission to death enables her to *become* a sentimental child and thus to generate the affective force of emotional voluntarism that must, in ideological terms, lie at the heart of the family.

In the last chapter, I argued that the eighteenth-century genre of the "marital gothic" produced wives as corpses. In somewhat related terms, one might say that sentimental fiction produces dead children. The narrative function of the dead child is to generate social meaning, but because the family is configured as enclosed and private—as, precisely, natural and hence resistant to the negotiations of sociality—only violence can penetrate the family to enable the circulation of social meaning. The family must be open for it to have social meaning (sociality is always public and private), yet it must cloak the moment of public generation and circulation of its meaning in order to preserve a sacrosanct claim to privacy. Of the three narratives I have considered here, the account of Harriot Wilson's death seems most clearly to exemplify the paradoxical closure of the sentimental family upon itself (the creation of intimacy and sublime bonds of affection and recognition) through the public execution of the beloved daughter. In 1822, I would suggest, we thus see the paradoxes of the sentimental family and its relation to the literary public sphere come sharply into focus. The final narrative I consider here is a third version of Elizabeth Wilson's tale, redacted by the well-known sentimental writer Lydia Maria Child and published in a gift book, *The Illustrated Ladies' Keepsake*, in 1852. In Child's version of the Wilson narrative, neither seduction nor conversion figure at all; rather, the nuclear family and, even more specifically, the violent rupture of its central bonds are the subject of the story. In a telling detail shared but revised slightly in each of the three Elizabeth Wilson narratives, the brother arrives shortly after the execution with a pardon from the governor. In the 1784 version of the tale, the brother arrives twenty-three minutes too late. In the 1822 Harriot Wilson story, the brother arrives a heart-rending five minutes too late. In Child's 1852 account, the brother arrives with a pardon so near to the time of execution as to witness it from a distant hilltop, though he is unable to intervene before his sister is dead. Across the three versions of the Wilson tale, then, we see a successively tighter winding of the nuclear family: the brother and sister are drawn increasingly closer in each of these narratives, but always in order to experience the same fatality. The family is drawn successively closer, yet the violence of its rupture is given increased emotional force in each new version of the tale. Like the Harriot Wilson narrative, then, Child's story portrays the sentimental family as the location of the violent abrogation of natural bonds. And like the other narratives, Child's tale ultimately offers us an account of Wilson's innocence. Yet unlike her predecessors,

Child is less clear that the social structure is innocent of violence and murder. Indeed, her narrative most clearly enacts the violent logic of closed sociality and comes the closest to indicting that very logic as well.

Child's account of the Elizabeth Wilson story is not about Elizabeth but about "Lizzy," a small child who, we learn immediately, has a fatal need for love:

> The earliest and strongest development of Lizzy's character was love. . . . A dozen times a day she would look earnestly into her mother's eyes, and inquire, most beseechingly, '*Does* you love your little Lizzy?' and if the final answer did not come as promptly as usual, her beautiful eyes, always plaintive in their expression, would begin to swim with tears. This 'strong necessity of loving,' which so pervades the nature of woman, the fair child inherited from her gentle mother; and from her, too inherited a deficiency of firmness, of which such natures have double need. . . . Such a being was of course born for sorrow.[37]

The sorrow promised here first takes shape in the death of Lizzy's mother, which occurs when the child is ten years old. Lizzy becomes extraordinarily attached to her brother William, with whom she mourns her mother's absence. Her father remarries, and shortly thereafter, the new stepmother has a child and sends both William and Lizzy away from home to work as servants. Lizzy's overly close relation with her mother has marked her as both a figure of sentimental value and the subject of sentimental suffering. Typically it is the loving child who dies in the sentimental text (as we've seen in the Harriot Wilson tale), and the child's death allows for the rearticulation of the family unit and family values around the absent, though now preserved, figure of the child. In Child's story, however, the mother dies before the child, and this death results in the destruction of domestic space rather than its circulation and affirmation. The particularity of the mother-child bond and its centrality to the domestic ideal is immediately evident in the story. When Lizzy's stepmother arrives, she is unable to serve as a substitute mother and maintain the domestic space of the family: specifically, she is unable to view her new husband's children as playful innocents and instead sees them as bodies able to perform work. She thus violates the central premise of sentimental love that structures domestic space—namely, its nonutilitarian (and thus "free") nature.

As Lizzy and William leave their home to become laborers, they walk together to their mother's grave: "'Oh, if dear mother was alive, Willie, we should not have to go away from home,'" (342) laments Lizzy. Without a mother to preserve the space of the home and the bonds within it from co-optation for the purposes of labor, there is effectively no longer any home for the two siblings. In proper sentimental fashion, the two seek to memorialize the home they have lost before parting: Willie gives Lizzy a sprig of wildflowers from their mother's grave, which Lizzy presses between the leaves of her Bible. Willie, in turn, asks Lizzy for a "soft, golden-brown ringlet, that nestled close to her ear" (342). Yet Lizzy refuses to part with the curl because her mother "would kiss that little curl in particular." Her refusal signals an interesting and ultimately significant failing: Lizzy refuses to allow for the circulation of affect that death (and memorialization) typically enables in the sentimental text. Lizzy's curl fetishizes her bond with her mother; the curl stands in for her mother in physical, metonymical terms rather than in the metaphorical and transferable fashion of the sentimental memento. As such, the curl signals Lizzy's incapacity to enter into any system of exchange or circulation. Her need for her mother's love, and no other, makes evident the singularity and centrality of the mother-child bond and thus indicates the closed nature of the nuclear family. It is as if Child has set out to literally enforce the sentimental code: she will show that Lizzy can find no substitute for an *original*, biological bond with her mother.

Lizzy's refusal or incapacity to engage in an exchange economy becomes more evident after she is forced to leave her father's home. Working listlessly in another family's home, Lizzy develops no new connection with anyone until, in her adolescence, she becomes an extraordinary beauty and is courted by a handsome man from the city. "This was the fairy-land of her young life," writes Child. "She had somebody now into whose eyes she could gaze, with all the deep tenderness of her soul, and ask, '*Do* you love your own Lizzy?'" (347). At this moment, it appears as if Lizzy has developed the capacity to transfer her bond of excessive (and identity-sustaining) love with her mother to another individual. Yet Child also indicates that Lizzy is not ready to circulate her affective connections as a form of social currency: when her new beloved asks for the fetishized curl as a token of their love, Lizzy again refuses to part with it, indicating her attachment to a singular object (a singular curl, a singular mother). Although his departure is not linked causally to Lizzy's refusal to relinquish the curl, her suitor subsequently abandons Lizzy for a wealthy woman, a woman who has currency that clearly can and does circulate. Lizzy is left desolate as well as pregnant and gives birth to a stillborn child. She spends many lonely years, emotionally sustained only by her attachment to her brother, William. At the age of twenty-three, she moves to Philadelphia to work for a family there; she returns pregnant and gives birth to twins. When the twins are several months old, she takes them on a trip to Philadelphia and arrives there without them. Shortly thereafter she is arrested for their murder, and is distracted to the point of incoherence—an incoherence that has, in fact, been more or less upon her since her mother's death. She seems not to understand that she has committed any crime. However, when she talks with her still-loving brother at one point, he asks her why she killed the babies. She responds, "*He* did it." "Who is *he*?" asks the brother gently. "The father," she replies (351). It is worth noting that the father of the twins appears nowhere in the text save in this singular reference. When Lizzy moves to Philadelphia, where she becomes pregnant, the sexual act that occurs there is described as unspeakable: "Important events followed this change [to Philadelphia], but a veil of obscurity rests over the causes that produced them" (350). In the absence of the mother's love, no account of connection between Lizzy and another individual seems able to be articulated. When Lizzy is imprisoned for the crime of infanticide, she recedes even further from the realm of speech, from the circulation of social meaning: "She spoke seldom . . . and often she did not appear to hear when she was spoken to. She sat on the little blue bench, gazing vacantly on the floor, like one already out of the body" (354). Unlike each of the other infanticidal mothers we have seen, Lizzy does not enter "into communion" during her imprisonment. Far from finding the words with which to secure social recognition, Lizzy retreats from language altogether.

Rather than demonstrating the innocence of the social structure with respect to infanticide, then, Child's story seems to indicate the failure of a series of social relays that are necessary to make cultural, economic, and biological reproduction possible. In her account of the rigidly closed sociality of the sentimentalized family, Child portrays a version of the nuclear family that collapses inward upon itself. Rather than serving as the site for establishing primary ties that then extend or transfer elsewhere to form sustaining structures of identity, the very force of the affective bond between mother and child here precludes the circulation of family relations as cultural currency. Because this family is so circumscribed, Lizzy is utterly incapable of functioning in a world of transference—in a world of market relations and reproductive familial relations. As such Child ambivalently seems to indict either the closed nature of the sentimental family or the demand for transference imposed by the capitalist economy. Whereas the Puritan conversion narrative worked to transform the marginal Esther Rogers into the exemplar of salvation, Child's circumscribed and enclosed family has no integrative capacity. The four narratives I have traced demonstrate the successively increased weight placed upon familial bonds as the location of establishing social meaning and value. The families become noticeably more enclosed, more normatively white and bourgeois, across the series of narratives as well, as less space is available for individuals external to the familial structure. Yet Child's narrative seems to point to the logical impossibility of finally embracing the mother-child bond as the naturalized locus of freedom, to the final implosion of the sentimental family that is charged with embodying liberal freedom.

'UNCLE TOM'S CABIN'

As we have seen in the sequence of infanticide narratives discussed above, the increased closure of the sentimental family tends to coincide with a racial whitening of the family. Differences of race and persons of color seen, for instance, in Esther Rogers's narrative, are written out of the more sentimental versions of the infanticide narrative as the family becomes more insistently closed and as the privacy and leisure of the family begin to figure as central modes of liberal freedom. The violence inherent in sentimentalism has thus been associated, to some extent, with the violence of an imperial, racializing agenda, a "tender violence" in Laura Wexler's words, which is the method of choice for propelling the "blind momentum of American domestication" at home and abroad.[38] Yet I have suggested that a somewhat different form of violence inheres in sentimentalism—one located more intimately within the domestic space and within the structure of the (liberal) sentimental bond itself. If this violence is disturbing, it is nonetheless also the sign of the necessarily open, flexible, and political nature of even the most private spaces within liberal society: violence is the marker of the necessary penetration of the family required when the family is asked to bear enormous cultural significance. As such, I want to suggest that progressive possibilities are (on occasion) to be found where structural violence is written into the sentimental text. As such, I suggest that suffering within the sentimental text can serve as an opening onto political modes of analysis.

The racial politics of nineteenth-century domestic ideology and sentimental literature have been the subject of extended debate among critics. While centered on domestic concerns, sentimentalism also aims to leverage the private domain of feeling into the public domain of politics, most specifically through creating a politics of fellow feeling, a politics based on identification. Sentimentalism thus invokes the traditional liberal narrative: affective bonds established in the prepolitical realm of the family become the basis for public and political forms of identity. By calling on the reader to extend affective bonds to outcast and socially marginalized figures such as children, drunks, and slaves, sentimental literature promises to break down established social boundaries such as those of class and race. Embracing the social other through the act of identification, sentimentalism is, some have argued, radically democratic. Thus Phil Fisher contends, "the political content of sentimentalism is democratic in that it experiments with the extension of full and complete humanity to classes or figures from whom it has been socially withheld."[39] Or as Elizabeth Barnes argues, sentimentalism "employ[s] a method of affective representation that dissolves the boundaries between 'self' and 'other.' ... In the sentimental scheme of sympathy, others are made real—and thus cared for—to the extent that they can be shown in *relation* to the reader."[40] Yet the ongoing critical debate about the political force of sentimental literature points to the vexed nature of the identification that sentimentalism so generously extends to the other. James Baldwin, as we have seen, focuses on the violence within a novel such as *Uncle Tom's Cabin*, arguing that the text is fundamentally cruel rather than generous in its parceling out of subjectivity: rather than extending subjectivity to blacks it imposes a model of white subjectivity and white redemption upon blacks. The extension of humanity to slaves, then, is no more than the imperialist imperative that the black become white, that alterity be erased. As Baldwin puts it, "The African, exile, pagan hurried off the auction block and into the fields, fell on his knees before that God in Whom he must now believe; who had made him, but not in His image. This tableau, this impossibility, is the heritage of the Negro in America: *Wash me*, cried the slave to his Maker, *and I shall be whiter, whiter than snow!* For black is the color of evil; only the robes of the saved are white."[41] Baldwin's analysis points to the problematic status of identification in sentimentalism: does identification involve the imposition of a model of identity on others, or does it involve the extension of notions of humanity and rights to the other? Are the bonds of sympathy, particularly when figured as primarily familial, transferable bonds? Child's infanticide narrative suggests that the mother-child bond is not subject to transference and that this marks a dangerous limit to domestic ideology; Baldwin, on the other hand, indicates that transference of the idealizing bonds of sympathy involves a form of violence. In what follows, I want to suggest that Stowe's novel, *Uncle Tom's Cabin*, offers a glimpse of one possible means out of this impasse—one version of open sociality that has its roots in the logic of domesticity but that also enables that logic to be rendered in flexible and negotiable terms.

According to Marianne Noble, identification in *Uncle Tom's Cabin* is not based upon a mimetic similarity between individuals or the imposition of a model of similarity between individuals. Rather, identification in the novel operates in relation to what Noble describes as the "sentimental wound": that is, subjects in *Uncle Tom's Cabin* identify with one another on the basis of shared pain.[42] Thus when the slave Tom is first told he will be sold and taken away from his wife and children, Stowe analogizes the pain he feels upon this separation to the pain the reader has felt upon losing a child:

> Sobs, heavy, hoarse, and loud, shook the chair, and great tears fell through his fin-
> gers on the floor; just such tears, sir, as you dropped into the coffin where lay your
> first born son; such tears, woman, as you shed when you heard the cries of your
> dying babe. For, sir, he was a man, —and you are but another man. And, woman,
> though dressed in silk and jewels, you are but a woman, and in life's great straits and
> mighty grief, ye feel but one sorrow![43]

The one sorrow felt here, then, is a reference to the fact that sorrow constitutes
a site of identification, that the pain felt by Tom is the same pain felt by the
reader upon losing a child. However, the nature of this wound is quite specific; it is the wound suffered by the parent upon losing a child. Mothers and children are repeatedly separated by death in *Uncle Tom's Cabin* as well as by the
social death of slavery. Indeed, this is Stowe's central claim concerning the evil
of slavery: slavery destroys the sacred relation—the natural bond—between
mother and child. However, the strength of this one pain, the oneness of the
shared sorrow of mother-child separation that Stowe insists that we feel as
readers, is predicated on the assumption that white women (readers) as well as
black women (slave mothers) are habitually separated from their children,
albeit through death rather than through slavery. In order to sustain the force
of this one sentimental wound, then, Stowe must repeatedly stage the death of
children in the novel, most famously, Little Eva, or, alternatively, invoke the
death of children in order to facilitate cross-racial identification.

Yet the repeated death and separation scenes that punctuate *Uncle Tom's
Cabin* provide more than just gratuitous scenes of cruelty and suffering
through which to channel a shared sorrow. Rather, Stowe repeatedly severs the
"natural" bond of mother and child in order to effect something of an opening in the gendered and racialized antebellum symbolic order. Despite the
codes of closed sociality that structure familial enclosure in the domestic
novel—or perhaps because of the very rigid nature of these codes—moments
of public, identificatory, and even radically open sociality emerge from the
rupture of the mother-child bond. The open nature of the sociality that arises
from the rupture occurs in part because the structure of identification the text
offers is not simply reflective: we are not asked to imagine ourselves in the
image of those whom we encounter in the text, and thus to assume a fixed
racialized or gendered identity in relation to these images. Rather, the reader is
asked to identify with a subjective experience of sorrow and thus to experience
a broken state of subjectivity that subsequently opens possibilities of alternative social reconstructions of identity. Stowe thus introduces a dislocation into
the structure of identity politics insofar as identification in the novel occurs

around moments of loss of selfhood. As such, she is able to reverse the narrative of liberalism: rather than positing a mother-child bond of sympathy and recognition that is then extended to others, Stowe destroys the mother-child dyad in its original (private, biological) form and reconstitutes this dyad outside the family. Once the "natural" mother-child bond is ruptured, unnatural, reconstructed versions of this bond are allowed to circulate: that is, culturally unauthorized and de-biologized versions of this bond are allowed to form and gain symbolic power in the text.

Near the beginning of the novel, Stowe models the process of ruptured identification between one Senator Bird, who has just lobbied Congress to pass the Fugitive Slave Bill, and a runaway slave, Eliza, who has arrived in his kitchen after crossing the ice on the Ohio River with her son in her arms. Senator Bird has just told his wife that sentiment is acceptable in the private sphere, but that the public sphere must be guided by interests of state rather than sympathy when he is called to witness Eliza in his kitchen. Senator Bird is stunned by his initial sight of Eliza, who lies, "with garments torn and frozen, with one shoe gone, and the stocking torn away from the cut and bleeding foot." Stowe writes, as we see Eliza through Bird's eyes, "There was the impress of the despised race on her face" (70). Neither the lost shoe, the cut foot, nor the face of Eliza, however, is able to generate the kind of cut or wound necessary to abrogate Bird's commitment to the separation of public obligation and private feeling. Yet Bird is eventually converted, and this moment occurs, as we might guess, when Eliza asks Mary Bird, "Ma'am, . . . have you ever lost a child?" "The question was unexpected," writes Stowe, "and it was a thrust on a new wound; for it was only a month since a darling child of the family had been laid in the grave" (72). In response to this question, Mrs. Bird bursts into tears, and, once Eliza has described her owner's attempts to sell her son Harry away from her, the entire scene in the kitchen dissolves into a flood of shared tears: Mrs. Bird, the senator, old Aunt Dinah, and the slave Cudjoe all weep copiously together. The one sorrow, signified in the uniform reaction of all listeners as they begin to cry, dissolves the boundaries among them and allows for the creation of a (momentarily) de-raced and de-gendered social sphere in the kitchen.

Yet the shared mourning for the mother-child separation generates more possibilities in the novel than just moments of collective weeping, and these moments occur as we see new versions of the mother-child bond formed in ways that emphasize the social (public, circulatory, metaphorical) rather than the biological nature of this relation. After Eliza insists that Mr. and Mrs. Bird identify with her loss of a child, Stowe turns to a description of the scene of Mrs. Bird's mourning. Stowe describes Mrs. Bird opening a drawer filled with the clothes and toys of her dead son: she removes these clothes in order to give them to Harry, the son Eliza has brought with her across the river.

> Mrs. Bird slowly opened the drawer. There were little coats of many a form and pattern, piles of aprons, and rows of small stockings; and even a pair of little shoes, worn and rubbed at the toes, were peeping from the folds of a paper. There was a toy horse and wagon, a top, a ball,—memorials gathered with many a tear and many a heart-break! She sat down by the drawer, and, leaning her head on her hands over it, wept till the tears fell through her fingers into the drawer; then suddenly raising her head, she began, with nervous haste, selecting the plainest and most substantial articles, and gathering them into a bundle. (75–76)

The opening of this drawer enacts a sort of movement to a personal and social unconscious, to what has been hidden away but remains foundational; this is the site of the particularized bond of the mother with her dead son, where his memorial has been established for Mrs. Bird. Moreover, Stowe insists that we, the readers, all have such drawers we might open: "And oh! mother that reads this, has there never been in your house a drawer, or a closet, the opening of which has been to you like the opening again of a little grave? Ah! happy mother that you are, if it has not been so" (75). Upon returning to this original scene of the mother-child bond, Stowe attempts to give it a circulatory and metaphorical force—she generalizes the experience of Mrs. Bird to all mothers as the basis of sentimental narrative force. Yet rather than simply celebrating a shared mother-child affective link, Stowe also reconfigures that link at this narrative moment. When Mrs. Bird opens the drawer and removes her dead son's clothes, she does so in order to place these clothes, and her maternal affect attached to them, back into circulation: specifically, she is donating both the clothing and her maternal affect to Harry, an African-American child. Mrs. Bird thus forges a symbolic link of motherhood to a black child: the text thus creates a cross-racial mother-child bond in response to the necessary and even universal rupture of the natural mother-child bond.

There are more than twenty scenes in *Uncle Tom's Cabin* that describe the destruction of the mother-child relation: scenes of slave children ripped from their mother's breasts, slave children sold at auction, and white and black children dying. Yet there are also multiple reconfigurations of the mother-child bond, indicating the repetitive work of reconstruction that Stowe performs as she circulates sentimental violence. In an instance perhaps more surprising than the Mrs. Bird–Harry coupling, Stowe places the slave Uncle Tom in an unlikely maternal position with respect to his white master, Augustine St. Clare, the father of Eva. Immediately following the dramatic and famous death scene of Eva, St. Clare turns, in his grief, to Uncle Tom, who suggests that he pray to ease his suffering. St. Clare tells Uncle Tom that he does not pray because he feels isolated when he does so: " 'I would [pray], Tom, if there was anybody there when I pray; but it's all speaking into nothing, when I do. But come, Tom, you pray, now, and show me how' " (263). St. Clare cannot pray because he has lost the affective bonds that would allow him to understand himself as existing in connection (with God, with family) rather than alone. Interestingly, he turns to Tom for assistance in reconstructing these bonds: "Tom's heart was full; he poured it out in prayer, like waters that have been long suppressed. One thing was plain enough; Tom thought there was somebody to hear, whether there were or not. In fact, St. Clare felt himself borne, on the tide of his faith and feeling, almost to the gates of heaven he seemed so vividly to conceive. It seemed to bring him nearer to Eva" (263–64). In this passage, we see Tom's powerful voice constructing—or perhaps better described, lending, transferring, circulating—the kinds of connections to God and family that St. Clare has lost. In the subsequent pages, Uncle Tom's voice more clearly emerges as channeling a maternal connection: that is, Tom is shown to stand in for a maternal voice and thus enables the reconstruction of the mother-child connection that St. Clare has lost for many years. The maternal figuration of Tom is primarily metonymic: St. Clare comes upon Tom reading the Bible and then begins, himself, to read a passage therein that reminds him of his mother. Thrown into a "deep reverie" St. Clare moves in a direction eerily similar to that of Mrs. Bird: he opens a drawer that contains the memorial objects—here, music books—that connect him to his dead mother. He returns, that is, to the site of the mother-child bond (here, he is the child) and draws forth an object that will now be placed into circulation. "[St. Clare] opened one of the drawers, took out an old music-book whose leaves were yellow with age, and began turning it over. 'There,' he said to Miss Ophelia, 'this was one of my mother's books.' . . . 'It was something she used to sing often,' said St. Clare. 'I think I can hear her now' " (271). With his mother's voice in his ears, St. Clare sits down at the piano and begins to play from the book, singing "Dies Irae." Whereas he could not, previously, pray because he lacked affective connection to others, he is able to voice a prayer in the form of his mother's song in this scene. He is able to voice a prayer because his mother, and Uncle Tom, are listening: "Tom, who was listening in the outer verandah, was drawn by the sound to the very door, where he stood earnestly. He did not understand the words, of course; but the music and manner of singing appeared to affect him strongly, especially when St. Clare sang the more pathetic parts" (271). Tom stands in for St. Clare's mother, listening to St. Clare's prayer and thus enabling the the him to pray.

The scene of St. Clare's recovery of a maternal connection occurs directly after the death of his child, Eva. The destruction of the white family thus becomes the staging ground for the creation of a cross-racial mother-child bond between Tom and St. Clare. The scene of Eva's death is one of the most famous in the novel and is the subject of a central critical debate over the political value of the novel and of sentimental writing in general. Ann Douglas argues that the "transcendence" of the deathbed scene is fundamentally self-indulgent and has little political force: "Sentimentalism provides a way to protest a power to which one has already in part capitulated. It is a form of dragging one's heels. It always borders on dishonesty. . . . We remember that Little Eva's beautiful death, which Stowe presents as part of a protest against slavery in no way hinders the working of that system."[44] Jane Tompkins, in response to Douglas, locates a reforming power in the suffering and transcendence of the death scene: "A pervasive cultural myth . . . invests the suffering and death of an innocent victim with just the kind of power that critics deny to Stowe's novel: the power to work in, and change, the world. This is the kind of action that little Eva's death in fact performs."[45] Tompkins and Douglas argue over modes of identification here: does the reader merely identify with the suffering of Eva (and thus weep), or does she identify with Eva's principles of racial equality and thus move forward from reading the novel with a new political agenda? Yet identification with Eva, in whatever form, may not be the most significant or salient response to sentimental violence suggested by the novel. In the interaction between Tom and St. Clare immediately following Eva's death, Stowe models the possibility of an open sociality that involves a resignification of the bond between mother and child. The death of Little Eva gives way to the re-creation of the mother-child bond in the form of a cross-racial, transgendered mothering—a stark revision of the seemingly biological bond that connects mother and child.

A final and significant example of cross-racial mothering—in which the circulatory power of mothering is placed into narrative play by the sentimental text—occurs when Cassy, the enslaved concubine of the evil Simon Legree, effects her escape from slavery by impersonating Legree's dead mother. Legree, the archetypal figure of the evil, uncaring master, *does* care or cannot not care, it seems, about his mother. His mother, "a fair-haired woman led him, at the sound of Sabbath bell, to worship and to pray" as a child, but he chose instead, a godless life of sin, rejecting the linked forms of Christian and maternal connection. Stowe writes that "one night, when his mother, in the last agony of her despair, knelt at his feet, he spurned her from him—threw her senseless on the floor, and, with brutal curses, fled to his ship" (323). The mother dies shortly thereafter, leaving Legree, in his wickedness, to be repeatedly terrified by the sight of her ghost—"that pale mother rising by his bedside" (323). As Eva Cherniavsky points out, Legree's rejection of his mother is entirely ineffectual within the codes of sentimentalism where identity is rooted in the original mirroring relation of mother and child: "Legree's susceptibility to his dead mother's haunting appearance suggests the structural function of maternal love in the economy of rational subjectivity. Maternal love can be rejected as well as embraced, but never escaped. . . . the relation to the mother (as origin) is inescapably a relation to (the ground of) [the child's] own social subjectivity."[46] As such, Legree's attempt to distance himself from his mother only makes her presence stronger, albeit in a threatening rather than reassuring manner. According to Cherniavksy, the cultural importance of the mother—her role in cementing the original identity of the child in private, domestic space—causes the mother to exceed her merely biological role and thus to function as a ghost that returns to haunt the son: in other words, the privacy of the original mother-son bond is never private since it must be circulated (it must return repeatedly) to insure the identity of the son as a full-fledged subject. Each iteration of the mother-son bond, however, enables the figure of the mother to accrue a new set of meanings—meanings that are not biological but cultural. Rather than simply citing the figure of the white, Christian mother as the cultural "ghost" of male identity, however, Stowe proposes an interesting literalization of this specter: Cassy dresses herself in a sheet and poses as the ghost of Legree's mother; she terrifies him to the extent that he is incapacitated in his role as "master" of the plantation and she is able to escape. It is worth noting that Legree is especially terrified by a lock of hair that he imagines belongs to his mother: his fetishized fear of her *particular* presence thus blinds him to the fact that another body is occupying the mother's position. While insisting on the power of the mother-child bond to control Legree's identity, Stowe revises the sentimental premise that this relation is always private, original, and biological. When Cassy steps into the position of Legree's mother, she produces herself as white and free, despite her status as a black slave. The open sociality enabled by the rupture of the mother-child bond is evident here in its most liberating form: Cassy frees herself from a social system that controls her as a racialized and gendered being.

As each of these reconfigured mother-child couplings demonstrates—Mrs. Bird and Harry; Uncle Tom and St. Clare; and Cassy and Simon Legree—the violent abrogation of the mother-child bond, which is structurally necessary for Stowe to stage the sentimental narrative, reveals radical social possibilities by disrupting the premise of closed sociality. Stowe's use of the dead child, then, enables a reconfiguration of identification that is potentially generative of change, potentially able to restructure the black/white play of identity and violence in racial relations of the antebellum period. I say potentially, however, because ultimately Stowe eradicates the very possibilities of open sociality that she has staged in the novel. By the close of the novel, Stowe renaturalizes the family such that it is configured in racially essentialized and biological terms. We see this most clearly in Cassy's case where her figurative habitation of the position of Legree's mother enables her to become free from slavery: yet upon escaping from Legree, she is ultimately reunited with her *biological* family—with her daughter Eliza, Eliza's husband George, and their children. As such, Cassy's biological motherhood is allowed to narratively supersede the metaphorical motherhood she established with respect to Legree. Indeed, her happy reunion with her own, natural family serves as a scene of closure for the entire novel. This kind of closure—the reunion of the black family torn apart by slavery—seems, in some respects, the obvious happy ending to a novel that has insisted that the most significant human relationship is that which ties mothers to their children. But in this reunion we also see the elimination of the political possibilities Stowe had earlier opened with respect to the mother-child bond. The mother-child bond, rendered transferable, translatable, and metaphorical in much of the text is retethered to the literal referent of biology and the oppressive racial politics of the "one-drop" rule in the final scenes of the novel.

When the African-American family is reunited, Stowe's political goal—that of humanizing slaves, of demonstrating their fundamental right to domesticity and the bonds of maternal connection—has apparently been achieved. Yet ironically, once the African-American family is reunited and rendered biologically whole and black, a range of political possibilities are foreclosed due to the reinstatement of liberal temporality and closed sociality. The black family can and should only exist, according to Stowe, in a black nation such as that of Liberia. According to the liberal narrative Stowe ultimately endorses, political identity is determined on the basis of prepolitical, private identity, and while blacks may be human (and have a right to domestic ties) they are not, it seems "naturally" to be given the status of citizens in the United States. While Stowe argues, politically, for the end of slavery in order that the family remain sacrosanct, she in turn argues that the right to political participation derives from familial and racial identity. As such, she presents George as infused with a desire to emigrate to Liberia: "My sympathies are not for my father's race," states the mulatto, George, "but for my mother's. . . . I have no wish to pass for an American, or to identify myself with them. It is with the oppressed, enslaved African race that I cast in my lot" (374). Ultimately, he wants to move to Africa:

"there it is my wish to go, and find myself a people" (374). In this passage, the bond between George and his mother is explicitly biological and racial. By insisting on the natural bond to the mother as the antidote to the social violence that caused a break with the mother, Stowe reinscribes a racist logic of identification, here clearly defined in terms of the one-drop rule in which racial status follows that of the mother. Moreover, when George speaks of finding a "people," and of an inability to identify with Americans, Stowe is clearly giving us an account of racially white America.

There is a deep irony to this ending: on the one hand, the basic humanity of the black slave requires that he have a home space, just like white Americans. Yet as it turns out, the reconstitution of that home space is precisely what grants someone like George the possibility of obtaining a political identity as a member of a nation (particularly for a male). Yet when we arrive at this political level—the nation—from this temporal direction (from private to public), the politics of identification (of one sorrow) that Stowe had set up seem to abruptly vanish into a separate but equal doctrine. African-Americans, she suggests, should move to Liberia. What the rupture of sentimental violence had opened is here closed again and reconstituted as a more familiar liberal narrative: once private, familial bonds are secure, they lose their political valence— or rather, their political valence becomes subsumed beneath that of biology. In turn, politics are then justifiably produced as a result of biology—nations are justly either black or white—and sociality no longer circulates cross-racial couplings, but prohibits them altogether.

While critics have condemned the scenes of suffering at the center of sentimental literature as dishonest and depoliticizing, I would suggest that violence and loss can be understood as operating in less conservative directions as well. Although Stowe's novel forecloses the possibilities violence opens in her text, there are also moments where alternative desires, alternative subjects, and alternative affective connections among individuals appear with great force in her text. Loss and violence generate the circulation of social meaning. As David Eng and David Kazanjian have recently argued, "the politics of mourning might be described as that creative process moderating a hopeful or hopeless relationship between loss and history."[47] The sentimental wound places loss at the center of its politics: this politics is reactive at the moment when it memorializes what is lost as the private origin of public meaning. At the moment when loss is circulated as social currency, however, the public process of transference, exchange, and circulation can also be recognized (to quote Eng and Kazanjian) as "active rather than reactive, prescient rather than nostalgic, abundant rather than lacking, social rather than solipsistic, militant rather than reactionary" (2). If we recognize sociality as an eminently public process—a process that is open to social negotiation—then privatization does not eradicate the possibility of politics.

In the nineteenth century, liberalism as we know it today begins to take shape with a marked emphasis on the family as the location of privacy and freedom. In this chapter, I have attempted to demonstrate the paradoxical nature of this formulation for liberalism: on the one hand, privacy is the site of freedom; on the other hand, privacy must be made publicly visible in order to perform the cultural work of representing the freedom of the liberal subject. I have argued throughout this book that the temporality of liberalism (a narrative movement from private to public identity) is fictive insofar as private identity is shaped by public forms of representation and recognition. Although this does not mean that privacy does not exist, it does mean that the terms in which private forms of identity register as meaningful are always subject to public, political negotiation. To the extent that this proposition is denied—when the sanctity of privacy is imagined as closed, prepolitical, and foundational—the structural contradiction intrinsic to this version of liberal privacy may register as violence. Looking forward to the twentieth century, it seems possible to correlate sentimental violence with what Mark Seltzer has described as a "wound culture" associated with a "pathological public sphere." Seltzer writes, "The spectacular public representation of violated bodies, across a burgeoning range of official, academic, and media accounts, in fiction and in film, has come to function as a way of imagining and situating our notions of public, social, and collective identity. . . . [Scenes of violence] have come to function as a way of imagining the relations of private bodies and private persons to public spaces."[48] The display of private persons—and particularly the display of the sanctity of privacy—seems abetted by violence or best represented as a spectacle of violence. Representational violence is not without productive possibilities, as I have suggested in reading scenes of loss and rupture in *Uncle Tom's Cabin*, but the murderous interface of public and private might also be meaningfully reconfigured by way of insisting upon the widening of an intermediate space between public and private—a space productive of social and civil forms of identity

As I have argued throughout this book, the creation of private subjectivity is a public and political process. I have adduced a series of literary-historical instances of this process, some of which announce the open sociality or the public creation of private identity, and some of which attempt to render sociality closed or invisible—all of which, however, demonstrate the shifting terms of the seemingly "ontological" categories of gender and race that ground private subjectivity. In these readings, I mean to have opened up a space for sociality itself to become visible, legible, and negotiable. The privatization of politics and social structure is indeed written into liberal narratives of identity, but alternative readings of this narrative (alternative temporalities, alternative affects, alternative origins) can locate politics and privacy as coextensive and thus reveal both terms as open to debate and negotiation.

Coda

Queering Marriage:
Emily Dickinson and the Poetics of Title

What might open sociality look like in political terms? How might one revise the temporality of liberalism such that femininity, marriage, and subject formation are not decisively linked to scripted versions of privacy? To what extent does the literary public sphere, as I have described it, offer an alternative to the divisions between public and private realms that structure liberal thought and policy? In the final section of this book, I turn briefly to the work of Emily Dickinson and to contemporary political debates concerning marriage to address these questions.

In 1996, the U.S. Congress passed the *Defense of Marriage Act*, an act designed specifically to deny federal recognition of same-sex marriages and thus to affirm heterosexuality and gender dimorphism between marriage partners. Included in the act is an explicit definition of marriage: "the word 'marriage' means only a legal union between one man and one woman as husband and wife."[1] The language of this act suggests that marriage remains a gendering machine; it affirms that a binary sexual division between partners is essential to the meaning of marriage, but we might also say that it *enacts* (with the power of a state apparatus) this division as central to the structure of marriage. As such, the *Defense of Marriage Act* not only denies state recognition to marriages that are not defined in terms of sexual difference and heterosexuality, but it also indicates the state's investment in producing gendered bodies ("one man and one woman") as an element of political legibility in relation to the mass body of the "people."

The concern of the federal government with forms of capitalist family formation is evident as well in a recent version of the welfare reform law titled the *Personal Responsibility, Work, and Family Promotion Act of 2003*, passed by the House in February of 2003.[2] This act authorizes continued funding, albeit with some significant changes, of the *Personal Responsibility and Work Opportunity Act of 1996*. One important shift in the newer version of the welfare law is writ large in its revised title: "family promotion" is now identified as a key aim of the new law. Goals of the new act include "end[ing] the dependence of needy families on government benefits and reduc[ing] poverty by promoting job preparation, work and marriage," as well as encouraging "healthy, 2-parent, married families and . . . responsible fatherhood."[3] The act provides $100 million per year (for six years) to fund programs designed to promote marriage, including "Public advertising campaigns on the value of marriage . . . [e]ducation in high schools on the value of marriage . . . [m]arriage education, marriage skills, and relationship skills programs, that may include parenting skills, financial management, conflict resolution, and job and career advancement, for non-married pregnant women and non-married expectant fathers."[4] An additional $102 million per year is set aside for programs on family formation, and $20 million per year is allocated to "promote responsible fatherhood." The language concerning fatherhood is particularly interesting insofar as it points to the gendered divisions of labor that are imagined to structure the healthy marriage and family: the legislation aims at "enhancing the abilities and commitment of unemployed or low-income fathers to provide material support for their families and to avoid or leave welfare" and "improving fathers' ability to manage family business affairs effectively," as well as "encouraging and supporting healthy marriages and married fatherhood."[5] Paternity is here associated with patriarchy; a healthy marriage evidently requires a father with the ability to pay bills and to "manage" the family business. What is striking about the welfare act, as a whole, is the amount of state authority (and money) that is directed toward creating the seemingly natural heterosexual marriage—a union that evidently does not come naturally enough to many citizens. While the *Defense of Marriage Act* aims to protect what its supporters described as the sacred, God-given nature of heterosexual marriage, the welfare act attempts to *create* the sexually dimorphic couple, thus demonstrating the state- (rather than God-) given nature of heterosexual family formation.[6]

Taken individually and together, the two legislative acts described here point to the reversal of the temporal narrative of liberalism: male and female individuals are not created in the private sphere and then united in the publicly recognized act of marriage. Rather, the public regulation of marriage seems aimed at instantiating forms of masculinity and femininity. The regulatory force of the marriage contract has been a key issue in debates over the desirability of legalizing same-sex marriage. Whereas advocates have argued that same-sex marriage will extend previously denied rights and recognition to homosexuals, queer theorists, in turn, have argued that marriage involves consenting to the disciplinary and normalizing force of the state. As Janet Halley argues, "To seek recognition is to concede the authority of those whose regard is sought. . . . The couple mixes its subjectivity with subjection the moment it makes its bid for recognition."[7] Marriage both confers privileges—the privilege of a particular status and the material benefits that accrue to that status—and calls upon the couple to assume obligations dictated less by love than by social normativity. The interest of the state in encouraging "healthy, 2-parent, married families" is related to moving the work of caretaking and support away from the state (welfare) and onto the family structure. Marriage might thus be viewed as a form of "private welfare" in which fixed gender roles become a resource for scripting the work of caretaking and family management (paternity as patriarchy, for instance).[8]

If queer theorists have argued for disrupting the generalized equation between marriage and rights, recognition, sexual privacy, and privatized welfare, straight feminists have, in turn, long imagined rescripting gender roles from within marriage—for example, reallocating the sexualized division of labor within marriage. As an alternative to either of these approaches, however, I want to consider Emily Dickinson's poetic treatment of the relation between marriage and entitlement—a treatment that seems to offer the possibility of queering marriage itself, and does so less by redefining gender roles within the private sphere of marriage than by redefining the relation between privacy and public recognition that structures marriage as it is conventionally conceived today. The work of Elizabeth Freeman on queer configurations of the wedding ceremony is instructive with respect to what queering marriage might look like. Freeman analyzes a variety of filmic and literary representations of weddings to demonstrate their performative richness—a richness that exceeds the couple form and is not coextensive with marriage as a state-sanctioned contract. Freeman finds that representations of many weddings

> [work] out fantasies about collectivity and publicity: the desire to be part of something publicly comprehensible *as* social, to create some group for which the bourgeois couple was not metonymic but antithetical or just irrelevant. . . . [T]he social alternatives that are exposed [in wedding scenes] . . . seem to resonate with a genuinely queer politics, one that insists on the mobility of identification and desire, on the ongoing production of shared meanings and unforeseen constituencies, and on exposing links between the "private" sphere and various "public" techniques of control.[9]

While Freeman clearly distinguishes the collectivities and forms of recognition played out in the wedding ceremony from the recognition associated with the marriage contract and the marital couple, I would suggest that something of her interest in "forms of belonging" that remain mobile and productive is at stake in Dickinson's concern with marriage as a structure of title and entitlement de-coupled from private modes of embodiment.

In Dickinson's poetry, marriage appears most prominently as a form of entitlement. As Susan Harris points out, many of Dickinson's poems concerning marriage are meditations on the "process of entitlement" or the *narrative* enactment of femininity, moving from girlhood to the empowered and conclusive goal of wifehood.[10] The model of adult femininity most available to Dickinson was that of married woman: marriage marked the transition from child to woman. Joanne Dobson thus argues that "in the cultural mythos a new and transcendent identity awaited the married woman—one that was not available to the single woman."[11] Yet difficulties with the progressive movement from child to entitled, married adult woman appear in the very poems in which Dickinson sketches out such a narrative, as in the poem below:

> I'm "wife"—I've finished that—
> That other state—
> I'm Czar—I'm "Woman" now—
>
> How odd the Girl's life looks
> Behind this soft Eclipse—
> I think that Earth feels so
> To folks in Heaven—now—
>
> This being comfort—then
> That other kind—was pain—
> But why compare?
> I'm "Wife"! Stop there!
>
> (T 199 / F 225)[12]

For Dickinson, marriage is most decidedly about achieving a publicly recognized and often quite feudal status, namely that of the "wife," a status that is likened here to that of a czar. The narrative in this poem clearly describes an ascent from the lesser to the greater of a series of binary positions—a movement from then to now, from girl to woman, from earth to heaven, from pain to comfort. The speaker's ascent is characterized in terms of her accession to the powerful title of "wife," a term Dickinson places in quotation marks throughout the poem, indicating that "wife" functions as a social category, a title, a term pronounced and recognized by others and thus cited by the speaker. Yet the speaker in the poem threatens to destroy the linear movement of ascent by turning backwards toward the past with too much attention. By the end of the poem, the secure title of "wife" seems insecure, threatened by the recursive movement of comparison. In looking backward and making the comparison that is foreclosed at the end of the poem ("why compare?"), the speaker of the poem intimates a sense of loss that runs counter to the narrative of gain asserted in the poem. This loss—a loss of girlhood, pain, and "that other state"—must be eclipsed, disavowed by the status of "wife" that the speaker forces herself to sustain in the imperative tone of the final lines of the poem against the desire to remain near to, faithful to that loss. Wifehood, we could say, thus *eclipses* rather than compensates for the loss that has been left behind, and this eclipse ultimately proves troubling.

In Dickinson's poems about marriage, as in this one, the title or status of wifehood is thus often accompanied by a sense of foreclosure or loss. According to Harris, the speaker in this poem, and in the marriage entitlement poems in general, finds it difficult to maintain "a stable, coherent 'Wife' identity" (48). As a result, Harris argues, Dickinson must redefine the meaning of "wife" in order to claim the title as her own: "The speaker who wants to make the transition from disenfranchised child to empowered adult discovers that simply claiming the name of wifehood will not entitle and will not transform her—she must earn her title by creating through her own poetry a concept of wifehood that will displace the cultural ideal that the word 'Wife' is assumed to represent" (48). Harris thus suggests that Dickinson works to redefine the signifier "wife" from within the realm of her own personal experience: "wife" will come to have a new meaning (ultimately, related to suffering) based on the coherence of her own (private) identity. I cite Harris's analysis because it bears resemblance to the feminist attempt to redefine marriage from within by rescripting the sexual division of labor in the household. More broadly, Harris's analysis adheres, as well, to the temporal movement of liberalism: the private experience of the subject, made public, is expected to generate a new form of recognition; the truth of public identity lies in the (suffering) private body. I would argue, however, that Dickinson's treatment of marriage and title operates in a different direction: rather than insisting on accurately representing private experience, Dickinson articulates a concept of title that is not linked to the truth of private, embodied forms of subjectivity. Indeed, Dickinson's concept of title and marriage is novel insofar as she de-couples marital recognition from a scripted marital privacy or even a rescripted version of the same.

A second poem related to marriage is "Rearrange a 'Wife's' affection!" Unlike "I'm 'wife,'" "Rearrange a 'Wife's' affection!" deals with an improper marriage, one that seems distant from rather than constricted to a normative definition of marriage. This impropriety, I would suggest, might be read as same-sex desire, and thus the poem posits not simply a discomfort with the norms of marriage but a disruption of and infidelity to these norms.

> Rearrange a "Wife's" affection!
> When they dislocate my Brain!
> Amputate my freckled Bosom!
> Make me bearded like a man!

> Blush, my spirit, in thy Fastness—
> Blush, my unacknowledged clay—
> Seven years of troth have taught thee
> More than Wifehood ever may!
>
> Love that never leaped its socket—
> Trust entrenched in narrow pain—
> Constancy thro' fire—awarded—
> Anguish—bare of anodyne!
>
> Burden—borne so far triumphant—
> None suspect me of the crown,
> For I wear the "Thorns" till *Sunset*—
> Then—my Diadem put on.
>
> Big my Secret but it's *bandaged*—
> It will never get away
> Till the Day its Weary Keeper
> Leads it through the Grave to thee.
>
> (J 1737 / F 267)

On Jane Donahue Eberwein's reading, this poem affirms a wife's commitment to a skeptical husband: "Denying the possibility of change in her feelings, she exclaims that he would have to transform her utterly—unsex her in fact—to alter her commitment. Far from expressing a desire for male traits, she sketches the metamorphosis in grotesque detail. Only if hacked to pieces and recombined as a manikin corpse would she betray her lover."[13] Yet wifehood in this poem is contrasted with "troth," suggesting that two kinds of marriage exist here: one that is publicly or conventionally referred to as wifehood, and a second kind of troth that is improper, unrecognized, yet more substantive than the conventional form of marriage; "Seven years of troth have taught thee / More than Wifehood ever may!" The speaker cites the position of "wife," yet the citation marks a degree of distance from this role: indeed, the quotation marks suggest that to become a "wife" is, precisely, to play a role or become a figure rather than to accede to a natural state. The speaker states that she has learned more from the troth she has plighted than the estate of wifehood can teach, further indicating that wifehood, or at least the conventional, natural version of this role, is not hers. To rearrange this troth, to make it conform to the normative and naturalized narrative of heterosexuality, would require that she become a man. If this poem refers to a homosexual union between two women, then the speaker would have to become a man in order to conform to the heterosexual convention of marriage, a possibility she imagines and rejects at once, just as she embraces marriage only to distance herself from it. If wifehood and marriage are accepted forms of social commitment between individuals, they are also unavailable between women, hence the poem's spurious fantasy of changing sexes to alter the commitment of the improper "wife." Yet part of the "wife's" commitment in this poem hinges on impropriety: she rejects the notion of altering her commitment to conform to wifehood and normative marriage because to do so would require the mutilation of precisely that to which she is committed—her private betrothal.

The "secret" of this unknown, redemptive marriage is one that is "bandaged," a term that indicates that the secret is hidden from view, but also that it bears some resemblance to a wound. Accordingly, bearing the secret of this improper marriage would seem to entail some sort of mutilation of the speaker after all. The poem thus might ultimately be seen to alternate between images of rearranging the narrative of marriage, as against its compulsory heterosexuality, and damaging the self—to alternate between the mutilation of the marriage narrative and the mutilation of the self. Although the initial verses of the poem cite and reject the normative terms of the marriage contract, suggesting that committed love and conventional "wifehood" are not naturally linked, the final verse of the poem suggests that sustaining a marriage that does not conform to convention, that cannot be signified, is painful and self-wounding. Accordingly, the poem invokes the tension between a deformation directed toward the cultural norm of heterosexual narrative and one directed toward the body of the speaker who cannot fully occupy this narrative.

In "Title divine—is mine!" we see a similar attempt to restage and rearrange the marriage contract, an attempt to signify what the normative form of the contract might foreclose. In this poem, the redemptive form of the heterosexual narrative is clearly rejected; however, some signifying power seems to arise from the rejection of this narrative. Unlike "Rearrange a 'Wife's' affection!" then, the process of dislodging the natural, normative marriage itself becomes a positive sign rather than merely a figure of mutilation that metonymically disfigures the speaker as well. Indeed, the poem begins by drawing a distinction between word and thing—between "wife" and "sign"—which immediately places the security of divine title in question.

> Title divine—is mine!
> The Wife—without the Sign!
> Acute Degree—conferred on me—
> Empress of Calvary!
> Royal—all but the Crown!
> Betrothed—without the swoon
> God sends us Women—
> When you—hold—Garnet to Garnet—
> Gold—to Gold—

> Born—Bridalled—Shrouded—
> In a Day—
> "My Husband"—women say—
> Stroking the Melody—
> Is *this*—the way?
>   (J 1072/ F 194)[14]

The emphatic claim with which the poem begins—the possessive claim to the title of "wife"—is described as one that lacks a "sign": the second line of the poem (the wife without the sign) thus invokes a Calvinist distinction between the unreliable signs of the visible world and the truth of a divine, invisible world. Indeed, the title "Empress of Calvary!" or queen of crucifixion itself suggests a redemptive Christian narrative: suffering on earth is redeemed in heaven. On the Calvinist model, suffering itself becomes the sign of redemption, thus securing the narrative movement from earthly suffering to divine redemption. Hence, for instance, the thorns worn by Christ become a crown: suffering on earth is thus transformed into *evidence* of divine title. As such, the relation between invisible truth and earthly signs is preserved rather than severed. Yet rather than transforming suffering into the proper sign of election, Dickinson's poem insists on the continued opposition and distance between divine election and earthly signification. For instance, rather than following her title "Empress of Calvary!" with a description of successful, redemptive signification (suffering as sign of election), she follows this line by a description of a hardening opposition between the signified and the signifier: the line "Royal—all but the Crown" suggests that, unlike Christ, the speaker wears no crown of thorns, no earthly sign of divine redemption. An increasing gap grows between the signified and the signifier: the narrative of redemption doesn't overcome this hiatus. The gap, moreover, asserts itself typographically in the dash that separates the two realms of meaning: divine/earthly, signified/signifier.

The marriage that results, moreover, is one that does not conform to a redemptive, narrative structure. Rather, the narrative of the convert/bride is contracted into a single exploded line—"Born—Bridalled—Shrouded—"—which occurs at once, "In a Day." The dashes that support the narrative links between birth, wedding, and death also attenuate or disrupt those same links: this disruptive connection is further emphasized by the condensed temporal frame of a single day. The temporal condensation intensifies the sequential moments of the conventional narrative, yet at the same time it destroys the redemptive, organizing effect of such a narrative. In other words, if narrative is used to make sense of events across time—to make sense of the events that define the lifetime of an individual from birth to death—then the temporal dislocation of this orderly progression of events also utterly destroys the organizing effect of such a narrative. Because birth, marriage, and death literally cannot occur in a day, these terms must be understood as distanced from their literal referents, as figurative in meaning. The identificatory female narrative ("Born—Bridalled—Shrouded—") thus loses its redemptive, organizing force once the temporal frame of the form is altered.

The ability to claim the redemptive title of divine marriage thus remains thoroughly in doubt by the end of the poem, which finally asks how one can signify a marriage that is not about redeeming female identity through associating it with a masculine, master signifier. In other words, the final question of the poem, "Is this—the way?" might be understood to ask, "Am I properly making my claim here? Am I properly displaying my titled status, just as other wives do when they say 'My Husband'?" or perhaps more ironically, "Is it possible or desirable to stake such a claim at all?"[15] The entire project of the poem to claim or signify divine title is thus placed in question in the final line: if divine title really has no sign, how then could a poem serve as the sign of such a title? While the poem begins by claiming "Title divine," it also ends by questioning whether this claim can be staked at all: the exclamation mark of the first line is thus transformed into a question mark in the final line. In short, then, the poem might be seen to ask how we signify that which cannot be signified.

In severing the relation between signifier and signified, between status and embodiment, Dickinson opens questions concerning the relation between textuality and embodiment that run throughout her poetry. More specifically, as Shira Wolosky argues, textual embodiment in the poem becomes a trope for physical embodiment, and Dickinson displays an ambivalent attitude toward both:

> This poem invests in a linguistic embodiment from which it also recoils. That embodiment includes both textuality and the (gendered) body, each a trope for the other, and with direct implications for Dickinson's incarnation of her work into a private manuscript-body while refusing the public exposure of publication. . . . She both would and would not incarnate herself in texts, which she would and would not finish and complete; would embody herself in manuscript but not in outward publication.[16]

Wolosky here posits an interesting link between the disrupted embodiment linked to title and marriage in "Title divine" and Dickinson's own refusal to publish her poetry. Only ten of Dickinson's poems appeared publicly in print during her lifetime; although she did circulate many poems in private letters written to those close to her, the vast majority of her poems were discovered after her death in handwritten, hand-sewn booklets (fascicles) that she evidently did not share with others.[17] Dickinson actively refused to publish her work and reportedly remarked, "I would as soon undress in public, as to give my poems to the world."[18] Dickinson's language here mirrors Hawthorne's claim, discussed in the first chapter, that for a woman to "appear" in print involves revealing herself as naked. Yet Dickinson's relation to publication and embodiment does not wholly reinforce Hawthorne's logic: rather, Dickinson indicates that appearing in print would not reveal her naked body so much as cause her body to be constructed as naked. In other words, Dickinson's complex and ambivalent relation to print and publication reveals a canny concern with avoiding the forms of embodiment that emerge out of the temporal narrative of liberalism.

In the pages of the fascicles, for example, Dickinson does not title her poems: the beginnings of her poems remain unmarked save for by an occasional long horizontal slash at the end of a poem that also indicates the beginning of a new poem.[19] This slash—a line that effectively replicates the repetitive dashes that break the interior of her poems—has proved too scant a formal boundary for the demands of publication and scholarship. Dickinson's first editors, Thomas Wentworth Higginson and Mabel Loomis Todd, simply added titles to the poems, a practice that Higginson defended as requisite to creating a public for Dickinson's odd poems: a title made each poem more familiar—more comprehensible—to the reader.[20] Dickinson's later editors have removed Higginson and Todd's titles, yet they have framed her work in an array of numerical indices. Thomas A. Johnson's complete edition of the poems literally encloses each poem in a set of numbers. His ordinal index stands in place of a title above the poem: the date of first publication of the poem is on the right, the date of presumed authorship is on the left. In his variorum edition, Johnson adds more numbers—namely, line numbers before each variant (absent in the manuscripts) to facilitate placing them in the poem. R. W. Franklin's more recent variorum edition adds titles back to the poems, redacting the first line of each poem slightly (omitting some punctuation and capitalization) and placing it in italics above the poem.[21] Dickinson's preference not to title, date, or publish her poems functions as a succinct rejection of the conventions and aims of editorial arrangement. As a result of Dickinson's practice, then, the poems assume a displaced or placeless quality—without titles, it is difficult to enclose the poems within topical boundaries, difficult to determine where they begin and end, and difficult to simply *refer* to the poems as an editor might want to in a table of contents or as a scholar might want to in a footnote.[22] Without dates of authorship or publication, moreover, it is difficult to place a given poem in the temporal context of Dickinson's biography.

Dickinson's preference not to title her works is not simply a problem for editors; rather, it is of a piece with a poetic practice that disturbs and obstructs the liberal subject's narrative of identity as well as the division between public and private upon which this narrative depends. In the liberal narrative, as we have seen, identity is often imagined to have been established in private, particularly in the domestic space of the home: subsequent to establishing a fixed and coherent identity in the space of the private realm, the individual is able to move into the public sphere in order to display, deploy, and even market (as Eliza Wharton was expected to) his or her identity in public. Dickinson's refusal to title her poems can be correlated with a refusal of the terms of this narrative on a number of levels. First, Dickinson does not ever "emerge" decisively from private identity into public display. Her practice of not titling her poems is of a piece with her refusal to publish her poems in print. In an interesting way, Dickinson's poems are simply incompatible with the norms of publication. Insofar as her poems are now in print, they trouble the conventions of literary publication and the meanings embodied in these conventions. A second, related disturbance of the liberal narrative appears as well: Dickinson's lack of titles and refusal to publish has also obscured access to a biographical understanding of her life or work. Because of the difficulty in dating the poems, critics have speculated for years on the relationship between the events of her life and the content of her poetry: without a set of poems clearly placed in public (at certain times, under certain titles), the shape of her private (or "real") identity has been difficult to discern as well. Most famously, critics have sought for years to attach the "Master" figure of letters and poems to a historical personage. More recently the uncertain referents in Dickinson's erotic and/or love poetry have excited debate over her sexuality: was Dickinson really lesbian, straight, or bisexual? Despite claims to the contrary, her poems offer little evidence to settle the issue.

In critical treatment of Dickinson's poems concerning marriage, the biographical impulse has thus proved powerful in part because Dickinson has so effectively blocked this path of analysis. Attempts to name Dickinson's naked desire have been numerous and inconclusive. For instance, Richard Sewall suggests that "Title divine—is mine!" is a poem in which Dickinson portrays herself as "the imagined wife of Samuel Bowles," in part because the poem was included in a letter Dickinson wrote to Bowles.[23] David Porter also describes the poem as a plea to Bowles—a plea for definition through the terms of the marriage contract:

> The poem Dickinson sent Bowles holds the great pathos of this need of hers for definition. . . . The terms for her search came first from her womanhood in which marriage would be a normal measure of identification. . . . The terms 'My Husband,'

'Wife,' and 'Women,' were part of a restless attempt to *name herself*, to find the sign that would stand for her, to give herself a title. But as with her titleless poems, she was not equipped by a sense of personal coherence to do the job of titling her self.[24]

Porter ascribes the failure of marriage in "Title divine—is mine!" to Dickinson's lack—her lack of personal coherence. Because she has no fixed personal identity, established, for instance, in the reality of marriage to a man, she is unable to express and display that coherence in public, unable to assume the title she seeks. Porter thus suggests that Dickinson can only achieve title by moving from personal identity to public display. Yet this biographical "solution" to the poem is complicated by the fact that Dickinson also included a version of the poem in a letter to her sister-in-law Susan Gilbert Dickinson. Ellen Louise Hart thus suggests that the poem may reference an imagined marriage between Dickinson and Sue.[25]

Read in the terms suggested by Hart, "Title divine—is mine!" might be seen as an effort to signify same-sex desire, albeit with the caveat that Dickinson is using the form against its most formal, normative constraint, namely heterosexuality. Dickinson, then, cites and displaces the terms of the normative narrative of female identity in lines such as "Born—Bridalled—Shrouded / In a Day." That Dickinson sees such a displacement as a success rather than a form of self-mutilation might be indicated in the variant version of the poem sent to Susan:

> Title divine, is mine.
> The Wife without the Sign—
> Acute Degree conferred on me—
> Empress of Calvary—
> Royal, all but the Crown—
> Betrothed, without the Swoon
> God gives us Women—
> When You hold Garnet to Garnet—
> Gold—to Gold—
> Born—Bridalled—Shrouded—
> In a Day—
> Tri Victory—
> "My Husband"—Women say
> Stroking the Melody—
> Is this the Way—
>
> (J 1072 / F194)

After the speaker is "Born—Bridalled—Shrouded—/ In a Day—" she announces a triple victory—"Tri Victory"—describing the *success* inherent in the disfiguration of the normative narrative of female identity.

Hart's reading of the poem seems aimed at exposing (or producing) the truth of Dickinson's private desire in the figure of Sue, yet the poem, read against the norms of heterosexual marriage, increasingly points to the inaccessible, figurative, and mobile nature of private desire. In other words, Hart's biographical solution meets with resistance from within the poem. The marriage in the poem places Garnet to Garnet and Gold to Gold, refiguring the traditional blazon that taxonomizes the female body in order for the male poet to take possession of it. Yet this title does not effect possession: Gold is faced with Gold, title is less referential than conventional, tautological. The referent for conventional marriage is heterosexual, procreative sexuality, coupled with essentialized gender roles that place a passive woman below an active male. By insisting on marriage as title without such a referent, Dickinson revises both the meaning of marriage and that of title. Title becomes conventional rather than mimetic: sexed and gendered vectors of desire become radically unknown and even unknowable. In placing "Garnet to Garnet," Dickinson places figure to figure, blazon to blazon, thus indicating the extent to which each "figure" in the couple is figuratively determined. Figure thus becomes less a means of pointing to an essentialized gender behind language than of pointing to the way in which figurality emerges from the relationship between signifiers—between one blazon and another.

In "Title divine—is mine!" desire and difference, I would argue, are generated by figurality rather than by the truth of a binarized sex and gender that lie behind figurative reference. In a letter to Susan Gilbert Dickinson, also dated by Johnson as "about 1884," Dickinson describes a complicated antithetical structure of desire between herself and her sister-in-law, Susan.

> Morning
> might come
> by Accident—
> Sister—
> Night comes
> by Event—
> To believe the
> final line of
> the Card would
> foreclose Faith—
> Faith is <u>Doubt</u>.
> Sister—
> Show me
> Eternity—and
> I will show
> you Memory—
> Both in one
> package lain

> And lifted
> back again—
> Be Sue—while
> I am Emily—
> Be next—what
> you have ever
> been—Infinity—
>   (L 912)[26]

In this letter, a series of antitheses is invoked: Morning/Night, Accident/Event, Faith/Doubt, Eternity/Memory, Sue/Emily. Yet while the poem relies on a structured series of oppositions, the nature of these oppositions is also the subject of interrogation throughout the poem. The poem begins, for instance, by invoking a set of parallel oppositions—morning/night, accident/event—that do not clearly or conventionally parallel one another. The morning/night opposition is both conventional and rooted in nature, yet the opposition between accident and event is neither. Moreover, no clear antithetical relation obtains between accident and event: an accident, after all, *is* an event. While the term "event" suggests, in the context of this poem, a sense of foreknowledge, or perhaps merely consciousness that is absent in the case of an accident, this very sense of the word "event" derives solely from its opposition to the term "accident." Thus in the letter/poem's initial coupling of morning/night and accident/event, the parallel structure of antithesis produces meaning: meaning does not generate antithesis. Accordingly, antithesis is shown to be both constructed (*derivative* of natural metaphors rather than simply natural) *and* constitutive of meaning.

The second opposition in the letter/poem—that between faith and doubt—explicitly points out the interdependence of antithetical terms. Indeed, this interdependence constitutes the virtual collapse of antithesis: as the speaker concludes, "Faith is Doubt." Dickinson's claim, in this instance, seems to be that faith depends upon doubt for its existence: in other words, faith is not necessary in the face of belief or fact, rather, faith is necessary in the face of disbelief. One needs to have faith precisely because one doubts. Dickinson's dialectic description of antithesis points to the play of identity and difference at work in oppositional structures of meaning. Moreover, the lines that precede the final claim—"Faith is Doubt"—suggest that to see only difference rather than identity within antithesis is to foreclose the dialectic that creates meaning: "To believe the / final line of / the Card would / foreclose Faith— / Faith is Doubt."[27] To believe in the finality (rather than mutability) of definitions rooted in antithesis is to foreclose the very play of identity and difference that enables meaning to arise from antithesis.

The next pair of "opposite" terms treated in the text, eternity and memory, are once again neither clearly nor conventionally antithetical. "Eternity" would seem to point to the future, to an unbounded temporal space, whereas "Memory" points to the past, to a finite period of time. Yet memory also infinitizes the past insofar as it allows the past to survive into the present and the future. In this latter sense, we might say that "Memory *is* Eternity." The closure implied in the conventional antithetical relation (that of, say, Morning and Night) has thus begun to elude us here. Indeed, the pairing of terms in antithetical relations, following what the poem has now taught us, both allows us to fix upon a particular sense of two words as well as to dismantle that very fixity. We are able, through antithesis, to lay two words such as "eternity" and "memory" in one package—to package their meaning according to the structure of antithesis—and, as the poem states, to "lift . . . [them] back again" from this package. That is, we both construct and deconstruct meaning through the antithetical structure we have been given.

The relation of Emily and Sue, the final opposition in the poem, partakes of both this construction and deconstruction. The temporal dimension of the imperative, "Be Sue—/ *while* I am Emily—" suggests the temporary or staged nature of this opposition. And indeed, the ontological status invoked in the context of the antithesis between the two women is restaged and refigured in the subsequent line: "Be next—what / you have ever/been—Infinity—". The packaging and "lift[ing] back again" of antithesis between the two women stages a stable relation of meaning, desire, and difference between the two women as well as the dissolution of this particular staging, a dissolution that prevents the foreclosure of desire. Insofar as Sue is "Infinity," she eludes the package of antithetical difference that enables the staging of desire: she also eludes the potential fixity of this antithesis and thereby reopens the play of meaning and difference between the two women. The letter/poem points, then, to precisely the necessity of understanding oppositional structures of meaning (and desire) as unstable, constructed, and mobile rather than fixed, final, and natural.

The language of difference is thus here restaged away from its fixed, natural referents to allow for both the staging of culturally proscribed desires (desire between women) and for the reinscription of difference as figurative and mutable. If we return to Dickinson's treatment of marriage, we can read precisely this design in her work, namely an effort to rearrange the natural, fixed reference to sexual difference between men and women in order to signify desire and difference between women as well as men and women. More importantly, perhaps, Dickinson's discussion of marriage insists that meaning can inhere in the entitlement attached to marriage in a way that does not rely upon a liberal narrative of identity that moves from private to public. Dickinson thus reforms marriage as status or as title. This reform takes the shape of "ghosting," as it were, the private referent of marriage, the act of desire, sexual union, or love that seemingly underwrites the consensual contract. Conventionally, marriage is seen to operate in precisely the opposite direction: marriage is viewed as a recognition or ratification of a loving bond established first and foremost in private. Yet as we have seen, the presumption that private love is established first and then simply sanctioned by the state ignores the power of a recognizing authority to shape that which it recognizes. In other words, we might say that the conventional understanding of marriage fails to attend to the figurative power of entitlement: the power to configure that which it bespeaks as already existing. Dickinson's queering of marriage, then, asks us to rethink the public role of titles by placing desire—heterosexual or homosexual—in a radically private and unknowable space: eroticism is signified as absent, not as present, as generated through figurative rather than literal or ontological grounds of entitlement.

In dissevering private behavior from public entitlement, Dickinson effects what we might call a "queering" of marriage. This claim runs counter to the arguments of queer theorists who have tended to define marriage as necessarily antithetical to the antiregulatory pursuits of queer theory. Yet I would argue that Dickinson demonstrates that title is itself available not simply as the location of regulation but as that of the negotiation—even politicization—of meaning. Dickinson thus shifts the burden of meaning away from gay or straight bodies, gay or straight desires, to the signifier that negotiates the production of private identity. Thus, as Nan Hunter argues, same-sex marriage is a proposition that concerns heterosexual marriage as well:

> The legalization of lesbian and gay marriage would not, of course, directly shift the balance of power in heterosexual relations. Gay marriage is no panacea. It could, however, alter the fundamental concept of the particular institution of marriage. Its potential is to disrupt both the gendered definition of marriage and the assumption that marriage is a form of socially, if not legally, prescribed hierarchy. . . . Whatever the impact that legalization of lesbian and gay marriage would have on the lives of lesbians and gay men, it has fascinating potential for denaturalizing the gender structure of marriage law for heterosexual couples.[28]

Although same-sex marriage remains the subject of ongoing debate within both gay and straight communities, Dickinson's queering of marriage has ramifications, as Hunter's analysis of gay marriage suggests, for understanding the gendered norms of social entitlement. In other words, in her focus on title or status rather than contract, Dickinson asks us to see marriage as necessarily remote from any natural, private referent. As overtly titular, marriage is necessarily public in nature and cannot be tethered to any normative, private sexuality. Dickinson thus splits apart the private and public faces of marriage, asking us to see the public function of marriage as unratified by any specific form of private activity.

By splitting apart the public and the private, Dickinson makes visible the space of sociality—the space in which public and private meanings are stitched together—either overtly or covertly. The third space, between public and private, is one that Dickinson's poetry habitually seeks to inhabit: as such, she both makes sociality visible and tends to disrupt the operations of liberal identity formation. Dickinson thus also points to the way in which we might recognize the political power of the literary public sphere. Liberalism tends to locate meaning and identity in private subject formation: this is one way that we might understand the force that "identity politics" has assumed in contemporary culture. One form of political response to the multiplication of private identities (gendered, racialized, sexualized) is to call for the increased public capacity for recognition of a variety of persons. Indeed, as Nancy Fraser argues, the culture wars have tended to focus on the "politics of recognition" or the pluralization of recognized identities within the public sphere.[29] Yet the difficulty with this response to the dynamics of liberalism is that it does not account for the fundamental politics of private identity formation in the first place. Rather than imagining that an increasingly capacious public sphere is the primary path to justice and equality, I would suggest that (taking our cue from Dickinson's poetics) we need to attend to the dynamics of sociality as they already occur, and have historically occurred, around us.

What does it mean for the speaker in a Dickinson poem to be a "wife"? On the one hand, it clearly gives her a title, that of "czar," that of an adult woman. Dickinson is not averse to the power conferred by title, to the value of laying claim to identity through linguistic acts. By the same token, she is aware of the control that title exerts in determining an individual from the outside: the title of "wife" makes a woman publicly readable or available for appropriation by others. Specifically, as I have argued, marriage is a gender-producing machine: it creates masculinity and femininity, and thus produces the "wife" as one woman standing in relation to one man. Dickinson, I would suggest, is not interested in being known this way: in refusing the marriage proposal of a suitor she tellingly writes, "Dont you know that 'No' is the wildest word we consign to Language?" (L 562). In preserving the wildness of language and a powerful mobility of desire, Dickinson emphasizes the force of title as nomination, but dissevers it from any ontological status, from the temporal narrative of liberalism in which identity is produced in private and acknowledged in public. Dickinson's poetics of title directly opposes identity politics, and particularly the call for increased public recognition of a variety of private, immutable identities. Rather than increased recognition, then, this reading of Dickinson's poetry points to the need for an increased politicization of the terms of entitlement. This would entail a loosening of ontological claims of identity rather than a strengthening and multiplication of them. Liberalism, as I have sought to demonstrate in this book, produces gendered bodies through the workings of the public sphere. At the moment when we locate this activity outside a public/private dichotomy—specifically in a middle ground of sociality—we can engage in politics not of recognition, but of open sociality, in which the opening of civil space is itself the grounds of title making.

Notes

Notes

Introduction

1. On performative speech acts and marriage see J. L. Austin, *How to Do Things with Words*.

2. Pamela Haag, *Consent*.

3. "Story of the First Beacon Hill Farm Bride," cited in Haag, *Consent*, 102.

4. On the history of the legal doctrine of privacy, see Lauren Berlant, "The Subject of True Feeling"; Caroline Danielson, "The Gender of Privacy and the Embodied Self"; David Garrow, *Liberty and Sexuality*; Deborah Nelson, *Pursuing Privacy in Cold War America*; and Brook Thomas, "The Construction of Privacy."

5. On the state's role in shaping marriage see Nancy Cott, *Public Vows*; and Michael Warner, "Beyond Gay Marriage."

6. See Zillah Eisenstein, *The Radical Future of Liberal Feminism*; and Carole Pateman, *The Sexual Contract*. For a discussion of the way in which contemporary liberal theorists fail to include women in their analyses, see Susan Moller Okin, "Humanist Liberalism."

7. Judith Shklar, "The Liberalism of Fear," 21, 24.

8. For useful historical work on women as writers and readers see Mary Kelley, *Private Woman, Public Stage* and "Reading Women/Women Reading." More recently, Paula Bennett has impressively catalogued and analyzed the strength and diversity of women's historical participation in the print public sphere in *Poets in the Public Sphere*.

9. Nathaniel Hawthorne, "Mrs. Hutchinson," 19 (emphasis added).

10. *Danny Lee Kyllo v. United States*, No. 99–8508 Supreme Court of the United States, 533 U.S. 27; 121 S. Ct. 2038 (June 11, 2001), 2046.

11. Jürgen Habermas, *The Structural Transformation of the Public Sphere*, 30.

12. Nancy Fraser, *Justice Interruptus*, 70.

13. Both Axel Honneth and Charles Taylor have written about the desire for recognition in relation to the dynamics of the public sphere. My concerns differ significantly from theirs, however, to the extent that I am less interested in describing or advocating increased access to the public sphere for unrecognized or excluded groups than understanding the extent to which privacy and individual subjectivity are constituted and articulated in circuits of exchange between the public and private spheres. The theoretical concern with a "struggle for recognition" has its roots in Hegelian thought and might be traced through a line of philosophers including Alexandre Kojève, Louis Althusser, Axel Honneth, and Charles Taylor. My own concerns are closer to those of

Althusser than Honneth or Taylor. See Althusser, "Ideology and Ideological State Apparatuses."

14. Iris Young, "Impartiality and the Civic Public," 72.

15. See Lauren Berlant, "The Subject of True Feeling" and "Poor Eliza."

Chapter 1: Gender, Liberal Theory, and the Literary Public Sphere

1. On the shift from contract to status, see Henry Sumner Maine, *Ancient Law*; and Amy Dru Stanley, *From Bondage to Contract*.

2. On the trope of the penetrable female body, see Sharon Marcus, "Fighting Bodies"; Gail Kern Paster, "Leaky Vessels"; and Jennifer Nedelsky, "Law, Boundaries, and the Bounded Self."

3. Phyllis Rackin thus argues, "As is well known, the body served as a map not of gender difference but of social and political hierarchy. The system of analogies that rationalized the social hierarchy included the subordination of women to men, but its essential axis of difference was social and political status rather than embodied sex" ("Foreign Country," 76).

4. Thomas Laqueur, *Making Sex*, 5.

5. Rackin, "Foreign Country," 74.

6. John Knox, "The First Blast of the Trumpet Against the Monstrous Regiment of Women," in *On Rebellion*, 12–13.

7. William Cobbett, *A Kick for a Bite*, 24.

8. Knox, "The First Blast of the Trumpet Against the Monstrous Regiment of Women," 12.

9. Lauren Berlant, "The Subject of True Feeling," 54.

10. Although it is customary to use the term "sex" to refer to biology and "gender" to refer to culture, I do not separate the two here since I am arguing that sex, precisely in its biological sense, is culturally determined. Although the binary model of sexual difference allows gender to be understood as the effect of biology, I am arguing that this grounding is itself the effect of culture and history.

11. Wendy Brown, *States of Injury*, 156–57 (emphasis added).

12. I borrow this phrase from Jacques Lacan's theory of the mirror stage in which the subject establishes his identity in a line of fiction ("une ligne de fiction") through imagining that the coherence and stability of the image of himself in the mirror accurately represent him. Although Lacan is primarily interested in the process of identification (a different line of fiction than the one I'm concerned with in liberalism), he does see this line of fiction as requiring a certain disavowal of the child's dependency. See Lacan, "Le stade du miroir," translated in *Écrits*, 1–7.

13. A feminist critique of Marxism has developed this argument in compelling terms, in part because the Marxist model of production discounts the domestic and reproductive labor of women: "The material base upon which patriarchy rests lies most fundamentally in men's control over women's labor power" (Heidi Hartmann, "The Unhappy Marriage of Marxism and Feminism," 101). See also Linda Nicholson, "Feminism and Marx"; Iris Young, "Beyond the Unhappy Marriage"; Ann Ferguson and Nancy Folbre, "The Unhappy Marriage of Patriarchy and Capitalism"; and Maria Mies, *Patriarchy and Accumulation on a World Scale*. The link between the symbolic function of women's bodies and their domestic labor is visible in the history of women's exclu-

sion from the political role of juror. Court rulings as late as 1994 have been required to insist on women's equal right and obligation to serve on jury trials. (See Kerber, *No Constitutional Right*, chapter 4; and Joanna Grossman, "Women's Jury Service.") The terms in which women were "excused" from jury service in the twentieth century rested upon equating femininity with a private, familial identity that stood in opposition to political participation. Ostensibly grounded in the language of biology, which identified women with childbearing and child raising, court rulings nonetheless limited the participation of *all* women in jury duty, not just pregnant women, women with small children, or even mothers. The language of these rulings references women's reproductive function, yet from this starting point, it clearly articulates the state's interest in maintaining a gendered segregation between the public labor of men and the private labor of women. Thus, as Linda Kerber argues, women's exclusion from jury duty seems more related to a division of labor between men and women than to physical constraint: "Women's exclusion from juries followed from a vision of the female who owed her primary service to her husband and their family. . . . Metaphors describing how women fulfilled their obligations to their husbands abounded in food imagery: with babies at their breasts or—as [a male state assistant attorney general] blurted out in court— 'cooking our dinners.' That pronoun 'our' . . . is key to understanding . . . the 'right' of women to be excused from jury service so that they could be free to cook 'our' dinners" (Kerber, *No Constitutional Right*, 217–18). The private nature of women's labor here follows a line of fiction—a chain of images in which the female body gives birth, produces milk, and cooks dinner. Cooking dinner for a state's attorney husband (an exemplary public sphere occupation) becomes metonymically associated with giving birth rather than with a division of labor upon which men depend for the freedom to function as political subjects. In court documents averring the state's interest in delimiting women's role to the domestic sphere, what becomes visible is not simply the exclusion of women from political participation, but their necessary location in the private sphere to enable the production of the public sphere. Women's private position in this narrative is thus crucial for the production of male agency, for providing for the material needs of men who then function as unconstrained by materiality.

14. Edmund Morgan, *American Slavery, American Freedom*, 381, 386. Along similar lines, Etienne Balibar points out that modern racism emerges out of liberal relations of equality: "it is necessary to include in the structural conditions . . . of modern racism the fact that the societies in which racism develops are at the same time supposed to be 'egalitarian' societies, in other words, societies which (officially) disregard status differences between individuals" ("Racism and Nationalism," 49).

15. Judith Butler, "Contingent Foundations," 4. See also Claude Lefort, who makes a related argument: "The political is thus revealed, not in what we call political activity, but in the double movement whereby the mode of institution of society appears and is obscured. It appears in the sense that the process whereby society is ordered and unified across its divisions becomes visible. It is obscured in the sense that the locus of politics (the locus in which parties compete and in which a general agency of power takes shape and is reproduced) becomes defined as particular, while the principle which generates the overall configuration is concealed" (*Democracy and Political Theory*, 11).

16. The literature on race and nineteenth-century science is extensive. For a useful overview, see Robyn Wiegman, *American Anatomies*, 43–78.

17. Saidiya Hartman's work on reconstruction-era liberalism and race indicates the

extent to which even the overt granting of political rights to African-American men through the fourteenth amendment could not overcome the effects of the biological essentialism that structures liberalism: "The legacy of slavery was evidenced by the intransigence of racism, specifically the persistent commitment to discriminatory racial classifications. . . . On one hand, the constraints of race were formally negated by the stipulation of sovereign individuality and abstract equality, and on the other, racial discriminations and predilections were cherished and protected as beyond the scope of the law" (*Scenes of Subjection*, 121). Biological essentialism relegates racial difference to a prepolitical realm; insofar as this is a structuring move of liberalism, the granting of political equality cannot eradicate racism without politicizing biology, or shifting the boundaries of the political.

18. At different points in U.S. history persons of color have been excluded from sharing in the privileges of liberal individualism. These persons include Native Americans, Asian-Americans, and Latinos as well as African-Americans. I focus on the racialized discourse concerning African-Americans in what follows, but related discourses developed with respect to other racialized groups that pertained to the specific historical circumstances of white/nonwhite relations in each instance.

19. Baker, "Critical Memory and the Black Public Sphere," 13. Despite barriers to access, many African-Americans did participate in the public sphere prior to the passage of the fourteenth amendment, but that participation often required an intervention in the racial terms that delimited the public sphere. Examples of two antebellum texts that overtly meditate on the racialized terms of political identity and public sphere access in the United States include *David Walker's Appeal* and Frederick Douglass's speech, "What to the Slave is the Fourth of July?"

20. Saidiya Hartman thus argues that whiteness metonymically becomes a form of property itself: "Whiteness was a valuable and exclusive property essential to the integrity of the citizen-subject and the exemplary self-possession of the liberal individual" (*Scenes of Subjection*, 119). This racial biological essentialism produces the mythical concept of "white blood," a substance that, despite its fundamentally nonempirical nature, functions as a juridical entity throughout the nineteenth and into the twentieth century, reified by law and circulated as a currency supporting white privilege and black dispossession. On whiteness as legal property in the postbellum period, see Eva Saks, "Representing Miscegenation Law." For an account of the Dred Scott decision and related documents, see Paul Finkelman, *Dred Scott v. Stanford*.

21. Hortense Spillers, "Mama's Baby, Papa's Maybe," 77–78.

22. As Robyn Wiegman argues, it is important to see "how thoroughly saturated is the *socio-symbolic structure* of sexual difference with the determinants of white racial supremacy. This structure of sexual difference was (and is) not reducible to the 'essential' components of male and female bodies, but refers instead to the processes and practices by which gendered subjectivity defines and inaugurates the modern subject, organizing 'civil' society by scripting it according to highly gendered roles and functions" (*American Anatomies*, 65–66).

23. For a philosophical discussion of the antinomies of liberalism, see Immanuel Kant, *The Critique of Judgement*.

24. See John E. Martin: "Reorganisation through enclosure created larger units of landholding and production and allowed the adoption of new methods of cultivation,

greater specialisation, and increased investment. . . . The emergence of absolute property allowed the detachment of land from traditional obligations and relationships, so
that it could be freely bought and sold" (*Feudalism to Capitalism*, 102). On the shift to
absolute property, see also Eugene Kamenka and R. S. Neale, *Feudalism, Capitalism, and
Beyond*; and Alan Ryan, *Property and Political Theory*.

25. J. G. A. Pocock, *Virtue, Commerce, and History*, 66.

26. The debate over the dominance of republican versus liberal politics in eighteenth-century England and the United States has animated much of the historiography in these fields for the past twenty years, with Pocock as a primary proponent of the
republican argument and C. B. Macpherson among those advancing the liberal argument. I treat the liberal/republican divide at greater length below in this chapter, as well
as extensively in the third chapter. With respect to property, one might schematize the
relation between the two as follows: republican property ownership sets the citizen free
from dependence and manipulation, allowing him to freely participate in the public
sphere where his actions are oriented toward pursuing the public good. Liberal property ownership also confers an autonomous status on its owner, but the liberal citizen
enters into the public sphere in order to protect his property and interests rather than
to pursue the public good. In republicanism, property ownership is a prerequisite to
virtuous public activity; in liberalism, property ownership is a palpable good and a
political right in and of itself. Pocock has also characterized the distinction between his
understanding of republican property ownership and Macpherson's as the difference
between a republican conception of fixed, real property and a liberal conception of
mobile, alienable property.

27. A. S. P. Woodhouse, *Puritanism and Liberty*, 82, cited by C. B. Macpherson, *The
Political Theory of Possessive Individualism*, 128. On the Putney debates, see also Peter
Linebaugh and Marcus Rediker, *The Many-Headed Hydra*, 104–42.

28. Woodhouse, *Puritanism and Liberty*, 83, cited by Macpherson, *The Political
Theory of Possessive Individualism*, 123.

29. Macpherson thus famously characterizes Locke's liberalism as "possessive individualism": what makes one an individual (a liberal subject) is the possession of property, including property in the self. As Macpherson also points out, Locke's theory of
liberalism posits the equal freedom of all individuals, yet Locke defines the mechanism
of consent to the social contract as the moment when one enters in agreements of property ownership, thus de facto limiting political subjectivity to property owners
(Macpherson, *The Political Theory of Possessive Individualism*, 249).

30. See Kirk Harold Porter, *A History of Suffrage in the United States*. On the franchise in relation to race and gender, see Joan Gunderson, "Independence, Citizenship,
and the American Revolution," and Rogers Smith, *Civic Ideals*.

31. On the relation between private property and liberal politics in the early
Republic, see Jennifer Nedelsky, *Private Property*, and, more generally, the essays in
Thomas Flanagan and Anthony Parel, *Theories of Property*.

32. John Locke, *Two Treatises of Government*, 314, 321, 322.

33. Carole Pateman, *The Sexual Contract*, 49.

34. Ibid., 93–94.

35. Pateman writes, "In all the telling of the [liberal origin] tales, and in the discussion and argument about the social contract, we are told only half the story. Political

theorists present the familiar account of the creation of civil society as a universal realm that (at least potentially) includes everyone and of the origins of political right in the sense of the authority of government in the liberal state. . . . But this is not the 'original' political right. . . . To uncover the latter, it is necessary to begin to tell the repressed story of the genesis of patriarchal political right which men exercise over women" (*Disorder of Women*, 33).

36. Judith Butler, "Contingent Foundations," 13. See also *Bodies That Matter* for a discussion of citationality or iteration in relation to performance. Here, Butler filters the notion of performativity through a deconstructive model of citation, arguing that power instantiates itself through citation and exclusion, yet each iteration is itself a displacement, a potential interrogation of the terms of exclusion upon which power is grounded.

37. Nathaniel Hawthorne, "Mrs. Hutchinson," 19. Hawthorne's concern to prevent women writers from committing acts of indecent exposure in print may have been motivated less by an interest in protecting "the loveliness of her sex" than in the desire to protect his own book sales. In economic terms, the division of labor between men and women might thus be seen to underwrite his understanding of women as essentially private beings.

38. Jürgen Habermas, *The Structural Transformation of the Public Sphere*, 36.

39. "Procedural rationality" is a term indicating the constitutive connection between reason and procedure—in this case, the procedure of public debate. Because ideas are exposed to debate and critique in public, they can be refined until they are unassailable or wholly reasonable. Any irrational, unreasonable, or personal bias embodied in a given concept would thus be winnowed out through the procedure of public debate.

40. Seyla Benhabib, "Models of Public Space," 88.

41. For discussions of the distinction between Habermas's earlier and later work, see Keith Michael Baker, "Defining the Public Sphere"; and Peter Uwe Hohendahl, "The Public Sphere: Models and Boundaries."

42. Joan Landes, *Women and the Public Sphere*, 7, 43.

43. Ibid., 88.

44. I would note here the explicitly liberal (rather than republican) bent of Habermas's description of the bourgeois public sphere. Liberalism, as I argue above (note 26), differs from republicanism insofar as it circles back upon privacy and property as the aim as well as the origin of autonomy. Republicanism, however, sees the public sphere as telos—as the site where virtue is established through concern with the public good (rather than with private property). Habermas makes the liberal structure of the bourgeois public sphere explicit when he contrasts it with the classical republican public sphere in the terms I use here (see Habermas, *The Structural Transformation of the Public Sphere*, 51–52). However, Habermas's normative public sphere (unlike the historical bourgeois public sphere) is often described and understood by critics in far more republican than liberal terms. For readings of a republican Habermas, see, for instance, Nancy Fraser, "Rethinking the Public Sphere," and Bruce Burgett, *Sentimental Bodies*. A canonical modern account of the republican public sphere can be found in Hannah Arendt, *The Human Condition*.

45. Pocock offers a somewhat analogous account of the effects of becoming

involved in an exchange economy:

> It was hard to see how [the citizen] could become involved in exchange relation-
> ships, or in relationships governed by the media of exchange (especially when these
> took the form of paper tokens of public credit) without becoming involved in
> dependence and corruption. The ideals of virtue and commerce could not therefore
> be reconciled to one another. . . . Virtue was redefined . . . with the aid of a concept
> of 'manners.' As the individual moved from the farmer-warrior world of ancient cit-
> izenship or Gothic *libertas*, he entered an increasingly transactional universe of
> 'commerce and the arts' . . . in which his relationships and interactions with other
> social beings, and with their products, became increasingly complex and various,
> modifying and developing more and more aspects of his personality. Commerce,
> leisure, cultivation and . . . the division and diversification of labor combined to
> bring this about; and if he could no longer engage directly in the activity and equal-
> ity of ruling and being ruled, but had to depute his government and defense to spe-
> cialized and professional representatives, he was more than compensated for his loss
> of antique virtue by an indefinite and perhaps infinite enrichment of his personali-
> ty, the product of the multiplying relationships, with both things and persons, in
> which he became progressively involved. (Pocock, *Virtue*, 48–49)

Pocock thus sees the exchange economy of capitalism as related to the cultivation of
personality, or what Habermas might call bourgeois subjectivity and interiority. Pocock
does not imagine this in terms of an "intimate sphere" as does Habermas, but does see
it as a depoliticization of previously political relations.

46. According to Karl Marx, individuals engaged in an exchange economy become
equalized as exchangers: "each of the subjects is an exchanger; i.e. each has the same
social relation towards the other that the other has towards him. As subjects of
exchange, their relation is therefore that of *equality*" (*Grundrisse*, 241).

47. Ibid., 247–48.

48. Adam Smith, *The Theory of Moral Sentiments*, 163–64.

49. John Bender, "Making the World Safe for Narratology," 30.

50. See Etienne Balibar, "Citizen Subject," for a useful account of this dual meaning
of the term "subject."

51. According to Habermas, women were active in the literary public sphere as readers (56). I would extend this claim to describe women as readers *and* writers of literature in the eighteenth century.

52. For a discussion of various taxonomies of public and private spheres, see Fraser,
"Rethinking the Public Sphere"; Bruce Robbins, "Introduction: The Public as
Phantom"; and Kathy Peiss, "Going Public."

53. Critics have challenged Habermas's account of women's exclusion from the public sphere and have also challenged his model of a monolithic public sphere. As Bruce
Robbins argues, "the lines between public and private are perpetually shifting."
Theorists have, accordingly, attempted "to pluralize and multiply the concept" of the
Habermasian public sphere and to construct models of "alternative public spheres and
counterpublics" ("Introduction," xv, xvii). In focusing on the *literary* public sphere in
particular, I mean to move away from a monolithic account of the public sphere and to
suggest, as well, that versions of the public sphere and the logic governing recognition
within such spheres are themselves the subject of continued contestation. For further

discussion of the mutable and plural nature of the public sphere, both historically and theoretically, see Geoff Eley, "Nations, Publics, and Political Cultures," and Lawrence Klein, "Gender and the Public/Private Distinction in the Eighteenth Century," as well as, more broadly, the following anthologies: Dario Castiglione and Lesley Sharpe, eds., *Shifting the Boundaries—Transformation of the Languages of Public and Private in the Eighteenth Century*; Johanna Meehan, ed., *Feminists Read Habermas*; Elizabeth Eger, Charlotte Grant, Clíona Ó Gallchoir, and Penny Warburton, eds., *Women, Writing and the Public Sphere, 1700–1830*; and Bruce Robbins, ed., *The Phantom Public Sphere*.

54. Habermas does offer some support for this idea:

> The process in which the state-governed public sphere was appropriated by the public of private people making use of their reason and was established as a sphere of criticism of public authority was one of functionally converting the public sphere in the world of letters already equipped with institutions of the public and with forums for discussion. With their help, the experiential complex of audience-oriented privacy made its way also into the political realm's public sphere. The representation of the interests of the privatized domain of a market economy was interpreted with the aid of ideas grown in the soil of the intimate sphere of the conjugal family. (51)

Here, Habermas suggests that the literary public sphere prepares the ground for a political public sphere. However, Habermas also argues that the bourgeoisie conflated the two spheres and the modes of subjectivity each one sustains:

> In the educated classes the one form of public sphere was considered to be identical with the other. . . . As soon as privatized individuals in their capacity as human beings ceased to communicate merely about their subjectivity but rather in their capacity as property-owners desired to influence public power in their common interest, the humanity of the literary public sphere served to increase the effectiveness of the public sphere in the political realm. *The fully developed bourgeois public sphere was based on the fictitious identity of the two roles assumed by the privatized individuals who came together to form a public: the role of property owners and the role of human beings pure and simple.* (56; emphasis in original)

Rather than see the literary public sphere as prior to the political public sphere, or even as conflated with it, I argue that the relation between the two is circular, or, to borrow a term from Mark Seltzer, is characterized by a form of "looping." For a discussion supporting this view, see Peter Uwe Hohendahl, "The Public Sphere: Models and Boundaries."

55. Kathryn Shevelow, *Women and Print Culture*, 14.

56. See Cathy Davidson, *Revolution and the Word*, ix, for a discussion of the fact that *Power of Sympathy* was first published at the time of Washington's inauguration.

57. For recent responses to Douglas, and discussion of the "feminization" narrative, see the 1999 special issue of *differences*, "America the Feminine," edited by Philip Gould and Leonard Tennenhouse, and especially Gould's introduction.

58. Warner is certainly less attached to the gendered terms of this narrative than is Douglas: indeed, he argues that the republican print public sphere contradicts its own premises insofar as it excludes women and nonwhite persons. Nevertheless, his account of the feminization of the citizen's relation to the nation in liberalism, together with the loss of a republican, active engagement in politics, seems to associate feminization with

a kind of unfortunate fall from republicanism into liberalism. The account of liberalism as the successor to republicanism in the United States has, of course, been the subject of a great deal of debate. For analyses by literary critics that challenge the model of republican-liberal succession, see Burgett, *Sentimental Bodies*; Julia Stern, *The Plight of Feeling*; and Elizabeth Barnes, *States of Sympathy*. For a more politically oriented challenge to Pocock and Gordon Wood on the demise of republicanism at the hands of liberalism, see Isaac Kramnick, *Republicanism and Bourgeois Radicalism*. I develop my position with respect to this debate at greater length in chapter 3 of this book.

59. I am not alone in doing so. The strongest examples of accounts that emphasize women as writers and readers in early American literature are Davidson, *Revolution and the Word*; Barnes, *States of Sympathy*; and Shirley Samuels, *Romances of the Republic*.

60. Michael Warner, *The Letters of the Republic*, xiii.

61. See Michael Warner, "The Mass Public and the Mass Subject," 383.

62. Smith, *The Theory of Moral Sentiments*, 161–62.

63. John Bender, *Imagining the Penitentiary*, 223.

64. Smith, *The Theory of Moral Sentiments*, 162.

65. As David Marshall argues, the fact that the "Enlightenment desires to discover universal principles" should not cause us "to overlook the implications of a perspective that casts people as spectators to each other" (*The Figure of Theater*, 169).

66. Lefort, *Democracy and Political Theory*, 17.

67. John Trenchard and Thomas Gordon, *Cato's Letters*, 56.

68. Pocock, *Virtue*, 114.

69. Ibid., 122.

70. For a discussion of the relation between the novel and Smithian models of sympathy and supposition, see Barnes and Bender. For more general discussion of the relation between the novel and probability, see Catherine Gallagher, *Nobody's Story*; Michael McKeon, *The Origins of the English Novel*; and Irene Tucker, *A Probable State*. See also James Thompson, *Models of Value*, who examines the relation of two forms of writing—the novel and economic theory—that were spawned at the same time in the eighteenth century.

71. In a later essay focusing on mass culture, Warner makes precisely this point, thus apparently revising his earlier argument that the structural determinants of a print public sphere correspond to republican premises. In the eighteenth century, Warner argues, "the discursive conventions of the public sphere had already made virtuous self-unity archaic" ("The Mass Public," 378). Warner's later essay seems, as well, to address the function of subjectification that occurs in this moment of abstraction: "Because the moment of special imaginary reference is always necessary," he writes, "the publicity of the public sphere never reduces to information, discussion, will formation, or any of the other scenarios by which the public sphere represents itself" (379). Here Warner argues against the premises of Benhabib's proceduralist public sphere: rather than imagining subjects who are preconstituted in privacy and who then emerge into the public with a clear account of their needs and desires at their disposal, Warner argues that the process of abstraction required for entering the public sphere is also a process of subject formation.

72. For a useful summary of this debate, see the "Introduction" to Glenn Hendler's *Public Sentiments*.

73. "Reflexivity" is Luhmann's term for what I have traced as Smithian sympathy or the *intersubjective* determination of the self in modern society.

74. Nancy Armstrong, *Desire and Domestic Fiction*, 5.

75. In this sense, Armstrong's argument bears an interesting resemblance to Locke's: one enters into the social contract by consenting to its existing institutions such as marriage and property ownership.

76. Seltzer, *Serial Killers*, 167.

77. Reva Siegel, "Why Equal Protection No Longer Protects," 1119.

Chapter 2: Puritan Bodies and Transatlantic Texts

1. For a recent and thorough historical account of the events of the antinomian crisis in Massachusetts Bay Colony, see Michael P. Winship, *Making Heretics*. Winship emphasizes that Hutchinson was not the leader of the "antinomian" or free grace faction; rather, he suggests, Henry Vane and John Wheelwright assumed more prominent roles in the political and theological debates that animated the crisis.

2. David Hall, *The Antinomian Controversy*, 348. The primary documents related to the antinomian controversy are collected in this anthology. Hutchinson was placed on trial twice: once in civil court, and later before the church. Hall's collection includes two versions of the civil trial, the first of which is a transcript first printed in Thomas Hutchinson's *History of the Colony and Province of Massachusetts Bay* (Boston, 1767). As Hall notes, Thomas Hutchinson (the great-great-grandson of Anne) relied upon an "ancient manuscript" that is no longer extant for this transcript. The second account of the civil trial appears in John Winthrop's report on the antinomian controversy, *A Short Story of the Rise, reign, and ruine of the Antinomians, Familists & Libertines*, which first appeared in England in 1644 and was published there by Thomas Weld. (The second section of this chapter deals extensively with the publishing history of *A Short Story*.) Hall's anthology includes both the transcript as redacted by Thomas Hutchinson and Winthrop's version. Differences between the transcript and Winthrop's account are numerous; some are discussed below. For further discussion of the differences, see Mary Beth Norton, *Founding Mothers & Fathers*, 359–400. Citations of the trial in my text refer to the Thomas Hutchinson transcript as it appears in Hall (rather than to Winthrop's version), save where explicitly noted. Page numbers refer to Hall's edition. Hall's collection also includes numerous other documents related to the controversy that are cited in the body of my text with Hall's pagination.

3. See, for example, Phillip Round, *By Nature and By Custom Cursed*: "Through their handling of the Hutchinson affair, [the ministers] worked to establish a gendered discursive center in the colony that effectively squeezed out women's forms of cultural production—prophecy, publication, and church-gathering—which were then beginning to flourish in some areas of the mother country" (127). For similar claims see Mary Maples Dunn, "Saints and Sisters"; Ann Kibbey, *The Interpretation of Material Shapes*; Jane Kamensky, *Governing the Tongue*; and Lyle Koehler, "The Case of the American Jezebels."

4. Koehler, "The Case of the American Jezebels," 65.

5. See Benedict Anderson, *Imagined Communities*.

6. John Winthrop, *The Journal of John Winthrop*, 208. Secondary sources on the the-

ological debates are numerous: see especially Norman Pettit, *The Heart Prepared*; William Stoever, *A Faire and Easie Way to Heaven*; and Perry Miller, *The New England Mind*.

7. On the important relation between speech and violence in the Bay Colony, see Kibbey, *The Interpretation of Material Shapes*; Kamensky, *Governing the Tongue*; Sandra Gustafson, *Eloquence Is Power*; and Cornelia Hughes Dayton, *Women Before the Bar*.

8. Numerous critics have demonstrated that Hutchinson's theological claims are internal to a fissiparous Puritanism rather than external or heretical. As Ross Pudaloff points out, the claim that Hutchinson follows Puritan doctrine is a long-standing one in treatments of the antinomian crisis: "Despite the 'errors' attributed to Mrs. Hutchinson in particular, the expressed beliefs of the Antinomians have appeared to fall within the mainstream of Puritan theology" ("Sign and Subject," 150). See also Perry Miller, *The New England Mind: The Seventeenth Century*; Larzer Ziff, *The Career of John Cotton*; Pettit, *The Heart Prepared*; Hall's introduction to *The Antinomian Controversy*; and Philip Gura, *A Glimpse of Sion's Glory* (cited below). In what follows, I seek to link the fairly well rehearsed terms of the theological debate to questions concerning colonialism and gender.

9. "For this was one of her tenents, that the whole Scripture in the Letter of it held forth nothing but a Covenant of works" (Winthrop in Hall, 264). Hutchinson denied this charge. See also Patricia Caldwell, "The Antinomian Language Controversy."

10. In Winthrop's *Short Story*, we see that all of the accused antinomians apparently adopted this strategy, arguing that no legitimate charges had been lodged against them and thus questioning the authority of the court to indict them.

11. For early legal history of the colony, see David Flaherty, ed., *Essays in the History of Early American Law*; Dayton, *Women Before the Bar*; and Bruce Mann and Christopher Tomlins, *The Many Legalities of Early America*.

12. Gura, *A Glimpse of Sion's Glory*, 239.

13. Stephen Foster, *The Long Argument*, 148. In a similar vein, see also Christopher Hill, *Change and Continuity in Seventeenth-Century England*: "The protestant emphasis on the heart helped to dissolve the hard crust of custom, tradition and authority . . . the appeal to inner conviction, and the rejection of the routine ceremonies through which the priesthood imposed its authority, could have liberating effects in any society" (98–99).

14. Perry Miller writes, "When the discipline was carried to America, it was immediately put to uses exactly opposite to those it had served in England. Instead of being the shield of an attacking party, it suddenly became the platform of a ruling oligarchy; instead of being invoked to delimit the sway of kings and prelates, it was now employed to rule a populace" (*Orthodoxy in Massachusetts*, 176). See also Kai Erikson, *Wayward Puritans*.

15. See R. H. Tawney, *Religion and the Rise of Capitalism*; A. S. P. Woodhouse, *Puritanism and Liberty*; Michael Walzer, *Revolution of the Saints*; Christopher Hill, *Change and Continuity in Seventeenth-Century England*; William Haller, *Liberty and Reformation in the Puritan Revolution*; and Alexis de Tocqueville, *Democracy in America*, 33. For criticism of these claims see C. H. George, "Puritanism as History and Historiography." George criticizes those who "transmute the base stuff of puritan piety into the gold of egalitarianism, individual liberty, and tolerance" (102). David Zaret similarly

argues against equating Puritanism with liberalism: see Zaret, *Origins of Democratic Culture*, 18–43. Both Zaret and George argue against equating Puritanism and liberalism on the basis of Puritan lack of tolerance for religious diversity. As I argue below, I see the internalization of law (God, reason) as more central to liberalism than toleration.

16. Vernon Parrington, *Main Currents in American Thought*, 15. For another version of this claim, see Larzer Ziff, whose primary concern, again, is religious toleration.

17. My argument here concurs in broad terms with that of Ross J. Pudaloff ("Sign and Subject"), who contends that the antinomian controversy marks a rupture between the Foucauldian organic and contractual epistemes and reveals the new dominance of the contractual episteme. According to Pudaloff, the antinomian controversy demonstrates the simultaneous production of a new form of subjectivity and the regulation of this subject through contractual relations: "Subject, subjectivity, and subjection, then, are entities produced simultaneously in the discourse of contractual relations" (160). My framework for understanding a contractual episteme is, however, less that of Foucault than Louis Althusser, or, perhaps (as discussed in the last chapter), Adam Smith. In other words, I view the contract less as a form of imposed discipline than as a structure through which desire circulates between the subject and a recognizing collectivity. For a useful account of Puritan subject formation in relation to the work of Althusser, see Ivy Schweitzer, *The Work of Self-Representation*, 30–32.

18. For an account of women as prophets see Phyllis Mack, *Visionary Women*. See also Keith Thomas, "Women and the Civil War Sects," 42–62; and Christopher Hill, *The World Turned Upside Down*, 27–260. Patricia Crawford argues that

> In many cases the voice of religious conscience triumphed over mere earthly wifely obedience. Conscience, as a woman's inward decision with reference to her view of God, stilled other conflicting voices. While the duty of wifely obedience was strongly preached and enforced, the voice of conscience, experienced as the commands of the Lord, could impel some women into public action. . . . Empowered by God, no social constraints could be allowed to restrict them. Conscience for women was no private matter to be left to one side or squared with public duty; it justified some women's wifely disobedience and their participation in English social and political life. (76)

See Patricia Crawford, "Public Duty, Conscience, and Women in Early Modern England."

19. For this view see, among others, Miller, *The New England Mind: Colony to Province*, 62. The significant exception to this view is Mary Beth Norton. Norton argues that the trial transcripts show that Hutchinson is not worn down and failing when she resorts to claims concerning revelation; rather, Norton argues, Hutchinson mentions her revelation at a moment of triumph, after leaving the ministers in disarray over the debate concerning taking oaths: "At that moment of triumph, she began to teach the court, as she had long taught the eager listeners in her household. And if she made a fatal mistake, it was that: emboldened by her success, she came to believe that she could convince most of the members of the General Court of the truth of her teachings" (*Founding Mothers*, 387).

20. Pudaloff, "Sign and Subject," 159.

21. Norton concurs that the content rather than the fact of her revelations is at issue.

22. During the trial, a Mr. Bartholomew mentions that Thomas Hooker had preached a sermon in England foretelling the destruction of England as revealed to him by God. Though John Eliot refutes the suggestion that Thomas Hooker made any such speech, David Hall notes that a printed record of Hooker's speech to that effect does exist. See also Andrew Delbanco, *The Puritan Ordeal*, on the continued use of revelation, as well as Marilyn Westerkamp, "Puritan Patriarchy and the Problem of Revelation." Megan Matchinske argues that women's prophecy would have been less readily accepted in England during this period than men's: see Matchinske, *Writing, Gender and State in Early Modern England*, 145–55.

23. On taking an oath, see David H. Flaherty, *Privacy in Colonial New England*, 223–27.

24. Mary Beth Norton points out the extent to which the debate between Winthrop and Hutchinson hinges upon competing definitions of the terms "public" and "private." For a summary of her definition of these terms, see *Founding Mothers*, 20–24. Norton speaks of an "informal public" versus a "formal public," terms that correspond roughly to what I identify below as a nascent oppositional public sphere, or liberal public sphere versus a state-identified notion of representative publicness. Norton's argument tends in a different direction than mine, however, insofar as she suggests that Hutchinson exerts her authority in a "Filmerian" (which is to say, hierarchical, or related to the theory of Sir Robert Filmer) rather than Lockean or liberal vein.

25. Zaret writes, "Restrictive norms of secrecy and privilege in prerevolutionary England precluded a public sphere in politics. Movement in this direction required communicative changes that created public opinion as both a nominal and real factor in politics" (*Origins of Democratic Culture*, 133).

26. Jürgen Habermas, *The Structural Transformation of the Public Sphere*, 27.

27. John Winthrop, *Winthrop Papers*, vol. 2, 293.

28. Winthrop, *The Journal of John Winthrop*, 167.

29. Habermas, *The Structural Transformation of the Public Sphere*, 27 (emphases added).

30. Note that the authority of the individual is granted not on the basis of individuality, but because of the individual's relation with God. In other words, authority resides in God, but access to this authority is now available by way of the individual rather than simply by way of figures of state or religious authority. Although this differs significantly from a later, liberal concept that values the rights of each individual, it is not as foreign as it might seem: Lockean liberalism grants the individual authority because he or she has a relation to reason, to an internal law that authorizes his or her actions. The internalization of reason in Lockean liberalism is analogous to a Protestant internalization of the individual's relation to God.

31. Christopher Hill, "Covenant Theology and the Concept of 'A Public Person,'" in *The Collected Essays of Christopher Hill*, vol. 3, 314, 316.

32. See also John Cotton's account in *The Way of Congregational Churches Cleared*: "what shee repeated and confirmed, was accounted sound, what shee omitted, was accounted Apocrypha" (Hall, *The Antinomian Controversy*, 413).

33. Patrick Collinson, *The Elizabethan Puritan Movement*, 372–82.

34. Foster, *The Long Argument*, 96.

35. Stephen Foster, "New England and the Challenge of Heresy," 627.

36. Winthrop, *The Journal of John Winthrop*, 234.

37. Stephen Foster succinctly summarizes the entwined relation of private or individual worship and collective Puritan identity as follows: "If the Puritan movement stood for anything on the eve of the Great Migration beyond simple opposition to certain aspects of the Church of England, it was the proposition that individual godliness is attained and practiced in company" ("New England and the Challenge of Heresy," 626).

38. Ibid., 627.

39. Collinson, *The Elizabethan Puritan Movement*, 379.

40. Winthrop, *The Journal of John Winthrop*, 242.

41. On migration to the colony in general, see Alison Games, *Migration and the Origins of the English Atlantic World*. On remigration, see David Cressy, *Coming Over*, 201; William L. Sachse, "The Migration of New Englanders to England, 1640–1660"; and Harry Stout, "The Morphology of Remigration."

42. Raymond Phineas Stearns, "The Weld-Peter Mission to England," 188–89.

43. A significant exception to this trend is the work of Phillip Round, *By Nature and by Custom Cursed*, discussed at greater length below.

44. See *Winthrop Papers*, vol. 3, 398.

45. According to David Hall, "The circumstances of the book's transmission to England remain a mystery" (200). A first version of the text, under the title *Antinomian and Familists Condemned By the Synod of Elders in New-England: with the Proceedings of the Magistrates against them, And their Apology for the same*, appeared in 1644 without Weld's preface and title. Second and third editions retitled and prefaced by Weld also appeared in 1644. The text cited here is the third edition, which is included in Hall's history.

46. As negative responses to the account of the crisis among English readers indicate, Winthrop and Weld's *Short Story* may not have been particularly effective as promotional material for the colony: although Winthrop saw in the colony's handling of the crisis evidence of effective governance, English audiences saw instead evidence of doctrinal disorder and religious intolerance.

47. For a reading of the antinomian crisis that emphasizes the significance of mercantile-capitalism and models of subjectivity linked to this economic formation, see Michelle Burnham, "Anne Hutchinson and the Economics of Antinomian Selfhood." Burnham argues that Hutchinson's connections to the merchant class locate her in a new subject position; my reading suggests that Winthrop is embedded in the financial relations of mercantile-capitalism as well.

48. Winthrop, *The Journal of John Winthrop*, 346.

49. See Robert Brenner, *Merchants and Revolution*, 271.

50. Ibid., 114–15.

51. This account relies on the analysis of Robert Brenner, who contends that the colonizing aristocrats were instrumental in securing a portable version of the charter. He cites Matthew Craddock and John Humfrey as crediting the aristocrats for securing the charter: "As John Humfrey remarked in 1630 at the end of the process, 'We are all much bound to Lord Saye for his cordial advice and true affections. As also my Lord of Warwick. Sir Nathaniel Rich deserves very much acknowledgement for his wise handling of Sir Ferdinando Gorges'" (ibid., 278). Frances Rose-Troup contends, on the

other hand, that the charter was never legally transferred, but a willful misreading of the language of the charter enabled the colonists to bring it with them to New England. In any event, it is clear that the Puritan aristocrats did assist in guiding the charter through state channels, even if not in securing any official endorsement of moving the charter to Massachusetts. See Rose-Troup, *The Massachusetts Bay Company*, 69–80.

52. See Bernard Bailyn, *New England Merchants*, 17–19. See also Edmund Morgan, *The Puritan Dilemma*, chapter 4.

53. The crown was increasingly uneasy about colonial independence and repeatedly threatened to withdraw the charter, eventually doing so in 1684 and creating the "Dominion" of New England. For discussion of the charter revocation, see Viola Barnes, *The Dominion of New England*. It is worth noting that one reason for revoking the charter and claiming control over the colony for the crown is the fact that New England shipping began to compete with British shipping.

54. David Zaret, "Religion, Science, and Printing," 223.

55. Winthrop, *The Journal of John Winthrop*, 56–57.

56. Cited in David Cressy, *Coming Over*, 18–19.

57. Winthrop, *Winthrop Papers*, vol. 3, 399.

58. Phillip Round, *By Nature and by Custom Cursed*, 33–34. Round here indirectly cites Annabel Patterson's work concerning censorship in England at the time: Round argues that similar forms of censorship occur in the colonies and in England.

59. Cressy, *Coming Over*, 20.

60. Stearns, "The Weld-Peter Mission to England," 193–94.

61. Hugh Peter also published Richard Mather's *Vindication of the Practices in New England*, and Weld published Winthrop's *Short Story*. William Sachse speculates that "it is possible that [Peter] and Weld were responsible for the printing of many of the tracts written by New Englanders in the forties" ("The Migration of New Englanders to England," 275–76).

62. Cited in Stearns, "The Weld-Peter Mission to England," 191.

63. Karen Ordahl Kupperman, "Errand to the Indies," 72. Robert Brenner makes claims to this effect as well. Note, too, that John Winthrop complains in his journal in 1640, for instance, that "it came over by divers letters and reports, that the Lord Say did labor, by disparaging this country, to divert men from coming to us, and so to draw them to the West Indies" (*The Journal of John Winthrop*, 324). Lord Say and Sele alleged "that this was a place appointed only for a present refuge, etc., and that, a better place being now found out, we were all called to remove thither" (ibid., 325). Winthrop, in turn, attempts to convince (if not threaten) Lord Say, arguing that New England is more than just a way station in greater Puritan colonization schemes: he writes to Lord Say of the providential signs indicating "how evident it was, that God had chosen this country to plant his people in, and therefore how displeasing it would be to the Lord, and dangerous to himself, to hinder this work, or to discourage men from supplying us, by abasing the goodness of the country" (ibid.). His threats were met with high-handed contempt from Lord Say, who had little patience for Winthrop's invocation of special providence for his embattled colony. Winthrop, it should be noted, reports with a fair amount of pleasure on the later demise of the Providence Island colony.

64. The errand argument is that advanced by Perry Miller. For criticism of this framework, see Kupperman, "Errand to the Indies."

65. Cited by Stearns, "The Weld-Peter Mission to England," 204.

66. On the print public sphere in England, see Zaret, *Origins of Democratic Culture*.

67. For the biography of Peter, see Raymond Phineas Stearns, *Strenuous Puritan*.

68. Ibid., 330–35.

69. As Stearns argues, Peter's politics were less oriented toward civil than ecclesiastical change: "The Levellers sought to establish the rule of the people; Hugh Peter endeavored to set up the rule of the saints" (ibid., 336). Nonetheless, during the Putney debates, for instance, Peter was evidently instrumental in framing a compromise on the issue of suffrage, advocating that the franchise be extended to all men who had assisted Parliament in the civil war (ibid., 316).

70. For a discussion of John Cotton's support of regicide once it had occurred, see Francis J. Bremer, "In Defense of Regicide."

71. Thomas Lechford, *Plain Dealing*, xxxi. Lechford was a lawyer who emigrated to Massachusetts Bay Colony in 1638. He was condemned by church leaders in the colony, however, for his religious writings, including his argument that "the office of apostleship doth still continew and ought soe to doe till Crist's coming, and that a Church hath now power to make apostles as our Crist had when hee was heere." As a result of his doctrinal disagreements, he was denied membership in the church and thus also denied the franchise and the right to hold public office. His employment prospects as a lawyer were limited as well. He complained that "I am kept from the Sacrament, and all place of preferment in the Common-Wealth and forced to get my living by writing things, which scarce finds me bread." In 1641, Lechford returned to England and in 1642 published *Plain Dealing; or, News from New England*, a text critical of Puritan church governance.

72. Cited in J. R. De Witt, *Jus Divinum*, 16.

73. Consider, for instance, Thomas Edwards's account of the antinomian controversy:

> New-England practising the way of Independencie, and not having Classes, Synods, that have authoritative power to call to account and censure such persons, were necessitated to make use of the Magistrates, and to give the more to them, a power of questioning for doctrines, and judging of errors; . . . (which now for want of Ecclesiasticall discipline and censure they knew not what to doe with) not as heresies and such opinions, but as breaches of the civill peace, and disturbances to the Common-wealth, (which distinction if the Parliament would have learned from you, and proceeded upon, they might long agoe have put downe all your Churches and Congregations . . .) . . . whereas the Presbyterians give the power in cases of heresies, errors, &c. that are not remedied in the particular Congregation, to Classes, Synods, Assemblies, to question, convince, judge of, censure and to apply spirituall remedies proper to spirituall diseases, which I am confident of, had such been in New-England in the Presbyteriall way, there had never beene so many imprisoned, banished for errors. (*Antapologia*, 165–66)

Edwards thus argues that the colonists were inappropriately forced to rely upon civil government to discipline the antinomian heretics because no functioning church government existed: this not only places control of spiritual matters outside church purview, but breeds spiritual disease within the church. More specifically, Edwards argues that without a governing hierarchy external and superior to the congregation (classes, synods, assemblies), any individual congregation may be infected by heretics and have no ecclesiastical remedy available to it.

74. James I, in a speech to parliament, states, "The king to his people is rightly compared to . . . the head of a body composed of divers members" (cited in James Schramer and Timothy Sweet, "Violence and the Body Politic in Seventeenth-Century New England," 4). Schramer and Sweet argue for the centrality of the body politic metaphor in seventeenth-century New England. I argue below that Puritans are moving away from this model during the same period. For further discussion of the body politic in New England at this time, see Jim Egan, *Authorizing Experience*. For a more general discussion of the history of the body politic metaphor in England, see David George Hale, *The Body Politic*.

75. Robert Baillie, *A Dissuasive From the Errours of the Time*, 185.

76. A more direct link between the antinomian faction in Massachusetts and doctrines of Lockean liberalism might be intimated from recent work on the figure of Henry Vane, the prominent former Massachusetts governor and Hutchinson supporter who returned to England to a seat in Parliament and an active role in the civil war. Vane was eventually executed during the Restoration for the crime of treason against the king. Michael Winship, in the final chapter of *Making Heretics*, argues for the influence of Vane's early experiences during the antinomian crisis in Massachusetts upon his later political career in England. Annabel Patterson, in turn, makes the case that Henry Vane's treason trial and writings were influential documents in the history of an early modern liberalism later transmitted from England to the United States, thus shaping the politics of the early Republic. See Patterson, *Early Modern Liberalism*, chapter 3.

77. Thomas Weld, *An Answer to W.R.*, 12.

78. Weld, *A Brief Narration of the Practice of the Churches in New England*, 3.

79. Ibid., 2–3.

80. Ibid., 4.

81. Weld's introduction to *A Short Story*, in Hall, 214, 215.

82. Ibid., 216 (emphasis added).

83. Ibid., 214.

84. Jim Egan points out that the headless fetus described by Weld and Winthrop in the *Short Story* is an image of what critics believe will happen to the English body in a colonial setting. See *Authorizing Experience*, 71.

85. Edward Johnson in *Wonder-Working Providence* describes the antinomian errors (and, implicitly, Hutchinson) as the many heads of a "Hidra" (93, 104). See also Samuel Gorton, *Simplicities Defence Against Seven-Headed Policy*, in which church government in the colony is described as a seven-headed hydra.

86. See *Newes From New-England of a Most Strange and Prodigious Birth*.

87. See Amy Schrager Lang: "By naming Hutchinson Eve or Jezebel, the historians of the controversy imply an immediate relationship between her heresy and her sexual identity" (*Prophetic Woman*, 65).

88. Egan, *Authorizing Experience*, 92.

89. Winthrop, *Winthrop Papers*, vol. 2, 289.

90. Winthrop, *A Short Story*, in Hall, 265.

91. Winthrop evidently sent an account of the fetus to England shortly after the

exhumation; this account was circulated amongst powerful supporters of the Puritan cause in England. In addition, Winthrop wrote letters to William Bradford and Roger Williams concerning the birth, and described it in his journal as well. In 1642, an account of the birth was published anonymously in England in a pamphlet called "Newes From New England of a Most Strange and Prodigious Birth." And in 1644, Thomas Weld published an account of the births in his introduction to Winthrop's *Short Story*. These texts, in turn, generated responses that cite the Dyer birth and recirculate its telling in the service of a variety of political and religious arguments. For further discussion of accounts from Winthrop circulating in England, see Valerie and Morris Pearl, "Governor John Winthrop on the Birth of the Antinomians' 'Monster.'"

92. John Wheelwright, *Mercurius Americanus*, 196.

93. Jonathan Gil Harris, *Foreign Bodies and the Body Politic*, 142.

94. Gail Kern Paster, *The Body Embarrassed*, 9.

95. Joyce Chaplin, *Subject Matter*, 156.

96. Ibid., 158.

97. John Wheelwright, *Mercurius Americanus*, 197, 199.

98. Edmund Morgan, *Visible Saints*, 89.

99. See Stephen Foster, *The Long Argument*, 173.

100. William Hubbard, *General History*, 274.

101. Charles Cohen, *God's Caress*, 152; see also Patricia Caldwell, *The Puritan Conversion Narrative*.

102. Michael Ditmore, "Preparation and Confession," 319.

103. Ann Kibbey, *The Interpretation of Material Shapes*, 118. Kibbey cites Darrett Rutman, *Winthrop's Boston*, 130.

104. Weld, *An Answer to W.R.*, 19.

105. See also Charles Cohen, *God's Caress*, 222, and the account of Ola Winslow, who describes Brother Hinsdell's wife in Dedham who "being fearfull & not able to speake in publike" fainted at the sound of her own voice (*Meetinghouse Hill*, 145). Winslow indicates that women may have been unaccustomed to speaking in public and thus have occasionally found it difficult to do so.

106. Cohen, *God's Caress*, 223.

107. See Amanda Porterfield, *Female Piety in Puritan New England*, 82–83, for discussion of this debate.

108. Fiske, *The Notebook of the Reverend John Fiske*, 4 (emphasis added).

109. For further background on the disputes in question, see Jane Kamensky, *Governing the Tongue*.

110. This passage and those cited below are from Robert Keayne, *Note-Book of the Boston Church, 1639–1642*, transcript by Merja Kytö (Uppsala University). Abbreviations such as "y^t" (for "that") and "&" ("and") have been expanded and are given in Present-day English; punctuation and related capitalization follow Present-day English, as far as possible.

111. Peter Bulkeley, cited in Edmund S. Morgan, "The Puritan's Marriage with God," 107.

112. See, for instance, Morgan, "The Puritan's Marriage with God," and Edmund Leites, *The Puritan Conscience and Modern Sexuality*.

113. John Winthrop, *The Journal of John Winthrop*, 588.

114. For further discussion of this passage, see Ivy Schweitzer, *The Work of Self-Representation*, 32.

115. Morgan, "The Puritan's Marriage with God," 107.

116. The extent to which liberalism is able to represent the subject's consent to social norms as a form of free choice has been explored at length by Sacvan Bercovitch. See Bercovitch, *The Rites of Assent*.

117. On the mortalist heresy, see J. F. Maclear, "Anne Hutchinson and the Mortalist Heresy."

118. Hall, *The Antinomian Controversy*, 362.

119. Ibid., 372.

Chapter 3: Contracting Marriage in the New Republic

1. Washington Irving, *The Legend of Sleepy Hollow*, 335, 333.

2. Jay Fliegelman, *Prodigals and Pilgrims*; Eric Slauter, "The State as a Work of Art." See also Shirley Samuels, *Romances of the Republic*, who notes images of threat to and dismemberment of the female body that coincide with the early national period.

3. Thomas Paine, *Common Sense*, 98.

4. Slauter notes that Paine uses this metaphor as a means of depersonalizing the state. See Slauter, "The State as a Work of Art," 82.

5. During the witchcraft crisis itself, the question of what sort of agency individual subjects wielded and where this agency lay was implicitly central to debates over the status of the "spectral evidence" used to convict many of the accused. Nancy Ruttenburg argues that the range of individuals claiming public authority at this moment indicates a democratic expansion of the public sphere or a broadening of access to representational power, albeit one marked by violence and upheaval. See Ruttenburg, *Democratic Personality*, chapter 1.

6. Claude Lefort, *Democracy and Political Theory*, 17, 19.

7. Alexis de Tocqueville, *Democracy in America*, 264.

8. Niklas Luhmann, *Love as Passion*, 12.

9. J. Aiken, "On the Choice of a Wife," 36.

10. For discussion of the historical shift toward voluntary, affectional marriage, see Carl Degler, *At Odds*; Fliegelman, *Prodigals and Pilgrims*; Jan Lewis, "The Republican Wife"; and (in an English rather American context) Lawrence Stone, *The Family, Sex and Marriage in England*.

11. "The Influence of the Female Sex on the Enjoyments of Social Life," 497.

12. "From the Genius of Liberty," 105–6.

13. Lewis, "The Republican Wife," 710.

14. See ibid., 699. In related terms, Jay Fliegelman argues that the shift toward consensual union (not union arranged by parents) mirrored the political liberation of the nation from the parental control of England: "the struggle for American independence and for subsequent federal union was intimately related to, and ideologically reflected in, a national affirmation of the sacred character of affectional and voluntaristic marriage" (*Prodigals and Pilgrims*, 129).

15. Ruth Bloch influentially argues that in the 1790s, the meaning of the term "virtue" shifts from association with masculine, political activity to an association with

feminine, private activity (including women's sexuality). See Bloch, "The Gendered Meanings of Virtue." More recently, Bloch has argued for understanding new patterns of marriage in the early Republic as indicative less of increased individual personal and political freedom than "as a fundamentally socializing experience"—a claim consonant with my discussion of marriage as a form of sociality ("Gender and the Public/Private Dichotomy," 166). For useful further discussion of the "feminization of virtue" (and particularly its privatization and depoliticization under liberalism), see Wai Chee Dimock, *Residues of Justice*. Dimock argues, "If the rise of modern liberalism marked the decline of political rationality . . . the feminization of virtue would seem to be simultaneously a symptom and a remedy. A cognitive revolution such as this one testifies both to the emerging irrationality of the political sphere and to a spirited attempt to repair that damage, to locate a rational ground outside the vicissitudes of politics, in a natural morality commensurate with the natural order" (53). Looking forward to nineteenth-century liberalism, then, the effects of an eighteenth-century privatization of virtue are related to forms of depoliticizing gender essentialism described in the first chapter of this book: "In mid-nineteenth-century America, gender is a field of symbolic order: a field where meanings are affixed, identities rationalized, distinctions maintained. . . . In the difficult transition from classical republicanism to modern liberalism, gender is invoked, above all, to restore a natural order to a newly denaturalized political order. Against the groundlessness of political institutions, gender works with the solidity of a natural fact" (47).

16. "On Conjugal Affection," 176.

17. Lewis argues that there has been no separation of public and private "spheres" at this point. Although this may be the case in the sense that men didn't leave the home in order to participate in an industrial workforce, it is nonetheless the case that the distinction between private and public realms had long been made and was indeed, as I am suggesting, central to the delineation of liberalism from the period of New England Puritanism forward. Note that many of the discussions of marriage in the 1790s employ language contrasting "public" and "private" roles of women (as do the Puritans, for that matter). For a more general discussion of separate spheres, see Nancy Cott, *The Bonds of Womanhood*, as well as the more recent special issue of *American Literature* 70, no. 3 (Sept. 1998), "No More Separate Spheres."

18. See Edmund Leites, *The Puritan Conscience and Modern Sexuality*, 92–100.

19. See Luhmann on the courtly love tradition, as well as Henry Abelove's claim in "Some Speculations on the History of Sexual Intercourse" that sex became more heterosexual, more reproductive in the eighteenth century.

20. Thomas Gataker, *A Marriage Praier*, 18–19.

21. Royall Tyler, "The Contrast," 29.

22. "On Conjugal Affection," 177.

23. "Domesticity cannot be described solely in terms of feelings, for the conversion of homes into centers of sociability required a shift in female work patterns. The change might be described as one of specialization: women's labor in behalf of home consumption gradually ceased being spread thinly over primary, intermediary, and final processes and became concentrated on the last stage. Cooking, sewing, decorating, cleaning, and childrearing are final processes, and the special attention devoted to these

activities is what domesticity was all about" (Carole Shammas, "The Domestic Environment in Early Modern England and America," 129).

24. See Carla Mulford, "Introduction."

25. Bruce Burgett, *Sentimental Bodies*, 15.

26. Dana Nelson, *National Manhood*, 33.

27. See Susan Juster, *Disorderly Women*.

28. See Caleb Crain, *American Sympathy*, 1–15.

29. *The Pennsylvania Magazine* 1 (Apr. 1775): 152, cited in Fliegelman, *Prodigals and Pilgrims*, 127.

30. *Royal American Magazine* 1 (Mar. 1774): 9, cited in Fliegelman, *Prodigals and Pilgrims*, 127.

31. See, for instance, Cathy Davidson, *Revolution and the Word*; Elizabeth Barnes, *States of Sympathy*; and Julia Stern, *The Plight of Feeling*, for discussions of incest in the early American novel.

32. We might call this the "people are Clarissa" claim. John Adams famously declared that England was Lovelace and "the people are Clarissa"—a declaration that has been cited to support the claim that America needed to protect its "virtue" from a dangerous British seducer, and that seduction novels served as allegories of this political predicament. Alternative readings by Stern and Barnes sketch out new directions in understanding novels of the period but leave the allegorical premise intact. For instance, Barnes sees the family as establishing familial feeling that is important to national feeling: the family is thus the allegory of the nation, or in her words is "conflated" with the nation. Stern argues that the novels of the 1790s are allegories for the pain of a national political formation in which many bodies (those of women and African-Americans) were cut out of the nation. According to Stern, scenes of seduction, incest, and gothic terror register this loss but as such, they remain allegorical of nation formation. The primary exception to this argument is the argument of Leonard Tennenhouse in "Libertine America," which I discuss below.

33. Michelle A. Massé uses the term "marital gothic" in her book, *In the Name of Love* in a somewhat related but different fashion. She describes the "marital gothic" as a version of the gothic in which women discover that marriage, far from liberating them from paternal authority, entraps them within a new version of it:

> Perfect love supposedly has cast out fear, and perfect trust in another has led to the omission of anxiety discussed above as an antecedent of trauma and repetition compulsion. Yet horror returns in the new home of the couple, conjured up by renewed denial of the heroine's identity and autonomy. The marriage that she thought would give her voice (because she would be listened to), movement (because her status would be that of an adult), and not just a room of her own but a house, proves to have none of these attributes. The husband who was originally defined by his opposition to the unjust father figure slowly merges with that figure. The heroine again finds herself mute, paralyzed, enclosed, and she must harrow the Gothic in an attempt to deal with that reality through repetition. (20)

While Massé's description of the marital gothic usefully points to what I have called the "structuring" force of marriage insofar as it is represented as a form of imprisonment or a trap, I do not use the term "marital gothic" to evoke the image of the female subject pitched against the social conventions of marriage and patriarchy, but to describe a more pointedly paradoxical relation (explored below) in which the subject is both created and killed in the same narrative movement.

34. Julie Ellison, *Cato's Tears and the Making of Anglo-American Emotion*, 25.

35. "A Lesson on Sensibility," 72.

36. Eve Sedgwick, in *The Coherence of Gothic Conventions*, notes that strict adherence to a set of defining conventions is itself a defining aspect of the gothic. In this sense, the gothic, as a genre, may perhaps always be "about" the power of convention.

37. "A New Way of Preserving a Wife," 375.

38. Nancy Armstrong, *Desire and Domestic Fiction*, 19–20.

39. The literature on the debate between liberal and republican views of the revolutionary and early national period is voluminous: articles that usefully summarize portions of this debate include Philip Gould, "Virtue, Ideology, and the American Revolution," and Richard Matthews, "Liberalism, Civic Humanism, and the American Political Tradition."

40. In a review of a number of books on the topic of liberalism and republicanism, Richard Matthews summarizes assumptions held in common by historians of the period as follows: "What, then, can be said about America's genesis? Republican, familial, or civic humanist ideals existed in America prior to 1787 where they exercised decreasing degrees of influence, until all but vanishing from the collective consciousness sometime after the turn of the century." See Matthews, "Liberalism, Civic Humanism, and the American Political Tradition," 1150.

41. I am not alone among critics in making this claim, though it strikes me as interesting that many of the historians and literary critics who tend to see less of a dichotomy between liberalism and republicanism are those who work on gender. A number of these arguments will be treated below. On gender and the liberal/republican divide, see Barnes, *States of Sympathy*; Lori Merish, *Sentimental Materialism*; and Rosemarie Zagarri, "The Rights of Man and Woman in Post-Revolutionary America." For further discussion of the related terms of liberalism and republicanism, see Gillian Brown, *The Consent of the Governed*, who focuses on Lockean liberalism and its relation to republicanism; Annabel Patterson, *Early Modern Liberalism*, who describes a liberal tradition transmitted textually from England to the founding fathers; Philip Hamburger, "Liberality," who proposes a model of "liberality" that is distinct from both liberalism and republicanism; Rogers Smith, *Civic Ideals*, who views ascriptive law as an important third tradition supplementing liberalism and republicanism; and Burgett, *Sentimental Bodies*, who describes a republican tradition that endures beyond the eighteenth century and that operates in ongoing tension with liberalism.

42. Linda Kerber, *Women of the Republic*, 285, 283.

43. Kerber notes that the invention of the "republican" mother is an American one without classical precedent and one that she describes as a synthesis of liberal and republican ideas. I discuss below Rosemarie Zagarri's claim that the roots of republican motherhood lie in the Scottish civil jurisprudence tradition. See Zagarri, "Morals, Manners, and the Republican Mother."

44. Pitkin, *Fortune Is a Woman*, 5.

45. Genevieve Lloyd, "Selfhood, War and Masculinity," 65.

46. Brown, *The Consent of the Governed*, 17.

47. Brown writes, "Probably even more widely read and circulated than the *Two Treatises of Government*, Locke's *Some Thoughts Concerning Education* provided the colonists in North America with an account of the making of consensual subjects. The influence of Locke also permeated the education of American colonists, which increasingly incorporated the tenets of Lockean pedagogy" (ibid., 17).

48. Lori Merish thus argues, "the emergence of middle-class domesticity was inseparable from the 'feminization of women': the (re)construction of 'woman' from the embodiment of demonic, irrational forces . . . into a paradigm of virtue, embodiment of moral sensibility, and shaper of 'civilized' society" (*Sentimental Materialism*, 16–17).

49. The debate over what constituted a citizen, and thus what the terms of the franchise would be, continued, of course, for many years. It is worth noting that the question of a religious test for the franchise was still a subject of debate during discussions concerning the constitution in the mid- to late eighteenth century. See Kirk Harold Porter, *A History of Suffrage*, on the broader history of the franchise; see John Hart, "'A Less Proportion of Idle Proprietors'"; and Jennifer Nedelsky, *Private Property and the Limits of Constitutionalism*, for reference to the debate over religious qualification for the franchise.

50. Dayton, *Women Before the Bar*, 8–9, 12.

51. Gordon Wood, *The Radicalism of the American Revolution*, 269, 270.

52. J. G. A. Pocock, "The Mobility of Property," 151.

53. Pocock, *Virtue, Commerce, and History*, 67.

54. Gordon Wood writes, "The American aristocracy, such as it was, was not only weaker than its English counterpart; it also had a great deal of trouble maintaining both the desired classical independence and its freedom from the marketplace. Few members of the American gentry were able to live idly off the rents of tenants as the English landed aristocracy did . . . Landlords were not able to preempt the produce of their tenants, and their rental income was often unreliable" (*The Radicalism of the American Revolution*, 113).

55. Isaac Kramnick, *Republicanism and Bourgeois Radicalism*, 179.

56. Hart, "'A Less Proportion of Idle Proprietors,'" 183.

57. Pocock, *Virtue, Commerce, and History*, 67.

58. Cited by Hart, "'A Less Proportion of Idle Proprietors,'" 168.

59. James Madison, *The Federalist Papers*, no. 10, 43–44.

60. For further discussion of Madison's Lockean understanding of property, see Nedelsky, *Private Property*, chapter 2. She cites Madison's claim that "the personal right to acquire property, which is a natural right, gives to property, when acquired, a right to protection, as a social right" (29). Though Pocock is correct that Madison spars with Hamilton over questions of national credit, paper money, and war debt, I would argue that it is incorrect to assimilate this debate to a republican/liberal divide over landed/mobile property. See also David Epstein, *The Political Theory of the Federalist*, 74, on Madison as Lockean.

61. According to Kramnick, in the eighteenth century, civic humanism is replaced by the notion that hard work equals virtue: "Citizenship and the public quest for the common good were replaced by economic productivity and hard work as the criteria of virtue. It is a mistake, however, to see this change simply as a withdrawal from public activity to a private, self-centered realm. The transformation also involved a shift in

emphasis on the nature of public behavior. Now the moral and virtuous man was defined not by his civic activity but by his economic activity. One's duty was still to contribute to the public good, but such contributions could best be made through economic activity, which actually aimed at private gain. Self-centered economic productivity, not public citizenship, became the badge of the virtuous man" (*Republicanism and Bourgeois Radicalism*, 196). See also Joyce Appleby's argument that "virtue" has a liberal rather than civic humanist meaning in the 1790s, in *Capitalism and a New Social Order*.

62. A great deal of scholarship has documented the influence of Scottish immigration and Scottish Enlightenment thought upon the United States: for a useful overview of this work, see Richard B. Sher's introduction to *Scotland and America in the Age of the Enlightenment*. In terms of gender and Scottish philosophy, the work of Lori Merish and Rosemarie Zagarri has been particularly helpful to my thinking on these matters.

63. Nicholas Phillipson, "Adam Smith as Civic Moralist," 201.

64. For discussion of the structural similarity of the North American colonies and Scotland, see John Clive and Bernard Bailyn, "England's Cultural Provinces: Scotland and America"; Andrew Hook, *Scotland and America*; and "Scottish Academia and the Invention of American Studies," in Robert Crawford, ed., *The Scottish Invention of English Literature*. See also Phillipson on Hook in "The Export of Enlightenment."

65. William Robertson (1769; 1817), *A View of the Progress of Society*, in *The Works of William Robertson*, vol. 4, 97.

66. Millar, *John Millar of Glasgow*, 386–87, 326.

67. J. G. A. Pocock, "Cambridge Paradigms and Scotch Philosophers," 240.

68. Pocock writes, "In the United States, this is not even on the agenda; the persistence of Jeffersonian values, in no matter how attenuated and nostalgic a form, is a major fact of intellectual history and cannot be understood without constant reference to the agrarian republicanism of the founders" (ibid., 244).

69. See Franklin Court, "The Early Impact of Scottish Literary Teaching in North America," 144.

70. See Forest McDonald, *Novus Ordo Seclorum*.

71. Merish, *Sentimental Materialism*, 35.

72. Smith, *The Theory of Moral Sentiments*, 161.

73. For a discussion of the relation between propriety and virtue in Smith, see Vincent Hope, "Smith's Demigod," 166–67. As Hope points out, Smith distinguishes between virtue and propriety, yet this distinction is effectively undercut by Smith's account of virtue in utilitarian terms that resemble his account of propriety.

74. Jean-Christophe Agnew, *Worlds Apart*, 185.

75. See Zagarri, "Morals, Manners, and the Republican Mother."

76. Leonard Tennenhouse, "Libertine America," 12.

77. Thomas Jefferson, cited in Joan Gunderson, "Independence, Citizenship, and the American Revolution," 64.

78. Ditz, "Shipwrecked; or Masculinity Imperiled," 65.

79. In similar terms, Dana Nelson outlines the logic of Pateman's claims with respect to the early Republic: "The symbolic female therein grounds the structural conditions for male-male relations in the early nation. Called to their 'common' manhood—in opposition to the 'monster' woman, or as guaranteed by the virgin woman who will produce those sons of liberty—men who might otherwise be rivals can turn

to each other as brothers in this sentimentalized region of pure masculine identity" (*National Manhood*, 48).

80. Betsy Erkkila, "Revolutionary Women," 219.

81. Charles Brockden Brown, *Edgar Huntly*, 9.

82. See Stephen Shapiro, "'Man to Man I Needed Not to Dread His Encounter.'"

83. For an argument that homosexuality emerges in relation to heterosexuality, see Henry Abelove, "Some Speculations on the History of Sexual Intercourse During the Long Eighteenth Century in England." See also Simon Richter, "The Ins and Outs of Intimacy": "the same ideology or fiction of the patriarchal conjugal family that confines the woman to the home also directs the intimacy between males into the closet, thus creating the space that will later, in the nineteenth century, be associated with the homosexual" (113).

84. Dana Luciano, "'Perverse Nature,'" 13.

85. See, in similar terms, Jared Gardner's reading of the primitivism of this scene as that which Huntly attempts to escape: "Having spontaneously degenerated to this lowest state of savagery, a state that even now he 'review[s] . . . with loathing and horror,' Edgar turns in disgust and begins his long journey back to civilization" (*Master Plots*, 69).

86. Warner, *The Letters of the Republic*, 41.

87. *Arthur Mervyn* was written and published in two separate volumes, the first of which appeared prior to *Edgar Huntly*, the second of which appeared subsequent to it. As such, critics have argued for a close relation among the three volumes. See David M. Larson, "*Arthur Mervyn*, *Edgar Huntly*, and the Critics."

88. The contagious model of identity and its association with the gothic genre is usefully explored by Luciano. Her discussion of the exchange of fluids between men in *Edgar Huntly*, as an aspect of this contagion, is also suggestive for my argument below.

89. Carroll Smith-Rosenberg, "Subject Female," 493.

90. Gardner, *Master Plots*, 69, 75. Smith-Rosenberg, in turn, contends that "[Huntly's] wanderings do not end until, killing the last American Indian, he buries his bayonet deep within the Indian's body. . . . It is only after repeatedly penetrating and then marking his sexual dominance over the Delaware warrior that Huntly can regain access to cultivated American land and America's civil society" (491).

91. Rogers Smith, *Civic Ideals*, 38.

92. John Robison, *Proofs of a Conspiracy Against All the Religions and Governments of Europe*, 100, cited in Michael Chandos Brown, "Mary Wollstonecraft, or, the Female Illuminati," 397.

93. Michael Chandos Brown, "Mary Wollstonecraft, or, the Female Illuminati," 400. On the Illuminati crisis in general, see Vernon Stauffer, *New England and the Bavarian Illuminati*.

94. William Cobbett, *Detection of a Conspiracy*, 4, cited in Gardner, *Master Plots*, 62.

95. Smith argues that Jefferson's Republican party resorts to ascriptive categories of identity as well, thus marking an important distinction between republican theory and Republican practice.

96. Cited in John C. Miller, *Crisis in Freedom*, 6, from the *York General Advertiser*, Aug. 1, 1798. Also cited in Gardner, *Master Plots*, 61.

97. Timothy Dwight, *Nature, Danger, of Infidel Philosophy, exhibited in Two Dis-*

courses, Addressed to the Candidates for the Baccalaureate, in Yale College (New Haven: George Bunce, 1798), cited by Michael Chandos Brown, "Mary Wollstonecraft, or, the Female Illuminati," 396.

98. David Shields, *Civil Tongues and Polite Letters in British America*, xiv.

99. It seems worth noting that Charles Brockden Brown participated in a New York society of intellectuals and writers known as the "Friendly Club": members of this group encouraged him to pursue a literary career. See Donald A. Ringe, *Charles Brockden Brown*, 5.

100. Hannah Webster Foster, *The Coquette*, 5.

Chapter 4: Sociality and Sentiment

1. Joanne Dobson, "Reclaiming Sentimental Literature," 267.

2. I refer here to Jacques Lacan's account of the moment when an infant, gazing into a mirror, accedes to a (fantasmatic) grasp of his own wholeness and identity. Without belaboring these terms, I would note that the language of psychoanalysis is eminently applicable to nineteenth-century sentimental texts, in part because, in sentimental fashion, psychoanalysis is constructed around an image of the family closed in upon itself.

3. Jürgen Habermas, *The Structural Transformation of the Public Sphere*, 46.

4. Louis Brandeis and Samuel D. Warren, "The Right to Privacy," 695.

5. Pamela Haag, *Consent*, 79.

6. Haag primarily emphasizes the way in which freedom was articulated in the twentieth century in relation to sexuality, pointing to the legal elaboration of the right to privacy in terms of (heterosexual and reproductive) sexuality. In using her framework to point backwards to sentimental discourse of the nineteenth century, I want to argue that familial emotion rather than reproductive sexuality is a central symbolic location of freedom prior to the twentieth century. For a discussion of legal formulations of privacy antedating Brandeis and Warren and focusing specifically on women, see Caroline Danielson, "The Gender of Privacy."

7. Ann Douglas, *The Feminization of American Culture*, 55.

8. See Jeanne Boydston, *Home and Work*, as well as Amy Dru Stanley, "Home Life and the Morality of the Market," and more broadly, Nancy Cott, *The Bonds of Womanhood*.

9. Reva Siegel, "Why Equal Protection No Longer Protects," 1119. On the legal sentimentalization of marriage in the nineteenth century, see Laura Korobkin, *Criminal Conversations*.

10. Harriet Beecher Stowe, *Uncle Tom's Cabin*, 122.

11. For a comparison of Rachel's utopian kitchen with the dystopian kitchen where the slave, Dinah, labors in *Uncle Tom's Cabin*, see Gillian Brown, *Domestic Individualism*.

12. Cott, *The Bonds of Womanhood*, xvii.

13. Amy Dru Stanley, *From Bondage to Contract*, 138, 157.

14. Douglas, *The Feminization of American Culture*, 74, 75.

15. See Jane Tompkins, *Sensational Designs*, and Lori Merish, *Sentimental Materialism*. For accounts of the important Tompkins-Douglas debate, see Mary Chapman and Glen Hendler's introduction to *Sentimental Men*, and Laura Wexler,

"Tender Violence," as well as, more generally, the essays in Shirley Samuels's edited volume, *The Culture of Sentiment*. For a recent discussion of Douglas, see the special issue of *differences* (11.3, 1999/2000) devoted to Douglas and sentimentalism.

16. See, for instance, Jacqueline Jones, *Labor of Love, Labor of Sorrow*, and Hazel Carby, *Reconstructing Womanhood*. Amy Dru Stanley's discussion of wage labor in *From Bondage to Contract* is also useful in demonstrating that the reality of leisure was not available to many laborers, though the ideology of domestic leisure structured a great deal of public and legal policy.

17. Thomas Hooker cited by Ross W. Beales Jr., "In Search of the Historical Child," 13; Daniel T. Rodgers, "Socializing Middle-Class Children," 127.

18. Rodgers, "Socializing Middle-Class Children," 126.

19. Karen Sánchez-Eppler, "Then When We Clutch Hardest," 64.

20. Frances Sargent Locke Osgood, "A Mother's Prayer in Illness," 72.

21. For additional discussion of the public nature of grief and its place in nineteenth-century U.S. culture, see Karen Halttunen, *Confidence Men and Painted Women*, and Martha Pike and Janice Armstrong, eds., *A Time to Mourn*.

22. Mary Louise Kete, *Sentimental Collaborations*, 55.

23. Karen Sánchez-Eppler, "Then When We Clutch Hardest," 66.

24. By this I mean to specify a kind of violence that is written into the form of sentimental narrative—a structural violence—that is different from the claims of sentimental imperialism or "tender violence" explored by Laura Wexler. See Wexler, "Tender Violence."

25. James Baldwin, "Everybody's Protest Novel," 496.

26. Lauren Berlant, "Poor Eliza," 641.

27. Adam Smith, *The Theory of Moral Sentiments*, 304, 305.

28. See William L. Langer, "Infanticide: A Historical Survey," and Mark Jackson's edited volume, *Infanticide: Historical Perspectives*.

29. Stephen Pinker, "Why They Kill Their Newborns."

30. On the historical incidence of infanticide and rates of prosecution in England and the United States, see Peter C. Hoffer and N. E. H. Hull, *Murdering Mothers*; Cornelia Hughes Dayton, *Women Before the Bar*; G. S. Rowe, "Infanticide, Its Judicial Resolution, and Criminal Code Revision in Early Pennsylvania"; Kenneth Wheeler, "Infanticide in Nineteenth-Century Ohio"; Josephine McDonagh, "Infanticide and the Nation"; and Helena Wall, *Fierce Communion*.

31. Laura Henigman, *Coming into Communion*, 60. See also Helena Wall's argument in *Fierce Communion* that there is an implicit responsibility on the part of the community to the pregnant woman: "the community . . . owed something to women in childbed" (95).

32. John Rogers, "Death the Certain Wages of Sin," page 2 of the unnumbered preface.

33. See Daniel Williams, "'Behold a Tragic Scene Strangely Changed into a Theater of Mercy.'"

34. *A Faithful Narrative of Elizabeth Wilson*, 3.

35. For publication information on this text, see Daniel Williams, "Victims of Narrative Seduction."

36. *The Victim of Seduction!*, 5.

37. Lydia Maria Child, "Elizabeth Wilson," 340.
38. Laura Wexler, *Tender Violence*, 8.
39. Philip Fisher, *Hard Facts*, 58.
40. Elizabeth Barnes, *States of Sympathy*, 4.
41. James Baldwin, "Everybody's Protest Novel," 500.
42. Marianne Noble, "The Ecstasies of Sentimental Wounding in *Uncle Tom's Cabin*."
43. Harriet Beecher Stowe, *Uncle Tom's Cabin*, 34–35.
44. Douglas, *The Feminization of American Culture*, 12.
45. Tompkins, *Sensational Designs*, 130.
46. Eva Cherniavsky, *That Pale Mother Rising*, 57.
47. David Eng and David Kazanjian, *Loss*, 2.
48. Mark Seltzer, *Serial Killers*, 21.

Coda: Queering Marriage

1. *Defense of Marriage Act of 1996*, Public Law 199, 104th Congress, 2d session (Sept. 21, 1996).
2. At this writing, the act awaits action in the Senate.
3. *Personal Responsibility, Work, and Family Promotion Act of 2003*, 108th Congress, 1st session, H.R. 4.
4. Ibid.
5. Ibid.
6. During House debates over the *Defense of Marriage Act*, Representative Charles Canady voiced one version of the claim that heterosexual marriage is natural and God-given:

> What is at stake in this controversy? Nothing less than our collective moral understanding—as expressed in the law—of the essential nature of the family—the fundamental building block of society. This is far from a trivial political issue. Families are not merely constructs of outdated convention, and traditional marriage laws were not based on animosity toward homosexuals. Rather, I believe that the traditional family structure—centered on a lawful union between one man and one woman—comports with nature and with our Judeo-Christian moral tradition. It is one of the essential foundations on which our civilization is based. Our law should embody an unequivocal recognition of that fundamental fact. (*Congressional Record*, 104th Congress, 2d session [July 11, 1996], vol. 142, pt. 102: H7441)

7. Janet Halley, "Recognition, Rights, Regulation, Normalisation," 99. For related arguments, see Michael Warner, "Beyond Gay Marriage," and Judith Butler, "Is Kinship Always Heterosexual?"
8. For a discussion of marriage as "private welfare," see Halley, "Recognition, Rights, Regulation, Normalisation," 110. As Warner suggests ("Beyond Gay Marriage"), one problem with correlating privilege and social welfare with marriage is the de facto denial of welfare to those who are not married, gay or straight.
9. Elizabeth Freeman, *The Wedding Complex*, xiv, xv.
10. Susan Harris, "Illuminating the Eclipse," 45.
11. Joanne Dobson, *Dickinson and the Strategies of Reticence*, 72.

12. I cite Dickinson's poems with both Thomas Johnson's numbers from the variorum edition (T 199), and those of R. W. Franklin's 1998 edition of the poems (F 225).

13. Jane Donahue Eberwein, *Dickinson*, 107–8.

14. This is the version of the poem sent to Samuel Bowles in 1862. A second version, quoted below, was sent to Susan Huntington Dickinson. Johnson dates the second version "perhaps as late as 1866" on the basis of the handwriting (*The Poems of Emily Dickinson*, 758).

15. Evan Carton argues for a similar reading: "We can read the speaker's closing question, at least in part, as a critical and self-conscious reflection on her poetic enterprise: 'Is it appropriate or purposeful for me to attempt the same sort of linguistic invocation of my object that other women so confidently perform by the words 'My Husband'?" (*The Rhetoric of American Romance*, 87).

16. Shira Wolosky, "Emily Dickinson's Manuscript Body," 95.

17. On the publication history of Dickinson's work, see R. W. Franklin, *The Editing of Emily Dickinson*.

18. Dickinson is quoted by Ellen E. Dickinson, the wife of her cousin Willie, to this effect in the *Boston Evening Transcript*, Oct. 12, 1895. Cited by Wolosky, "Emily Dickinson's Manuscript Body," 95.

19. Out of her 1,775 poems, Dickinson gave titles to twenty-four. Most of these titles are supplied in the text of letters accompanying poems sent to friends. For a list of the titled poems see Thomas H. Johnson, "Appendix 8," in *The Poems of Emily Dickinson*, vol. 3, 1206.

20. See Franklin, *The Editing of Emily Dickinson*, 25–26.

21. See Johnson, *The Poems of Emily Dickinson*, and Franklin, *The Poems of Emily Dickinson*.

22. The difficulty of enclosing Dickinson's poems within fixed boundaries is compounded by her practice of including variant words, marked with asterisks, even in the presumably final versions of the poems written in the fascicles. For an excellent reading of the effect of the variants within the fascicles see Sharon Cameron, *Choosing Not Choosing*.

23. Richard Sewall, *The Life of Emily Dickinson*, 405.

24. David Porter, *Dickinson: The Modern Idiom*, 208–9.

25. See Ellen Louise Hart, "Encoding Homoerotic Desire," as well as, more broadly, Hart and Martha Nell Smith's impressive edited volume of Dickinson's correspondence with Susan Huntington Dickinson, *Open Me Carefully*.

26. I cite the letter number that is supplied in Thomas H. Johnson and Theodora Ward's edition of *The Letters of Emily Dickinson*. However, I cite the lineation and punctuation provided by Hart and Smith in *Open Me Carefully*, 256–57, which replicates the lineation of the original manuscript. Hart and Smith reframe many of the letters Emily sent to Susan as poems and make a convincing argument for doing so. In "The Encoding of Homoerotic Desire," Hart reads this letter/poem as evidence of the enduring love between Dickinson and Sue as against biographers who have claimed that a permanent break in the relationship occurred in the late 1850s.

27. Hart argues that the reference to the "Card" in this line is "the poem's most ambiguous image. It may refer to a message previously sent on a card or to a printed greeting card, a playing card, or a fortune-telling card; it may represent a map or a chart

since a circular piece of cardboard, marked with the points of a mariner's compass, is known as a card of the sea. The 'Card' may even refer to the Bible, the 'great card and compass' and guide to faith" ("Encoding Homoerotic Desire," 263). My reading here emphasizes the word "final," a reading consonant with any of Hart's suggestions, all of which describe the "Card" as a fixed, even directional text. The final line of a fixed text is thus the site of fixity and closure, a fixity to which Dickinson objects.

28. Nan Hunter, "Marriage, Law, and Gender," 112.

29. See Nancy Fraser, *Justice Interruptus*, chapter 1.

Works Cited

Abelove, Henry. "Some Speculations on the History of Sexual Intercourse During the Long Eighteenth Century in England." *Genders* 6 (1989): 125–30.

Agnew, Jean-Christophe. *Worlds Apart: The Market and the Theater in Anglo-American Thought, 1550–1750.* Cambridge: Cambridge University Press, 1986.

Aiken, J. "On the Choice of a Wife." *The New York Magazine, or Literary Repository* (Jan. 1795): 35–39.

Althusser, Louis. "Ideology and Ideological State Apparatuses." In *Lenin and Philosophy, and Other Essays.* New York: Monthly Review Press, 1971.

Anderson, Benedict R. O'G. *Imagined Communities: Reflections on the Origin and Spread of Nationalism.* London: Verso Editions / NLB, 1983.

Appleby, Joyce Oldham. *Capitalism and a New Social Order: The Republican Vision of the 1790s.* New York: New York University Press, 1984.

Arendt, Hannah. *The Human Condition.* Chicago: University of Chicago Press, 1969.

Armstrong, Nancy. *Desire and Domestic Fiction: A Political History of the Novel.* New York: Oxford University Press, 1987.

Austin, J. L. *How to Do Things with Words.* Cambridge, Mass.: Harvard University Press, 1962.

Baillie, Robert. *A Dissuasive from the Errours of the Time.* London: Printed for Samuel Gellibrand . . . , 1646.

Bailyn, Bernard. *The New England Merchants in the Seventeenth Century.* New York: Harper & Row, 1964.

Baker, Houston. "Critical Memory and the Black Public Sphere." In *The Black Public Sphere: A Public Culture Book*, ed. Black Public Sphere Collective, 5–37. Chicago: University of Chicago Press, 1995.

Baker, Keith Michael. "Defining the Public Sphere in Eighteenth-Century France: Variations on a Theme by Habermas." In *Habermas and the Public Sphere*, ed. Craig Calhoun, 181–208. Cambridge, Mass: MIT Press, 1997.

Baldwin, James. "Everybody's Protest Novel." In *Uncle Tom's Cabin*, ed. Elizabeth Ammons, 495–501. New York: Norton, 1994.

Balibar, Etienne. "Citizen Subject." In *Who Comes after the Subject?* ed. Eduardo Cadava, Peter Connor, and Jean-Luc Nancy, 33–57. New York: Routledge, 1991.

———. "Racism and Nationalism." In *Race, Nation, Class: Ambiguous Identities*, ed. Etienne Balibar and Immanuel Maurice Wallerstein, 37–67. London: Verso, 1991.

Barnes, Elizabeth. *States of Sympathy: Seduction and Democracy in the American Novel.* New York: Columbia University Press, 1997.

Barnes, Viola Florence. *The Dominion of New England: A Study in British Colonial Policy.* New Haven, Conn.: Yale University Press, 1923.

Beales, Ross W., Jr. "In Search of the Historical Child: Miniature Adulthood and Youth in Colonial New England." In *Growing up in America: Children in Historical Perspective,* ed. N. Ray Hiner and Joseph M. Hawes, 7–24. Urbana: University of Illinois Press, 1985.

Bender, John B. *Imagining the Penitentiary: Fiction and the Architecture of Mind in Eighteenth-Century England.* Chicago: University of Chicago Press, 1987.

———. "Making the World Safe for Narratology: A Reply to Dorrit Cohn." *New Literary History* 26, no. 1 (1995): 29–33.

Benhabib, Seyla. "Models of Public Space: Hannah Arendt, the Liberal Tradition, and Jürgen Habermas." In *Habermas and the Public Sphere,* ed. Craig J. Calhoun, 73–98. Cambridge, Mass.: MIT Press, 1997.

Bennett, Paula Bernat. *Poets in the Public Sphere: The Emancipatory Project of American Women's Poetry, 1800–1900.* Princeton, N.J.: Princeton University Press, 2003.

Bercovitch, Sacvan. *The Rites of Assent: Transformations in the Symbolic Construction of America.* New York: Routledge, 1993.

Berlant, Lauren. "Poor Eliza." *American Literature* 70, no. 3 (1998): 635–68.

———. "The Subject of True Feeling: Pain, Privacy, and Politics." In *Cultural Studies and Political Theory,* ed. Jodi Dean, 42–62. Ithaca, N.Y.: Cornell University Press, 2000.

Bloch, Ruth. "Gender and the Public/Private Dichotomy in American Revolutionary Thought." In *Gender and Morality in Anglo-American Culture, 1650–1800,* 154–66. Berkeley: University of California Press, 2003.

———. "The Gendered Meanings of Virtue in Revolutionary America." *Signs: Journal of Women in Culture and Society* 13, no. 1 (1987): 37–58.

Boydston, Jeanne. *Home and Work: Housework, Wages, and the Ideology of Labor in the Early Republic.* New York: Oxford University Press, 1990.

Brandeis, Louis, and Samuel Warren. "The Right to Privacy." *Harvard Law Review* 4, no. 5 (1890).

Bremer, Francis J. "In Defense of Regicide: John Cotton on the Execution of Charles I." *William and Mary Quarterly,* 3d series 37, no. 1 (1980): 103–24.

Brenner, Robert. *Merchants and Revolution: Commercial Change, Political Conflict, and London's Overseas Traders, 1550–1653.* Princeton, N.J.: Princeton University Press, 1993.

Brown, Chandos Michael. "Mary Wollstonecraft, or, the Female Illuminati: The Campaign against Women and 'Modern Philosophy' in the Early Republic." *Journal of the Early Republic* 15 (1995): 389–424.

Brown, Charles Brockden. *Arthur Mervyn: Or, Memoirs of the Year 1773.* Kent, Ohio: Kent State University Press, 1980.

———. *Edgar Huntly Or, Memoirs of a Sleep-Walker.* Ed. Norman Grabo. New York: Penguin USA, 1988.

Brown, Gillian. *The Consent of the Governed: The Lockean Legacy in Early American Culture.* Cambridge, Mass.: Harvard University Press, 2001.

———. *Domestic Individualism: Imagining Self in Nineteenth-Century America.* The New Historicism, vol. 14. Berkeley: University of California Press, 1990.

Brown, Wendy. *States of Injury: Power and Freedom in Late Modernity*. Princeton, N.J.: Princeton University Press, 1995.

Brown, Wendy, and Janet Halley, eds. *Left Legalism / Left Critique*. Durham, N.C.: Duke University Press, 2002.

Brown, William Hill, and Hannah Webster Foster. *The Power of Sympathy: The Coquette*. New Haven, Conn.: College & University Press, 1970.

Burgett, Bruce. *Sentimental Bodies: Sex, Gender, and Citizenship in the Early Republic*. Princeton, N.J.: Princeton University Press, 1998.

Burnham, Michelle. "Anne Hutchinson and the Economics of Antinomian Selfhood in Colonial New England." *Criticism* 39, no. 3 (1997): 337–58.

Butler, Judith. *Bodies That Matter: On the Discursive Limits of "Sex."* New York: Routledge, 1993.

———. "Contingent Foundations: Feminism and the Question of 'Postmodernism.'" In *Feminists Theorize the Political*, ed. Judith P. Butler and Joan Wallach Scott, 3–21. New York: Routledge, 1992.

———. "Is Kinship Always Already Heterosexual?" In *Left Legalism / Left Critique*, ed. Wendy Brown and Janet Halley, 229–58. Durham, N.C.: Duke University Press, 2002.

Caldwell, Patricia. "The Antinomian Language Controversy." *Harvard Theological Review* 69 (1976): 345–67.

———. *The Puritan Conversion Narrative: The Beginnings of American Expression*. Cambridge: Cambridge University Press, 1983.

Calhoun, Craig J. "Introduction." In *Habermas and the Public Sphere*, ed. Craig J. Calhoun, 1–48. Cambridge, Mass.: MIT Press, 1997.

Cameron, Sharon. *Choosing Not Choosing: Dickinson's Fascicles*. Chicago: University of Chicago Press, 1992.

Campbell, Jill. *Natural Masques: Gender and Identity in Fielding's Plays and Novels*. Stanford, Calif.: Stanford University Press, 1995.

Carby, Hazel V. *Reconstructing Womanhood: The Emergence of the Afro-American Woman Novelist*. New York: Oxford University Press, 1987.

Carton, Evan. *The Rhetoric of American Romance: Dialectic and Identity in Emerson, and Dickinson, Poe, and Hawthorne*. Baltimore, Md.: Johns Hopkins University Press, 1985.

Castiglione, Dario, and Lesley Sharpe, eds. *Shifting the Boundaries: Transformation of the Languages of Public and Private in the Eighteenth Century*. Exeter: University of Exeter Press, 1995.

Chaplin, Joyce E. *Subject Matter: Technology, the Body, and Science on the Anglo-American Frontier, 1500–1676*. Cambridge, Mass.: Harvard University Press, 2001.

Chapman, Mary, and Glen Hendler, eds. *Sentimental Men: Masculinity and the Politics of Affect in American Culture*. Berkeley: University of California Press, 1999.

Cherniavsky, Eva. *That Pale Mother Rising: Sentimental Discourses and the Imitation of Motherhood in 19th-Century America*. Bloomington: Indiana University Press, 1995.

Child, Lydia Maria. "Elizabeth Wilson." In *The Illustrated Ladies' Keepsake*, ed. Asahel Abbott, 339–55. New York: John S. Taylor, 1852.

Clive, John, and Bernard Bailyn. "England's Cultural Provinces: Scotland and America." *William and Mary Quarterly* 11 (1954): 200–213.

Cobbett, William. *Detection of a Conspiracy Formed by the United Irishmen: With the*

Evident Intention of Aiding the Tyrants of France in Subverting the Government of the United States of America. Philadelphia, Penn.: William Cobbett, 1798.

———. *A Kick for a Bite; or Review Upon Review; With a Critical Essay, on the Works of Mrs. S. Rowson; in a Letter to the Editor, or Editors, of the American Monthly Review.* Philadelphia, Penn.: Printed by Thomas Bradford no. 8 South Front Street, 1796.

Cohen, Charles Lloyd. *God's Caress: The Psychology of Puritan Religious Experience.* New York: Oxford University Press, 1986.

Collinson, Patrick. *The Elizabethan Puritan Movement.* Berkeley: University of California Press, 1967.

Coquillette, Daniel R. "Radical Lawmakers in Colonial Massachusetts: The 'Countenance of Authoritie' and the *Lawes and Libertyes.*" *New England Quarterly* 67, no. 2 (June 1994): 179–211.

Cott, Nancy F. *The Bonds of Womanhood: "Woman's Sphere" in New England, 1780–1835.* 2d ed. New Haven, Conn: Yale University Press, 1997.

———. *Public Vows: A History of Marriage and the Nation.* Cambridge, Mass.: Harvard University Press, 2000.

Court, Franklin E. "The Early Impact of Scottish Literary Teaching in North America." In *The Scottish Invention of English Literature,* ed. Robert Crawford, 134–63. Cambridge: Cambridge University Press, 1998.

Crain, Caleb. *American Sympathy: Men, Friendship, and Literature in the New Nation.* New Haven, Conn.: Yale University Press, 2001.

Crawford, Patricia. "Public Duty, Conscience, and Women in Early Modern England." In *Public Duty and Private Conscience in Seventeenth-Century England,* ed. Paul Slack, John Morrill, and Daniel Woolf, 57–76. Oxford: Clarendon, 1993.

Crawford, Robert. *The Scottish Invention of English Literature.* Cambridge: Cambridge University Press, 1998.

Cressy, David. *Coming Over: Migration and Communication between England and New England in the Seventeenth Century.* New York: Cambridge University Press, 1987.

Danielson, Caroline. "The Gender of Privacy and the Embodied Self: Examining the Origins of the Right to Privacy in U.S. Law." *Feminist Studies* 25, no. 2 (1999): 311–44.

Davidson, Cathy N. *Revolution and the Word: The Rise of the Novel in America.* New York: Oxford University Press, 1986.

Dayton, Cornelia Hughes. *Women Before the Bar: Gender, Law, and Society in Connecticut, 1639–1789.* Chapel Hill: University of North Carolina Press, 1995.

De Witt, John Richard. *Jus Divinum: The Westminster Assembly and the Divine Right of Church Government.* Kampen, The Netherlands: J. H. Kok, 1969.

Defense of Marriage Act of 1996, Public Law 199, 104th Congress, 2d session (Sept. 21, 1996).

Degler, Carl N. *At Odds: Women and the Family in America from the Revolution to the Present.* New York: Oxford University Press, 1980.

Delbanco, Andrew. *The Puritan Ordeal.* Cambridge, Mass.: Harvard University Press, 1989.

Dickinson, Emily. *The Letters of Emily Dickinson.* Ed. Thomas H. Johnson and Theodora Ward. 3 vols. Cambridge, Mass.: Belknap Press of Harvard University Press, 1958.

Dickinson, Emily, and R. W. Franklin. *The Poems of Emily Dickinson.* Variorum ed. Cambridge, Mass.: Belknap Press of Harvard University Press, 1998.

Dickinson, Emily, Ellen Louise Hart, and Martha Nell Smith. *Open Me Carefully: Emily*

Dickinson's Intimate Letters to Susan Huntington Dickinson. Ashfield, Mass.: Paris Press, 1998.

Dickinson, Emily, and Thomas Herbert Johnson. *The Poems of Emily Dickinson: Including Variant Readings Critically Compared with All Known Manuscripts*. Cambridge, Mass.: Belknap Press of Harvard University Press, 1955.

Dimock, Wai Chee. *Residues of Justice: Literature, Law, Philosophy*. Berkeley: University of California Press, 1996.

Ditmore, Michael. "Preparation and Confession: Reconsidering Edmund S. Morgan's *Visible Saints*." *New England Quarterly* 67, no. 2 (1994): 298–319.

Ditz, Toby L. "Shipwrecked; or Masculinity Imperiled: Mercantile Representations of Failure and the Gendered Self in Eighteenth-Century Philadelphia." *The Journal of American History* 81, no. 1 (1994): 51–80.

Dobson, Joanne. *Dickinson and the Strategies of Reticence: The Woman Writer in Nineteenth-Century America*. Bloomington: Indiana University Press, 1989.

———. "Reclaiming Sentimental Literature." *American Literature* 69, no. 2 (1997): 263–88.

Douglas, Ann. *The Feminization of American Culture*. New York: Noonday Press / Farrar Straus and Giroux, 1998.

Douglass, Frederick. "What to the Slave Is the Fourth of July?" In *Narrative of the Life of Frederick Douglass*, ed. William L. Andrews, 116–27. New York: Norton, 1997.

Dunn, Mary Maples. "Saints and Sisters: Congregational and Quaker Women in the Early Colonial Period." *American Quarterly* 30, no. 5 (1978): 582–601.

Eberwein, Jane Donahue. *Dickinson: Strategies of Limitation*. Amherst: University of Massachusetts Press, 1985.

Edwards, Thomas. *Antapologia: Or, a Full Answer to the Apologeticall Narration of Mr Goodwin, Mr Nye, Mr Sympson, Mr Burroughs, Mr Bridge, Members of the Assembly of Divines*. London: Printed by G.M. for John Bellamie, 1644.

Egan, Jim. *Authorizing Experience: Refigurations of the Body Politic in Seventeenth-Century New England Writing*. Princeton, N.J.: Princeton University Press, 1999.

Eger, Elizabeth, Charlotte Grant, Clíona Ó Gallchoir, and Penny Warburton, eds. *Women, Writing and the Public Sphere, 1700–1830*. Cambridge: Cambridge University Press, 2001.

Eisenstein, Zillah R. *The Radical Future of Liberal Feminism*. Boston, Mass.: Northeastern University Press, 1993.

Eley, Geoff. "Nations, Publics, and Political Cultures." In *Habermas and the Public Sphere*, ed. Craig J. Calhoun, 289–339. Cambridge, Mass.: MIT Press, 1997.

Ellison, Julie K. *Cato's Tears and the Making of Anglo-American Emotion*. Chicago: University of Chicago Press, 1999.

Eng, David, and David Kazanjian, eds. *Loss: The Politics of Mourning*. Berkeley: University of California Press, 2002.

Epstein, David F. *The Political Theory of the Federalist*. Chicago: University of Chicago Press, 1984.

Erikson, Kai T. *Wayward Puritans: A Study in the Sociology of Deviance*. New York: Wiley, 1966.

Erkkila, Betsy. "Revolutionary Women." *Tulsa Studies in Women's Literature* 6, no. 2 (1987): 189–223.

A Faithful Narrative of Elizabeth Wilson. Philadelphia, Penn.: n.p., 1786.

Ferguson, Ann, and Nancy Folbre. "The Unhappy Marriage of Patriarchy and Capitalism." In *Women and Revolution: A Discussion of the Unhappy Marriage of Marxism and Feminism*, ed. Lydia Sargent, 313–338. Boston, Mass.: South End Press, 1981.

Finkelman, Paul, ed. *Dred Scott v. Sanford: A Brief History with Documents*. Boston, Mass.: Bedford Books, 1997.

Fisher, Philip. *Hard Facts: Setting and Form in the American Novel*. New York: Oxford University Press, 1985.

Fiske, John. *The Notebook of the Reverend John Fiske, 1644–1675*. Ed. Robert G. Pope. Publications of the Colonial Society of Massachusetts, vol. 47. Boston: Colonial Society of Massachusetts, 1974.

Flaherty, David H. *Privacy in Colonial New England*. Charlottesville: University Press of Virginia, 1972.

Flaherty, David H., ed. *Essays in the History of Early American Law*. Chapel Hill: University of North Carolina Press, 1969.

Flanagan, Thomas, and Anthony Parel, eds. *Theories of Property: Aristotle to the Present*. Waterloo, Ont.: Wilfrid Laurier University Press, 1979.

Fliegelman, Jay. *Prodigals and Pilgrims: The American Revolution against Patriarchal Authority, 1750–1800*. Cambridge: Cambridge University Press, 1982.

Foster, Hannah Webster. *The Coquette*. Ed. Cathy N. Davidson. New York: Oxford University Press, 1986.

Foster, Stephen. *The Long Argument: English Puritanism and the Shaping of New England Culture, 1570–1700*. Chapel Hill: University of North Carolina Press, 1991.

———. "New England and the Challenge of Heresy, 1630 to 1660: The Puritan Crisis in Transatlantic Perspective." *William and Mary Quarterly*, Third Series, 38, no. 4 (1981): 624–60.

Franklin, R. W. *The Editing of Emily Dickinson: A Reconsideration*. Madison: University of Wisconsin Press, 1967.

Fraser, Nancy. *Justice Interruptus: Critical Reflections on the 'Postsocialist' Condition*. New York: Routledge, 1997.

———. "Rethinking the Public Sphere: A Contribution to the Critique of Actually Existing Democracy." In *The Phantom Public Sphere*, ed. Bruce Robbins, 1–32. Minneapolis: University of Minnesota Press, 1993.

Freeman, Elizabeth. *The Wedding Complex: Forms of Belonging in Modern American Culture*. Durham, N.C.: Duke University Press, 2002.

"From the Genius of Liberty." *Key* (Apr. 14, 1798): 105–6.

Gallagher, Catherine. *Nobody's Story: The Vanishing Acts of Women Writers in the Marketplace, 1670–1820*. The New Historicism, vol. 31. Berkeley: University of California Press, 1994.

Games, Alison. *Migration and the Origins of the English Atlantic World*. Cambridge, Mass.: Harvard University Press, 1999.

Gardner, Jared. *Master Plots: Race and the Founding of an American Literature 1787–1845*. Baltimore, Md.: Johns Hopkins University Press, 1998.

Garrow, David. *Liberty and Sexuality: The Right to Privacy and the Making of Roe V. Wade*. New York: Macmillan, 1994.

Gataker, Thomas. *A Marriage Praier*. London: Fulke Clifton and James Bowler, 1624.

George, C. H. "Puritanism as History and Historiography." *Past and Present* 41 (1968): 77–104.

Gorton, Samuel. *Simplicities Defence Against Seven-Headed Policy, or, Innocency Vindicated, Being Unjustly Accused, and Sorely Censured by that Seven-headed Church-government United in New-England*. London: Printed by John Macock, 1646.

Gould, Philip. "Virtue, Ideology, and the American Revolution: The Legacy of the Republican Synthesis." *American Literary History* 5, no. 3 (1993): 564–77.

Grossman, Joanna L. "Women's Jury Service: Right of Citizenship or Privilege of Difference?" *Stanford Law Review* 46 (1994).

Gunderson, Joan. "Independence, Citizenship, and the American Revolution." *Signs: Journal of Women in Culture and Society* 13, no. 1 (1987): 59–77.

Gura, Philip F. *A Glimpse of Sion's Glory: Puritan Radicalism in New England, 1620–1660*. Middletown, Conn.: Wesleyan University Press, 1984.

Gustafson, Sandra M. *Eloquence Is Power: Oratory and Performance in Early America*. Chapel Hill: University of North Carolina Press, 2000.

Haag, Pamela. *Consent: Sexual Rights and the Transformation of American Liberalism*. Ithaca, N.Y.: Cornell University Press, 1999.

Habermas, Jürgen. *The Structural Transformation of the Public Sphere: An Inquiry into a Category of Bourgeois Society*. Trans. Thomas Burger. Studies in Contemporary German Social Thought. Cambridge, Mass.: MIT Press, 1989.

Hale, David George. *The Body Politic: A Political Metaphor in Renaissance English Literature*. The Hague, the Netherlands: Mouton, 1971.

Hall, David D. *The Antinomian Controversy, 1636–1638: A Documentary History*. 2d ed. Durham, N.C.: Duke University Press, 1990.

Haller, William. *Liberty and Reformation in the Puritan Revolution*. New York: Columbia University Press, 1955.

Halley, Janet. "Recognition, Rights, Regulation, Normalisation: Rhetorics of Justification in the Same-Sex Marriage Debate." In *Legal Recognition of Same-Sex Partnerships: A Survey of National European and International Law*, ed. Robert Wintemute and Mads Andenaes, 97–111. Oxford: Hart Publishing, 2001.

Halttunen, Karen. *Confidence Men and Painted Women: A Study of Middle-Class Culture in America, 1830–1870*. New Haven, Conn.: Yale University Press, 1982.

Hamburger, Philip. "Liberality." *Texas Law Review* 78 (2000): 1215–86.

Harris, Jonathan Gil. *Foreign Bodies and the Body Politic: Discourses of Social Pathology in Early Modern England*. Cambridge: Cambridge University Press, 1998.

Harris, Susan. "Illuminating the Eclipse: Dickinson's 'Representative' and the Marriage Narrative." *The Emily Dickinson Journal* 4, no. 2 (1995): 44–61.

Hart, Ellen Louise. "The Encoding of Homoerotic Desire: Emily Dickinson's Letters and Poems to Susan Dickinson, 1850–1886." *Tulsa Studies in Women's Literature* 9, no. 2 (1990): 251–72.

Hart, Ellen Louise, and Martha Nell Smith, eds. *Open Me Carefully: Emily Dickinson's Intimate Letters to Susan Huntington Dickinson*. Ashfield, Mass.: Paris Press, 1998.

Hart, John F. "'A Less Proportion of Idle Proprietors': Madison, Property Rights, and the Abolition of Fee Tail." *Washington & Lee Law Review* 58 (2001): 167–95.

Hartman, Saidiya V. *Scenes of Subjection: Terror, Slavery, and Self-Making in Nineteenth-Century America*. New York: Oxford University Press, 1997.

Hartmann, Heidi. "The Unhappy Marriage of Marxism and Feminism: Towards a More Progressive Union." In *The Second Wave: A Reader in Feminist Theory*, ed. Linda J. Nicholson, 97–122. New York: Routledge, 1997.

Hawthorne, Nathaniel. "Mrs. Hutchinson." In *Tales and Sketches*, 18–24. New York: Literary Classics of the United States, 1982.

Hendler, Glenn. *Public Sentiments: Structures of Feeling in Nineteenth-Century American Literature*. Chapel Hill: University of North Carolina Press, 2001.

Henigman, Laura. *Coming into Communion: Pastoral Dialogues in Colonial New England*. Albany: State University of New York Press, 1999.

Hill, Christopher. *Change and Continuity in Seventeenth-Century England*. London: Weidenfeld and Nicolson, 1974.

———. *The Collected Essays of Christopher Hill*. Amherst: University of Massachusetts Press, 1985.

———. *The World Turned Upside Down: Radical Ideas During the English Revolution*. London: Penguin Books, 1991.

Hoffer, Peter C., and N. E. H. Hull. *Murdering Mothers: Infanticide in England and New England, 1558–1803*. New York: New York University Press, 1981.

Hohendahl, Peter. "The Public Sphere: Models and Boundaries." In *Habermas and the Public Sphere*, ed. Craig J. Calhoun, 99–108. Cambridge, Mass.: MIT Press, 1997.

Hook, Andrew. *Scotland and America: A Study of Cultural Relations, 1750–1835*. Glasgow: Blackie, 1975.

———. "Scottish Academia and the Invention of American Studies." In *The Scottish Invention of English Literature*, ed. Robert Crawford, 164–79. Cambridge: Cambridge University Press, 1998.

Hope, Vincent. "Smith's Demigod." In *Philosophers of the Scottish Enlightenment*, ed. Vincent Hope, 157–67. Edinburgh: Edinburgh University Press, 1984.

Hubbard, William. *A General History of New England, From the Discovery to MDCLXXX*. Published by the Massachusetts Historical Society. Cambridge, Mass.: Hilliard & Metcalf, 1815.

Hunter, Nan. "Marriage, Law and Gender: A Feminist Inquiry." In *Sex Wars: Sexual Dissent and Political Culture*, ed. Lisa Duggan and Nan D. Hunter, 107–22. New York: Routledge, 1995.

"The Influence of the Female Sex on the Enjoyments of Social Life." *The Christian's, Scholar's, and Farmer's Magazine* (Oct.–Nov. 1789).

Irving, Washington. *The Legend of Sleepy Hollow and Other Stories in the Sketch Book*. New York: Signet, 1981.

Jackson, Mark, ed. *Infanticide: Historical Perspectives on Child Murder and Concealment, 1550–2000*. Aldershot, U.K.: Ashgate, 2002.

Johnson, Edward. *Wonder-Working Providence of Sions Saviour in New England (1654) and Good News from New England (1648)*. Delmar, N.Y.: Scholars' Facsimiles & Reprints, 1974.

Jones, Jacqueline. *Labor of Love, Labor of Sorrow: Black Women, Work, and the Family from Slavery to the Present*. New York: Basic Books, 1985.

Juster, Susan. *Disorderly Women: Sexual Politics & Evangelicalism in Revolutionary New England*. Ithaca, N.Y.: Cornell University Press, 1994.

Kamenka, Eugene, and R. S. Neale. *Feudalism, Capitalism and Beyond*. London: E. Arnold, 1975.

Kamensky, Jane. *Governing the Tongue: The Politics of Speech in Early New England*. New York: Oxford University Press, 1997.

Kant, Immanuel. *The Critique of Judgement*. Trans. James Creed Meredith. Oxford: Clarendon Press, 1952.

Keayne, Robert. *Note-Book of the Boston Church, 1639–1642*. Transcribed by Merja Kytö (Uppsala University).

Kelley, Mary. *Private Woman, Public Stage: Literary Domesticity in Nineteenth-Century America*. New York: Oxford University Press, 1984.

———. "Reading Women / Women Reading: The Making of Learned Women in Antebellum America." *The Journal of American History* 83, no. 2 (1996): 401–24.

Kerber, Linda K. *No Constitutional Right to Be Ladies: Women and the Obligations of Citizenship*. New York: Hill and Wang, 1998.

———. *Women of the Republic: Intellect and Ideology in Revolutionary America*. Chapel Hill: University of North Carolina Press, 1980.

Kete, Mary Louise. *Sentimental Collaborations: Mourning and Middle-Class Identity in Nineteenth-Century America*. Durham, N.C.: Duke University Press, 2000.

Kibbey, Ann. *The Interpretation of Material Shapes in Puritanism: A Study of Rhetoric, Prejudice, and Violence*. Cambridge: Cambridge University Press, 1986.

Klein, Lawrence. "Gender and the Public/Private Distinction in the Eighteenth Century: Some Questions About Evidence and Analytic Procedure." *Eighteenth-Century Studies* 29 (1996): 97–109.

Knox, John. *On Rebellion*. Ed. Roger A. Mason. Cambridge: Cambridge University Press, 1994.

Koehler, Lyle. "The Case of the American Jezebels: Anne Hutchinson and Female Agitation During the Years of Antinomian Turmoil, 1636–1640." *William and Mary Quarterly* 31 (1974): 55–78.

Korobkin, Laura. *Criminal Conversations: Sentimentality and Nineteenth-Century Legal Stories of Adultery*. New York: Columbia University Press, 1998.

Kramnick, Isaac. *Republicanism and Bourgeois Radicalism: Political Ideology in Late Eighteenth-Century England and America*. Ithaca, N.Y.: Cornell University Press, 1990.

Kupperman, Karen Ordahl. "Errand to the Indies: Puritan Colonization from Providence Island through the Western Design." *William and Mary Quarterly* 45, no. 1 (1988): 70–99.

Lacan, Jacques. *Écrits: A Selection*, trans. Alan Sheridan. New York: Norton, 1977.

———. "Le stade du miroir." *Revue française de psychanalyse*, no. 4 (Oct.–Dec. 1949): 449–55.

Landes, Joan B. *Women and the Public Sphere in the Age of the French Revolution*. Ithaca, N.Y.: Cornell University Press, 1988.

Lang, Amy Schrager. *Prophetic Woman: Anne Hutchinson and the Problem of Dissent in the Literature of New England*. Berkeley: University of California Press, 1987.

Langer, William L. "Infanticide: A Historical Survey." *History of Childhood Quarterly* 1 (1974): 353–66.

Laqueur, Thomas Walter. *Making Sex: Body and Gender from the Greeks to Freud*. Cambridge, Mass.: Harvard University Press, 1990.

Larson, David M. "*Arthur Mervyn, Edgar Huntly*, and the Critics." *Essays in Literature* 15 (1988): 206–19.

Lechford, Thomas. *Plain Dealing, or, News from New England.* Ed. J. Hammond Trumbull. Boston, Mass.: J. K. Wiggin & Wm. Parsons Lunt, 1867.

Lefort, Claude. *Democracy and Political Theory.* Cambridge: Polity Press in association with Basil Blackwell, 1988.

Leites, Edmund. *The Puritan Conscience and Modern Sexuality.* New Haven, Conn.: Yale University Press, 1986.

"A Lesson on Sensibility." *The Weekly Magazine of Original Essays, Fugitive Pieces, and Interesting Intelligence* (May 19, 1798): 71–76.

Lewis, Jan. "The Republican Wife: Virtue and Seduction in the Early Republic." *William and Mary Quarterly* 44, no. 4 (1987): 689–721.

Linebaugh, Peter, and Marcus Buford Rediker. *The Many-Headed Hydra: The Hidden History of the Revolutionary Atlantic.* Boston, Mass.: Beacon Press, 2000.

Lloyd, Genevieve. "Selfhood, War, and Masculinity." In *Feminist Challenges: Social and Political Theory,* ed. Elizabeth Gross and Carole Pateman, 63–76. Boston, Mass.: Northeastern University Press, 1987.

Locke, John. *Two Treatises of Government.* Ed. Peter Laslett. Cambridge: Cambridge University Press, 1988.

Locke, John, John W. Yolton, and Jean S. Yolton. *Some Thoughts Concerning Education.* Oxford: Clarendon Press and Oxford University Press, 1989.

Luciano, Dana. "'Perverse Nature': *Edgar Huntly* and the Novel's Reproductive Disorders." *American Literature* 70, no. 1 (1998): 1–27.

Luhmann, Niklas. *Love as Passion: The Codification of Intimacy.* Trans. Jeremy Gaines and Doris L. Jones. Stanford, Calif.: Stanford University Press, 1998.

Mack, Phyllis. *Visionary Women: Ecstatic Prophecy in Seventeenth-Century England.* Berkeley: University of California Press, 1992.

Maclear, J. F. "Anne Hutchinson and the Mortalist Heresy." *New England Quarterly* 54, no. 1 (1981): 74–103.

Macpherson, C. B. *The Political Theory of Possessive Individualism: Hobbes to Locke.* London: Oxford University Press, 1964.

Madison, James, Alexander Hamilton, and John Jay. *The Federalist Papers.* Ed. Garry Wills. New York: Bantam Books, 1982.

Maine, Henry Sumner. *Ancient Law: Its Connection with the Early History of Society and Its Relation to Modern Ideas.* Boston, Mass.: Beacon Press, 1963.

Mann, Bruce, and Christopher Tomlins, eds. *The Many Legalities of Early America.* Chapel Hill: University of North Carolina Press, 2001.

Marcus, Sharon. "Fighting Bodies, Fighting Words: A Theory and Politics of Rape Prevention." In *Feminists Theorize the Political,* ed. Judith P. Butler and Joan Wallach Scott, 385–403. New York: Routledge, 1992.

Marshall, David. *The Figure of Theater: Shaftesbury, Defoe, Adam Smith, and George Eliot.* New York: Columbia University Press, 1986.

Martin, John E. *Feudalism to Capitalism: Peasant and Landlord in English Agrarian Development, Studies in Historical Sociology.* Atlantic Highlands, N.J.: Humanities Press, 1983.

Marx, Karl. *Grundrisse: Foundations of the Critique of Political Economy.* Trans. Martin Nicolaus. New York: Random House, 1973.

Massé, Michelle A. *In the Name of Love: Women, Masochism, and the Gothic.* Reading Women Writing. Ithaca, N.Y.: Cornell University Press, 1992.

Matchinske, Megan. *Writing, Gender and State in Early Modern England: Identity Formation and the Female Subject.* Cambridge: Cambridge University Press, 1998.

Matthews, Richard K. "Liberalism, Civic Humanism, and the American Political Tradition: Understanding Genesis." *Journal of Politics, Southern Political Science Association* 49, no. 4 (1987): 1127–53.

McDonagh, Josephine. "Infanticide and the Nation: The Case of Caroline Beale." *New Formations* 3, no. 2 (1997): 11–21.

McDonald, Forrest. *Novus Ordo Seclorum: The Intellectual Origins of the Constitution.* Lawrence: University Press of Kansas, 1985.

McKeon, Michael. *The Origins of the English Novel, 1600–1740.* Baltimore, Md.: Johns Hopkins University Press, 1987.

Merish, Lori. *Sentimental Materialism: Gender, Commodity Culture, and Nineteenth-Century American Literature.* Durham, N.C.: Duke University Press, 2000.

Mies, Maria. *Patriarchy and Accumulation on a World Scale: Women in the International Division of Labour.* Third World Books. London: Zed Books, 1986.

Millar, John, and William Christian Lehmann. *John Millar of Glasgow, 1735–1801: His Life and Thought and His Contributions to Sociological Analysis.* London: Cambridge University Press, 1960.

Miller, John C. *Crisis in Freedom: The Alien and Sedition Acts.* Boston, Mass.: Little, Brown, 1951.

Miller, Perry. *The New England Mind: From Colony to Province.* Cambridge: Harvard University Press, 1953.

———. *The New England Mind: The Seventeenth Century.* New York: Macmillan Company, 1939.

———. *Orthodoxy in Massachusetts, 1630–1650.* Gloucester, Mass.: P. Smith, 1965.

Morgan, Edmund Sears. *American Slavery, American Freedom: The Ordeal of Colonial Virginia.* New York: Norton, 1975.

———. *The Puritan Dilemma: The Story of John Winthrop.* Boston, Mass.: Little Brown, 1958.

———. "The Puritan's Marriage with God." *South Atlantic Quarterly* 49 (1949): 107–12.

———. *Visible Saints: The History of a Puritan Idea.* New York: New York University Press, 1963.

Mulford, Carla. "Introduction." In *Power of Sympathy by William Hill Brown; and the Coquette by Hannah Webster Foster,* ed. Carla Mulford. New York: Penguin Books, 1996.

Nedelsky, Jennifer. "Law, Boundaries, and the Bounded Self." *Representations* 30 (1990): 162–89.

———. *Private Property and the Limits of American Constitutionalism: The Madisonian Framework and Its Legacy.* Chicago: University of Chicago Press, 1990.

Nelson, Dana D. *National Manhood: Capitalist Citizenship and the Imagined Fraternity of White Men.* Durham, N.C.: Duke University Press, 1998.

Nelson, Deborah. *Pursuing Privacy in Cold War America.* New York: Columbia University Press, 2002.

"A New Way of Preserving a Wife." *The Weekly Magazine of Original Essays, Fugitive Pieces, and Interesting Intelligence* (Mar. 30, 1799): 374–77.

Newes from New-England of a Most Strange and Prodigious Birth. London: Printed for John G. Smith, 1642.

Nicholson, Linda J. "Feminism and Marx: Integrating Kinship with the Economic." In *The Second Wave: A Reader in Feminist Theory*, ed. Linda J. Nicholson, 129–45. New York: Routledge, 1997.

Noble, Marianne. "The Ecstasies of Sentimental Wounding in *Uncle Tom's Cabin*." *Yale Journal of Criticism* 10, no. 2 (1997): 295–320.

Norton, Mary Beth. *Founding Mothers & Fathers: Gendered Power and the Forming of American Society*. New York: Alfred A. Knopf, 1996.

Okin, Susan Moller. "Humanist Liberalism." In *Liberalism and the Moral Life*, ed. Nancy L. Rosenblum, 39–53. Cambridge, Mass.: Harvard University Press, 1989.

"On Conjugal Affection." *The Lady's Magazine, and Repository for Entertaining Knowledge* (Sept. 1792): 175–79.

Osgood, Frances Sargent Locke. "A Mother's Prayer in Illness." In *Nineteenth-Century Women Poets: An Anthology*, ed. Paula Bernat Bennett, 71–72. Malden, Mass.: Blackwell, 1998.

Paine, Thomas. *Agrarian Justice*. Philadelphia, Penn.: Printed by R. Folwell, for Benjamin Franklin Bache, 1797.

———. *Common Sense*. Ed. Isaac Kramnick. New York: Penguin, 1979.

Parrington, Vernon Louis. *Main Currents in American Thought: An Interpretation of American Literature from the Beginnings to 1920*. New York: Harcourt Brace and Company, 1927.

Paster, Gail Kern. *The Body Embarrassed: Drama and the Disciplines of Shame in Early Modern England*. Ithaca, N.Y.: Cornell University Press, 1993.

———. "Leaky Vessels: The Incontinent Women of City Comedy." *Renaissance Drama* 18 (1987): 43–65.

Pateman, Carole. *The Disorder of Women: Democracy, Feminism and Political Theory*. Stanford, Calif.: Stanford University Press, 1989.

———. *The Sexual Contract*. Stanford, Calif.: Stanford University Press, 1988.

Patterson, Annabel M. *Censorship and Interpretation: The Conditions of Writing and Reading in Early Modern England*. Madison: University of Wisconsin Press, 1984.

———. *Early Modern Liberalism*. Cambridge: Cambridge University Press, 1997.

Pearl, Valerie, and Morris Pearl. "Governor John Winthrop on the Birth of the Antinomians' 'Monster': The Earliest Reports to Reach England and the Making of a Myth." *Proceedings of the Massachusetts Historical Society* 102 (1990): 21–37.

Peiss, Kathy. "Going Public: Women in Nineteenth-Century Cultural History." *American Literary History* 3 (1991): 817–28.

Pettit, Norman. *The Heart Prepared: Grace and Conversion in Puritan Spiritual Life*. Middletown, Conn.: Wesleyan University Press, 1989.

Phillipson, Nicholas. "Adam Smith as Civic Moralist." In *Wealth and Virtue: The Shaping of Political Economy in the Scottish Enlightenment*, ed. Istvan Hont and Michael Ignatieff, 179–202. Cambridge: Cambridge University Press, 1983.

———. "The Export of Enlightenment." *Times Literary Supplement* (July 2, 1976): 823–24.

Pike, Martha V., and Janice Gray Armstrong. *A Time to Mourn: Expressions of Grief in Nineteenth-Century America*. Brooklyn, N.Y.: Museums at Stony Brook, 1980.

Pinker, Stephen. "Why They Kill Their Newborns." *New York Times*, Nov. 2, 1997, 52–54.

Pitkin, Hanna Fenichel. *Fortune Is a Woman: Gender and Politics in the Thought of Niccolò Machiavelli*. Berkeley: University of California Press, 1984.

Pocock, J. G. A. "Cambridge Paradigms and Scotch Philosophers." In *Wealth and Virtue: The Shaping of Political Economy in the Scottish Enlightenment*, ed. Istvan Hont and Michael Ignatieff, 235–52. Cambridge: Cambridge University Press, 1983.

———. "The Mobility of Property and the Rise of Eighteenth-Century Sociology." In *Theories of Property: Aristotle to the Present*, ed. Anthony Parel and Thomas Flanagan, 141–66. Waterloo, Ontario: Wilfred Laurier Press, 1979.

———. *Virtue, Commerce, and History: Essays on Political Thought and History, Chiefly in the Eighteenth Century*. Cambridge: Cambridge University Press, 1985.

Porter, David T. *Dickinson: The Modern Idiom*. Cambridge, Mass.: Harvard University Press, 1981.

Porter, Kirk Harold. *A History of Suffrage in the United States*. New York: AMS Press, 1971.

Porterfield, Amanda. *Female Piety in Puritan New England: The Emergence of Religious Humanism*. New York: Oxford University Press, 1992.

Pudaloff, Ross J. "Sign and Subject: Antinomianism in Massachusetts Bay." *Semiotica* 54, no. 1/2 (1985): 147–63.

Rackin, Phyllis. "Foreign Country: The Place of Women and Sexuality in Shakespeare's Historical World." In *Enclosure Acts: Sexuality, Property, and Culture in Early Modern England*, ed. Richard Burt and John Michael Archer, 68–95. Ithaca, N.Y.: Cornell University Press, 1994.

Richardson, Samuel. *Pamela; or, Virtue Rewarded*. New York: Garland, 1974.

Richter, Simon. "The Ins and Outs of Intimacy: Gender, Epistolary Culture, and the Public Sphere." *German Quarterly* 69, no. 2 (1996): 111–24.

Ringe, Donald A. *Charles Brockden Brown*. Rev. ed. Twayne's United States Authors Series, vol. 98. Boston, Mass.: Twayne Publishers, 1991.

Robbins, Bruce. "Introduction: The Public as Phantom." In *The Phantom Public Sphere*, ed. Bruce Robbins, vii–xxvi. Minneapolis: University of Minnesota Press, 1993.

Robertson, William. *A View of the Progress of Society, from the Subversion of the Roman Empire to the Beginning of the Sixteenth Century*. In *The Works of William Robertson D.D.*, vol. 4, 1–230. London: Cadell & Davies, 1817.

Robison, John. *Proofs of a Conspiracy against All the Religions and Governments of Europe: Carried on in the Secret Meetings of Free Masons, Illuminati, and Reading Societies*. New-York: Printed and sold by George Forman No. 64 Water-Street between Coenties and the Old-Slip, 1798.

Rodgers, Daniel T. "Socializing Middle-Class Children: Institutions, Fables, and Work Values in Nineteenth-Century America." In *Growing up in America: Children in Historical Perspective*, ed. N. Ray Hiner and Joseph M. Hawes, 119–32. Urbana: University of Illinois Press, 1985.

Rogers, John. *Death the Certain Wages of Sin*. Boston, Mass.: B. Green and J. Allen for Samuel Phillips, 1701.

Rose-Troup, Frances. *The Massachusetts Bay Company and Its Predecessors*. New York: Grafton Press, 1930.

Round, Phillip H. *By Nature and by Custom Cursed: Transatlantic Civil Discourse and New England Cultural Production, 1620–1660*. Hanover, N.H.: University Press of New England, 1999.

Rowe, G. S. "Infanticide, Its Judicial Resolution, and Criminal Code Revision in Early

Pennsylvania." *Proceedings of the American Philosophical Society* 135, no. 2 (1991): 200–232.

Rutman, Darrett Bruce. *Winthrop's Boston: Portrait of a Puritan Town, 1630–1649*. Chapel Hill: University of North Carolina Press, 1965.

Ruttenburg, Nancy. *Democratic Personality: Popular Voice and the Trial of American Authorship*. Stanford, Calif.: Stanford University Press, 1998.

Ryan, Alan. *Property and Political Theory*. Oxford: B. Blackwell, 1984.

Sachse, William L. "The Migration of New Englanders to England, 1640–1660." *American Historical Review* 53, no. 2 (1948): 251–78.

Saks, Eva. "Representing Miscegenation Law." *Raritan* 8, no. 2 (1988): 39–69.

Samuels, Shirley. *The Culture of Sentiment: Race, Gender, and Sentimentality in Nineteenth-Century America*. New York: Oxford University Press, 1992.

———. *Romances of the Republic: Women, the Family, and Violence in the Literature of the Early American Nation*. New York: Oxford University Press, 1996.

Sánchez-Eppler, Karen. "Then When We Clutch Hardest: On the Death of a Child and the Replication of an Image." In *Sentimental Men: Masculinity and the Politics of Affect in American Culture*, ed. Mary Chapman and Glen Hendler, 64–85. Berkeley: University of California Press, 1999.

Schiebinger, Londa L. *Nature's Body: Gender in the Making of Modern Science*. Boston, Mass.: Beacon Press, 1993.

Schramer, James, and Timothy Sweet. "Violence and the Body Politic in Seventeenth-Century New England." *Arizona Quarterly* 48, no. 2 (1992): 1–32.

Schweitzer, Ivy. *The Work of Self-Representation: Lyric Poetry in Colonial New England*. Chapel Hill: University of North Carolina Press, 1991.

Sedgwick, Eve Kosofsky. *The Coherence of Gothic Conventions*. New York: Arno Press, 1980.

Seltzer, Mark. *Serial Killers: Death and Life in America's Wound Culture*. New York/ London: Routledge, 1998.

Sewall, Richard Benson. *The Life of Emily Dickinson*. New York: Farrar Straus and Giroux, 1974.

Shammas, Carole. "The Domestic Environment in Early Modern England and America." In *The American Family in Social-Historical Perspective*, ed. Michael Gordon, 113–35. New York: St. Martin's Press, 1983.

Shapiro, Stephen. "'Man to Man I Needed Not to Dread His Encounter': *Edgar Huntly's* End of Erotic Pessimism." In *Revising Charles Brockden Brown: Culture, Politics, and Sexuality in the Early Republic*, ed. Mark Kamrath, Philip Barnard and Stephen Shapiro. Knoxville: University of Tennessee Press, forthcoming.

Sher, Richard B., and Jeffrey R. Smitten, eds. *Scotland and America in the Age of the Enlightenment*. Princeton, N.J.: Princeton University Press, 1990.

Shevelow, Kathryn. *Women and Print Culture: The Construction of Femininity in the Early Periodical*. London: Routledge, 1989.

Shields, David S. *Civil Tongues and Polite Letters in British America*. Chapel Hill: University of North Carolina Press, 1997.

Shklar, Judith N. "The Liberalism of Fear." In *Liberalism and the Moral Life*, ed. Nancy L. Rosenblum, 21–37. Cambridge, Mass.: Harvard University Press, 1989.

Shrick, Ernest. "The Mother's Prayer." *Godey's Lady's Book* 15, no. 2 (1855): 157.

Siegel, Reva. "Why Equal Protection No Longer Protects: The Evolving Forms of Status-Enforcing State Action." *Stanford Law Review* 49 (1997): 1111–48.

Slauter, Eric. "The State as a Work of Art: Politics and the Cultural Origins of the Constitution." Stanford University, 2000.

Smith, Adam. *The Theory of Moral Sentiments.* Amherst, N.Y.: Prometheus Books, 2000.

Smith, Rogers M. *Civic Ideals: Conflicting Visions of Citizenship in U.S. History.* New Haven, Conn.: Yale University Press, 1997.

Smith-Rosenberg, Carroll. "Subject Female: Authorizing American Identity." *American Literary History* 5, no. 3 (1993): 481–511.

Spillers, Hortense. "Mama's Baby, Papa's Maybe: An American Grammar Book." *Diacritics* 17, no. 2 (1987): 64–81.

Stanley, Amy Dru. *From Bondage to Contract: Wage Labor, Marriage, and the Market in the Age of Slave Emancipation.* New York: Cambridge University Press, 1998.

———. "Home Life and the Morality of the Market." In *The Market Revolution in America,* ed. Stephen Conway and Melvyn Stokes. Charlottesville: University Press of Virginia, 1996.

Stauffer, Vernon. *New England and the Bavarian Illuminati.* New York: Columbia University Press, 1918.

Stearns, Raymond Phineas. *The Strenuous Puritan: Hugh Peter, 1598–1660.* Urbana: University of Illinois, 1954.

———. "The Weld-Peter Mission to England." *Publications of the Colonial Society of Massachusetts* 32 (1937): 188–246.

Stern, Julia A. *The Plight of Feeling: Sympathy and Dissent in the Early American Novel.* Chicago: University of Chicago Press, 1997.

Stoever, William K. B. *A Faire and Easie Way to Heaven: Covenant Theology and Antinomianism in Early Massachusetts.* Middletown, Conn.: Wesleyan University Press, 1978.

Stone, Lawrence. *The Family, Sex and Marriage in England, 1500–1800.* New York: Harper & Row, 1977.

"Story of the First Beacon Hill Farm Bride." In Day Missions records, Emily Hartwell papers, Yale University Divinity School archives.

Stout, Harry. "The Morphology of Remigration: New England University Men and Their Return to England, 1640–1660." *Journal of American Studies* 10 (1976): 151–72.

Stowe, Harriet Beecher. *Uncle Tom's Cabin: Authoritative Text, Backgrounds and Contexts, Criticism,* ed. Elizabeth Ammons. New York: Norton, 1994.

Tawney, R. H. *Religion and the Rise of Capitalism: A Historical Study.* New York: New American Library, 1954.

Tennenhouse, Leonard. "Libertine America." *differences* 11, no. 3 (1999/2000): 1–28.

Thomas, Brook. "The Construction of Privacy in and Around *The Bostonians.*" *American Literature* 64 (1992): 719–47.

Thomas, Keith. "Women and the Civil War Sects." *Past and Present* 13 (1958): 42–62.

Thompson, James. *Models of Value: Eighteenth-Century Political Economy and the Novel.* Durham, N.C.: Duke University Press, 1996.

Tocqueville, Alexis de. *Democracy in America.* New York: A. Knopf, 1994.

Tompkins, Jane P. *Sensational Designs: The Cultural Work of American Fiction, 1790–1860.* New York: Oxford University Press, 1985.

Trenchard, John, and Thomas Gordon. *Cato's Letters; or, Essays on Liberty, Civil and Religious, and Other Important Subjects*. Ed. Ronald Hamowy. Indianapolis, Ind.: Liberty Fund, 1995.

Tucker, Irene. *A Probable State: The Novel, the Contract, and the Jews*. Chicago: University of Chicago Press, 2000.

Tyler, Royall. *The Contrast: A Comedy in Five Acts*. New York: Lenox Hill, 1970.

The Victim of Seduction!: Some Interesting Particulars of the Life and Untimely Fate of Miss Harriot Wilson. Boston, Mass.: J. Wilkey, 1822.

Walker, David. *David Walker's Appeal*. New York: Hill and Wang, 1965.

Wall, Helena M. *Fierce Communion: Family and Community in Early America*. Cambridge, Mass.: Harvard University Press, 1990.

Walzer, Michael. *The Revolution of the Saints: A Study in the Origins of Radical Politics*. New York: Atheneum, 1972.

Warner, Michael. "Beyond Gay Marriage." In *Left Legalistm/Left Critique*, ed. Wendy Brown and Janet Halley, 259–89. Durham, N.C.: Duke University Press, 2002.

———. *The Letters of the Republic: Publication and the Public Sphere in Eighteenth-Century America*. Cambridge, Mass.: Harvard University Press, 1990.

———. "The Mass Public and the Mass Subject." In *Habermas and the Public Sphere*, ed. Craig Calhoun, 377–400. Cambridge, Mass.: MIT Press, 1997.

Weld, Thomas. *An Answer to W.R. His Narration of the Opinions and Practises of the Churches Lately Erected in New-England*. London: Printed by T. Paine for H. Overton, 1644.

———. *A Brief Narration of the Practice of the Churches in New-England: Written in Private to One That Desired Information Therein; by an Inhabitant There, a Friend to Truth and Peace*. London: n.p., 1651.

Westerkamp, Marilyn. "Puritan Patriarchy and the Problem of Revelation." *Journal of Interdisciplinary History* 23 (1992–93): 571–95.

Wexler, Laura. *Tender Violence: Domestic Visions in an Age of U.S. Imperialism*. Chapel Hill: University of North Carolina Press, 2000.

———. "Tender Violence: Literary Eavesdropping, Domestic Fiction, and Educational Reform." In *The Culture of Sentiment: Race, Gender, and Sentimentality in Nineteenth-Century America*, ed. Shirley Samuels, 12–32. New York: Oxford University Press, 1993.

Wheeler, Kenneth H. "Infanticide in Nineteenth-Century Ohio." *Journal of Social History* 31, no. 2 (1997): 407–18.

Wheelwright, John. *John Wheelwright His Writings, Including His Fast-Day Sermon, 1637, and His Mercurius Americanus, 1645: With a Paper Upon the Genuineness of the Indian Deed of 1629 and a Memoir, Publications of the Prince Society*. Ed. Charles Henry Bell. Boston, Mass.: Printed for the Prince Society, 1876.

Wiegman, Robyn. *American Anatomies: Theorizing Race and Gender*. New Americanists. Durham, N.C.: Duke University Press, 1995.

Williams, Daniel. " 'Behold a Tragic Scene Strangely Changed into a Theater of Mercy': The Structure and Significance of Criminal Conversion Narratives in Early New England." *American Quarterly* 38 (1986): 827–47.

Williams, Daniel E. "Victims of Narrative Seduction: The Literary Translations of Elizabeth (and 'Miss Harriot') Wilson." *Early American Literature* 28 (1993): 148–70.

Winship, Michael P. *Making Heretics: Militant Protestantism and Free Grace in Massachusetts, 1636–1641*. Princeton, N.J.: Princeton University Press, 2002.

Winslow, Ola Elizabeth. *Meetinghouse Hill, 1630–1783*. New York: Macmillan, 1952.

Winthrop, John. *The Journal of John Winthrop, 1630–1649*. Ed. Richard S. Dunn, James Savage, and Laetitia Yandle. Abridged ed. Cambridge, Mass.: Belknap Press of Harvard University Press, 1996.

———. *Winthrop Papers*. 5 vols. Boston, Mass.: Massachusetts Historical Society, 1929–47.

Wolosky, Shira. "Emily Dickinson's Manuscript Body: History/Textuality/Gender." *The Emily Dickinson Journal* 8, no. 2: 87–99.

Wood, Gordon S. *The Radicalism of the American Revolution*. New York: Vintage Books, 1993.

Woodhouse, A. S. P. *Puritanism and Liberty, Being the Army Debates (1647–9) from the Clarke Manuscripts with Supplementary Documents*. Chicago: University of Chicago Press, 1951.

Young, Iris. "Beyond the Unhappy Marriage: A Critique of Dual Systems Theory." In *Women and Revolution: A Discussion of the Unhappy Marriage of Marxism and Feminism*, ed. Lydia Sargent, 43–69. Boston, Mass.: South End Press, 1981.

———. "Impartiality and the Civic Public: Some Implications of Feminist Critiques of Moral and Political Theory." In *Feminism as Critique: On the Politics of Gender*, ed. Seyla Benhabib and Drucilla Cornell, 56–76. Minneapolis: University of Minnesota Press, 1987.

Zagarri, Rosemarie. "Morals, Manners, and the Republican Mother." *American Quarterly* 44, no. 2 (1992): 192–215.

———. "The Rights of Man and Woman in Post-Revolutionary America." *William and Mary Quarterly* 55, no. 2 (1998): 203–30.

Zaret, David. *Origins of Democratic Culture: Printing, Petitions, and the Public Sphere in Early-Modern England, Princeton Studies in Cultural Sociology*. Princeton, N.J.: Princeton University Press, 2000.

———. "Religion, Science, and Printing in the Public Spheres in Seventeenth-Century England." In *Habermas and the Public Sphere*, ed. Craig Calhoun, 212–35. Cambridge: MIT Press, 1997.

Ziff, Larzer. *The Career of John Cotton: Puritanism and the American Experience*. Princeton, N.J.: Princeton University Press, 1962.

Index

In this index an "f" after a number indicates a separate reference on the next page, and an "ff" indicates separate references on the next two pages. A continuous discussion over two or more pages is indicated by a span of page numbers, e.g., "57–59." *Passim* is used for a cluster of references in close but not consecutive sequence.